A HANDBOOK OF ISLAM

Reviews of *The Religion of Islam* when published in 1936

Marmaduke Pickthall, translator of the Quran into English:

"Probably no man living has done longer or more valuable service for the cause of Islamic revival than Maulana Muhammad Ali of Lahore. … the present volume is his finest work. … It is a description of Al-Islam by one well-versed in the Sunna who has on his mind the shame of the Muslim decadence of the past five centuries … Such a book is greatly needed at the present day when in many Muslim countries we see persons eager for the reformation and revival of Islam making mistakes through lack of just this knowledge. … his premises are always sound, we are always conscious of his deep sincerity; and his reverence for the holy Quran is sufficient in itself to guarantee his work in all essentials."

Sir Shahab-ud-Din, Speaker, Punjab Legislative Assembly:

"The 'Religion of Islam' is the latest masterpiece from the pen of Maulana Muhammad Ali. … It is a mine of very useful information on the principles, doctrines and laws of the Muslim religion. It is a monumental collection of exceptional merit. It contains very full, detailed and reliable information on all questions dealt with in it."

Dr Allama Sir Muhammad Iqbal:

"I have glanced through parts of it, and find it an extremely useful work almost indispensable to the students of Islam. You have already written a number of books; one cannot but admire your energy and power of sustained work."

Chief Justice S.M. Suleman, High Court, Allahabad:

"…a great and comprehensive work, embodying Islamic philosophy and jurisprudence and embracing Muslim theology as well as the cardinal points of Muslim Law. This exhaustive work contains a vast store of information … the product of great learning, deep scholarship and enormous labour."

Sir Shafaat Ahmad Khan, Indian Muslim leader:

"…written in a highly scholarly manner and is proof of the learned author's high ability and ingenuity. In it the learned author has thrown sufficient light on the important Islamic issues and in explaining them has displayed the highest capability. I hope this will prove to be an authentic and unequalled book on Islam."

A Handbook of Islam

Sources, Principles and Practices of Islam

Being an Abridged Edition of the renowned work

The Religion of Islam

by

Maulana Muhammad Ali

Renowned author of several classic works on Islam

Edited by

Zahid Aziz

Ahmadiyya Anjuman Lahore Publications, U.K.

2020

Editions of the full work *The Religion of Islam* printed and published in Lahore:

First Edition, 1936
Second (Reprint) Edition, 1950
Third (Revised) Edition, 1971
Fourth (Reprint) Edition, 1973
Fifth (Retypeset) Edition, 1983

Printed and published from U.S.A.:
Sixth (Revised) Edition, 1990
Subsequent reprints of above Edition

This abridged edition *A Handbook of Islam,*
published online under title *A Handbook of Islam,* 2015
Revised edition, 2020
This printing (with small changes), 2022

Copyright © 2020
By Ahmadiyya Anjuman Lahore Foundation, U.K.
15 Stanley Avenue, Wembley, U.K., HA0 4JQ

Websites: `www.ahmadiyya.org`
e-mails: `info@ahmadiyya.org`

This book is available on the Internet at the above website.

ISBN: 978-1-906109-23-3

Preface to the Abridged Edition

The Religion of Islam by Maulana Muhammad Ali is a comprehensive, almost encyclopaedic, work, first published in 1936. It was immediately hailed by renowned Muslim scholars and intellectual leaders in their reviews as "greatly needed at the present day", "exhaustive, bold and authentic", "almost indispensable to the students of Islam", and as revealing "great learning, deep research and a thorough mastery of the subject".[1] Marmaduke Pickthall, famous British Muslim and a translator of the Quran into English, began his review of this book with the words: "Probably no man living has done longer or more valuable service for the cause of Islamic revival than Maulana Muhammad Ali of Lahore".[2] He added that "in many Muslim countries we see persons eager for the reformation and revival of Islam, making mistakes through lack of just this knowledge", the knowledge contained in this book.

As the author related in his Preface, he was approached to write this book by his friend Chaudhry Sir Shahab-ud-Din, President of the Punjab Legislative Council in British India.[3] Upon publication, Sir Shahab-ud-Din described this book as "a monumental collection of exceptional merit". His request to Maulana Muhammad Ali to write this book, and his endorsement of it, shows that this publication had the approval of the highest level of Muslim leadership and was tantamount to being a work commissioned by them.

A second edition of *The Religion of Islam* was published in 1950, during the author's lifetime, with insignificant changes. In a brief note to that edition, he stated that he had been unable to add the two chapters, on *The Ethics of Islam* and *The Muslim State,* which he had promised in the preface of the first edition to add to a later edition. He had, however, dealt with these subjects briefly in some later books, to which he referred the reader for information on these topics.

The third edition of *The Religion of Islam* appeared in 1971. It was revised by the author's son, Muhammad Ahmad. The major part of the revision was to use Maulana Muhammad Ali's later, 1951, edition of the English translation and commentary of the Quran, for the quotations in this book, and to add or amend some footnotes in accordance with that later work. Also, the two chapters, as mentioned above, were added from some of the Maulana's later books. There were also some stylistic revisions. Certain points of detail were moved from the main text to footnotes, the language in some places was made more formal,[4] and some Arabic terms were replaced by English equivalents, for example replacing "Hadith" by "Tradition".

Subsequent editions of *The Religion of Islam* have been reprints of the 1971 edition, with corrections to some references.

This abridged edition

Due to the all-comprehensive and highly detailed nature of the book, a need has been felt for an abridged version, more suiting the general reader. The book treated certain topics to a great depth, necessary only for researchers and scholars. On the other hand, it provided full details regarding the practices of Islam, such as prayer, which were not readily available in English at the time. In this abridgment, discussions of both these kinds have been curtailed or omitted.

The source of this abridgment is the third revised edition of 1971, but the original edition of 1936 has also been carefully kept in view. In a few cases the 1971 revisions have been undone, for example in reverting to using "Hadith" instead of "Tradition".

Near the end of the book, three short chapters from the original book have been combined to form the chapter 17, *Economics and Finance*. The chapters on *Penal Laws* and the *State* have been combined as one, and under Penal Laws a supplement by the Editor has been added, in a small typesize, to correct widespread misconceptions relating to Islamic laws in four areas. The material on the State and Ethics, as added in the 1971 edition, has been rechecked from the Maulana's later books from which it had been added, and has been revised and expanded from the same books.

Most of the references to original sources have been rechecked, and references to the 'Six Reliable' collections of Hadith are now provided to easily accessible editions in both Arabic and English. See the section *Sources and References* at page 450. An extensive index of subjects has also been compiled in this edition.

As regards the formatting, quotations have been laid out as indented blocks for ease of reading; only very short quotations are set inside paragraphs of the author's own text. Notes containing references and extra material for each chapter are grouped together at the end of the chapter. Any substantial note added by the Editor is prefixed as *Editor's Note*, while other explanatory notes are from the author's own writing. I wish to thank Mr Shaukat Ali, Coordinator of the Ahmadiyya Anjuman Lahore for the Asia and Pacific Region, for helping me in the proof reading and making several useful suggestions.

Zahid Aziz, Dr.
Editor,
April 2015

Note to the 2020 edition

The edition produced in 2015, as mentioned in my note above, was only published in digital formats. Essentially the same work, with some revisions, is now being published both digitally and in print. I have also simplified the presentation of the references to the 'Six Reliable' collections of Hadith.

Zahid Aziz, Dr.
Editor,
July 2020

Notes to this Preface:

1. From reviews by, respectively, Marmaduke Pickthall, Shaikh Mushir Husain Kidwai, Sir Muhammad Iqbal, and Justice Abdur Rashid.

2. *Islamic Culture,* Hyderabad Deccan, India, October 1936, pp. 659–660.

3. Chaudhry Sir Shahab-ud-Din (d. 1949) was President of the Punjab Legislative Council three times between 1925 and 1936, later Speaker of the first Punjab Legislative Assembly, 1937–1945. These bodies were the Punjab provincial legislature under British rule of India.

4. For example, amending the informal style of writing "as I have said above" to the formal "as stated above".

Preface to the First Edition

There could be no better comment on the prevalent Muslim lethargy towards Islam than the fact that non-Muslim contributions to Islamic religious literature in English are by far in excess of the Muslim. It is true that much of this literature draws a distorted picture of Islam, but even here the Muslim is more to blame than the non-Muslim, for it is his duty to place the right kind of material before a world whose thirst for knowledge is insatiable. But whatever may be said as to the superficiality of one part of this literature and the prejudicial tenor of another, it cannot be denied that Europe has made a most valuable contribution to research work in connection with the religion of Islam and the history of the Muslims. The Muslims are also turning their attention to the producing of religious literature in English, but the attempt is, as yet, a very weak one, directed more to appealing to the market than to serious efforts requiring hard work and critical acumen.

The Religion of Islam is the name of a book written by the Rev. F. A. Klein and published in 1906. It was through the courtesy of a friend that this book fell into my hands in the year 1928. He had read it with pain, he said, on account of the distorted picture of Islam that it contained, and he suggested that I should write a comprehensive work containing a true picture of Islam and dealing in detail with its teachings. More than twenty years before this, and just about the time when this book had been published in London, on the 13th of February 1907 to be exact, the Founder of the Ahmadiyya Movement, Hazrat Mirza Ghulam Ahmad of Qadian, had charged me with the writing of an English book which should contain all that was necessary for a Muslim, or a non-Muslim, to know about the religion of Islam, and to give a true picture of the religion which was largely misrepresented. The multifarious duties which I had to perform as President of the Ahmadiyya Anjuman Isha‘at Islam were a great hindrance, but the call of duty overcame these difficulties, and I set to work immediately, after going through Klein's book, and the work is now being published under the same name.

Had I been able to devote myself entirely to this task, it should not have taken more than three years. But seven years have passed, and still I am not satisfied that the book is as complete a picture as I had wished it to be. It has been my good fortune, from one point of view, to contribute to the literary activities of Islam and to be the head of a society which aims at the propagation of Islam, as the two works are so closely associated; but from another point of view it is a misfortune, since each of these works requires entire devotion to itself, to the exclusion of the other. I turned to the author's work again and again, amidst the many duties which I was required to perform as the head of a newly established society, but always to be recalled to some other task which the urgency of the moment forced on my attention. An author's singleness of purpose was not vouchsafed to me, and I have to confess that the work may, perhaps, suffer somewhat from this handicap.

There is yet another circumstance which may detract from the value of the book. I fell ill, rather seriously, in March 1935, and my medical advisers ordered complete rest for some time. Even after convalescence, I was advised to give up hard work, a direction which, to be candid, I have not been able to carry out, since the publication could not be delayed any longer. So I had to hurry on the work; and, more than that, I had to relinquish two chapters which I originally intended to include.* Besides, the concluding chapters have not been dealt with as exhaustively as I had wished. I only hope that these and other deficiencies will be removed if I am spared to bring out a second edition.

Islam, as I have pointed out in the Introduction to this book, is a religion which deals not only with the ways of devotion and the means which make man attain communion with God, but also with a vast variety of problems relating to the world around us and questions that pertain to the social and political life of man. In a treatise which aims at giving a true picture of Islam, it was necessary not only to discuss all the laws and regulations of the system but also to throw full light on the principles on which it is based, and even upon the

---

* *The Ethics of Islam* and *The Muslim State.*

sources from which its teachings, principles and laws are derived. I have, therefore, divided this book into three parts. The first part deals with the sources from which the teachings of Islam are drawn, and which can serve the purpose of guiding the Muslim world in its present and future needs; the second describes the creed of Islam or the fundamental doctrines of the religion; while the third treats of the laws and regulations of Islam which govern not only a Muslim's domestic, social and international relations but also his relations with God, which are the mainspring of the development of his faculties. An introduction has been added dealing with some questions relating to religion in general and Islam in particular.

A work of this nature would have carried little weight if it did not give full references to original authorities, and this had made the work laborious, for it contains over 2,500 references and quotations. The Holy Quran, being the original source on which all principles and laws of Islam are based, occupies the first place in this list, and next to it comes Bukhari, the most reliable book of Hadith. It is on these two authorities that the present work is chiefly based, but others, besides these, have been freely quoted and referred to where necessary.

In conclusion, I wish to express my indebtedness to the Honourable Chaudhri Sir Shahab-ud-Din, President of the Punjab Legislative Council, who is the friend, referred to above, and who, besides drawing my attention to the need of such a book, has helped me with valuable suggestions.

MUHAMMAD ALI
President,
Ahmadiyya Anjuman Isha'at Islam, Lahore
Ahmadiyya Buildings,
Lahore
21st November, 1935.

Contents

Introduction

Significance of the name *Islām*

Among the great religions of the world Islam enjoys the distinction of bearing a significant name, a name that points to its very essence. Muhammad was the name of the Holy Prophet through whom this religion was revealed, but its name as stated in the Quran is *Islām*,[1] and the one who follows it is called a *Muslim*.[2] So far from the system being named after its founder, as in the case of Christianity, Buddhism, Confucianism etc., the Prophet Muhammad is himself called a Muslim.[3] In fact, earlier prophets of God are spoken of in the Quran as being "submitting ones" (literally, "Muslims"),[4] thus showing that what is called "Islam" is the true religion for the whole of humanity, the various prophets being the preachers of that religion among different nations in different times and the Holy Prophet Muhammad its last and most perfect exponent.

The root-meaning of the word *Islām* is *to enter into peace,* and a *Muslim* is *one who makes his peace with God and man.* Peace with God implies complete submission to His will, and peace with man is not only to refrain from evil or injury to another but also to do good to him; and both these ideas find expression in the Holy Quran itself as the true essence of the religion of Islam:

> "No, whoever submits himself entirely to Allah and he is the doer of good [to others], he has his reward from his Lord, and there is no fear for such nor shall they grieve." — 2:112

Islam is thus, in its very inception, the religion of peace, and its two basic doctrines, the unity of God and the unity or brotherhood of the human race, afford positive proof of its being true to its name. Not only is Islam stated to be the true religion of all the prophets of God, as pointed out above, but even the involuntary but complete submission to Divine laws which is witnessed in nature, is indicated by the same word *aslama.* This wider significance is also retained in the strictly legal usage of the word, for, in law, Islam has a two-fold significance: a simple profession of faith — a declaration that "there is no god but Allah and Muhammad is the Messenger of Allah" (the *Kalimah*) — and a complete submission to the Divine will which is only attainable through spiritual perfection. Thus, the person who simply accepts the religion of Islam, the mere novice, is a Muslim, as well as the one who completely submits himself to the Divine will and practises all the Divine commandments.

Place of Islam among world religions

Islam is the last of the great religions — those mighty movements which have revolutionized the world and changed the destinies of nations. But it is not only the last, it is an all-inclusive religion which contains within itself all religions which came before it. One of its most striking characteristics is that it requires its followers to believe that all the great religions of the world that preceded it have been revealed by God:

> "And [Muslims are those] who believe in what has been revealed to you [O Muhammad] and what was revealed before you…" — 2:4

> "Say: We believe in Allah and in what has been revealed to us, and in what was revealed to Abraham, and Ishmael and Isaac and Jacob and the tribes, and in what was given to Moses and Jesus, and in what was given to the prophets from their Lord, we make no distinction between any of them…" — 2:136

> "The Messenger believes in what has been revealed to him from his Lord, and [so do] the believers. They all believe in Allah and His angels and His Books and His messengers. We make no distinction between any of His messengers." — 2:285

Thus a Muslim believes not only in the Prophet Muhammad but in all other prophets as well. And prophets were, according to the express teachings of the Holy Quran, raised up among all the nations:

> "And there is not a people but a warner has gone among them." — 35:24

Similarly, its sacred Book, the Holy Quran, is spoken of as a combination of all the sacred scriptures of the world:

"Pure pages in which are all the right books." — 98:2–3

In addition to being the last and an all-inclusive religion, it is the perfect expression of the Divine will. Thus Allah says in the Holy Quran:

> "This day have I perfected for you your religion and completed My favour on you and chosen for you Islam as a religion." — 5:3

Like every other form of consciousness, the religious consciousness of man has developed slowly and gradually down the ages, and the revelation of the great Truth from on high was thus brought to perfection in Islam. It is to this great truth that the words of Jesus Christ allude:

> "I still have many things to say to you but you cannot bear them now. However, when he, the spirit of truth, has come, he will guide you into all truth." [5]

Thus it is the great mission of Islam to bring about peace in the world by establishing a brotherhood of all the religions, to bring together all the religious truths contained in previous religions, to correct their errors and to sift the true from the false, to preach the eternal verities which had not been preached before on account of the special circumstances of any race or society in the early stages of its development, and, last of all, to meet all the moral and spiritual requirements of an ever-advancing humanity.

New meaning introduced into religion

With the advent of Islam, religion has received a new significance. Firstly, it is to be treated not as a dogma, which one must accept in order to escape everlasting damnation, but as a science based on the universal experience of humanity. It is not a particular nation that becomes the favourite of God and the recipient of Divine revelation; on the contrary, revelation is recognized as a necessary factor in the evolution of man; hence while in its crudest form it is the universal experience of humanity, in its highest, that of prophetical revelation, it has been a Divine gift bestowed upon all nations of the world. And the idea of the scientific in religion has been further strengthened by presenting its doctrines as principles of human conduct and action. There is not a single religious doctrine which is not made the basis of action for the development of man to higher and yet higher stages of life.

Secondly, the sphere of religion is not confined to the next world; its primary concern is rather with this life: that man, through a righteous life here on earth, may attain to the consciousness of a higher existence. And so it is that the Holy Quran deals with a vast variety of subjects which affect man's life in this world. It deals not only with the ways of devotion, the forms of worship, and the means which make man attain communion with God, but also, and in richer detail, with the problems of the world around us, with questions of relations between human beings, their social and political life, institutions of marriage, divorce and inheritance, division of wealth and relations of labour and capital, administration of justice, military organization, peace and war, national finance, debts and contracts, rules for the service of humanity and even treatment of animals, laws for the help of the poor, the orphan and the widow, and hundreds of other questions the proper understanding of which enables a person to lead a happy life.

It lays down rules not only for individual progress but also for the advancement of society as a whole, of the nation and even of humanity. It throws light on problems regarding relations not only between individuals but also among the different tribes and nations into which humanity is divided. And all these rules and laws are made effective by a faith in God. It prepares man for another life, it is true, but only through making him capable of holding his own in the present one.

Religion is a force in the moral development of man

A cursory glance at the history of human civilization will show that religion has been the supreme force in the development of mankind to its present condition. It is through the teachings of this or that prophet that man has been able to conquer his lower nature and to set before himself the noblest ideals of selflessness and the service of humanity. A study of the noble sentiments that inspire man today will show their origin in the teachings and example of some great sage who had a deep faith in God and through whom was sown the seed of faith in other human hearts. The moral and ethical development of man to his present state, if due to any one cause, is due to religion. Humanity has yet to find out whether the lofty emotions which inspire man today will survive after a generation or two of Godlessness, and what sentiments materialism will bring in its train.

It is often said that religion is responsible for much of the hatred and bloodshed in the world, but a cursory glance at the history of religion will show that this is a monstrous misconception. Love, concord, sympathy, kindness to one's fellow human beings, have been the message of every religion, and every nation has learnt these essential lessons in their true purity only through the spirit of selflessness and service which a faith in God has inspired. If there have been selfishness and hatred and bloodshed, those have been there in spite of religion, not as a consequence of the message of love which religion has brought. They have been there because human nature is too prone to these things; and their presence only shows that a still greater religious awakening is required, that a truer faith in God is yet the crying need of humanity. That man sometimes turns to low and unworthy things does not show that the nobler sentiments are worthless, but only that their development has become a more urgent necessity.

Islam as the greatest unifying force in the world

Islam is undoubtedly the greatest civilizing force the world has ever known. In the seventh century C.E. it was Islam that saved it from crashing into an abyss of savagery, that came to the help of a civilization whose very foundations had collapsed, and that set about laying a new foundation and rearing an entirely new edifice of culture and ethics. A new idea of the unity of the human race as a whole, not of the unity of this or that nation, was introduced into the world — an idea so mighty that it welded together nations which had warred with one another since the world began. It not only cemented together the warring tribes of one country but also established a brotherhood of all nations of the world, even uniting those which had nothing in common except their common humanity. It obliterated differences of colour, race, language, geographical boundaries and even of culture. It united man with man as such, and the hearts of those in the far east began to beat in unison with the hearts of those in the farthest west. Indeed, it proved to be not only the greatest but the only force unifying man, because, whereas other religions had succeeded merely in unifying the different elements of a single race, Islam actually achieved the unification of many races, and harmonized the jarring and discordant elements of humanity.

Islam laid the basis of a unity of the human race beyond which human conception cannot go. It recognized the equality not only of the civil and political rights of people, but also of their spiritual rights. "Mankind is a single nation" [6] is the fundamental doctrine of Islam, and for that reason every nation is recognized as having received the spiritual gift of revelation.

Islam as the greatest spiritual force of the world

Equally great is the unparalleled transformation which Islam has brought about in the world; for it has proved itself to be a spiritual force the equal of which the human race has never known. Its miraculous transformation of world conditions was brought about in an incredibly short time. It swept away the vilest superstitions, the crassest ignorance, the rank immorality, the old evil habits of centuries over centuries in less than a quarter of a century. That its spiritual conquests are without parallel in history is an undeniable fact, and it is because of the unparalleled spiritual transformation effected by him that the Holy Prophet Muhammad is admitted to be the "most successful of all prophets and religious personalities." [7]

Islam offers a solution of the great world problems

Islam is not only the most civilizing and the greatest spiritual force of the world but also offers a solution of the most baffling problems which confront mankind today. Materialism, which has become humanity's ideal in modern times, can never bring about peace and mutual trust among the nations of the world. Islam is the only force which has already succeeded in blotting out race and colour distinctions and it is through Islam only that this great problem of the modern world can be solved.

Islam is, first and foremost, an international religion, and it is only before its grand international ideal — the ideal of the equality of all races and of the unity of the human race — that the curse of nationalism, which has been and is responsible for the troubles of the ancient and the modern worlds, can be swept away. But even within the boundaries of a nation or a country there can be no peace as long as a just solution of the two great problems of wealth and sex cannot be found.

Modern nations have gone to two extremes on the wealth question: capitalism and communism. There is either the tendency to concentrate wealth among the great capitalists, or, by community of wealth, to bring the indolent and the industrious to one level. Islam offers the true solution by ensuring to the worker the reward of his work, great or small, in accordance with the merit of the work, and also by allotting to the poor a share in the wealth of the rich. Thus, while the rights of property are maintained in their true sense, arrangements are made for equalizing conditions by taking a part of the wealth of the rich and distributing it among the poor.

Similarly, Islam's solution of the sex question is the only one that can ensure ultimate peace to the family. There is neither the free-love which would loosen all ties of social relations, nor the indissoluble binding of man and woman which turns many a home into a veritable hell. And, by solving these and a hundred other problems, Islam — as its very name indicates — can bring true happiness to the human race.

Misconceptions underlying criticism of religion

Three chief objections to religion are raised by modern anti-religious movements:

1. That religion helps in the maintenance of the present social system, which has borne the fruit of capitalism with the consequent crushing of the aspirations of the poor.
2. That it keeps the people subject to superstition and thus hinders the advance of sciences.
3. That it teaches people to pray for their needs instead of working for them and thus it makes them indolent.

So far as Islam is concerned, the facts are entirely contrary to these allegations. Islam came as the friend of the poor and the destitute, and as a matter of fact it has accomplished an upliftment of the poor to which history affords no parallel. It raised people from the lowest rung of the social ladder to the highest positions of life, it made of slaves not only leaders in thought and intellect but actual rulers of state. Its social system is one of an equality which is quite unthinkable in any other nation or society. It lays down as one of the fundamental principles of religion that the poor have a *right* in the wealth of the rich, a right exercised through the state which collects annually a fortieth of the wealth amassed by the rich, to be distributed among the poor.[8]

The second allegation, that religion discourages the advancement of science and learning, is equally devoid of truth. Islam gave an impetus to learning in a country which had never been a seat of learning and was sunk in the depths of superstition. Even as far back as the caliphate of Umar,[9] the Islamic state undertook the education of the masses, while the Muslims carried the torch of learning to every country where they gained political ascendancy; schools, colleges and universities sprang up everywhere as a result of the Muslim conquest. It is no exaggeration to say that it was through Islam that the Renaissance came about in Europe.

The third allegation that religion makes people idle by teaching them to pray is also belied by the history of Islam. Not only does the Quran teach people to work hard for success in life, and lays down in plain words that "man can have nothing but what he strives for",[10] but it actually made the Arabs — the then most backward nation in the world — a nation of great leaders in all phases of life. And this great revolution was brought about only by awakening in them a desire for work and a zest for hard striving. Islam does teach man to pray, but prayer, instead of making him idle, is intended to fit him for a still harder struggle, and to carry on that struggle in the face of failure and disappointment, by turning to God Who is the Source of all strength. Thus prayer in Islam is only an incentive to work, and not a hindrance.

Notes to the Introduction

1. "This day have I perfected for you your religion and completed My favour on you and chosen for you Islam as a religion" (5:3). "Surely the (true) religion with Allah is Islam" (3:19).

2. "He named you Muslims before and in this" (22:78), where *before* refers to prophecies of earlier prophets about Muslims, and *this* refers to the Quran.

3. "And I am the first of those who submit" (6:163).

    Editor's Note: The word translated as "those who submit" is *muslimīn* in the original, which is the plural of *muslim*. By "first" is meant that the Holy Prophet Muhammad is the foremost, and ahead of all, in submitting.

4. "And the same did Abraham enjoin on his sons and so did Jacob: O my sons, surely Allah has chosen for you (this) religion, so die not unless you are

submitting ones" (2:132). "We revealed the Torah, in which was guidance and light; with it the prophets who submitted themselves (*aslamū*) judged matters for those who were Jews" (5:44).

Editor's Note: In 2:132 the word translated as "submitting ones" is *muslimūn* in the original, which is the plural of *muslim*. As the prophets submitted themselves to God through the revelation which had come to them, they were "Muslims" of their time.

5. Gospel of John, 16:12–13.

6. The Quran, 2:213.

7. *Encyclopaedia Britannica,* 11th edition, Art. 'Koran', opening paragraph. It is stated in this paragraph: "…it has been truly described as the most widely-read book in existence. This circumstance alone is sufficient to give it an urgent claim on our attention, whether it suit our taste and fall in with our religious and philosophical views or not. Besides, it is the work of Mahomet, and as such is fitted to afford a clue to the spiritual development of that most successful of all prophets and religious personalities."

8. *Editor's Note:* In addition to this tax on the wealth of the rich for the benefit of the poor, Islam has declared it as the second most important duty of Muslims, after prayer, to spend out of what they possess to help the destitute by money and all other means.

9. The period 634–644 C.E.

10. The Quran, 53:39.

1. The Holy Quran

How and when the Quran was revealed

The original source from which all principles and ordinances of Islam are drawn is the Holy Book called *al-Qur'ān.*[1] Generally the sources are said to be four: the Quran, the *Sunnah* or Hadith (Doings and Sayings of the Prophet Muhammad as preserved in various recognized collections), *Ijmā'* or *unanimous agreement* of the Muslim community and *Qiyās* or *reasoning.* But as *ijmā'* and *qiyās* are based on the Quran and the Hadith, and the latter is itself only an explanation of the Quran, as will be shown later on, the Quran is actually the real foundation on which the whole superstructure of Islam rests, and the only, absolute and final authority in every discussion relating to the principles and laws of Islam.

The name *Qur'ān* is frequently mentioned in the book itself[2] which also states to whom, how, why, when, and in what language, it was delivered. It was revealed to Muhammad:

> "And those who believe and do good and believe in that which has been revealed to Muhammad — and it is the Truth from their Lord." — 47:2

Its revelation commenced in the month of Ramadan on a certain night which, from then on, received the name of the *Night of Majesty* (*Lailat al-Qadr*):

> "The month of Ramadan is that in which the Quran was revealed…" — 2:185

> "We revealed it on a blessed night…" — 44:3

> "Surely We revealed it on the Night of Majesty." — 97:1

It was revealed in the Arabic language:

> "So We have made it easy in your tongue [O Prophet] that they may be mindful." — 44:58

> "Surely We have made it an Arabic Quran that you [O people] may understand." — 43:3

It was revealed in portions, every portion being written and committed to memory as soon as it was revealed, and the revelation was spread over twenty-three years of the Holy Prophet's life, during which time he was occupied solely with the reformation of a benighted world:

> "And it is a Quran which We have made distinct, so that you may read it to the people by slow degrees, and We have revealed it in portions." — 17:106

It was not the Prophet who spoke under influence of the Holy Spirit; it was a Divine Message brought by the angel Gabriel, and delivered in words to the Holy Prophet who communicated it to mankind. He is told in the Quran:

> "And surely this is a revelation from the Lord of the worlds. The Faithful Spirit has brought it on your heart that you may be a warner, in plain Arabic language." — 26:192–195

> "Whoever is an enemy to Gabriel — for surely he revealed it to your heart by Allah's command…" — 2:97

> "The Holy Spirit has revealed it from your Lord with the truth…" — 16:102

The Quran uses the words Holy Spirit and Gabriel interchangeably. Both the Quran and Hadith make it clear that Divine revelation was brought to the Holy Prophet, and to the prophets before him, by the angel Gabriel who is also called the Holy Spirit or the Faithful Spirit. The Jewish concept was also that the Holy Spirit brought inspiration to the prophets, and Jesus and his disciples used the word in exactly the same sense.[3] The orthodox Christian conception of the Holy Spirit was unknown to the Jewish mind and the Holy Ghost is peculiar to the New Testament writers.

It is the highest form of revelation

Though the Holy Quran was revealed piecemeal through Gabriel, yet the entire revelation is one whole, delivered in one and the same manner. Revelation, we are told in the Quran, is granted to man in three forms:

> "And it is not granted to a mortal that Allah should speak to him, except by revelation (*wahy*) or from behind a veil, or by sending a messenger and revealing by His permission what He pleases." — 42:51

The first of these three modes is called *wahy,* which is generally translated as meaning *revelation.* Since the different kinds of revelation are spoken of here, the word *wahy* is obviously used in its literal sense, its primary significance being a hasty suggestion. Hence the inspired word, which enters the hearts of the prophets and of the righteous, is called *wahy* because it is like a sudden suggestion made directly to the heart of the inspired one. It is not a message in words but simply an idea which comes like a flash and clears up a doubt or difficulty, and it is not the result of the thought process. The second mode is described as speaking from behind a veil — a scene, carrying a deeper significance, is shown as in a vision or in a dream or words are heard by the person spoken to, as if coming from behind a veil. The third mode is that in which the angel bearing the message is sent to the recipient of the Divine revelation, and the message is delivered in words, and this is the highest form of revelation.

As already stated, the angel entrusted with the Divine message in words is Gabriel or the Holy Spirit, and this third mode of revelation is limited to the prophets of God only — to men entrusted with important Divine messages to humanity — while the first two lower forms of revelation are common to prophets as well as those who are not prophets. For the delivery of the higher message which relates to the welfare of mankind, a higher form of revelation is chosen, a form in which the message is not simply an idea but is clothed in actual words. The prophet's faculty of being spoken to by God is so highly developed that he receives the messages, not only as ideas instilled into the mind or in the form of words uttered or heard under the influence of the Holy Spirit, but actually as Divine messages in words delivered through the latter. In the terminology of Islam this is called "revelation that is recited" (*wahy matluww*), and the Holy Quran was, from beginning to end, delivered in this form to the Holy Prophet, as the quotations earlier given from the Book itself make it abundantly clear. It does not contain any other form of revelation. It is in its entirety *waḥy matluww* or revelation recited to the Holy Prophet distinctly in words, and is thus wholly the highest form of Divine revelation.

Other forms of Divine revelation to human beings

As stated above, prophets also received the two lower forms of Divine revelation. For example, we are told in Hadith reports that before the higher message came to the Prophet Muhammad — i.e., before he received the first Quranic revelation — he used to have clear and true visions:

> "The first of revelations that came to the Messenger of Allah were good visions so that he did not see a vision but it came out true as the dawn of the day." [4]

This is the second mode of revelation mentioned earlier. The details of laws as later expounded by Holy Prophet, and as met with in his practice, belong to the first form of revelation, an idea instilled into the mind, which is called "inner revelation" (*waḥy khafiyy*).

In the lower forms, revelation is still granted to the righteous from among the followers of the Holy Prophet and even to others, for, as will be shown later, revelation in the lowest form is the universal experience of humanity. There is also a difference as to the method in which the different kinds of revelation are received. While the two lower forms of revelation involve but little change in the normal condition of a person, whether awake or asleep, and he is only occasionally transported to a state of trance, the highest form, which is that peculiar to the prophets, brings with it a violent change; it does, in fact, require a real passing from one world to the other, while the recipient is in a state of perfect wakefulness, and the burden of revelation is not only felt by him but is also visible to those who see him.

The Holy Prophet's experience of revelation

The Holy Prophet first experienced the higher revelation while he was alone in the cave of Hira. Before this, he had from time to time seen visions, but when the angel came with the higher message, he found himself quite exhausted:

> "He [Gabriel] seized me and squeezed me to such an extent that I was quite exhausted",

and this was repeated three times.[5] And even after he reached home, the effect of exhaustion was still upon him and he had to lie down, covered over, before he could relate what had befallen. It was an equally hard experience when the second message came to him after an interval of some months. And even afterwards, the effect of the Spirit upon him was so great that on the coldest of days perspiration would run down his forehead: "I saw", says Aishah, his wife, "revelation coming down upon him in the severest cold, and when that condition was over, perspiration ran down his forehead".[6] Zaid ibn Thabit relates that he was sitting with his leg under that of the Holy Prophet when revelation came down upon him, and he felt as if his leg would be crushed under the weight.[7]

Nature of the Holy Prophet's revelation

When it was once enquired of the Holy Prophet how revelation came to him, he replied:

> "It comes to me sometimes as the ringing of a bell and this is hardest on me, then he [the angel] leaves me and I remember from him what he says; and sometimes the angel comes in the shape of a man and he talks to me and I remember what he says." [8]

These are the only two forms in which the Quranic revelation came to the Holy Prophet. In both cases, the angel came to him and was seen by him; in both cases, a certain message was delivered in words which he at once committed to memory. That is the essence of the whole question. The only difference between the two cases was that in one case the angel appeared in the shape of a human being and uttered the words in a soft tone as a man talks to another; in the other case, it is not stated in what form he came, but we are told that the words were uttered like the ringing of a bell, that is to say, in a harsh, hard tone, which made it a heavier task for the Prophet to receive them. But still it was the angel who brought the message, as is shown by the use of the personal pronoun *he* in the first part of the report. In both cases the Prophet was transported, as it were, to another world, and this transportation caused him to go through a severe experience which made him perspire even on a cold day, but this experience was harder still when the deliverer of the message did not appear in human shape and there remained no affinity between the deliverer and the recipient. But whether the angel appeared in human shape or not, whether the message was delivered in a hard or soft tone, the one thing certain is that it was a message delivered in words; and therefore the Quranic revelation is entirely one message delivered in one form.

It should be noted that the Holy Prophet often received the message while sitting with his Companions, but the latter never saw the angel nor ever heard the words of revelation. It was, therefore, with other than the normal human senses that the Prophet saw the angel and heard his words, and it was really the granting of these other senses that is called transportation to another world.

Arrangement of the Quran

Though the Holy Quran was revealed in portions, it did not remain long in that fragmentary condition. As its name implies, it was a book from the first, and though it could not be complete until the last verse was revealed, it was never without some form of arrangement. There is the clearest testimony, internal as well as external, that every single verse or part of a verse and every chapter that was revealed had its own definite place in the Book. The Quran is itself clear on this point:

> "And those who disbelieve say: Why has not the Quran been revealed to him all at once? Thus [it is] that We may strengthen your heart by it, and We have arranged it well in arranging." — 25:32

The arrangement of the Quran was thus a part of the Divine scheme. Another verse showing that the collection of the Book was a part of the Divine scheme runs thus:

> "Surely on Us rests the collecting of it and the reciting of it." — 75:17

It appears from this that just as the Quran was recited by Gabriel to the Holy Prophet, in like manner, the collecting of its various parts was effected by the Prophet under the guidance of the Holy Spirit. History also bears testimony to the truth of this statement, for not only are there numerous anecdotes showing that this or that portion of the Quran was put to writing under the orders of the Holy Prophet, but we are clearly told by Uthman, the third Caliph, that every portion of the Book was written, and given its specified place, at the bidding of the Prophet:

> "It was customary with the Messenger of Allah (may peace and the blessings of Allah be upon him) that when portions of different chapters were revealed to him, and when any verse was revealed, he called one of those persons who used to write the Quran and said to him: Write this verse in the chapter where such and such verses occur." [9]

Arrangement in oral recitation

In fact, if we bear in mind the use that was made of the Holy Quran, we cannot for an instant entertain the idea that the Book existed without any arrangement of its verses and chapters in the lifetime of the Holy Prophet. It was not only recited in prayers but committed to memory and regularly recited to keep it fresh in the mind. Now if an arrangement of verses and chapters had not existed, it would have been impossible either to recite it in public prayers or to commit it to memory. The slightest change in the place of a verse by the man leading the prayers would at once call forth a correction from the audience, as it does at the present day. Since no one could take the liberty of changing a word or the place of a word in a verse, no one could change a verse or the place of a verse in a chapter; and so the committing of the Quran to memory by so many of the Companions of the Holy Prophet, and their constant recitation of it, would have been impossible unless a known order was followed. The Holy Prophet could not teach the Quran to his Companions nor the Companions to each other, nor could he or anyone else lead the public prayers, in which long portions of the Book were recited, without following a known and accepted order.

Complete written copies of the Quran

The Holy Quran thus existed in a complete and ordered form in the memories of men, but no complete written copy of it existed at the time, nor could such a copy be made while the Holy Prophet was alive, and still receiving revelations. But the whole of the Quran in one arrangement was safely preserved in the memories of reciters.

It happened, however, that many of the reciters fell in the famous battle of Yamama, in the caliphate of Abu Bakr,[10] and it was then that

Umar[11] urged upon him the necessity of compiling a standard written copy, so that no portion of the Quran should be lost even if all the reciters were to die. And this copy was compiled, not from the hundreds of copies that had been made by individual Companions for their own use but from the manuscripts written under the direction of the Holy Prophet himself, and the arrangement adopted was that of the oral recitation as followed in his time. Zaid ibn Thabit was chosen for the task of collecting and compiling the Quranic writings since, during the Holy Prophet's life at Madinah, he had done by far the greater part of the work of writing his revelations.[12]

Thus a standard written copy was prepared, which was entrusted to the care of Hafsah, wife of the Prophet.[13] But still no arrangement had been made for securing the accuracy of the numerous copies that were in circulation. This was done by Uthman[14] who ordered several copies to be made of the copy prepared in the time of the first Caliph, and these were then sent to the different Islamic centres so that all copies made by individuals should be compared with the standard copy at each centre.

Standardization of the Quran

Thus Abu Bakr ordered a standard copy to be prepared from the manuscripts written in the presence of the Holy Prophet, following the order of chapters which was followed by the reciters under the directions of the Holy Prophet, and Uthman ordered copies to be made from this standard copy. If there was any variation from that standard copy, it went no further than this that where the Quraish wrote a word in one way and Zaid ibn Thabit wrote it in another way, Uthman's order was to write it in the manner of the Quraish. This was because Zaid belonged to Madinah while his colleagues were Quraish, which was the leading tribe of Makkah, the Holy Prophet Muhammad himself belonging to the Banu Hashim branch of this tribe.

Differences of readings

There were slight differences in the spoken language of different tribes, that of the Quraish being the model for the literary language. The Holy Quran was revealed in the dialect of the Quraish, the literary language of Arabia. But when, towards the close of the Holy Prophet's life, people from different Arabian tribes accepted Islam in large numbers, it was found that they could not pronounce certain words in the idiom of the Quraish, being habituated from childhood to their own idiom, and it was then that the Holy Prophet allowed them to pronounce a word according to their own peculiar idiom. This permission was given only to facilitate the recitation of the Quran. The written Quran was one; it was all in the chaste idiom of the Quraish, but certain people belonging to other tribes were allowed to pronounce it in their own way.

There may have been certain revelations in which an optional reading was permitted. Readings belonging to this class can only be accepted on the most unimpeachable evidence, and the trustworthiness of the Hadith reports containing such readings must be established beyond all doubt. But even these readings do not find their way into the written text, which remains permanently one and the same. Their value is only explanatory: they only show what significance is to be attached to the word used in the text; they are never at variance with the text. They are known to very few even of the learned, to say nothing of the general readers of the Holy Book, and are considered to have the value of an authentic Hadith report in explaining the meaning of a certain word occurring in the text.

Thus, the so-called different readings were either dialectic variations, which were never meant to be permanent and intended only to facilitate the reading of the Quran in individual cases, or explanatory variations meant to throw light on the text. The former ceased to exist with the spread of education in Arabia, and the latter have still the same explanatory value as they originally had.

Collective testimony of the purity of the Quranic text

Random reports that a certain verse or chapter, not to be met with in the Quran, was part of the text, have no value at all as against the conclusive and collective testimony which establishes the purity of the text of the Holy Quran. It is a fact that every verse of the Quran was, when revealed, promulgated and made public; it became a part of the public prayer and was repeated day and night to be listened to by an audience of hundreds. When the written manuscripts of the Quran were first collected into one volume in the time of the first Caliph Abu Bakr, and later on when copies were made from that original in the time of the third Caliph Uthman, there was the unanimous testimony of all the Companions that every verse that found a place in that collection was part of the Divine revelation. Such testimony of overwhelming numbers cannot be set aside by the evidence of one or two, but, as a matter of fact, all reports quoted as affecting the purity of the text ascribe a certain statement to only one man, and in not a single case is there a second person to support that assertion.

The theory of abrogation

That certain verses of the Holy Quran are abrogated by others is now an exploded theory. The two passages on which it was supposed to rest refer, really, to the abrogation, not of the passages of the Quran but of the previous revelations whose place the Holy Book had taken. The first verse is contained in the 16th chapter (*al-Nahl*) — a Makkah revelation — and runs thus:

> "And when We change a message for a message — and Allah knows best what He reveals — they say: You are only a forger." — 16:101

It is a fact that details of the Islamic law were revealed at Madinah and it is in relation to these details that the theory of abrogation has been broached. Therefore, a Makkah revelation would not speak of abrogation. But the reference in the above verse is to the abrogation, not of the Quranic verses but of the previous Divine messages or revelations, consequent upon revelation of the Quran. The context shows this clearly to be the case, for the opponents are here made to say that the Prophet was a forger. He was so accused by the opponents not because he announced the abrogation of certain verses of the Quran but because he claimed that the Quran was a Divine revelation which had taken the place of previous revelations. They argued that it was not a revelation at all: "Only a mortal teaches him" (16:103). According to them the whole of the Quran, and not merely a particular verse of it, was a forgery. The theory of abrogation, therefore, cannot be based on this verse which speaks only of one revelation or one law taking the place of another.

The other verse which is supposed to lend support to the theory runs thus:

> "Whatever message We abrogate or cause to be forgotten, We bring one better than it or one like it." — 2:106

A reference to the context will show that the Jews or the followers of previous revelations are here addressed. Of these it is said:

> "…they say: We believe in that which was revealed to us; and they deny what is besides that." — 2:91

So they were told that if a certain revelation was abrogated, it was only to give place to a better one. And there is mention not only of abrogation but also of something that was forgotten. The words "or cause to be forgotten" cannot refer to the Quran at all because no portion of it could be said to have been forgotten so as to require a new revelation in its place. There is no point in supposing that God should first make the Holy Prophet forget a verse and then reveal a new one in its place. Why not, if he really had forgotten a verse, remind him of the one forgotten? But even if it is supposed that his memory ever failed in retaining a certain verse (which really never happened), that verse was quite safely preserved in writing, and the mere failure of the memory could not necessitate a new revelation. That the Holy Prophet never forgot what was recited to him by the Holy Spirit is plainly stated in the Quran:

> "We shall make you recite, so you shall not forget". — 87:6

History also bears out the fact that he never forgot any portion of the Quranic revelation. Sometimes the whole of a very long chapter would be revealed to him in one portion, as in the case of the sixth chapter which extends over 165 verses, but he would have it written down without delay, and make his Companions learn it by heart, and recite it in public prayers, and that without the change of even a letter, despite the fact that he himself could not read from a written copy, nor did the written copies, as a rule, remain in his possession. It was a miracle indeed that he never forgot any portion of the Quran, though other things he might forget, and it is to his forgetfulness in other things that the words *except what Allah pleases,* in the next verse (87:7), refer. On the other hand, it is a fact that parts of the older revelations had been utterly lost and forgotten, and thus the Holy Quran was needed to take the place of that which was abrogated, and that which had been forgotten by the world.

Hadith on abrogation

It is quite strange that the theory of abrogation has been accepted by writer after writer without ever thinking that not a single report in

Hadith, however weak, touching on the abrogation of a verse, was traceable to the Holy Prophet. It never occurred to the upholders of this theory that the Quranic verses were promulgated by the Holy Prophet, and that it was he whose authority was necessary for the abrogation of any Quranic verse; no Companion, not even Abu Bakr or Ali, could say that a verse was abrogated. The Holy Prophet alone was entitled to say so, and there is not a single hadith to the effect that he ever said so; it is always some Companion or a later authority to whom such views are to be traced.

In most cases, where a report is traceable to one Companion who held a certain verse to have been abrogated, there is another report traceable to another Companion to the effect that the verse was not abrogated.[15] Even among later writers we find that there is not a single verse on which the verdict of abrogation has been passed by one without being questioned by another; and while there are writers who would lightly pass the verdict of abrogation on hundreds of verses, there are others who consider not more than five to be abrogated, and even in the case of these five the verdict of abrogation has been seriously impugned by earlier writers.

Use of the word *naskh*

The theory of abrogation has in fact arisen from a misunderstanding of the use of the word *naskh* (abrogation) by the Companions of the Holy Prophet. When the significance of one verse was limited by another, the former was sometimes spoken of as having been "abrogated" (*nusikhat*) by the latter. Similarly when the words of a verse gave rise to a misconception, and a later revelation cleared up that misconception, the word "abrogation" was metaphorically used in connection with it, the idea underlying its use being not that the first verse was abrogated but that a certain conception to which it had given rise was abrogated. Earlier authorities admit that abrogation means *explanation* metaphorically. It is an abrogation, but not an abrogation of the words of the Quran; rather it is the abrogation of a misconception of their meaning. This is further made clear by the application of abrogation to verses containing statements of facts, whereas, properly speaking, abrogation could only take place in the case of verses containing a commandment or a prohibition. This use of the word "abrogation" by the earlier authorities regarding state-ments of facts shows that they were using the word to signify the removal of a wrong conception regarding, or the placing of a limitation upon, the meaning of a certain verse. At the same time, it is true that the use of this word soon became indiscriminate, and when anyone found himself unable to reconcile two verses, he would declare one of them to be abrogated by the other.

Basis of abrogation

The principle on which the theory of abrogation is based is unacceptable, being contrary to the clear teachings of the Quran. A verse is considered to be abrogated by another when the two cannot be reconciled with each other; in other words, when they appear to contradict each other. But the Quran destroys this foundation when it declares that no part of it is at variance with another:

> "Will they not then meditate on the Quran? And if it were from any other than Allah, they would have found in it many a discrepancy." — 4:82

It was due to lack of reflection that one verse was thought to be at variance with another; and hence it is that in almost all cases where abrogation has been upheld by one person, there has been another who, being able to reconcile the two, has repudiated the alleged abrogation.

Later commentators on abrogation

It is only among the later commentators that we meet with the tendency to augment the number of verses thought to have been abrogated, and by some of these the figure has been placed as high as five hundred. In this connection, Suyuti, one of the well-known commentators, says: "Those who multiply [the number of abrogated verses] have included many kinds — one kind being that in which there is neither abrogation, nor any particularization [of a general statement], nor has it any connection with any one of them, for various reasons." Suyuti himself brings the number of verses which he thinks to be abrogated down to twenty-one, but he admits that there is a difference of opinion even about these.[16]

A later writer, however, the famous Shah Wali-ullah of India, commenting on this in his *Fauz al-Kabīr,* says that abrogation cannot be proved in the case of sixteen out of Suyuti's twenty-one verses, but in the case of the remaining five he is of the opinion that the verdict of abrogation of one verse by another is final.

However, an examination of these five verses shows that in two of them some early commentators themselves reject abrogation, and in the other three it is due to a misunderstanding.[17]

Thus the theory of abrogation falls to the ground on all considerations.

Interpretation of the Quran

The rule as to the interpretation of the Quran is thus given in the Holy Book itself:

> "He it is Who has revealed the Book to you; some of its verses are decisive — they are the basis of the Book — and others are allegorical. Then those in whose hearts is perversity follow the part of it which is allegorical, seeking to mislead, and seeking to give it [their own] interpretation. And none knows its interpretation except Allah, and those firmly rooted in knowledge. They say: We believe in it, it is all from our Lord. And none are mindful except those who have understanding." — 3 : 7

In the first place, it is stated here that there are two kinds of verses in the Holy Quran, namely, the decisive and the allegorical — the latter being those which are capable of different interpretations. Next we are told that the decisive verses are the basis of the Book, that is, that they contain the fundamental principles of religion. Hence whatever may be the differences of interpretation, the fundamentals of religion are not affected by them, all such differences relating only to secondary matters. The third point is that some people seek to give their own interpretation to allegorical statements and are thus misled. In other words, serious errors arise only when a wrong interpretation is placed on words which are susceptible of two meanings. Lastly, in the concluding words, a clue is given as to the right mode of interpretation in the case of allegorical statements: "It is all from our Lord" — meaning that there is no disagreement between the various portions of the Book. This statement has in fact been made elsewhere also, as already quoted (see 4 : 82).

The important principle to be borne in mind in the interpretation of the Quran, therefore, is that the meaning should be sought from within the Quran, and never should a passage be interpreted in such a manner that it may be at variance with any other passage, but more especially with the basic principles laid down in the decisive verses. This principle, says the Holy Quran, is followed by "those firmly rooted in knowledge."

The following rules may, therefore, be laid down:

-   The principles of Islam are enunciated in decisive words in the Holy Quran; and, therefore, no attempt should be made to establish a principle on the strength of an allegorical passage, or of words susceptible of different meanings.

-   The explanation of the Book should in the first place be sought in the Quran itself; for, whatever it has stated briefly, or merely hinted at, in one place, will be found expanded and fully explained elsewhere in it.

-   The Holy Quran contains allegory and metaphor along with what is plain and decisive, and the only safeguard against being misled by what is allegorical or metaphorical is that the interpretation of such passages must be strictly in consonance with what is laid down in clear and decisive words, and not at variance therewith.

-   When a law or principle is laid down in clear words, any statement carrying a doubtful significance, or a statement apparently opposed to the law so laid down, must be interpreted subject to the principle enunciated.

Value of Hadith and commentaries in interpreting the Quran

Hadith also affords an explanation of the Holy Quran but a report can only be accepted when it is reliable and not opposed to what is clearly stated in the Quran. As regards commentaries, a word of warning is necessary against the tendency to regard what is stated in them as being the final word on interpretation, since by so doing the great treasures of knowledge which an exposition of the Holy Quran in the new light of modern progress reveals are shut out, and the Quran becomes a sealed book to the present generation. The learned men of old all freely sought its meaning according to their understanding and circumstances, and the same right belongs to the present generation. It must also be added that though the commentaries are valuable stores of learning for a knowledge of the Quran, the numerous anecdotes and legends with which many of them are filled can only be accepted with the greatest caution and after the most careful sifting.

Divisions of the Quran

The Holy Quran is divided into 114 chapters, each of which is called a *sūrah,* meaning literally *eminence* or *high degree* and also *any degree of a structure.* The chapters are of varying length, the longest comprising one-twelfth of the entire Book. All the chapters, with the exception of the last thirty-five, are divided into sections, each section or *rukū'* dealing generally with one subject, and the different sections being interrelated to each other.[18] Each section contains a number of verses, a verse being known as an *āyah.* The total number of verses is more than 6000.

For the purpose of recitation, the Quran is divided into thirty equal parts (*juz'*), each of these being again subdivided into four equal parts. Another division is into seven portions (*manzil*), which is designed for the completion of its recital in seven days. These divisions for the purpose of recitation have nothing to do with the subject-matter of the Holy Quran.

Makkah and Madinah chapters

An important division of the Quran relates to the Makkah and Madinah chapters. After the Divine Call to prophethood, the Holy Prophet passed 13 years at Makkah, and was then forced to migrate with his Companions to Madinah where he spent the last ten years of his life. Out of the total of 114 chapters of the Book, 92 were revealed during the Makkah period and 22 during the Madinah period, but the Madinah chapters, being generally longer, contain about one-third of the Holy Book. In arrangement, the Makkah revelation is intermingled with that of Madinah.

On referring to the subject-matter of the Makkah and Madinah revelations, we find the following three broad features distinguishing the two groups of chapters. Firstly, the Makkah revelation deals chiefly with faith in God and is particularly devoted to grounding the Muslims in that faith, while the Madinah revelation is mainly intended to translate that faith into action. It is true that exhortations to good and noble deeds are met with in the Makkah revelation, and in the Madinah revelation faith is still shown to be the foundation on which the structure of deeds should be built, but, in the main, stress is laid in the former on faith in an Omnipotent and Omnipresent God Who requites every good and every evil deed, and the latter deals chiefly with what is good and what is evil, in other words, with the details of the law. The second feature distinguishing the two revelations is that while that of Makkah is generally prophetical, that of Madinah deals with the fulfilment of prophecy. Thirdly, while the former shows how true happiness of mind may be sought in communion with God, the latter points out how man's dealing with man may also be a source of bliss and comfort to him. Hence a rational arrangement of the Quran must of necessity rest on the intermingling of the two revelations, blending of faith with deeds, of prophecy with fulfilment of prophecy, of Divine communion with man's relation to and treatment of man.

The place of the Quran in world literature
That the Quran occupies a place of eminence in Arabic literature which has not fallen to the lot of any other book goes without saying; but we may say more and assert with confidence that the place so occupied has not been attained at any time by any book anywhere. For what book is there in the whole history of the human race that, through so many centuries, has not only remained admittedly the standard of the language in which it is written but has also originated a world-wide literature?

The feat accomplished by the Holy Quran is unique in the whole history of the written word. It transformed a dialect, spoken in a very limited area of a forgotten corner of the world into a world-wide language which became the mother-tongue of vast countries and mighty empires, and produced a literature which is the basis of the culture of powerful nations from one end of the world to the other. There was no literature, properly speaking, in Arabic before the Holy Quran; the few pieces of poetry that did exist never soared beyond the praise of wine or woman, or horse or sword. It was with the Quran that Arabic literature originated, and through it that Arabic became a powerful language spoken in many countries and casting its influence on the literary histories of many others. Without the Quran, the Arabic language would have been nowhere in the world.

There are other considerations which entitle the Quran to a place of eminence to which no other book can aspire. It throws light on all the fundamentals of religion, the existence and unity of God, the reward of good and evil, the life after death, paradise and hell, revelation, etc. In addition to expounding to us the mysteries of the unseen, it offers a solution of the most difficult problems of this life, such as the distribution of wealth, the sex-problem, and all other questions on which depends in any degree the happiness and advancement of man. And the value of this copiousness of ideas is further enhanced when it is seen that it does not confront man with dogmas but gives reasons for every assertion made, whether relating to the spiritual or the physical life. There are hundreds of topics on which it has enriched the literature of the world, and whatever questions it discusses, it adopts a rational approach and convinces by argument and not by dogma.

More wonderful still is the effect which the Holy Quran has produced. The transformation which it brought about is unparalleled in the history of the world. A complete change was wrought in the lives of a whole nation in an incredibly short time — a period of no more than twenty-three years. The Quran found the Arabs worshippers of idols, unhewn stones, trees and heaps of sand, yet in less than a quarter of a century the worship of the One God ruled the whole land and idolatry had been wiped out from one end of the country to the other. It swept all superstitions before it and, in their place, gave the most rational religion the world could dream of. The Arab who had been wont to pride himself on his ignorance had been transformed into the lover of knowledge, drinking deep at every fountain of learning to which he could gain access. And this was directly the effect of the teaching of the Quran, which not only appealed to reason, ever and again, but declared man's thirst for knowledge to be insatiable. And along with superstition went the deepest vices of the Arab, and in their place the Holy Book put a burning desire for the best and noblest deeds in the service of humanity.

Yet it was not the transformation of the individual alone that the Holy Quran had accomplished; equally was it a transformation of the family, of society, of the very nation itself. From the warring elements of the Arab race, it welded a nation, united and full of life and vigour, before whose onward march the greatest kingdoms of the world crumbled as if they had been but toys before the reality of the new faith. Thus the Holy Quran effected a transformation of humanity itself — a transformation material as well as moral, an awakening intellectual as well as spiritual. There is no other book which has brought about a change so miraculous in the lives of people.

Notes to Chapter 1

1. The word *Qur'ān* means 'a book that is recited'. It calls itself *al-kitāb* or 'the book' in many places, as in 2:2, 2:151, 3:3, etc. It is from a root *qara'a,* meaning 'collecting things together'. This may refer to the Quran gathering together in itself the fruits of all Books of God; see 98:2–3.

2. The Quran, 2:185, 10:37, 10:61, 17:106, etc.

3. See Matthew 22:43, Mark 12:36, and see also Luke 11:13.

4. Bukhari, book 1: 'The beginning of revelation', ch. 3, h 3.

5. *Ibid.*

6. *Ibid.,* book 1, ch. 2, h. 2. Some misdirected critics have represented this extraordinary experience of the coming of the revelation as an epileptic fit. The question is whether an epileptic could, when the fit came on, utter those grand religious truths which are met with in the Quran, or indeed make any coherent statement at all; or possess the unparalleled energy which we witness in every phase of the Holy Prophet's life; whether hundreds of thousands of men possessing the Arabs' independence of character would have taken him for a leader whose orders were obeyed in the minutest details of life?

7. Bukhari, book 8: 'Prayer', ch. 12 heading (above h. 371).

8. Bukhari, book 1: 'How revelation began', ch. 2, h. 2.

9. Abu Dawud, book 2: 'Prayer', ch. 127, h. 786. Tirmidhi, book 47: 'Commentary on the Quran', h. 3086 (MDS: book 44, ch. 9).

10. Abu Bakr was the first Caliph of Islam, ruling from 632 to 634 C.E.

11. Umar was the second Caliph, from 634 to 644 C.E.

12. The account is given by Zaid himself. See Bukhari, book 65: 'Commentary on the Quran', h. 4679 (on *Surah* 9, v. 128).

13. Bukhari, book 66: 'Virtues of the Quran', ch. 3, h. 4986.

14. Uthman was the third Caliph, from 644 to 656 C.E.

15. Some examples, taken only from chapter 2, may be noted here — 2:180 is held by some to have been abrogated while others have denied it; 2:184 is considered by Ibn Umar as having been abrogated while Ibn Abbas says it was not (Bukhari, book 65, h. 4506 and h. 4505 on *Surah* 2, v. 184); 2:240 was abrogated according to Ibn Zubair while Mujahid says it was not (Bukhari, book 65, h. 4530 on *Surah* 2, v. 240 and h. 4531 on v. 234).

16. *Itqān fī 'Ulūm al-Qur'ān* by Jalal-ud-Din Suyuti, v. 2, pp. 22, 23.

17. *Editor's Note:* In *The Religion of Islam* Maulana Muhammad Ali has fully dealt with these five verses. Here we have summed up his conclusion.

18. *Editor's Note:* The sub-division of chapters into sections is only found in certain parts of the Muslim world, such as the Indian subcontinent.

2. The Hadith

Sunnah and *Ḥadīth*

Sunnah or *Ḥadīth* (the practice and the sayings of the Holy Prophet Muhammad) is the second and undoubtedly secondary source from which the teachings of Islam are drawn. In its original sense *Sunnah* indicates the doings and Hadith the sayings of the Holy Prophet; but in effect both cover the same ground and are applicable to his actions, practices, and sayings, Hadith being the narration and record of the *Sunnah* but containing, in addition, various prophetical and historical elements.

Any student of the Quran will see that the Holy Book generally deals with the broad principles or essentials of religion, going into details in rare cases. The details were supplied by the Holy Prophet himself, either by showing in his practice how an injunction was to be carried out, or by giving an explanation in words. The two most important religious institutions of Islam, for instance, are prayer and the compulsory charity known as *zakāt;* yet when the injunctions relating to these were delivered — and they are repeatedly met with both in Makkah and Madinah revelations — no details were supplied. It was the Holy Prophet himself who by his own actions gave the details of the prayer service and the rules and regulations for the collection and payment of *zakāt*. These are but two examples; but since Islam covered the whole sphere of human activity, hundreds of points had to be explained by the Holy Prophet by his example in action and word, while on the moral side, his was the pattern which every Muslim was required to follow.[1] Whoever, therefore, embraced Islam stood in immediate need of both the Quran and the *Sunnah*.

Transmission of Hadith in Holy Prophet's lifetime

The transmission of the practices and sayings of the Holy Prophet, from one person to another, thus became necessary during the Prophet's lifetime. In fact, the Holy Prophet himself used to give instructions about the transmission of what he taught. Thus when a deputation of the tribe of Rabi'ah came to wait upon him in the early days of Madinah, he concluded his instructions to them with the words:

> "Remember this and report it to those whom you have left behind." [2]

There is another report according to which, on the occasion of a pilgrimage, the Holy Prophet, after enjoining on the Muslims the duty of holding sacred each other's life, property and honour, added:

> "He who is present here should carry this message to him who is absent." [3]

Again, there is ample historical evidence that whenever a people embraced Islam, the Holy Prophet used to send them one or more of his missionaries who not only taught them the Quran but also explained to them how its injunctions were to be carried out in practice. And the Companions of the Prophet knew full well that his actions and practices were to be followed, should no express direction be met with in the Quran. It is related that when Mu'adh ibn Jabal, on being appointed Governor of Yaman by the Holy Prophet, was asked how he would judge cases, his reply was, "by the Book of Allah." Asked what he would do if he did not find a direction in the Book of Allah, he replied "by the *Sunnah* of the Messenger of Allah".[4] The *Sunnah* was, therefore, recognized in the very lifetime of the Holy Prophet as affording guidance in religious matters.

Preservation of Hadith in Holy Prophet's lifetime

The preservation of what the Holy Prophet did or said was not an after-thought on the part of the Muslims, for the Companions while translating into practice most of his sayings, endeavoured also to preserve them in memory as well as on paper. They were conscious of the fact that these things must be preserved for future generations. When one of the Companions complained to the Holy Prophet of his inability to remember what he heard from him, the Holy Prophet's reply was that he should seek the help of his right hand, referring to the use of pen.[5] Another well-known report is from Abdullah ibn Amr:

> "I used to write everything that I heard from the Messenger of Allah, intending to commit it to memory. [On some people taking objection to this] I spoke about it to the Messenger of Allah ... who said: 'Write down, for I only speak the truth'." [6]

These and other reports show that while generally Hadith was committed to memory, it was occasionally, when there was need for it, written down. The Prophet sometimes did object to the writing down of his sayings, but this was due to his fear lest his sayings be mixed up with the revealed word of the Quran and the purity of the text of the Quran might be affected. However, there was nothing essentially wrong in writing these down nor did the Holy Prophet ever forbid this being done. On the other hand, as late as the conquest of Makkah, we find him giving orders himself for the writing down of a certain saying at the request of a hearer.[7] He also wrote letters, and treaties were put down in writing too.

Memory was by no means an unreliable mode for the pre-servation of Hadith, for the Quran itself was safely preserved in the memory of the Companions of the Holy Prophet in addition to being committed to writing. The Arabs had a wonderfully retentive memory in which to store up knowledge of countless things. It was in this safe custody that all the poetry of the pre-Islamic days had been kept alive and intact. Hundreds and even thousands of verses could be recited from memory by one man, and the reciters would also remember the names of the persons through whom those verses had been transmitted to them. Later on, the famous Bukhari trusted to memory alone for the retention of as many as six hundred thou-sand sayings of the Holy Prophet and many students corrected their manuscripts by comparing them with what he had only retained in his memory.

Collection of Hadith: First stage

The first steps for the preservation of Hadith were thus taken in the lifetime of the Holy Prophet, but all his followers were not equally interested in the matter, nor had all equal chances of being so. There was, however, a party of students called the *Aṣḥāb al-Ṣuffah* who lived in the mosque itself, and who were specially equipped for the teaching of religion to the tribes outside Madinah. Some of these would go to the market and do a little work to earn livelihood; others would not care to do even that. Of this little band, the most famous was Abu Hurairah, who would remain in the Holy Prophet's company at all costs, and store up in his memory everything which the Holy Prophet said or did. He himself is reported to have said once:

"You say, Abu Hurairah is profuse in narrating hadith from the Messenger of Allah; and you say, How is it that the Refugees (*Muhājirīn*) and the Helpers (*Anṣār*) do not narrate hadith from the Messenger of Allah like Abu Hurairah? The truth is that our brethren from among the Refugees were occupied in transacting business in the market and I used to remain with the Prophet having filled my belly; so I was present when they were absent and I remembered what they forgot; and our brethren from among the Helpers were occupied with work on their lands, and I was a poor man from among the poor inmates of the Suffah, so I retained what they forgot." [8]

Aishah, the Holy Prophet's wife, was also one of those who sought to preserve the practice of the Prophet. She too had a marvellous memory, and was, in addition, gifted with a clear intellect, by virtue of which she refused to accept anything which she did not understand: "she never heard anything she did not recognize but she questioned about it again and again".[9] In other words, she accepted nothing, even from the lips of the Holy Prophet himself, until she was fully satisfied as to its meaning. Abdullah ibn Umar and Abdullah ibn Abbas are two other Companions who were specially engaged in the work of preserving and transmitting the knowledge of the Quran and the Hadith, as also was Abdullah ibn Amr who used to write down the sayings of the Holy Prophet. And in addition to these, every Companion did his utmost to preserve such of his words and deeds as came to his knowledge.

"Let him who is present deliver to him who is absent" [10] is the concluding sentence of many of his most important utterances, which afford a clear proof that the work of preservation and transmission of the practice and sayings of the Holy Prophet had begun in his lifetime.

Collection of Hadith: Second stage

With the Holy Prophet's death, the work of the collection of Hadith entered a second stage. Every case that came up for decision had now to be referred either to the Quran or to some judgment or saying of the Holy Prophet, which judgments or sayings, therefore, obtained a wide reputation. There are numerous cases on record in which a right was claimed on the basis of a judgment or saying of the Holy Prophet, and evidence was demanded as to the authenticity of that saying. Thus the multiple needs of a rapidly growing and widely spreading community, whose necessities had increased greatly, brought into prominence a large number of Hadith reports, knowledge of which had been limited to one or a few only, with the seal of confirmation on their truth, because at that time direct evidence of that truth was available.

Moreover, the influx into Islam of large numbers of people who had never seen the Prophet himself, but who could behold for themselves the astounding transformation brought about by him, formed in itself an important factor in the general eagerness to discover everything which the great man had said or done. It was natural that each new convert should be anxious to know all there was to know about the great Teacher who had infused a new life into a dead world. Everyone who had seen him would thus become a source of knowledge for the later converts and since the incidents were fresh in the memories of the Companions they would be conveyed with fair accuracy to the new generation.

It must be remembered that the wonderful success which Islam achieved within so short a time, and the rapidity with which the reputation of its Prophet advanced, were the very reasons which led to the preservation of the actual facts concerning him. The personality of the Holy Prophet and his religion assumed an unparalleled importance in Arabia within twenty years of the day on which he began the work of a reformer, and within ten years of his death Islam spread to many countries beyond the borders of Arabia. Everything relating to the Holy Prophet, therefore, became a matter of discussion among Arabs and non-Arabs, friends and foes. Every incident of his life had become public property before it could be forgotten.

Another important factor was that, to the Companions, the religion brought by the Holy Prophet was the greatest gift of God, and to carry it to other people had become the supreme object of their lives. The great Master had also laid, on those who saw him and listened to his words, the duty of carrying what they saw and heard to those who were absent, to those who came after him. And they were faithful to this duty. They travelled in all directions, and wherever they went, they carried with them the Quran and the Hadith. Individuals like Aishah, Abu Hurairah, Abdullah ibn Abbas,

Abdullah ibn Umar, Abdullah ibn Amr, Anas ibn Malik and many others, whose first object in life was to preserve the sayings and practice of the Holy Prophet, became, as it were, centres to whom people resorted from different quarters of the kingdom of Islam to gain knowledge of Islam and its Prophet. The zeal of the new generation for the acquisition of knowledge was so great that students were wont to travel from one place to another to complete their religious studies, and some would journey long distances to obtain first-hand information about one hadith only.

Collection of Hadith: Third stage

With the passing of the generation that had seen and heard the Holy Prophet, the work of the collection of Hadith entered upon a third stage. There were no more reports to be investigated from different persons, and the whole of Hadith was now the property of teachers who taught at various centres, and, therefore, it could all be learnt by visiting these centres.

At this stage, moreover, the writing of Hadith became more common. The large number of the students at different centres, having abundance of material to digest, to which was also added the further task of remembering the names of the transmitters, sought aid from the pen, so that the work might be easier. There was now no fear of the Hadith being confused with the Quran. However, at this stage the Hadith reports were written merely as an aid to memory; the mere fact that a report was found among the manuscripts of a person was no evidence of its authenticity, which could be established only by tracing it to a reliable transmitter.

Umar ibn Abdul Aziz, commonly known as Umar II, the Umayyad Caliph, who ruled towards the close of the first century of Hijrah, was the first man to issue definite orders to the effect that written collections of Hadith reports should be made. But he died after a short reign of two and a half years, and his successor does not seem to have been interested in the matter. Even if a collection had been made in pursuance of these orders, which is very doubtful, no copy has reached us. But the work was taken up independently of government patronage in the next century.

Collection of Hadith: Fourth stage

Before the middle of the second century of Hijrah, Hadith started to assume a more permanent shape, and written collections began to appear. Hundreds of students were engaged in the work of learning Hadith in the various centres, but with every new teacher and student the work of preserving the name of the transmitter along with the text was becoming more difficult. Written collections had thus become indispensable. By far the most important of these collections is the *Muwaṭṭā* of Imam Malik ibn Anas (d. 179 A.H., 795 C.E.). All these books, however, were far from being exhaustive. In the first place, the object of their compilation was simply the collection of such reports as touched on the daily life of the Muslims. Reports relating to a large number of topics, such as faith, knowledge, the life of the Holy Prophet, wars, and comments on the Quran, were outside their scope. And secondly, every author collected only such reports as were taught at the centre where he worked. These works were, however, a great advance on oral transmission in the work of collecting Hadith.

Collection of Hadith: Fifth stage

This great work was brought to completion in the third century of Hijrah. It was then that two kinds of collections were made, *Musnad* (the earlier type) and *Jāmi‘* or *Muṣannaf. Musnad* is derived from *sanad* meaning *authority,* and the *isnād* of a Hadith report meant the tracing of it back through various transmitters to the Companion of the Holy Prophet on whose authority it rested. The *Musnad* collections were arranged, not according to the subject-matter of the report, but under the name of the Companion on whose final authority the report rested. The most important of the works of this class is the *Musnad* of Imam Ahmad ibn Hanbal (d. 241 A.H., 855 C.E.), which contains about thirty thousand reports.

It is to the *Jāmi‘* or *Muṣannaf* that the honour is due of bringing the knowledge of Hadith to perfection. The word *Jāmi‘* means 'one that gathers together' and *Muṣannaf* is something 'compiled together'. The *Jāmi‘* not only arranges reports according to their subject-matter but is also of a more critical tone.

Six books are recognized generally under the heading, being the collections made by:

1. Muhammad ibn Ismail, commonly known as Bukhari (d. 256 A.H., 870 C.E.)
2. Muslim ibn al-Hajjaj (d. 261 A.H., 875 C.E.)
3. Tirmidhi (d. 279 A.H., 892 C.E.)
4. Abu Dawud (d. 275 A.H., 889 C.E.)
5. Ibn Majah (d. 273 A.H., 887 C.E.)
6. Nasa'i (d. 303 A.H., 915 C.E.).[11]

These books classified reports under various subjects and thus made Hadith easy for reference, not only for lawyers and judges but also for students and research scholars, thus giving a further impetus to the study of Hadith.[12]

Bukhari

Among the six collections mentioned above, known collectively as *Ṣiḥāḥ Sittah* or the 'six reliable collections', *Bukhārī* holds the first place in several respects while *Muslim* comes second. Firstly, Bukhari has the unquestioned distinction of being first, all the others modelling their writings on his. Secondly, he is the most critical of all. He did not accept any report unless all its transmitters were reliable and until there was proof that the later transmitter had actually met the first; the mere fact that the two were contemporaries, which is the test adopted by Muslim, did not satisfy him. Thirdly, in his acumen he surpasses all. Fourthly, he heads the more important of his chapters with text from the Quran, and thus shows that Hadith is only an explanation of the Quran, and as such a secondary source of the teachings of Islam.

Method of counting reports

There is a wrong impression that the compilers of Hadith were faced with a vast mass of spurious reports and they did not credit more than one or two per cent of the prevailing mass as being genuine, the majority of the reports being fabrications. It is true that Bukhari took cognizance of 600,000 reports and knew some 200,000 of these by heart. It is also a fact that his book contains no more than 9,000 reports. But it is not true that he found the other 591,000 reports to be false or fabricated. It must be clearly understood that those who were engaged in the dissemination and study of Hadith looked upon every report as different when even a single transmitter was changed. For instance, a report from Abu Hurairah may have been reported by, say, ten of his disciples with or without any variation. Each of these reports would, according to the collectors, form a separate hadith. Again, suppose each of the transmitters of Abu Hurairah's report had two reporters, the same would then be counted as twenty different reports. The number would thus go on increasing as the number of reporters increased. By the time of Bukhari, in a chain of ordinarily four or five transmitters, consider the number of reports that would arise from the same basic report and it is easy to understand that 600,000 did not mean so many reports relating to various subjects, but so many reports coming through different transmitters, many of them referring to the same incident or conveying the same subject-matter with or without variation of words.

Reports in biographies and commentaries

Western criticism of Islam has often mixed up Hadith with the reports met with in the biographies of the Holy Prophet and in the commentaries on the Quran.[13] No Muslim scholar has ever attached the same value to the biographical reports as to hadith narrated in the above-mentioned collections. On the other hand, all Muslim critics recognize that the biographers never made much effort to sift truth from error. Imam Ahmad ibn Hanbal sums up the Muslim point of view as regards the trustworthiness of the biographical reports when he declares that the biographies "are not based on any principle"[14] and Hafiz Zain-ud-Din Iraqi says that "they contain what is true and what is false".

The same is true of the reports met with in the commentaries of the Quran, which are still more unreliable. Many careless commentators confounded Hadith with Jewish and Christian stories, and made free use of the latter as if they were so many reports. Speaking of the commentaries, Ibn Khaldun says:

> "Their books and their reports contain what is bad and what is good and what may be accepted and what should be rejected, and the reason of this is that the Arabs were an ignorant race without literature and without knowledge, and desert life and ignorance were their chief characteristics, and whenever they desired, as mortals do desire, to obtain knowledge of the cause of existence and the origin of creation and the mysteries of the universe, they turned for information to the followers of the Book, the Jews and such of

the Christians as practised their faith. But these people of the Book were like themselves, and their knowledge of these things went no further than the knowledge of the ignorant masses. … So when these people embraced Islam, they retained their stories which had no connection with the commandments of the Islamic law, such as the stories of the origin of creation, and things relating to the future and the wars, etc. … Commentaries on the Quran were soon filled with these stories of theirs." [15]

Shah Wali-ullah writes in a similar strain:

> "It is necessary to know that most of the Israelite stories that have found their way into the commentaries and histories are copied from the stories of the Jews and the Christians, and no commandment or belief can be based upon them." [16]

In fact, in some of the commentaries, the reports cited do not make sense. Even the commentary of Ibn Jarir, with all its value as a literary production, cannot be relied upon. Ibn Kathir's commentary is, however, an exception, as it contains chiefly reports taken from reliable collections.

Canons of criticism of Hadith as accepted by Muslims

There is no doubt that the collectors of Hadith attached the utmost importance to the trustworthiness of the narrators. As Alfred Guillaume says:

> "Inquiries were made as to the character of the guarantors, whether they were morally and religiously satisfactory, whether they were tainted with heretical doctrines, whether they had a reputation for truthfulness, and had the ability to transmit what they had themselves heard. Finally, it was necessary that they should be competent witnesses whose testimony would be accepted in a court of civil law." [17]

More than this, they tried their best to find out whether each report was actually traceable to the Holy Prophet through the various necessary stages. Even the Companions did not accept any report which was brought to their notice until they were fully satisfied that it came from the Holy Prophet. But the collectors went beyond the narrators, and they had rules of criticism which were applied to the subject-matter. In judging whether a certain report was spurious or genuine, the collectors not only made a thorough investigation of the trustworthiness of the transmitters but also applied other rules of criticism which are in no way inferior to modern methods. For example, a report was not accepted if it was opposed to recognized historical facts; or it was of such a nature that to know it and act upon it was incumbent upon all but it was reported only by one individual; or it was against reason or against the plain teachings of Islam; or it mentioned an incident which, had it happened, would have been reported by large numbers, while it was not reported by anyone except the particular reporter; or if it contained an accusation against the Companions by a Shiah reporter, or against a member of the Holy Prophet's family by a reporter who was a Khariji, and such a report was not corroborated by independent testimony.

The Quran as the greatest test for judging Hadith

In addition to these rules of criticism, there is another very important test whereby the trustworthiness of Hadith may be judged, and it is a test the application whereof was commanded by the Holy Prophet himself:

> "There will be narrators after me reporting sayings from me, so judge the sayings by the Quran; if it agrees with the Quran, accept it; otherwise, do not accept it." [18]

The genuineness of this saying is beyond all question, as it stands on the soundest basis. It is a fact that Hadith was in vogue in the time of the Holy Prophet, as already shown, and the authority of the Quran was treated as higher than that of Hadith, as appears from numerous occasions. There is a saying of the Holy Prophet:

> "My sayings do not abrogate the word of Allah, but the word of Allah can abrogate my sayings." [19]

The hadith relating to Mu'adh which has been quoted earlier (see page 30) places the Quran first, and the Hadith after that. Aishah used to quote a verse of the Quran on hearing words reported from the Holy Prophet when she thought that the purport of what the Prophet reportedly said did not agree with the Quran. The great Imam Bukhari quotes a verse of the Quran whenever he finds one suiting his text, before citing a saying, thus showing that the Quran holds precedence over Hadith; and by common consent of the Muslim community,

Bukhari's collection, considered to be the most trustworthy of all collections of Hadith, is called the most reliable of books *after* the Book of Allah. This verdict is enough proof that even if something in Bukhari disagrees with the Quran, it is the former that must be rejected and not the Book of God.

Hadith is only an explanation of the Quran, and for this reason also the latter must have precedence. Moreover, both Muslim and non-Muslim historians are agreed that the Quran has been handed down intact, every word and every letter of it, while Hadith cannot claim that purity. Since the Quran deals with the principles of the Islamic law while Hadith deals with its details, it is just and reasonable that only such details should be accepted as are in consonance with the principles. Again, as the Holy Prophet is plainly represented in the Quran as following "only what is revealed" to him and as not disobeying a word of what was revealed to him,[20] it follows clearly that if there is anything in Hadith which is not in consonance with the Quran, it could not have proceeded from the Holy Prophet, and must, therefore, be rejected.

How far did the Collectors apply these tests?

But the question arises as to whether all the collectors paid equal regard to the above canons of criticism. It is clear that they did not. The earliest of them, Bukhari, is, by a happy coincidence, also the soundest. He was not only most careful in accepting the trustworthiness of the narrators but he also paid the utmost attention to the last of the critical tests enumerated above: the test of judging Hadith by the Quran. Many of his books and chapters are headed by Quranic verses, and occasionally he has contented himself with a verse of the Quran in support of his text. This shows that his criticism of Hadith was not limited to a mere examination of the guarantors but that he also applied other tests. The act of criticism was, of course, applied mentally and one should not expect a record of the processes of that criticism in the book itself.

Other collectors too followed the necessary rules of criticism but were not all equally careful, nor did they all possess equal critical acumen or experience. Indeed, they sometimes intentionally relaxed the rules of criticism, both as regards the examination of the narrators and the critical tests. They also made a distinction between reports relating to matters of jurisprudence and others, such as those having to do with past history or with prophecies, or with other material which had no bearing on the practical life of man. They were stricter in matters of jurisprudence, relating to what is allowed and what is prohibited, than in other reports.

It must, however, be admitted that most of the collectors paid more attention to the investigation of the narrators than to the other critical tests. Their object was to produce reliable collections and, therefore, their first concern was to see that the reports could be authentically traced back to the Holy Prophet through a trustworthy chain of narrators. This part of the criticism was more essential, as the longer the chain of narrators, the more difficult would it have been to test their reliability. The passing away of another century would have rendered the task of the examination of the chain of narrators practically impossible. Hence the collectors rightly focussed their attention on this test. Nor did the work of collecting the Hadith close the door to further criticism. The collectors contented themselves with producing collections reliable in the main, leaving the rest of the work of criticism to future generations. They never claimed, nor does any Muslim claim on their behalf, infallibility of judgment, even in the case of Bukhari. In fact, they had started a work which was to continue in future.

We must also remember that the collectors set to work with minds absolutely free from bias or external influence. They would lay down their lives rather than swerve from what they deemed to be the truth. Many of the famous religious personalities, facing bitter opposition from the vested interests of the Muslim ruling houses of the time, preferred punishment or jail to uttering a word against their beliefs. Many of them, in order to retain their independence, refused to accept any employment or office from the government.

Notes to Chapter 2

1. See the Quran, 33:21.
2. Mishkat, book 1: 'Faith', ch. 1, sec. 1, h. 15 (v. 1, p. 19).
3. Bukhari, book 3: 'Knowledge', ch. 37, h. 104, h. 105.
4. See page 44 for the full quotation.
5. Tirmidhi, book 41: 'Knowledge', ch. 12, h. 2666 (MDS: book 39).
6. Abu Dawud, book 26: 'Knowledge', ch. 3, h. 3646 (MDS: book 24).
7. Bukhari, book 3: 'Knowledge', ch. 39, h. 112.

8. Bukhari, book 34: 'Sales and Trade', ch. 1, h. 2047.

9. Bukhari, book 3: 'Knowledge', ch. 36, h. 103.

10. *Ibid.,* ch. 37, chapter heading and h. 104, h. 105.

11. The works of Abu Dawud, Ibn Majah and Nasa'i are more generally known by the name of *Sunan* (pl. of *sunnah*).

12. The Shiahs have separate collections of Hadith which they recognize.

13. The term for a biography of the Holy Prophet is *Sīrat,* and for a commentary of the Quran is *Tafsīr.*

14. *Mauḍū'āt* by Mulla Ali Qari, p. 85.

15. *Muqaddamah* by Ibn Khaldun, Cairo 1329 A.H., v. 1, p. 481, chapter *'Ulūm-ul-Qur'ān.*

16. *Ḥujjatullāh al-Bālighah,* Brailey, India, 1286 A.H., v. 1, p. 171.

17. Alfred Guillaume, *Traditions of Islam,* Oxford, 1924, p. 83.

18. *Sunan Al-Dāra Quṭnī,* under *Letter of Umar to Abu Musa al-Ash'ari.* In the Urdu translation of this work by Hafiz Faizullah Nasir, published 2015, see report 4476 in vol. 3, p. 425.

19. Mishkat, book 1: 'Faith', ch. 6, sec. 3, h. 184 (v. 1, p. 62).

20. See the Quran, 6:50, 7:203, 46:9; and 6:15, 10:15.

3. *Ijtihād* or Exercise of Judgment

Ijtihād is the third source from which the laws of Islam are drawn. It literally means 'exerting oneself to the utmost' and applies technically to the exerting of mind to the utmost by a lawyer to form an opinion in a case of law in regard to a difficult point.[1]

Value of reason recognized

Reasoning or the exercise of judgment, in theological as well as in legal matters, plays a very important part in the religion of Islam, and the value of reason is expressly recognized in the Holy Quran. It appeals to reason again and again, and is full of exhortations such as the following: "Do you not reflect?" "Do you not understand?" "Have you no sense?" "There are signs in this for a people who reflect;" "There are signs in this for a people who understand;" and so on. Those who do not use their reasoning faculty are compared to animals, and spoken of as being deaf, dumb and blind:

> "And the parable of those who disbelieve is as the parable of one [i.e., the Prophet] who calls out to that which hears no more than a call and a cry. Deaf, dumb, blind, so they have no sense." — 2:171

> "They have hearts with which they do not understand, and they have eyes with which they do not see, and they have ears with which they do not hear. They are as cattle; rather, they are more astray." — 7:179

> "The vilest of beasts in Allah's sight are the deaf, the dumb, who do not understand." — 8:22

> "Or do you think that most of them hear or understand? They are only as the cattle; rather, they are farther astray from the path." — 25:44

While those who do not exercise their reason or judgment are condemned, those who do it are praised:

"In the creation of the heavens and the earth, and the alternation of the night and the day, there are surely signs for those who have understanding, those who remember Allah standing and sitting and [lying] on their sides, and reflect on the creation of the heavens and the earth." —3:190–191

The Quran does recognize revelation as a source of knowledge higher than reason, but at the same time admits that the truth of the principles established by revelation may be judged by reason, and hence it is that it repeatedly appeals to reason and denounces those who do not use their reasoning faculty. It also recognizes the necessity of the exercise of judgment in order to arrive at a decision:

"But if any news of security or fear comes to them, they spread it about. And if they had referred it to the Messenger and to those in authority among them, those of them who can *search out the knowledge* of it would have known it." — 4:83

The verse recognizes the principle of the exercise of judgment, and though the occasion on which it is mentioned is a particular one, the principle recognized is general.

The Prophet allowed exercise of judgment in religious matters

The exercise of judgment (*Ijtihād*) is expressly recognized in Hadith as the means by which a decision may be arrived at when there is no direction in the Quran or Hadith. The following report is regarded as the basis of *Ijtihād* in Islam:

"When the Messenger of Allah decided to send Mu'adh to Yaman [as Governor], he asked him how he would decide cases. Mu'adh replied: 'By the Book of Allah'. He asked: 'But if you do not find [any direction] in it'. He replied: 'Then by the practice (*Sunnah*) of the Messenger of Allah'. 'But if you do not find [any direction] in the *Sunnah*', he asked. 'Then I will exercise my judgment (*ajtahidu*) and spare no effort', Mu'adh replied. … The Messenger of Allah said: 'Praise be to Allah Who has granted the messenger of His Messenger what pleases the Messenger of Allah'." [2]

This report shows not only that the Holy Prophet approved of the exercise of judgment, but also that his Companions were well aware of the principle, and that reasoning or exercise of judgment by others was freely resorted to when necessary, even in the Holy Prophet's lifetime.

Exercise of Judgment by the Companions

After the Holy Prophet's death, the principle of *Ijtihād* obtained a wider prevalence, and as new areas were added to the material and spiritual realm of Islam, the need of resorting to the exercise of judgment became greater. Nor did the Caliphs arrogate all authority to themselves. They had a council to which every important case was referred, and its decision by a majority of votes was accepted by the Caliph as well as by the Muslim public. Thus Suyuti writes in his *History of the Caliphs:*

> "When a case came before Abu Bakr [the first Caliph], he used to consult the Book of Allah; if he found anything in it by which he could decide, he did so; if he did not find it in the Book, and he knew of a practice or saying of the Messenger of Allah, he decided according to it; and if he was unable to find anything there, he used to question the Muslims if they knew of any decision of the Prophet in a matter of that kind, and a company of people thus gathered round him, every one of whom stated what he knew from the Prophet, and Abu Bakr would say, 'Praise be to Allah Who has kept among us those who remember what the Prophet said'; but if he was unable to find anything in the practice of the Prophet, he gathered the heads of the people, and the best of them, and consulted them, and if they agreed upon one opinion [by a majority] he decided accordingly." [3]

The same rule was followed by Umar, the second Caliph, who resorted to *Ijtihād* very freely, but took care always to gather the most learned Companions for consultation. When there was a difference of opinion, the decision of the majority was acted upon. Besides this council, there were great individual teachers, such as Aishah, Ibn Abbas, Ibn Umar and others, whose opinion was highly revered. Decisions were given and laws made and promulgated subject only to the one condition that they were neither contrary to the Holy Quran nor to the practice of the Holy Prophet.

The four great jurists

In the second century of the Hijrah arose the great jurists who codified the Islamic law according to the need of their time. The first of these, and the one who claims the allegiance of the greater part of the Muslim world, was Imam **Abu Hanifah** (d. 150 A.H., 767 C.E.). The basis of his analogical reasoning (*qiyās*) was the Holy Quran, and he accepted Hadith only when he was fully satisfied as to its authenticity; and, as the collectors of Hadith had not yet commenced the work of collection, naturally Abu Hanifah accepted very few reports, and always resorted to the Holy Quran for his juristic views. Later on when Hadith was collected, and was more in vogue, the followers of the Hanafi system — as Abu Hanifah's school of thought was called — introduced into it more of its reports.

Abu Hanifah had two famous disciples, Muhammad and Abu Yusuf, and it is mostly their views of the great master's teaching that now form the basis of the Hanafi system. This system is not only the first in point of time but is also the one which claims allegiance from the great majority of Muslims, and a development of which on the right lines would have resulted in immense benefit to the Muslim world. It was he who first directed attention to the great value of ana-logical reasoning in legislation. He also laid down the principle of equity, whereby not only could new laws be made, but even logical conclusions could be controverted when proved inequitable.

Imam **Malik ibn Anas** (d. 179 A.H., 796 C.E.), the second famous jurist, was born in Madinah. He limited himself almost entirely to the Hadith reports which he found in Madinah, relating more especially to the practice which prevailed there, and his system of jurisprudence is based entirely on the traditions and practices of the people of Madinah. He was scrupulously careful in giving judg-ment, and whenever he had the least doubt as to the correctness of his decision, he would say: "I do not know". His book, *Muwaṭṭā,* though a comparatively small collection of Hadith, and limited only to the Hadith reports and practices of the people of Madinah, is the first work of its kind, and one of the most authoritative.

The third jurist, Imam **al-Shafi'i** (d. 204 A.H., 820 C.E.), worked for the most part in Egypt. He was intimately acquainted with the Hanafi and the Maliki schools of thought, but that which he himself founded was based largely on Hadith, as distinguished from the

Hanafi system which was founded on the Holy Quran and made very little use of Hadith. Over the Maliki system, which is also based on *Sunnah*, it had this advantage that the Hadith made use of by Shafi'i was more extensive, and was collected from different centres, while Malik contented himself only with what he found at Madinah.

Imam **Ahmad ibn Hanbal** (d. 241 A.H., 855 C.E.), the last of the four great jurists, was born and died in Baghdad. He too made a very extensive study of Hadith. His famous work on the subject, the *Musnad* of Ahmad ibn Hanbal, containing nearly thirty thousand reports, was prepared by his son Abdullah, based on the material collected by the Imam himself. In the *Musnad,* however, as already remarked, Hadith reports are not arranged according to subject-matter but according to names of the Companions to whom they are ultimately traced. Though it contains a large number of reports, it does not apply those strict rules of criticism favoured by collectors like Bukhari and Muslim. Accordingly, the *Musnad* of Ahmad cannot claim the same reliability as regards its material as can the collections of the other famous collectors.

From the very nature of his exertions, it is evident that Ahmad ibn Hanbal made very little use of reasoning, and as he depended almost entirely on Hadith, the result was that he admitted even the weakest report. It would thus appear that from the system of Abu Hanifah, who applied reasoning very freely and sought to deduce all questions from the Holy Quran by the help of reason, the system of Ahmad ibn Hanbal is distinguished by the fact that it makes the least possible use of reason, and thus there was a marked falling off in the last of the four great jurists from the high ideals of the first, so far as the application of reason to matters of religion is concerned. Even the system of Abu Hanifah himself deteriorated on account of the later jurists of that school not developing the master's high ideal, with the consequence that the world of Islam gradually shut the door to *Ijtihād* or Exercise of Judgment and stagnation reigned in the place of healthy development.

Different methods of formulating new laws
The four Jurists (or *Imams*) who are accepted by the entire Sunni world of Islam are thus agreed in giving an important place in legislation to *Ijtihād,* and the Shiahs attached to it an even greater importance.

Ijmā' or 'consensus of opinion' (see later), which means really the *Ijtihād* of many, and *Ijtihād* are thus looked upon as two more sources of the Islamic law along with the Quran and the *Sunnah*. However, only the Quran and the *Sunnah* are regarded as absolute arguments or authorities, while *Ijtihād* and *Ijmā'* are called "arguments obtained by exertion".

The sphere of *Ijtihād* is very wide since it seeks to fulfil all the requirements of the Muslim community which are not met with expressly in the Holy Quran and the Hadith. The great jurists of Islam have endeavoured to meet these demands by various methods, as briefly described below.

Qiyās, which may be described as 'reasoning based on analogy', is the most important of these methods, and has almost a universal sanction. When a case comes up for decision, which is not expressly provided for either in the Holy Quran or in Hadith, the jurist looks for a case resembling it in the Quran or in Hadith, and, by reasoning on the basis of analogy, arrives at a decision. Thus it is an extension of the law as met with in the Quran and Hadith, and no infallibility is claimed for such analogical deductions or laws based on them. A jurist may err in his judgment and hence it is that so many differences of juristic deductions exist even among the highest authorities. By its very nature, the reasoning of one generation may be rejected by a following generation.

Istiḥsān, in the terminology of the jurists, is the exercise of private judgment, not on the basis of analogy but on that of public good or the interest of justice. According to the Hanafi school, when a deduction based on analogy is not acceptable either because it is against the broader rules of justice or because it is not in the interest of the public good, and is likely to cause undue inconvenience to those to whom it is applied, the jurist is at liberty to reject the same, and to adopt instead a rule which is conducive to public good, or is in consonance with the broader rules of justice. This method is peculiar to the Hanafi system, but owing to strong opposition from the other schools of thought, it has not, even in that system, been developed to its full extent. The principle underlying it is, however, a very sound one and is quite in accordance with the spirit of the Holy Quran. There is, moreover, less liability to error in this method than in far-fetched analogy, which often leads to narrow results opposed to the broad spirit of the Holy Book. In the school of Imam Malik, a similar rule is adopted under the name of *istiṣlāḥ* which means 'a deduction of law based on considerations of public good'.

Istidlāl literally signifies the 'inferring of one thing from another', and the two chief sources recognized for such inferences are customs and usages, and the laws of religions revealed before Islam. Customs and usages, when not opposed to the spirit of the teachings of the Quran, or not forbidden by it, would be admissible, because, according to a well-known maxim of the jurists, "permissibility is the original principle"; therefore what has not been declared unlawful is permissible. The Hanafi law lays special stress on the value of customs and usages. As regards laws revealed previous to Islam, the Hanafi school holds that those laws of the previous religions are binding which have been mentioned in the Quran without being abrogated.

Ijmā' or Consensus of Opinion

In the terminology of the Muslim jurists, *Ijmā'* means a consensus of opinion or an agreement of the Muslim jurists of a particular age on a question of law. The agreement may be inferred from their word, their practice, or silence when recognized jurists do not controvert an opinion expressed by one or more of them. It is generally held that *Ijmā'* means the consensus of opinion of jurists only, but some are of the opinion that it means the agreement of all Muslims. Most authorities require the unanimity of opinion of all the jurists of a particular age, but others have held the opposite view. However, it is generally agreed that if there is an overwhelming preponderance of jurists holding a certain view, that view is valid and binding, though not absolute. One *Ijmā'* may be repealed by another in the same age or in a subsequent age, with this reservation that the *Ijmā'* of the Companions of the Holy Prophet cannot be reversed by any later generation.

Ijmā' is not an independent source of the laws of Islam. It is essentially *Ijtihād* or exercise of judgment, on which all or the majority of the jurists of a certain generation are agreed. There is no denying the fact that, if many jurists are agreed on a certain question, their opinion would carry greater weight than that of a single one, but even the opinion of many, or of all, is not infallible. *Ijmā'*, after all, is only *Ijtihād* on a wider basis, and like the latter it is always open to correction.

To differ with majority is no sin

It may be added here that the sense in which the word *Ijmā'* is commonly used nowadays is quite erroneous, for it is taken to mean the opinion of the majority, and it is generally thought that it is a sin on the part of a Muslim to differ with the views of the majority. But honest difference of opinion, instead of being a sin, is called a mercy by the Holy Prophet, who is reported to have said: "The differences of my people are a mercy".[4] Difference of opinion is called a mercy because it is only through encouraging it that the reasoning faculty is developed, and the truth ultimately discovered. There were many differences of opinion among the Companions, and there were also matters on which a single man used to express boldly his dissent from all the rest. *Ijtihād* is encouraged by a saying of the Holy Prophet, which promises reward even to one who makes an error in it:

> "When the judge gives a judgment and he exercises his reasoning faculty and is right, he has a double reward, and when he gives a judgment and exercises his reasoning faculty and makes a mistake, there is a reward for him." [5]

The door of *Ijtihād* is still open

Later jurists regard the door of every degree of *Ijtihād* to have been closed after the sixth century of Hijrah. It is said that after the immediate disciples of the first four Imams,[6] there can only be followers (*muqallidīn*) who may only quote a decision (*fatwā*) from any of the earlier authorities, or when there are differing opinions of the earlier jurisconsults they can choose one of them, but they cannot question the correctness of what has been said. Thus *Ijtihād,* which was never considered to be an absolute authority by the great Imams or their immediate disciples, is now practically placed on the same level with the Holy Quran and the Hadith and hence no one now is considered to be fit for *Ijtihād.*

It is, however, a mistake to suppose that the door of *Ijtihād* was closed in any way after the four Imams mentioned above. It is quite clear that the free exercise of judgment was allowed by the Holy Quran, while both the Quran and the Hadith explicitly allowed analogical deduction, and it was on the basis of these directions that the Muslim world continued to exercise its judgment in making laws for itself. The Companions made use of it even in the Holy Prophet's lifetime, when it was not convenient to refer a matter to him personally; and after his death, as new circumstances arose, new laws were made by the majority of the Caliph's council and new decisions given by the learned among the Companions; the next generation added up to the knowledge of the Companions; and each succeeding generation, not satisfied with what the previous one had achieved, freely applied its judgment. The second century saw the four great luminaries appear on the horizon of *Ijtihād,* and the appearance of these great jurists one after another, each evidently dissatisfied with what his predecessor had achieved, is another conclusive argument that Islam permitted human judgment to be exercised freely to meet new circumstances.

Ijtihād was a great blessing to the Muslim people; it was the only way through which the needs of succeeding generations and the requirements of different races merging into Islam could be met. Neither the Holy Prophet, nor any of his Companions, nor any of the great jurists ever said that Muslims were forbidden to apply their own judgment to new circumstances and the ever changing needs of a growing community after a certain time. What happened was that the attention of the great intellects of the third century was directed towards the collection and criticism of Hadith. On the other hand, the four Imams rose so high above the ordinary jurists that the latter were dwarfed into insignificance, and the impression gained ground gradually that no one could exercise his judgment independently of the former. This impression in its turn led to limitations upon *Ijtihād* and the independence of thought to which Islam had given an impetus. Being thus restrained by a false impression, the intellect of Islam suffered a heavy loss and the increasing demand of knowledge being brought to a standstill, stagnation and ignorance took its place.

Independence of thought recognized

The Holy Quran expressly recognizes independence of opinion for one and all, and requires that absolute obedience be given only to God and His Messenger:

> "O you who believe, obey Allah and obey the Messenger and those in authority from among you; then if you quarrel about anything, refer it to Allah and the Messenger..." — 4:59

This verse speaks of obedience to those in authority (*ulu-l-amr*), along with the obedience to the Messenger, and then mentions disputes which, it says, must be settled by referring them to God and His Messenger. The omission of *ulu-l-amr* from the latter portion of the verse shows clearly that the *quarrel* here spoken of relates to differences with *ulu-l-amr,* and in the case of such a difference the only authority is that of God and the Messenger, or the Quran and the Hadith. Every authority in Islam, whether temporal or spiritual, is included in *ulu-l-amr,* and independence of thought for every Muslim is thus recognized by allowing him to differ with all except the Quran and the Hadith. The Companions, the Collectors of Hadith, the four Imams and the other jurists being thus included in *ulu-l-amr,* must be obeyed ordinarily, but to differ with any one or all of them, when one has the authority of the Quran and the Hadith is expressly permitted. And since the ultimate test of the correctness of Hadith is the Quran itself, the conclusion is evident that Islam allows independence of thought subject only to one condition, that the principles laid down in the Quran are not contravened.

It will thus be seen that any Muslim community has the right to make any law for itself, the only condition being that such law shall not contravene any principle laid down by the Holy Quran. The impression prevailing in the Muslim world at present that no one has the right, even in the light of the new circumstances which a thousand years of the world's progress have brought about, to differ with the four Imams, is entirely a mistaken one. The right to differ with the highest of men below the Holy Prophet is a Muslim's birthright, and to take away that right is to stifle the very existence of Islam. Under the present circumstances, when conditions have quite changed and the world has been moving on for a thousand years, while Muslims have more or less stagnated, it is the duty of Muslim states and Muslim peoples to apply their own judgment to the changed conditions, and find out the ways and means for their temporal salvation.

Notes to Chapter 3

1. Lane's Lexicon.
2. Abu Dawud, book 25: 'Judgment (*Al-Aqḍiyya*)', ch. 11, h. 3592 (MDS: book 23).

3. *Tārīkh al-Khulafā'*, edition published in Lahore, 1870, p. 40.

4. *Jāmi' al-Ṣaghīr* by Imam Jalal-ud-Din Suyuti, Cairo, p. 11.

5. Mishkat, book 17: 'Governing and Judgment', ch. 3, sec. 1, h. 3560 (v. 2, p. 203).

6. Of Muhammad and Abu Yusuf, the two famous disciples of Abu Hanifah, it is said that their unanimous opinion on any point must be accepted, even if it goes against that of their master.

4. Faith

Faith and action

The religion of Islam may be broadly divided into two parts — the theoretical, or what may be called its articles of faith or its doctrines, and the practical, which includes all that a Muslim is required to do, that is to say, the practical course to which he must conform his life. In the Holy Quran the two broad divisions are repeatedly referred to as *īmān* (faith or belief) and *'amal* (deed or action) and the two words are often used together to describe a believer; "those who believe and do good" is the oft-recurring description of true believers. The relation of faith with deeds must be constantly borne in mind in order to understand the true meaning of Islam.

In the terminology of later Muslim theologians, the articles of faith are called *uṣūl* or the 'roots', and the regulations or ordinances are called *furū'* or the 'branches', because the branches grow from the roots just as action springs from faith.

Use of the word *īmān* in the Quran

The word *īmān* (faith or belief), as used in the Holy Quran, signifies either simply a confession of the truth with the tongue, or simply an assent of the heart and a firm conviction of the truth brought by the Holy Prophet, or the doing of good deeds and carrying into practice of the principle accepted, or it may signify a combination of the three.

In the following two verses, for example, the words "who believe" refer to those who do nothing more than confess with the tongue that they believe in Muhammad:

> "Surely those *who believe* and those who are Jews, and the Christians, and the Sabians,[1] whoever believes in Allah and the Last Day and does good, they have their reward with their Lord..."[2] — 2:62

> "O you who believe! Believe in Allah and His Messenger and the Book which He has revealed to His Messenger..." — 4:136

In the following verse, belief stands for assent of the heart:

> "The dwellers of the desert say: 'We believe.' Say [to them]:
> You do not believe, but [rather] say, 'We submit'; and faith
> has not yet entered into your hearts." — 49:14

In the following verse, "believe in Allah" means *make sacrifices
in the cause of truth:*

> "What reason have you that you do not believe in Allah, and
> the Messenger invites you that you may believe in your Lord
> and He has indeed made a covenant with you if you are
> believers." — 57:8

It is also used to imply the condition in which a confession with
the tongue is accompanied by *both* an assent of the heart and the
carrying into practice of what is believed, as in this verse:

> "And those who believe in Allah and His Messengers, they
> are the truthful and the faithful ones[3] with their Lord." —
> 57:19

Generally, however, it is employed to indicate an assent of the
heart, combined, of course, with a confession with the tongue, to
what the prophets bring from God, as distinguished from the doing
of good deeds, and hence it is that the righteous, as already remarked,
are spoken of as those *who believe and do good.*

The word *īmān* in Hadith

In Hadith, the word *īmān* is frequently used in its wider sense, that is
to say, as including good deeds, and sometimes simply as standing
for good deeds. Thus the Holy Prophet is reported to have said:

> "Faith (*īmān*) has over sixty branches, and modesty is a
> branch of faith." [4]

> "Faith (*īmān*) has over seventy branches, the highest of
> which is [the belief] that nothing deserves to be worshipped
> except Allah (*Lā ilāha ill-Allāh*), and the lowest of which is
> the removal from the way of that which might cause injury
> to anyone." [5]

> "One of you has no faith unless he loves for his brother what
> he loves for himself." [6]

"One of you has no faith unless he has greater love for me
than he has for his father and his son and all the people." [7]

Unbelief (*kufr*)

Just as faith (*īmān*) is the acceptance of the truth brought by the
Prophet, so unbelief (*kufr*) is its rejection, and as the practical acceptance of the truth or the doing of a good deed is called *īmān* or part
of *īmān,* so the practical rejection of the truth or the doing of an evil
deed is called *kufr* or part of *kufr*. There is a report that when someone
related that he had abused a man, addressing him as the son of a black
woman, the Holy Prophet told him:

"You find fault with him because of his mother. Surely you
are a man in whom is *jāhiliyyah*." [8]

Now *jāhiliyyah* (lit. *ignorance*), in the terminology of Islam, means
the "time of ignorance" before the advent of the Holy Prophet, and is
thus synonymous with *kufr* or unbelief. Thus the mere act of finding
fault with a man on account of his racial origin is called *jāhiliyyah* or
kufr. According to another hadith, the Holy Prophet is reported to
have warned his Companions in the following words:

"Beware, do not become unbelievers (*kuffār,* pl. of *kāfir*)
after me, so that some of you should strike off the necks of
others." [9]

Here the slaying of Muslims by Muslims is condemned as an act of
unbelief. In another hadith, it is said:

"Abusing a Muslim is transgression and fighting with him is
unbelief (*kufr*)." [10]

Yet in spite of the fact that in these reports the fighting of Muslims with one another is called *kufr* — and those who fight among
themselves are even termed *unbelievers* (singular, *kāfir*) — the Holy
Quran speaks of two parties of Muslims at war with one another as
believers (*mu'minīn*).[11] It is, therefore, clear that such conduct is
called an act of unbelief (*kufr*) simply as being an act of disobedience.
This point has been explained by Ibn Athir in his well-known dictionary of Hadith, the *Nihāyah*. Writing under the word *kufr,* he says:

"*Kufr* (unbelief) is of two kinds: one is denial of the faith
itself, and that is the opposite of faith; and the other is denial

of a branch of the branches (*furū‘*) of Islam, and on account of it a man does not get out of the faith itself."

As already shown, the *furū‘* of Islam are its ordinances, and thus the practical rejection of an ordinance of Islam, while it is called *kufr,* is not *kufr* in the technical sense, i.e., a denial of Islam itself. Thus it is clear that a Muslim remains a Muslim though he may be guilty of an act of unbelief (*kufr*).

A Muslim cannot be called a *kāfir* (unbeliever)

As stated above, a Muslim cannot properly be called a *kāfir* (un-believer). Every evil deed or act of disobedience being part of *kufr,* even a Muslim may commit an act of unbelief. And the opposite is equally true, namely, that since every good deed is a part of faith, even an unbeliever may perform an act of faith. There is nothing paradoxical in these statements. The dividing line between a Muslim and an unbeliever is confession of the Unity of God and the prophet-hood of Muhammad — *Lā ilāha ill-Allāh, Muḥammad-ur Rasūl-ullāh.* One becomes a Muslim or a believer by making this confession and as long as he does not renounce his faith in it, he remains a Muslim or a believer technically, in spite of any opinion he may hold on any religious question, or any evil which he may commit; and someone who does not make this confession is a non-Muslim or unbeliever technically. It does not mean that the evil deeds of the Muslim are not punished, or that the good deeds of the non-Muslim are not rewarded. As the Holy Quran puts it in very clear words:

> "So whoever does an atom's weight of good will see it, and whoever does an atom's weight of evil will see it." — 99:7–8

A believer is capable of doing evil and an unbeliever is capable of doing good, and each shall be requited for what he does. But no one has the right to expel anyone from the brotherhood of Islam so long as he confesses the Unity of God and the prophethood of Muhammad. The Quran and the Hadith are quite clear on this point. Thus in the Holy Quran we have:

> "And do not say to anyone who offers you salutation: You are not a believer." — 4:94

The Muslim form of salutation — *as-salāmu ‘alaikum,* or "peace be to you" — is thus considered a sufficient indication that the one who offers it is a Muslim, and no one has the right to say to him that he is not a believer, even though he may be insincere.

The Holy Quran speaks of two parties of Muslims fighting with each other, and yet of both as believers (singular *mu'min*):

> "And if two groups of the believers fight with each other, make peace between them.... The believers are brethren so make peace between your brethren..." — 49:9–10

Even those who were known to be hypocrites were treated as Muslims by the Holy Prophet and his Companions, though they refused to join the Muslims in the struggle in which the latter had to engage in self-defence, and when the reputed chief of these hypocrites, the notorious Abdullah ibn Ubayy, died, the Holy Prophet offered funeral prayers on his grave and treated him as a Muslim.

Hadith is equally clear on this point. The Holy Prophet is reported to have said:

> "Whoever offers prayers as we do and turns his face to our *Qiblah* and eats the animal slaughtered by us, he is a Muslim for whom is the covenant of Allah and His Messenger, so do not violate Allah's covenant." [12]

> "Three things are the basis of faith: [the first is] to withhold from one who confesses faith in *Lā ilāha ill-Allāh* ('There is no god but Allah'), you should not call him *kāfir* for any sin, nor expel him from Islam for any deed." [13]

> "Whoever calls the people of *Lā ilāha ill-Allāh* as *kāfir* is himself nearer to unbelief (*kufr*)." [14]

By the people of *Lā ilāha ill-Allāh,* or the upholders of the Unity of God, are clearly meant Muslims, and it is made quite evident that anyone who makes a confession of the *Kalimah,* that there is no god but Allah and Muhammad is His Messenger, becomes a Muslim, and to call him a *kāfir* is the greatest of sins.

Thus it will be seen that membership of the brotherhood of Islam is a thing not to be tested by some great theologian, well-versed in logical quibbling, but rather by the man in the street, by the man of commonsense, or even by the illiterate man who can judge of another by his very appearance, who is satisfied with even a greeting in the

Muslim style, who requires no further argument when he sees a man turn his face to *Qiblah,* and to whom Islam means the confession of the Unity of God and the prophethood of Muhammad.

Despite the schisms and differences that arose afterwards among Muslims, the principle stated above is upheld by all authorities on Islam:

> "The generality of the theologians and the jurists are agreed that none of the *Ahl Qiblah* (the people who recognize the Ka'bah as *qiblah*) can be called a *kāfir.*" [15]

> "Trustworthy Imams from among the Hanafis and the Shafi'is and the Malikis and the Hanbalis and the Ash'aris hold that none of the *Ahl Qiblah* can be called a *kāfir.*" [16]

And the famous Abu-l-Hasan Ash'ari writes:

> "After the death of their Prophet, the Muslims became divided on many points, some of them called others *ḍāll* (straying from the right path), and some shunned others, so that they became sects entirely separated from each other, and scattered parties, but Islam gathers them all and includes them all in its sphere." [17]

The words *īmān* and *islām*

Originally the word *īmān* signifies *conviction of the heart,* while the word *islām* signifies *submission* and hence relates primarily to action. This difference in the original meaning finds expression both in the Quran and the Hadith, though in ordinary use they both convey the same significance, and *mu'min* ('believer') and Muslim are generally used interchangeably. An example of the distinction in their use in the Quran is afforded in 49:14:

> "The dwellers of the desert say: 'We believe' (*āmannā,* from *īmān*). Say: You do not believe, but say, 'We submit' (*aslam-nā,* from *islām*); and faith has not yet entered into your hearts. And if you obey Allah and His Messenger, He will not diminish anything of your deeds; for Allah is Forgiving, Merciful."

This does not mean, of course, that they did not believe in the prophethood of Muhammad. The significance of faith entering into the heart is made clear in the very next verse:

> "The believers are those only who believe in Allah and His
> Messenger, then they do not doubt, and struggle hard with
> their wealth and their lives in the way of Allah. Such are the
> truthful ones." — 49:15

In fact, both the words *īmān* and *islām* are used to signify two
different stages in the spiritual growth of man. A person is said to
have believed (*āmana*) when he simply declares his faith in the Unity
of God and the prophethood of Muhammad, which in fact is the first
stage of belief; and he is also said to have believed (*āmana*) when he
carries into practice to their utmost extent the principles in which he
has declared his faith, the faith having entered into the depths of the
heart and brought about the change required. Examples of the first
use are 2:62 and 4:136 (see page 54); an example of the latter use is
49:15 quoted above. The same is the case with the use of the word
islām; in its first stage it is simply a willingness to submit, as in the
verse 49:14 quoted above; in its last it is entire submission, as in
2:112:

> "No, whoever submits himself (*aslama*) entirely to Allah,
> and he is the doer of good [to others], he has his reward from
> his Lord, and there is no fear for such nor shall they grieve."

Thus both *īmān* and *islām* are the same in their first and last stage
— from a simple declaration they have developed into perfection —
and cover all the intermediate stages. They have both a starting point
and a goal; and the one who is at the starting point and the one who
has attained the goal, in spite of all the differences between them, are
both called *mu'min* or Muslim, as are also those who are on their way
at different stages of the journey.

Principles of faith

The whole of the religion of Islam is briefly summed up in the two
short sentences, *Lā ilāha ill-Allāh,* i.e., there is no god but Allah, or,
nothing deserves to be made an object of love and worship except
Allah, and *Muḥammad-ur Rasūl-ullāh,* Muhammad is the Messenger
of Allah. It is simply by bearing witness to the truth of these two
simple propositions that anyone enters the fold of Islam. The first part
of the creed is the constant theme of the Quran, as for example in the
verse "Know that there is no god but Allah" (47:19), and a faith in
the Unity of God, that there is no god except Allah, is repeatedly

mentioned as the basic principle, not only of Islam but of every religion revealed by God. The second part of the creed, concerning the messengership of the Holy Prophet Muhammad, is also a constant theme of the Quran and the very words *Muḥammad-ur Rasūl-ullāh* occur in 48:29. From Hadith too, it appears that the essential condition of the acceptance of Islam was the acceptance of these two component parts of the creed.

The above, in the terminology of the later theologians, is called "a brief expression of faith" (*īmān mujmal*), while the detailed expression of faith, which the later theologians call *mufaṣṣal,* is set forth in the very beginning of the Quran as follows: a belief in the Unseen (i.e. God), a belief in that which was revealed to the Holy Prophet Muhammad and in that which was revealed to the prophets before him, and a belief in the Hereafter.[18] Further on in the same chapter, five principles of faith are clearly mentioned:

> "...that one should believe in Allah and the Last Day and the angels and the Book and the prophets..." — 2:177

Again and again, the Quran makes it clear that it is only in relation to these five that belief is required. In the Hadith there is a slight variation. Bukhari has it as follows:

> "That you believe in Allah and His angels and in the meeting with Him and His messengers and that you believe in the life after death." [19]

It will be seen that a belief in the meeting with God is mentioned distinctly here, and while this is included in the belief in God in the Quran in the verse quoted above, it is also mentioned distinctly on many occasions, as in verse 13:2 etc. Again, in the Hadith, the books are not mentioned distinctly and are included in the word "messengers". Thus the basis of belief rests on five principles, according to the Holy Quran and Hadith: God, His angels, His prophets, His books, and a life after death.[20]

Significance of faith

The above discussion on the words *īmān* and *islām* leads us also to the conclusion that there are no dogmas in Islam, no mere beliefs forced upon a person for his alleged salvation. Belief, according to Islam, is not only a conviction of the truth of a given proposition, but it is essentially the acceptance of a proposition as a basis for action. While the proposition of the existence of devils is as true as that of the existence of angels according to the Holy Quran, yet a belief in angels is again and again mentioned as part of a Muslim's faith, whereas a *disbelief* in devils is equally clearly mentioned as necessary:

> "So whoever disbelieves in the devil and believes in Allah, he indeed has laid hold on the firmest handle…" — 2:256

The words used here for believing in God and disbelieving in devils are, respectively, *īmān* and *kufr*. If *īmān* meant simply a belief in the existence of a thing, and *kufr* the denial of its existence, a disbelief in devils could not have been spoken of as necessary along with a belief in God. But while we must believe in God and His angels, we must disbelieve in the devil. This is because the angel, according to the Quran, is the being that prompts the doing of good, and the devil is the being that prompts the doing of evil, so that a belief in angels means really acting upon the promptings to do good, and a disbelief in the devil means refusing to entertain evil promptings.

Thus *īmān* (belief) really signifies the acceptance of a principle as a basis for action, and every doctrine of Islam answers to this description. There are no dogmas, no mysteries, no faith which does not require action; for every article of faith means a principle to be carried into practice for the higher development of man.

Allah is the Being Who possesses all the perfect attributes, and when a person is required to believe in Allah, he is really required to make himself possessor of the highest moral qualities, his goal being the attainment of the Divine Attributes. He must set before himself the highest and purest ideal which the heart of a human being can conceive, and make his conduct conform to that ideal. Belief in the angels means that the believer should follow the good impulses which are inherent in him, for the angel is the being who prompts the doing of good. Belief in the books of God signifies that we should follow the directions contained in them for the development of our inner faculties. Belief in messengers means that we are to model ourselves on their noble example and sacrifice our lives for humanity even as they did. Belief in the Hereafter or the Last Day tells us that physical or material advancement is not the end or goal of life; but that its real purpose is an infinitely higher one, of which the Resurrection, or the Last Day, is but the beginning.

Notes to Chapter 4

1. *Editor's Note:* The Sabians followed a religion akin to Judaism and Christianity.

2. *Editor's Note:* The whole verse means that salvation cannot be attained by applying a label to oneself, whether it is Muslim, Jew, Christian, or any other, but only by true belief in God and doing good deeds. That is the principle. It is a different matter that true belief and doing of good deeds to the highest degree is only attainable through the teachings of the Prophet Muhammad.

3. *Editor's Note:* "Truthful" refers to those in whose hearts belief is confirmed, and "faithful" refers to those who put belief into practice.

4. Bukhari, book 2: 'Belief', ch. 3, h. 9.

5. Muslim, book 1: 'Faith', ch. 12, h. 35b (MDS: ch. 12, h. 153).

6. Bukhari, book 2: 'Belief', ch. 7, h. 13.

7. *Ibid.,* ch. 8, h. 15.

8. *Ibid.,* ch. 22, h. 30.

9. Bukhari, book 25: 'Pilgrimage', ch. 132, h. 1739 and h. 1741.

10. Bukhari, book 2: 'Belief', ch. 36, h. 48.

11. The Quran, 49:9.

12. Bukhari, book 8: 'Prayer', ch. 28, h. 391.

13. Abu Dawud, book 15: 'Jihad', ch. 35, h. 2532 (MDS: ch. 33).

14. *Ṭabarānī,* reported from Ibn Umar.
    The Holy Prophet is also reported as saying: "Do not call those who follow your *Qiblah* (*ahl Qiblah*) disbelievers" (*Al-Nihāyah* under *Kufr*).

15. *Al-Mawāqif* by Qazi Abdur Rahman ibn Ahmad, Cairo, p. 600.

16. *Miftāḥ al-Saʿādah* by Ahmad ibn Mustafa, Hyderabad Deccan, v. 1, p. 46.

17. *Maqālāt al-Islāmiyyīn wa Ikhtilāfāt al-Muṣallīn,* p. 1, 2.

18. The Quran, 2:2–4.

19. Bukhari, book 2: 'Belief', ch. 37, h. 50.

20. In some Hadith reports the words are added: "That you believe in *qadar*", meaning 'the measure', but commonly thought of as predestination. *Qadar* is, no doubt, spoken of in the Quran as a law of God, but never as an article of faith, and all the Divine laws are accepted as true by every Muslim. See chapter 10, page 175, on '*Taqdīr* or Predestination'.

5. The Divine Being

Section 1: *The Existence of God*

Material, inner and spiritual experience of humanity

In all religious scriptures the existence of God is taken almost as an axiomatic truth. The Holy Quran, however, advances numerous arguments to prove the existence of a Supreme Being Who is the Creator and Controller of this universe. These are, broadly speaking, of three kinds. Firstly, there are the arguments drawn from the creation, which relate to the lower or material experience of humanity; secondly, the evidence of human nature, which concerns the inner experience of humanity; and thirdly, there are arguments based on Divine revelation to man, which may be called the higher or spiritual experience of humanity.

It will be seen, from what is said further on, that as the scope of experience is narrowed down, so the arguments gain in effectiveness. The argument from creation simply shows that there *must be* a Creator of this universe, Who is also its Controller, but it does not go so far as to show that there *is* a God. The testimony of human nature proceeds a step further, since there is in it a consciousness of Divine existence, though that consciousness may differ in different natures according to whether the inner light is bright or dim. It is only revelation that discloses God in the full splendour of His light, and shows the sublime attributes which man must emulate if he is to attain perfection, together with the means whereby he can hold communion with the Divine Being.

The law of evolution as an evidence of purpose and wisdom

The first argument, drawn from the creation, centres round the word *Rabb*. In the very first revelation that came to the Prophet, he was told to "read in the name of the *Rabb* Who created" (96:1). The word *Rabb,* generally translated as 'Lord', combines two senses, that of *fostering, bringing up* or *nourishing,* and that of *regulating, completing* and *accomplishing.*[1] Thus its underlying idea is that of fostering things from the crudest state to that of highest perfection, in other words, the idea of evolution. According to Raghib,[2] *Rabb* signifies *the fostering of a thing in such a manner as to make it attain one condition after another until it reaches its goal of perfection.* There is, thus, in the use of the word *Rabb,* an indication that everything created by God bears the impress of Divine creation, in the characteristic of moving on from lower to higher stages until it reaches perfection. This argument is expanded in another very early revelation as follows:

> "Glorify the name of your *Rabb,* the Most High, Who creates, then makes complete, and Who measures, then guides." — 87:1–3

The full meaning of *Rabb* is explained here: He creates things and brings them to perfection; He makes things according to a measure and shows them the ways whereby they may attain to perfection. The idea of evolution is fully developed in the first two actions, the creation and the completion, so that everything created by God must attain to its destined completion. The last two actions show how the completion or evolution is brought about. Everything is made according to a measure, that is to say, certain laws of development are inherent in it; and it is also shown a way, that is to say, it knows the line along which it must proceed, so that it may reach its goal of completion. It thus appears that the creative force is not a blind force but one possessing wisdom and acting with a purpose. Even to the ordinary eye, wisdom and purpose are observable in the whole of the Divine creation, from the tiniest particle of dust or blade of grass to the mighty spheres moving in the universe on their appointed courses, because everyone of them is travelling along a certain line to its appointed goal of completion.

One law prevails in the whole universe

A further point upon which the Holy Quran lays special stress is the fact that, despite its immensity and variety, there is but one law for the whole universe:

> "[Allah is He] Who created the seven heavens alike. You see no anomaly in the creation of the Beneficent God. Then look again: can you see any disorder? Then look again and again — your sight will return to you confused, while it is fatigued." — 67:3–4

Here we are told that there is in creation neither incongruity, whereby things belonging to the same class are subject to different laws, nor disorder, whereby the law cannot work uniformly; so that the miraculous regularity and uniformity of law in the midst of the unimaginable variety of conflicting conditions existing in the universe is also evidence of a Divine purpose and wisdom in the creation of things.

From the smallest particle to the largest heavenly body, everything is held under control and is subject to a law; no one thing interferes with the course of another or hampers it; while, on the other hand, all things are helping each other on to attain perfection. The Quran stresses this fact frequently:

> "The sun and the moon follow a reckoning. And the herbs and the trees adore [Him]." — 55 : 5 – 6

> "And the sun moves on to its destination. That is the ordinance of the Mighty, the Knower. And the moon, We have ordained for it stages till it becomes again as an old dry palm branch. Neither is it for the sun to overtake the moon, nor can the night outstrip the day. And all float on in an orbit." — 36 : 38 – 40

> "Then He directed Himself to the heaven and it was a vapour, so He said to it and to the earth: Come both, willingly or unwillingly. They both said: We come willingly." — 41 : 11

> "Allah is He Who made subservient to you the sea that the ships may glide in it by His command, and that you may seek of His grace, and that you may give thanks. And He has made subservient to you whatsoever is in the heavens and whatsoever is in the earth, all from Himself. Surely there are signs in this for a people who reflect." — 45 : 12 – 13

> "And He created the sun and the moon and the stars, made subservient by His command; surely His is the creation and the command." — 7 : 54

All these verses show that, inasmuch as everything is subject to command and control for the fulfilment of a certain purpose, there must be an All-Wise Controller of the whole.

Guidance afforded by human nature

The second kind of argument for the existence of God relates to the human soul. In the first place, there is in it the consciousness of the existence of God. There is an inner light within each one telling him that there is a Higher Being, a God, a Creator. This inner evidence is often brought out in the form of a question. It is like an appeal to man's inner self. The question is sometimes left unanswered, as if one is called upon to give it a deeper thought:

> "Or were they created without a [creative] agency? Or are they the creators [of their own souls]? Or did they create the heavens and the earth?" — 52:35–36

Sometimes the answer is given:

> "And if you ask them, Who created the heavens and the earth, they would say: The Mighty, the Knowing One, has created them." — 43:9

On one occasion, the question is put direct to the human soul by God Himself:

> "And when your Lord brought forth from the children of Adam, from their loins, their descendants and made them bear witness about themselves: Am I not your Lord (*Rabb*)? They said: Yes, we bear witness." — 7:172

This is clearly the evidence of human nature which is elsewhere spoken of as being "the nature made by Allah in which He has created mankind" (30:30).

Sometimes this consciousness on the part of the human soul is mentioned in terms of its unimaginable nearness to the Divine Spirit:

> "We are nearer to him than his life-vein." — 50:16

> "We are nearer to it [the soul] than you, but you do not see." — 56:85

The idea that God is nearer to man than his own self only shows that the consciousness of the existence of God in the human soul is even clearer than the consciousness of its own existence.

If, then, the human soul has such a clear consciousness of the existence of God, how is it, the question may be asked, that there are people who deny the existence of God? Here, two points must be borne in mind. In the first place, the inner light within each person, which makes him conscious of the existence of God, is not equally clear in all cases. With some, as with the great divines of every age and country, that light shines forth in its full glory, and their consciousness of the Divine presence is very strong. In the case of ordinary people, this consciousness is generally weaker and the inner light more dim; there may even be cases in which that consciousness is only in a state of inertia, and the inner light has almost gone out. Secondly, even the atheist or the agnostic recognizes a First Cause, or a Higher Power, though he may deny the existence of a God with particular attributes; and occasionally that consciousness is awakened in him, and the inner light asserts itself, especially in times of distress or affliction. It looks very much as though ease and comfort, like evil, cast a veil over the inner light of man, and the veil is removed by distress — a fact to which the Quran has repeatedly called attention:

> "And when We show favour to man, he turns away and withdraws himself; but when evil touches him, he is full of lengthy supplications." — 41:51

> "And when harm afflicts people, they call upon their Lord, turning to Him." — 30:33.

> "And when a wave like awnings covers them they call upon Allah, being sincere to Him in obedience. But when He brings them safe to land, some of them follow the middle course." — 31:32

> "And whatever good you have, it is from Allah; then when evil afflicts you, to Him do you cry for aid." — 16:53

There is in the human soul something more than mere consciousness of the existence of God; there is in it a yearning after its Maker — the instinct to turn to God for help;[3] there is implanted in it the love of God for Whose sake it is ready to make every sacrifice.[4] Finally, it cannot find complete contentment without God.[5]

Guidance afforded by Divine revelation

The third group of arguments found in the Holy Quran, to prove the existence of God, relates to Divine revelation — the clearest and surest evidence — which not only establishes the truth of the existence of God but also casts a flood of light on the Divine attributes without which the existence of the Divine Being would remain mere dogma. It is through this disclosure of the Divine attributes that belief in God becomes the most important factor in the evolution of man, since a knowledge of those attributes enables him to set before himself the high ideal of imitating Divine morals; and it is only thus that man can rise to the highest moral eminence. God is the Nourisher of everything in the creation, so His worshipper will do his utmost to serve the cause not only of humanity but of all creation. God is Loving and Affectionate to His creatures, so one who believes in Him will be moved by the impulse of love and affection towards His creation. God is Merciful and Forgiving, so His servant must be merciful and forgiving to his fellow-beings. A belief in a God possessing the perfect attributes made known by Divine revelation is the highest ideal which a human being can place before himself; and without this ideal there is a void in his life, a lack of all earnestness and every noble aspiration.

In another way, Divine revelation brings man closer to God and makes His existence felt as a reality in his life, and that is through the example of the perfect man who holds communion with the Divine Being. That God is a Reality, a Truth — in fact, the greatest reality in this world; that man can feel His presence and realize Him in each hour of his everyday life, and have the closest relations with Him; that such a realization of the Divine Being works a change in the life of man, making him an irresistible spiritual force in the world, is not the solitary experience of one individual or of one nation, but the universal experience of people in all nations, all countries and all ages. Abraham, Moses, Christ, Confucius, Zoroaster, Rama, Krishna, Buddha and Muhammad, each and every one of these luminaries brought about a moral, and in some cases also a material, revolution in the world, which the combined resources of whole nations were powerless to resist, and lifted up humanity from the depths of degradation to the greatest heights of moral, and even material, prosperity. This only shows to what heights the human soul may rise if only it works in true relationship with the Divine Being.

One example may be considered in greater detail — that of the Holy Prophet Muhammad. A solitary man arose in the midst of a whole nation which was sunk in all kinds of vice and degradation.

He had no power at his back, not even a man to second him, and without any preliminaries at all, he set his hand to the unimaginable and apparently impossible task of the reformation, not merely of that one nation but, through it, of the whole of humanity. He started with that one Force, the Force Divine, which makes possible the impossible:

> "Read in the name of your Lord!" (96:1); "Arise and warn, and your Lord do magnify [Him]" (74:2–3).

The cause was Divine, and it was on Divine help that its success depended. With every new dawn the task grew harder, and the opposition waxed stronger, until, to an onlooker, there was nothing but disappointment everywhere. Nonetheless, his determination grew stronger with the strength of the opposition and, while in the earlier revelation there were only general statements of the triumph of his cause and the failure of the enemy, those statements became clearer and more definite as the prospects, to all outward appearance, grew more hopeless.

Some of these verses in the order of their revelation are:

> "By the grace of your Lord you are not mad. And yours is surely a reward never to be cut off." — 68:2–3

> "Surely We have given you abundance of good." — 108:1

> "Surely with difficulty is ease." — 94:5

> "And surely the later state is better for you than the earlier, and soon will your Lord give you so that you will be well pleased." — 93:4–5

> "Surely it is the word of an honoured Messenger, the possessor of strength, having an honourable place with the Lord of the Throne". — 81:19–20

> "And during a part of the night, keep awake by it [i.e., the Quran]… maybe your Lord will raise you to a position of great glory." — 17:79

> "O man! We have not revealed the Quran to you that you may be unsuccessful". — 20:1–2

> "And on that day the believers will rejoice in Allah's help." — 30:4–5

"We certainly help Our messengers, and those who believe, in this world's life and on the day when the witnesses arise." — 40:51

"Blessed is He Who, if He please, will give you what is better than this: Gardens in which flow rivers. And He will give you palaces." — 25:10

"Allah has promised to those of you who believe and do good that He will surely make them rulers in the earth as He made those before them rulers, and that He will surely establish for them their religion, which He has chosen for them, and that He will surely give them security in exchange after their fear." — 24:55

"He it is Who has sent His Messenger with the guidance and the Religion of Truth that He may make it prevail over all religions." — 48:28

In like manner, the end of opposition is described more clearly in the later revelations than in the earlier, although that opposition grew more and more powerful as days went on. The following three verses belong to three different periods:

"...till when they see what they are promised, they will know who is weaker in helpers and smaller in number." — 72:24

"Or do they say: We are an army allied together to help each other? Soon shall the armies be routed, and they will show [their] backs." — 54:44–45

"Say to those who disbelieve: You shall soon be defeated..." — 3:12

And all this did happen a few years after these things had been foretold, though at that time there was nothing to justify such prophecies and all the circumstances were against them. No man could possibly have foreseen what was so clearly stated as certain to come about, and no human power could have brought to utter failure the whole nation with all its resources ranged against a solitary man and determined to destroy him. Divine revelation thus affords the clearest and surest testimony of the existence of God, in Whose knowledge, past, present and future are alike and Who controls both the forces of nature and the destiny of human beings.

Section 2: *The Unity of God*

The Unity of God

All the basic principles of Islam are fully dealt with in the Holy Quran, and so is the doctrine of faith in God, of which the cornerstone is belief in the Unity of God (*tauḥīd*). The best-known expression of Divine Unity is that contained in the declaration of *lā ilāha ill-Allāh*. It is made up of four words: *lā* (no), *ilāh* (that which is worshipped), *illā* (except) and *Allāh* (the proper name of the Divine Being). Thus these words, which are commonly rendered into English as meaning "there is no god but Allah" convey the significance that there is nothing which deserves to be worshipped except Allah. It is this confession which, when combined with the confession of the prophethood of Muhammad (*Muḥammad-ur Rasūl-ullāh*) admits one into the fold of Islam.

The Unity of God, according to the Holy Quran, implies that God is One in His person, One in His attributes and One in His works. His Oneness in His person means that there is neither plurality of gods nor plurality of persons in the Godhead; His Oneness in attributes implies that no other being possesses one or more of the Divine attributes in perfection; His Oneness in works implies that none can do what God has done, or what God may do. The doctrine of Unity is beautifully summed up in one of the shortest and earliest chapters of the Holy Quran:

> "Say: He, Allah, is One. Allah is He on Whom all depend. He has no offspring, nor is He born [of anyone]; and none is like Him." — ch. 112

The gravity of *shirk*

The opposite of Unity is *shirk*,[6] implying *partnership*. In the Holy Quran, *shirk* is used to signify the associating of gods with God, whether such association be with respect to the person of God or His attributes or His works, or with respect to the obedience which is due to Him alone. *Shirk* is said to be the gravest of all sins:

> "Surely *shirk* is a grievous wrong." — 31:13

> "Allah does not forgive that a partner should be set up with Him,[7] and forgives all besides that to whom He pleases." — 4:48

This is due to the fact that *shirk* demoralizes man, while Divine Unity brings about his moral elevation. According to the Holy Quran, man is God's vicegerent[8] on earth, and this shows that he is gifted with the power of controlling the rest of the earthly creation:

> "Allah is He Who made subservient to you the sea that the ships may glide in it by His command, and that you may seek of His grace, and that you may give thanks. And He has made subservient to you whatsoever is in the heavens and whatsoever is in the earth, all from Himself. Surely there are signs in this for a people who reflect." — 45:12–13

If, then, man has been created to rule the universe and is gifted with the power to subdue everything and to turn it to his use, does he not degrade himself by taking other things for gods, by bowing before the very things which he has been created to conquer and rule? This is an argument which the Holy Quran has itself advanced against *shirk*. Thus the words, "Shall I seek a lord other than Allah, while He is the Lord of all things" (6:164), are followed in the next verse by: "And He it is Who has made you successors in the land". And again: "Shall I seek for you a god other than Allah, while He has made you excel all created things?" (7:140). *Shirk* is, therefore, of all sins the most serious because it degrades man and renders him unfit for attaining the high position destined for him in the Divine scheme.

Various forms of *shirk*

The various forms of *shirk* mentioned in the Holy Quran are an indication of the ennobling message underlying the teaching of Divine Unity. These are summed up in the verse:

> "…that we shall serve none but Allah and that we shall not set up any partner with Him and that some of us shall not take others for lords besides Allah." — 3:64

These are really three forms of *shirk* — a fourth is mentioned separately. The most palpable form of *shirk* is that in which anything besides God is worshipped, such as stones, idols, trees, animals, tombs, heavenly bodies, forces of nature, or human beings who are supposed to be demi-gods or gods or incarnations of God or sons or daughters of God. The second kind of *shirk,* which is less palpable, is the setting up of partners with God, that is, to suppose that other things and beings possess the same attributes as the Divine Being. The beliefs that there are three persons in the Godhead, and that the Son and the Holy Ghost are eternal, Omnipotent and Omniscient like God Himself, as in the Christian creed, or that there is a Creator of Evil along with a Creator of Good, as in Zoroastrianism, or that matter and soul are co-eternal with God and self-existing like Himself, as in Hinduism — all come under this head. The last kind of *shirk* is that in which some people take others for their lords, meaning that they blindly obey their religious leaders in what they declare as right or wrong, or as commanded or forbidden by God.

The fourth kind of *shirk* is referred to in the verse:

> "Have you seen him who takes his low desires for his god?" — 25:43, 45:23

Here the blind submission to one's own desires is described in words used for *shirk.* Thus belief in the Unity of God means that true obedience is due to God alone, and whosoever obeys either anyone else, or his own low desires, in preference to the Divine commandments, is really guilty of *shirk.*

Idolatry

Of the different forms of *shirk,* idolatry is cited more frequently than all the others, and is denounced in the most scathing terms in the Holy Quran. This is because idolatry is the most heinous form of *shirk* and also was the most rampant throughout the world at the advent of Islam. Not only is idolatry condemned in its gross form, which takes it for granted that an idol can cause benefit or do harm, but the idea is also controverted that there is any meaning underlying this gross form of worship:

> "And those who choose protectors besides Him [say]: We serve them only that they may bring us nearer to Allah. Surely Allah will judge between them in that in which they differ." — 39:3

It is sometimes said, in explanation of idolatry, that an idol is used only to enable a worshipper to concentrate his attention, and become more deeply engrossed in Divine contemplation. This idea is controverted in the verse quoted above — "that they may bring us nearer to Allah". But even in this case the worshipper must believe that the idol on which he centres his attention is a symbol of the Divine Being, which is a grossly false notion; and, moreover, it is the idol on which the worshipper's attention is centred, not the Divine Being. It is also wrong to suppose that a material symbol is necessary for concentration, for attention can be just as easily concentrated on a spiritual object, and it is only when the object of attention is spiritual that concentration helps the development of will-power. Along with idol-worship, the Holy Quran also prohibits dedication to idols (6:137).

Nature worship

Another form of prevailing *shirk* denounced in the Holy Quran is the worship of the sun, the moon, the stars, in fact of everything which might appear to control the destinies of man. This is expressly forbidden:

> "And of His signs are the night and the day and the sun and the moon. Do not adore the sun nor the moon, but adore Allah Who created them…" — 41:37

The argument advanced against the worship of the sun and the moon not only applies to all heavenly bodies but also, and equally well, to all the forces of nature, which are in fact again and again mentioned as being made subservient to man.

Trinity

The Trinity is also denounced as a form of *shirk:*

> "So believe in Allah and His messengers. And do not say, Three. Refrain [from it], it is better for you. Allah is only One God." — 4:171

It is sometimes alleged that the Quranic conception of the Trinity is a mistaken one, because it speaks of Jesus and Mary as having been taken for two gods:

> "O Jesus, son of Mary, did you say to people, Take me and my mother for two gods besides Allah?" — 5:116

The reference here is not to Trinity but to Mariolatry. That Mary was worshipped is a fact, and the Quran's reference to it is significant, but it should be noted that neither the Holy Quran nor the Holy Prophet has anywhere said that Mary was the third person of the Trinity. Where the Quran denounces the Trinity, it speaks of the doctrine of sonship but does not speak of the worship of Mary at all; and where it speaks of the worship of Mary, it does not refer to the Trinity.[9]

Doctrine of sonship

Another form of *shirk,* refuted in the Holy Quran, is the doctrine that God has sons or daughters. The pagan Arabs ascribed daughters to God while Christians hold that God has a son. Though the doctrine of ascribing daughters to God is mentioned in the Quran several times,[10] yet it is against the Christian doctrine that the Holy Book speaks with gravest emphasis:

> "And they say: The Beneficent God has taken to Himself a son. Certainly you have made a detestable assertion! The heavens may almost be torn apart at it, and the earth split, and the mountains crumble down in pieces, that they ascribe a son to the Beneficent God!" — 19:88–91

The doctrine is denounced repeatedly, even in the earliest revelations,[11] which shows that from the very first the Holy Quran set before itself the correction of this great error. It will be observed that a mention of the doctrine of sonship is often followed by the word *subḥāna-hū* ("glory be to Him"), which is used to indicate the purity of God from all defects. The reason for this is that the doctrine of sonship is due to the supposition that God cannot forgive sins unless He receives some satisfaction therefor, and this satisfaction is supposed to have been afforded by the crucifixion of the Son of God, who alone is said to be sinless. The doctrine of sonship is thus practically a denial of the quality of forgiveness in God, and this amounts to attributing a defect to Him. It is for this reason also that a most forcible denunciation of the doctrine of sonship, quoted above, is followed by the words:

> "And it is not worthy of the Beneficent God (*Raḥmān*) that He should take to Himself a son." — 19:92

The word *Raḥmān* signifies originally the Lord of immeasurable mercy Who requires no satisfaction or compensation for a display of the quality of mercy which is inherent in Him, and the attribute of being *Raḥmān* negatives the doctrine of sonship.

Significance underlying the doctrine of Unity

The various kinds of *shirk* mentioned in the Holy Quran show that, in the doctrine of Unity, it gives to the world an ennobling message of advancement all round, physical as well as moral and spiritual. Man is freed not only from slavery to animate and inanimate objects, but also from subservience to the great and wondrous forces of nature which, he is told, he can subdue for his benefit. It goes further and delivers man from that greatest of slaveries, slavery to man. It does not allow to any mortal the dignity of Godhead, or of being more than a mortal; for the greatest of mortals is commanded to say:

> "I am only a mortal like you; it is revealed to me that your God is One God." — 18:110

Thus all the bonds which fettered the mind of man were broken, and he was set on the road to progress. A slave mind, as the Quran plainly says, is incapable of doing anything good and great (16:75–76), and hence the first condition for the advancement of man was that his mind should be set free from the trammels of all kinds of slavery, which was accomplished in the message of Divine Unity.

Unity of human race underlies Unity of God

The doctrine of the Unity of God, besides casting off the bonds of slavery which had enthralled the human mind, and thus opening the way for its advancement, carries another significance equally great, if not greater, namely, the idea of the unity of the human race. God is *Rabb al-'ālamīn* — the Lord of all the nations. This signifies that all the nations of the world are, as it were, the children of one Father, and that He takes equal care of all, bringing all to their goal of completion by degrees.[12] Hence God is spoken of in the Quran as granting not only His physical but also His spiritual sustenance, His revelation, to all the nations of the world:

> "And for every nation there is a messenger." — 10:47

> "There is not a people but a warner has gone among them." — 35:24

We further find that the Quran upholds the idea that God, being the God of all nations, deals with all of them alike. He hearkens to the prayers of all, whatever their religion or nationality. He is equally merciful to all and forgives the sins of all. He rewards the good deeds of the Muslim and the non-Muslim alike; and not only does He deal with all nations alike, but we are further told that He created them all alike, in the Divine nature:

> "…the nature made by Allah in which He has created mankind." — 30:30

And this unity of the human race, which is thus a natural corollary of the doctrine of the Unity of God, is further stressed in the plain words that "Mankind is a single nation" (2:213) and that humanity is "but a single nation" (10:19).

Section 3: *The Attributes of God*

Nature of the Divine attributes

In the Holy Quran, God is plainly stated to be above all material conceptions:

> "Vision cannot comprehend Him, and He comprehends all vision." — 6:103

And He is not only above all material limitations but even above the limitation of metaphor:

> "Nothing is like a likeness of Him." — 42:11

To indicate His love, power, knowledge and other attributes, the same words had to be used as are in ordinary use for human beings, and therefore God is spoken of in the Holy Quran as seeing, hearing, speaking, being displeased, loving, being affectionate, possessing control, etc.; but the conception is not quite the same. God sees and hears, but that does not mean He has eyes and requires light to see things, or has ears and requires some medium, such as air, to convey sound to Him. God creates, but that does not mean He has hands like a man and needs material with which to make things. The "hands" of God are spoken of in the Holy Quran (5:64), but it is simply to give expression to His unlimited power in bestowing His favours on whom He will, and this is in accordance with the Arabic idiom.

God's Throne (*'arsh*) is spoken of in the Holy Quran, but it does not signify any place, rather representing His control of things as a monarch's throne is a symbol of his power to rule. The phrase "He is established on the Throne"[13] is used after mentioning the creation of the heavens and the earth, and in relation to the Divine control of creation, and the law and order to which the universe is made to submit by its great Author. It is nowhere said in the Quran that God sits on the *'arsh;* it is always His controlling power that is mentioned in connection therewith. Similarly, His *kursī*,[14] literally 'chair', means His knowledge.

Proper name of the Divine Being

Allāh is the proper or personal name of the Divine Being, as distinguished from all other names which denote His attributes. It is also known as the greatest name of God (*ism a'ẓam*). Being a proper name it does not carry any significance, but being the proper name of the Divine Being it comprises all the attributes which are contained separately in the attributive names. Hence the name Allah is said to gather together in itself all the perfect attributes of God.

The word *Allāh* is not derived from any other word. Nor has it any connection with the word *ilāh* (god or object of worship). It is sometimes said that *Allāh* is a contracted form of *al-ilāh,* meaning 'the god', but that is a mistake, for if *al* in *Allāh* were an additional prefix, the form *yā Allāh* for addressing Him ("O Allah"), which is a correct form, would not have been permitted, since *yā al-ilāh* or *yā al-Raḥmān* are not correct. Moreover, this supposition would mean that there were different gods, one of which became gradually known as *al-ilāh* (the god) and was then contracted into *Allāh*. This is against facts, since *Allāh* has ever been the name of the Eternal Being. Nor has the word *Allāh* ever been applied to any but the Divine Being, according to all authorities on Arabic lexicology. The Arabs had numerous *ilāh*s or gods but none of them was ever called *Allāh,* while a Supreme Being called *Allāh* was recognized above them all as the Creator of the universe,[15] and no other deity, however great, was so regarded.

Four chief attributes

Among the attributive names of the Divine Being occurring in the Holy Quran, four stand out prominently, and these four are exactly the names mentioned in the opening chapter *al-Fātiḥah*, which by a consensus of opinion, and according to a saying of the Holy Prophet, is the quintessence of the Book. The chapter opens with the proper name Allah, and then follows the greatest of all attributive names *Rabb* which, for want of a proper equivalent, is translated "Lord". Its real significance, according to the best authority on Quranic lexicology, is the *Fosterer of a thing in such a manner as to make it attain one condition after another until it reaches its goal of completion* (see p. 65). *Rabb,* therefore, means the Lord Who brings all that is in this universe to a state of perfection through various stages of growth, and as these stages include the lowest and the remotest, which, as we go back farther and farther, dwindle into nothingness, the word *Rabb* carries with it the idea of the Author of all existence. *Rabb* is thus the chief attribute of the Divine Being, and hence it is that prayers are generally addressed to *Rabb,* and begin with the words *Rabba-nā,* that is, "our Lord". Indeed after the proper name Allah, the Quran has given the greatest prominence to the name *Rabb.*

The order adopted by the Holy Quran in speaking of the Divine attributes is quite logical. Allah, the proper name, comes first of all in the opening chapter, and this is followed by *Rabb,* the most important of the attributive names. While the name Allah is found in the Holy Quran some 2800 times, *Rabb* occurs about 960 times, no other name being so frequently mentioned.

Next in importance to *Rabb* are the names *Raḥmān* (Beneficent), *Raḥīm* (Merciful) and *Mālik* (Master), which follow *Rabb* in the opening chapter. These three names in fact show how the attribute of bringing to perfection by fostering, is brought into play. Both *Raḥmān* and *Raḥīm* are derived from the same root, conveying the ideas of love and mercy. *Raḥmān* signifies that love is so predominant in the Divine nature that He bestows His favours and shows His mercy even though man has done nothing to deserve them. The granting of the means of subsistence for the development of physical life, and of Divine revelation for man's spiritual growth, are due to this attribute of unbounded love in the Divine Being. Then follows the stage in which man takes advantage of these various means which help the development of his physical and spiritual life, and turns them to his use. It is at this stage that the third attribute of the Divine Being, *Raḥīm,* comes into play, whereby He rewards every effort made by man in the right direction; and since man is making constant and continual efforts, the attribute of mercy conveyed in the name *Raḥīm* is also displayed continually. This is true both as regards the physical and spiritual development of man.

As submission to the law results in the advancement of man which brings reward, disobedience to the law must result in retarding his progress or bringing down punishment upon him. In fact, punishment is only a different phase of the exercise of the attribute of fostering; for ultimate good is still the object. Therefore, just as *Raḥīm* is needed to bring his reward to one who does good or submits to the law, there must be another attribute to bring about the requital of evil. Hence in the opening chapter of the Quran, *Raḥīm* is followed by *Māliki yaum-id-dīn* or "Master of the Day of Recompense". The adoption of the word *Mālik,* or Master, in connection with the requital of evil, is significant, as ordinarily it would be expected that there should be a judge to mete out the requital of evil. The essential difference between a judge and a master is that the former is bound to do justice and must punish the evil-doer for every evil, while the latter can exercise his discretion, and may either punish the evil-doer or forgive him and pass over even the greatest of his iniquities.

This idea is fully developed in the Quran, where we are repeatedly told that while good is rewarded ten times over or even more, evil is either forgiven or requited with its equivalent. In one place, indeed, the unbounded mercy of the Divine Being is said to be so great that "He forgives sins altogether" (39:53). Hence the attributive name *Mālik* is introduced to link the idea of requital with that of forgiveness. That is why, while the opening chapter mentions the name *Mālik* as the next in importance to *Raḥīm,* in the body of the Quran it is the name *Ghafūr* (Forgiving) which occupies that place of importance, as in its various forms it is the next, in frequency of occurrence, after *Raḥmān* and *Raḥīm* in their various forms. Hence it will be seen that the Quran gives prominence to the attributes of love and mercy in God to an extent the parallel of which is not to be found in any other revealed book.

Other names of God

From their mention in the opening chapter of the Quran, and the frequency of their mention in the Holy Book, to which no approach is made by any other name, it is clear that the four names *Rabb, Raḥmān, Raḥīm* and *Mālik* are the chief attributive names of the

Divine Being, and all His other attributes are only offshoots of these four essential attributes. In a Hadith report, which is regarded as weak, ninety-nine names of God are generally mentioned, the hundredth being Allah; but while some of them occur in the Quran, others are only inferred from some act of the Divine Being, as finding expression in the Holy Book. There is, however, no authority whatsoever for the practice of repeating these names on a rosary or otherwise. Neither the Holy Prophet nor any of his Companions ever used a rosary.

In the Holy Quran, it is said:

> "And Allah's are the best names, so call on Him thereby, and leave alone those who violate the sanctity of His names."
> — 7:180

Calling on God by His excellent names only means that nothing derogatory to His dignity should be attributed to Him, and the violation of the sanctity of the Divine names has been clearly explained to mean either ascribing to God attributes which do not befit His high dignity, or ascribing Divine attributes to that which is not Divine. Hence calling on God by His excellent names merely means that only those high attributes should be ascribed to Him which befit His dignity.

Among the names of God mentioned in the Holy Quran are the following:

1. As relating to His person:
   al-Wāhid (the One), *al-Haqq* (the Truth), *al-Samad* (on Whom all depend while He does not depend on any), *al-Hayy* (the Ever-living), *al-Qayyūm* (the Self-subsisting).

2. As relating to the act of creation:
   al-Khāliq (the Creator), *al-Bāri'* (the Creator of the soul), *al-Bādī* (the Originator).

3. As relating to the attributes of love and mercy (besides the chief attributes mentioned above):
   al-Tawwāb (the Oft-returning to mercy), *al-Halīm* (the Forbearing), *al-'Afuww* (the Pardoner), *al-Salām* (the Author of peace), *al-Barr* (the Benign).

4. As relating to His greatness and glory:

    al-'Aẓīm (the Grand), *al-'Azīz* (the Mighty), *al-'Aliyy* (the Exalted or the High), *al-Kabīr* (the Great), *al-Ḥamīd* (the Praiseworthy), *al-Majīd* (the Glorious).

5. As relating to His knowledge:

    al-'Alīm (the Knowing), *al-Ḥakīm* (the Wise), *al-Sam 'ī* (the Hearing), *al-Baṣīr* (the Seeing), *al-Raqīb* (the Watcher), *al-Bāṭin* (the Knower of hidden things).

6. As relating to His power and control of things:

    al-Qādir or *Qadīr* (the Powerful), *al-Waliyy* (the Guardian), *al-Malik* (the King), *al-Mālik* (the Master), *al-Ḥāsib* or *al-Ḥasīb* (the One Who takes account).

Predominance of love and mercy in Divine nature

It will be seen that the attributes of God given above have nothing to do with the autocracy, inexorability, vengeance and cruelty which Western critics of Islam have generally associated with the picture of Him as drawn in the Holy Quran. On the contrary, the qualities of love and mercy in God are emphasized in the Quran more than in any other sacred book. Not only does every chapter open with the two names *Raḥmān* and *Raḥīm,* thus showing that the qualities of love and mercy are predominant in Divine nature, but the Holy Book goes further and lays the greatest stress in explicit words on the immeasurable vastness of the Divine mercy. The following may be taken as examples:

> "He has ordained mercy on Himself." — 6:12, 6:54

> "Your Lord is the Lord of all-encompassing mercy." — 6:147

> "And My mercy encompasses all things." — 7:156

> "Except those on whom your Lord has mercy, and for this did He create them." — 11:119

> "O My servants who have been reckless against their own souls, do not despair of the mercy of Allah, surely Allah forgives sins altogether." — 39:53

> "Our Lord! You embrace all things in mercy and know-
> ledge…" — 40:7

So great is the Divine mercy that it encompasses believers and unbelievers alike as the above verses show. Even the enemies of the Holy Prophet are spoken of as having mercy shown to them:

> "And when We make people taste of mercy after an afflic-
> tion touches them, lo! they devise plans against Our
> messages." — 10:21

The idol-worshippers are repeatedly spoken of as calling upon God when in distress, and God as removing their distress. The picture of the Divine attributes portrayed in the Quran is, first and last, a picture of love and mercy, and while these are mentioned under many different names and repeated hundreds of times, His attribute of punishment — Exactor of retribution — occurs but four times in the whole of the Quran.[16] It is true that the punishment of evil is a subject on which the Quran is most emphatic, but its purpose in this case is simply to impress upon man that evil is a most hateful thing which ought to be shunned; and, by way of set-off, not only does it lay great stress on the reward of good deeds, but goes further and declares over and over again that evil is either forgiven or punished only with the like of it, but that good is rewarded tenfold, and hundredfold, or even without measure.

At the same time it must be borne in mind that punishment itself, as described in the Holy Quran, is of a remedial nature, and has in it nothing of vengeance — it is the treatment of a disease which a person has brought upon himself. It is still love, for its object is still to set a person on the road to spiritual progress by healing the disease. God does bring about distress, but this is only in the limited sense that it is a punishment for wrong-doing with the underlying object of reformation: "We seized them with distress and affliction in order that they might humble themselves" (6:42, 7:94).

Divine attributes as the great ideal to be attained

Just as belief in the Unity of God is a source of man's uplift, making him conscious of the dignity of human nature, and inspiring him with the grand ideas of the conquest of nature and of the equality of human beings, so the numerous attributes of the Divine Being, as revealed in the Holy Quran, are really meant for the perfection of human character. The Divine attributes really serve as an ideal to which man must strive to attain. God is *Rabb al-'ālamīn,* the Fosterer and Nourisher of the worlds; keeping that as an ideal before himself, man must endeavour to make the service of humanity, even that of dumb creation, the object of his life. God is *Rahmān,* conferring benefits on man and showing him love without his having done anything to deserve it; the one who seeks to attain to perfection must do good even to those from whom he has not himself received, and does not expect to receive, any benefit. God is *Rahīm,* making every good deed bear fruit; man must also do good for any good that he receives from another. God is *Mālik,* requiting evil, not in a spirit of vengeance or even of unbending justice, but in a spirit of forgiveness; so must man be forgiving in his dealings with others, if he will attain to perfection.

So it is with all His other attributes. As to love and mercy, God is Affectionate, Oft-returning to mercy, Forbearing, Pardoner, Multiplier of rewards, Author of peace, Granter of security, Restorer of loss, Benign, Bestower of sustenance and so on; all this man must also try to be. Again let us take His attributes of knowledge. God is Knowing, Wise, Aware, Seeing, Knower of hidden things; man must also try to perfect his knowledge of things and acquire wisdom. In fact, where man is spoken of as having been made a vicegerent of God, his chief characteristic, that which marks him out as the ruler of creation, is stated to be a knowledge of things.[17] Then there are His attributes of power and greatness and control of all things. Man is told again and again that everything in the heavens and in the earth has been made subservient to him.

It is true that man's love, mercy, knowledge, wisdom, and control of things are all insignificant as compared with their Divine models, but however imperfectly he may achieve it, the fact remains that he has before him the ideal of Divine morals, which he must try to imitate.

Notes to Chapter 5

1. Lane's Lexicon.
2. The famous classical lexicologist of the Quran in his dictionary *Al-Mufradāt fī Gharīb al-Qur'ān.*

3. The Quran, 1:4.

4. The Quran, 2:177, 76:8.

5. The Quran, 13:28.

6. Properly transliterated, the word *shirk* should be <u>*shirk*</u>.

7. *Editor's Note:* Those who set up partners with God themselves believe that He does not have the power to forgive them without the mediation of such partners. How can He forgive them when they do not believe that He alone possesses that power?

8. The term in the Quran is <u>*khalīfa*</u>. See 2:30.

9. Deism is another doctrine refuted in the Holy Quran: "And Allah has said: Do not take two gods. He is only one God" (16:51).

10. See the Quran, 16:57, 17:40, 37:149.

11. See the Quran, 2:116, 6:102–104, 10:68, 17:111, 18:4–5, 19:35, 19:91–92, 23:91, 37:151–152, 112:3. Of these, ch. 112 is undoubtedly one of the earliest revelations, while the 17th, 18th and 19th chapters also belong to the early Makkah period.

12. See the meaning of *Rabb* on page 65.

13. The Quran, 7:54, etc.

14. The Quran, 2:255.

15. The Quran, 29:61.

16. The Quran, 3:4, 5:95, 14:47, 39:37.

   Editor's Note: In the above verses, the name of God as "Exactor of retribution" is <u>*Dhu-ntiqām*</u>. A related name of God is *muntaqim,* taken from *muntaqimūn* ("We shall exact retribution"), which occurs three times in the Quran, in 32:22, 43:41 and 44:16.

17. The Quran, 2: 30–31.

6. Angels

Angels are immaterial beings

The Arabic word for angel is *malak,* of which the plural form is *malā'ika.*[1] The Holy Quran speaks of the creation of man from dust and of the creation *of jinn* from fire, but it does not speak of the origin of *angels.* There is, however, a Hadith report according to which the Holy Prophet said that the *jinn* are created from fire (*nār*), and that the angels are created from light *(nūr).*[2] This shows that angels are immaterial beings, and further, that the *jinn* and the angels are two different classes of beings, and that it is a mistake to consider them as belonging to one class.

In the Holy Quran angels are spoken of as "messengers flying on wings" (35:1). Their description has reference to their spiritual function of bearing Divine messages. Sacred history, indeed, represents angels as possessing wings, but so far as the Quran is concerned, it would be a grievous mistake to confuse the wing of an angel with the fore-limb of a bird which fits it for flight. The wing is a symbol of the *power* which enables those immaterial beings to execute their functions with all speed; and in Arabic, the word here for 'wing', *janāḥ,* is used in a variety of senses. In birds it is the wing, and in man his hand is spoken of as his *janāḥ.* The word has further been used metaphorically in the Quran in several places where the "lowering of the wing" stands for "being kind".[3] Angels are immaterial beings, and in them a material wing cannot be thought of; it is simply the symbol of a *power* which is speedily brought into action.

Can angels be seen?

It is commonly thought that the immaterial beings, whom we call angels, can assume any shape they like, but the Holy Quran gives no support to this idea. On the contrary, it is repeatedly stated in answer to the demands of the Holy Prophet's opponents, who desired to see an angel or to have an angel as a messenger, that angels could not be seen and that an angel would have been sent as a messenger if angels, and not human beings, lived on earth:

> "And nothing prevents people from believing, when the guidance comes to them, except that they say: Has Allah raised up a mortal to be a messenger? Say: If there had been in the earth angels walking about secure, We would have sent down to them from the heaven an angel as messenger."
> — 17:94–95

Twice it is related in the Quran that the angelic hosts sent to help Muslims were not seen by human eye:

> "Then Allah sent down His calm upon His Messenger and upon the believers, and sent armies which you did not see…"
> — 9:26

> "Call to mind the favour of Allah to you when armies came against you, so We sent against them a strong wind and forces that you did not see." — 33:9

There is, however, a story related in the Holy Quran about Abraham's guests[4] who first came to him and gave him the good news of a son, Isaac, and then went to Lot and bade him leave the city along with his followers, since punishment was about to overtake his people. It is generally supposed that these were angels, as angels alone are deputed to deliver messages to prophets, and the Bible says that they were angels. But the Quran speaks of them only as the guests of Abraham and as "Our messengers", and nowhere says that they were angels. Had they been angels, they would have delivered the Divine message to Abraham and Lot in the manner in which the angels deliver such messages, which is by revealing the Divine message to the heart of the prophet; and the angel, though he may come in the shape of a man, is not seen by the physical eye of the prophet but by his spiritual eye. Therefore, if the guests spoken of were angels, their appearance to both Abraham and Lot must have been in a vision, the state in which revelation comes to the prophets of God; but if it was with the physical eye that Abraham and Lot beheld them, then they were men and not angels.

Nature of angels

Though angels are spoken of as *beings,* they are not endowed with powers of discrimination like those of human beings; in this respect, indeed, they may be said to partake more of the attributes of the powers of nature than of man. Their function is to obey and they cannot disobey. The Holy Quran says plainly:

> "They do not disobey Allah in what He commands them, but do as they are commanded." — 66:6

As man is endowed with a will while the angel is not, man is superior to the angel. This superiority is also evident from the fact that angels were commanded to make submission to him.[5]

The angel's coming to the Holy Prophet

It is true that the angel Gabriel is spoken of as coming to the Holy Prophet with the Divine revelation, but as has been already shown (page 15), it was with the spiritual senses that the Holy Prophet received the revelation, and therefore it was not with the physical eye that he beheld Gabriel. The angel came to him sometimes in the shape of a man; the Prophet heard the words of revelation, on occasions, with the force of the ringing of a bell; yet those who were sitting next to him, while fully conscious of the change coming over him, neither saw the angel, nor heard the words of the revelation. And even when Gabriel came to him at other times, it was always with the spiritual eye that the Holy Prophet saw him.

The Holy Prophet's wife Aishah is very explicit on this point. It is related that on a certain occasion the Holy Prophet said to her:

> " 'O Aishah! Here is Gabriel offering salutation to you'. She said: 'And on him be peace and the mercy and blessings of Allah; you see what I do not see'." [6]

This shows that even Aishah never saw Gabriel, whether he came with revelation or on other occasions.

There are, however, a few stray incidents, related in certain Hadith reports, from which inference is drawn that others besides the Holy Prophet saw Gabriel, but, from what has been stated above, it is clear that either it was in a vision, and therefore it was with the spiritual senses that the few people present with the Holy Prophet shared his vision, or that there had been some misunderstanding in relating the incident.

Angelic function

In the Holy Quran, angels are generally described as having a connection with the spiritual state of man. It was an angel, Gabriel by name, who brought revelation to the Holy Prophet (2:97, 26:193–194) and the prophets before him (4:163). The same angel is mentioned as strengthening the prophets (2:87) and the believers (58:22). While angels generally are spoken of as descending on believers and comforting them (41:30), they are also intermediaries in bringing revelation to those who are not prophets, as in the case of Zacharias (3:39) and Mary (3:42, 45). Angels were sent to help the believers against their enemies (3:124–125, 8:12); they pray for blessings on the Holy Prophet (33:56) and on the believers (33:43); they ask forgiveness for all human beings, believers as well as non-believers (42:5); they cause believers to die (16:32) and also non-believers (4:97, 16:28); they write down the deeds of human beings (82:10, 12) and will intercede for them on the Day of Judgment (53:26). There is no clear reference to their function in the physical world unless the causing of death may be treated as such, but it should be classed as a spiritual function because death makes both the believers and unbelievers enter a new life. It may be added here that Hadith mentions an angel of birth, that is an angel appointed for everyone while he is in the mother's womb.[7]

There are, however, verses in the Holy Quran which show that the angelic hosts have some sort of connection with the physical world. The most important of these verses are those which speak of the creation of man (Adam). When God wished to create man, He communicated His wish to the angels (2:30, 15:28, 38:71). This shows that the angels were there before man was created, and, therefore, must have had some sort of connection with the physical world and with the forces which brought about the creation of man. Unless they are treated as intermediaries carrying out the Divine will, the communication to them of the Divine will to create man is meaningless. These verses, therefore, lead us to the conclusion that the laws of nature find expression through angels. It is due to this function of theirs that they are called messengers (22:75, 35:1). Expression of the Divine will is a Divine message, and the angels as bearers of that message carry it into execution. Their description as bearers of the Throne of the Lord (40:7, 69:17) leads to the same conclusion; for, as already stated, the Throne (*'arsh*) stands for the Divine control of the universe, and the angels, the bearers of that control, are in fact the intermediaries through whom that control is exercised.

Vastly greater importance is, however, attached to the angelic function in the spiritual world, because it is primarily with the spiritual development of man that the Holy Quran is concerned. To put it briefly, the function of the angel in the spiritual world is the same as his function in the physical world — to serve as an intermediary in carrying out the Divine will which, in the latter case, is to bring about the evolution of creation, and in the former, the evolution of man. According to the teachings of Islam, the angel has a close connection with the life of man from his birth, even from the time he is in the mother's womb till his death, and even after death, in his spiritual progress in Paradise and his spiritual treatment in Hell. The different functions of the angel in connection with the spiritual life of man may be broadly divided into the classes which are detailed below.

1. Angels as intermediaries in bringing revelation

The most important and, at the same time, the most prominent function of the angel, in the spiritual realm, is the bringing down of Divine revelation or the communication of Divine messages to the prophets. The prophet not only sees the angel but also hears his voice, and the angel is to him, therefore, a reality. This has been the universal experience of humanity in all ages. As the angel is an immaterial being, the prophet sees him sometimes in the shape of a human being and sometimes in other forms.

According to the Quran, the angel who brought revelation to the Holy Prophet is known by the name of Gabriel (2:97), the Arabic form of which is *jibrīl*. Gabriel is also mentioned in the Quran as *Rūḥ al-Amīn* or the Faithful Spirit (26:193), and *Rūḥ al-Qudus* or the Holy Spirit (16:102). In all these places, Gabriel or the Faithful Spirit or the Holy Spirit is said to have revealed the Quran to the Holy Prophet. The revelation to the prophets who appeared before him is said to have been granted in a similar manner (4:163). Gabriel is also called the messenger (*rasūl*) through whom God speaks to His prophets (42:51).

Angels generally are said to bring revelation to other righteous servants of God:

> "He sends down angels with revelation (*al-rūḥ*) by His command on whom He pleases of His servants…" — 16:2

> "Exalter of degrees, Lord of the Throne of Power, He casts

the spirit (*al-rūḥ*) by His command on whom He pleases of His servants…" — 40:15

These are general statements. In the case of Mary who was undoubtedly not a prophet, the angels are also spoken of as bearing Divine messages:

"And when the angels said: O Mary, surely Allah has chosen you and purified you…" — 3:42, see also 3:45.

Also in the case of Zacharias, the father of John the Baptist:

"So the angels called to him as he stood praying in the sanctuary: Allah gives you good news of John…" — 3:39

And the believers generally are thus spoken of:

"As for those who say, Our Lord is Allah, then continue in the right way, the angels descend upon them, saying: Do not fear, nor grieve, and receive good news of the Garden which you were promised." — 41:30

2. Angels as intermediaries in strengthening believers

The second function of the angels, as revealed in the Holy Quran, is to strengthen the righteous servants of God, prophets as well as others, and to give them comfort in trials and affliction. Jesus Christ, because of the serious allegations of the Jews against him, is mentioned as being strengthened with the Holy Spirit which, as shown earlier (page 11), is another name of Gabriel. And the believers generally are said to be strengthened with the Holy Spirit:

"These are they into whose hearts He has impressed faith, and strengthened them with a Spirit from Himself." — 58:22

Again we find in the Holy Quran that the angels are spoken of as friends or guardians of the faithful in this life and in the Hereafter (41:31). It was in this sense, i.e., to strengthen the believers, that the angels were sent to help them in their struggle against the unbelievers, as in the verse:

"When you sought the aid of your Lord, so He answered you: I will assist you with a thousand of the angels…" — 8:9

The Holy Quran itself explains why the angels were sent:

> "And Allah made it only a good news for you and that your hearts might be at ease thereby." — 3:126, 8:10

It was through the strengthening of the believers' hearts that the angels worked (8:12). These angelic hosts were sent when the Muslims had to fight in defence against heavy odds, and the strengthening of the heart through the angels is, therefore, a solid fact of history.

3. Angels as intermediaries in carrying out Divine punishment

Closely allied with this strengthening of the believers is the third function of the angels — that of executing Divine punishment against the wicked, because in the contest between the righteous and the wicked the punishment of the latter and the help of the former are identical. Often would those who sought to extirpate the truth by physical force say that if there were a God Whose messenger the Prophet was, and if there were angels who could help his cause, why did they not come? For example:

> "Why have not angels been sent down to us, or why do we not see our Lord?" — 25:21 (see also 2:210, 16:33, 6:158.)

To these demands, the Holy Quran replies in the following words:

> "And on the day when the heaven bursts apart with clouds, and the angels are sent down, as they are sent. The Kingdom on that day rightly belongs to the Beneficent, and it will be a hard day for the disbelievers."
> — 25:25–26

And on one occasion, the demand and the answer are thus put together:

> "And they say ... Why do you not bring the angels to us if you are truthful? We do not send angels but with truth, and then they would not be given respite." — 15:6–8

4. Angels' intercession and prayers for people

Another very important function of the angels is that of intercession — an intercession which includes all, both the believer and the unbeliever. As God "has ordained mercy on Himself" (6:12), and His "mercy encompasses all things" (7:156) — in fact, it was to show mercy that "He created them" (11:119) — it was necessary that His angels, who are intermediaries carrying out His will, should include everyone in their intercession. The intercession of the angels is mentioned in the Holy Quran on one occasion in particular:

> "And how many angels are there in the heavens whose intercession does not avail except after Allah gives permission to whom He pleases and chooses." — 53:26

Now intercession is really a prayer to God on behalf of the sinners on the Day of Judgment, but we are told that the angels pray for people even in this life:

> "…the angels celebrate the praise of their Lord and ask forgiveness for those on earth." — 42:5

"Those on earth" include both the believer and the unbeliever. And while this prayer by the angels is all-comprehensive, it grows stronger in the case of believers:

> "Our Lord, You embrace all things in mercy and knowledge, so protect those who turn to You and follow Your way… and make them enter the Gardens of perpetuity which You have promised them and such of their fathers and their wives and their offspring as are good… and guard them from evil." — 40:7–9

As a result of the prayers of the angels, the faithful are actually guided forth from every kind of darkness into light:

> "He it is Who sends His blessings on you and [so do] His angels, that He may bring you forth out of darkness into light." — 33:43

And as regards the Prophet, the angels bless him:

> "Surely Allah and His angels bless the Prophet. O you who believe, call for blessings on him…" — 33:56

Thus the angels' connection with man grows stronger as he advances in righteousness. As regards people generally, the angels pray for their forgiveness so that punishment in respect of their evil deeds may be averted; as regards the faithful, they lead them forth from darkness into light, and thus enable them to make progress spiritually; and as regards the Prophet, they bless him and are thus helpful in advancing his cause in the world.

5. Angels' promptings to noble deeds

Every good and noble deed is the result of the promptings of the angel. The Holy Quran speaks of the angel and the devil as leading man to two different courses of life: the former, as shown above, to a good and noble life aiming at the development of the human faculties, and the latter, as will be shown later, to a base and wicked life tending to the deadening of those faculties. Every person is said to have two associates, an associate angel and an associate devil. The first is called a "witness" (_shahīd_) and the second a "driver" (_sā'iq_):

> "And every soul comes, with it a driver and a witness. You [O soul] were indeed heedless of this, but now We have removed from you your veil, so that your sight is sharp this day." — 50:21–22

The _driver_ is the devil who makes evil suggestions and leads man to a state of degradation, and the _witness_ is the angel who helps man on to a good and noble end. Man is said to be heedless of it here, there being a veil over his eyes, so that he cannot see to what condition he is being led, but he will see the result clearly on the Day of Judgment. In Hadith we are told that every human being has an associate angel and an associate devil. Thus there is a report in Sahih Muslim:

> "The Prophet said: There is not one among you but there is appointed over him his associate from among the jinn and his associate from among the angels. The Companions said: And what about you, Prophet of Allah? He said: The same is the case with me, but Allah has helped me over him [i.e., over the associate jinn], so he has submitted and does not command me anything but good." [8]

6. Angels recording deeds of human beings

Another spiritual function of the angels, on which special stress is laid in the Holy Quran, is the recording of the good and evil deeds of man. These angels are called "honourable recorders", the words being taken from the verse of the Quran:

> "And surely there are keepers over you, honourable recorders (_kirām-an kātibīn_), they know what you do." — 82:10–12

and elsewhere we have:

> "When the two receivers receive, sitting on the right and on the left. He utters not a word but there is by him a watcher at hand." — 50:17–18

> "Alike [to Him] among you is he who conceals the word and he who speaks openly, and he who hides himself by night and who goes forth by day. For him are angels guarding the consequences [of his deeds], before him and behind him, who guard him by Allah's command." — 13:10–11

The guarding in the last verse refers to the guarding of man's deeds. The angels are immaterial beings, and hence also their recording is effected in a different manner from that in which a human being would prepare a record. In fact, their record exists, as elsewhere stated, in the form of the effect which an action produces:

> "And We have made every human being's actions cling to his neck, and We shall bring forth to him on the Day of Resurrection a book which he will find wide open." — 17:13

The clinging of a man's actions to his neck is clearly the effect which his actions produce and which he is powerless to obliterate, and we are told that this effect will be met with in the form of an open book on the Resurrection Day, thus showing that the angel's recording of a deed is actually the producing of an effect.

Faith in angels

The different functions of angels in the spiritual world are thus connected, in one way or another, either with the awakening of the spiritual life in man or its advancement and progress. Herein lies the reason why faith in angels is required along with a faith in God:

> "…righteous is the one who believes in Allah, and the Last Day, and the angels, and the Book and the prophets." — 2:177

> "The Messenger believes in what has been revealed to him from his Lord, and so do the believers. They all believe in Allah and His angels and His books and His messengers." — 2:285

Faith or belief in any doctrine, according to the Holy Quran, is essentially the acceptance of a proposition as a basis for action. Faith in angels, therefore, means that there is a spiritual life for man, and that he must develop that life by working in accordance with the promptings of the angel and by bringing into play the faculties which God has given him; and that is why — though the existence of the devil, who makes the evil suggestions, is as much a fact as the existence of the angel who makes the good suggestions — the Holy Quran requires a belief in angels but a disbelief in devils.[9] The significance is that one must obey the commandments of God and refuse to follow the suggestions of the devil. Faith in the angels, therefore, only means that every good suggestion — and such is the suggestion of the angel — must be accepted, because it leads to the spiritual development of man.

Iblīs is not an angel but one of the jinn

There is a popular misconception that *Iblīs* or the Devil is one of the angels. This has arisen from the fact that where the angels are commanded to make submission to Adam, there is also mention of *Iblīs* and his refusal to make the submission:

> "And when We said to the angels, Be submissive to Adam, they submitted, but *Iblīs* [did not]. He refused and was proud, and he was one of the disbelievers." — 2:34

From these words it is clear enough that *Iblīs* or the Devil was one of the unbelievers and refused to obey, and therefore he could not be an angel, because, regarding the angels, it is plainly said that:

> "They do not disobey Allah in what He commands them, but do as they are commanded." — 66:6

And elsewhere it is stated of *Iblīs:*

> "He was from among the jinn, so he transgressed the commandment of his Lord." — 18:50

Now jinn and angels are two different classes of beings; their origin and their functions have nothing in common. It is, therefore, an obvious error to look upon the jinn as being a branch of the angelic creation or *Iblīs* as an angel.

The *Jinn* — first sense

The word *jinn* is derived from *janna* meaning *he covered* or *concealed* or *hid* or *protected.* The word *jinn* has been used in the Holy

Quran distinctly in two senses. It is applied in the first place to the spirits of evil or the beings that invite man to evil, as opposed to the angels who invite him to good, both being imperceptible with the senses. The origin of these beings is said to be fire, and their function is described as that of exciting evil passions or low desires. The Holy Quran is explicit on both these points. As regards the creation of jinn, it says:

> "And the jinn We created before of intensely hot fire." — 15:27

> "And He created the jinn of a flame of fire." — 55:15

And to show that the jinn and the devils are one, the devil is spoken of as saying:

> "I am better than he [i.e., man]; You have created me of fire while him You did create of dust." — 7:12

As regards the function of jinn, the Holy Quran is equally clear:

> "...the slinking devil who whispers into the hearts of people, from among the jinn and mankind." — 114:4–6

A Hadith report has already been quoted showing that every person has with him an associate from among the angels who inspires him with good and noble ideas, and an associate from among the jinn who excites his baser passions.

The devil

The question is often asked, why has God created beings which lead man astray? There is a misunderstanding in this question. God has created every human being with two kinds of passions, the higher which awaken in him a higher or spiritual life, and the lower which relate to his physical existence; and corresponding to these two passions there are two kinds of beings, the angels and the devils. The lower passions are necessary for a person's physical life, but they become a hindrance to him in his advancement to a higher life when they run riot and are out of control. Man is required to keep these passions in control. If he can do so, they become a help to him in his advancement instead of a hindrance. This is the meaning underlying the Holy Prophet's reply in the report already quoted (see page 95), when he was asked if he too had an associate jinn. Yes, he said, "but

Allah has helped me over him, so he has submitted and does not command me anything but good." That is to say, he became a help to him in the development of his higher life.

Such is the true significance underlying the story of Adam. The devil at first refuses to make obeisance to man, i.e., to become helpful in his spiritual advancement, and is determined, by hook or by crook, to set him on the wrong course and excite his baser passions.[10] But he is subdued by the help of the Divine revelation, and those who follow the revelation have no fear of the devil's misleading:

> "Then Adam received [revealed] words from his Lord, and He turned to him mercifully… Surely a guidance from Me will come to you, then whoever follows My guidance, no fear shall come upon them, nor shall they grieve." —2:37–38

The presence of the devil thus indicates that, in the earlier stages of spiritual development, man has to contend with him by refusing to obey his evil promptings, and anyone who makes this struggle is sure to subdue the evil one; while in the higher stages, the lower passions having been brought into subjection, the devil actually becomes helpful, "not commanding anything but good," so that even physical desires become a help in the spiritual life of man. Without struggle there is no advancement in life, and thus even in the earlier stages, the devil is the ultimate means of man's good, unless, of course, man chooses to follow instead of stubbornly resisting him.

The word *jinn* as applied to humans — second sense

The other use of the word *jinn* is with regard to men of a certain category. Even the word *devil* (*shaiṭān*), or *devils* (*shayāṭīn*), has been applied to men in the Holy Quran, and the leaders of evil are again and again called devils.[11] But the use of the word *jinn* when speaking of certain persons was recognized in Arabic literature before Islam. It is said that *Arabs liken a man who is sharp and clever in affairs to a jinni and a shaiṭān.*[12] In pre-Islamic poetry the word *jinn* has also been used to denote great or brave men. In addition to this, the *word jinn* is explained by Arabic lexicologists as meaning *the bulk of mankind.*[13] In the mouth of an Arab, the main body of men would mean the non-Arab world. They called all foreigners *jinn* because they were concealed from their eyes.

It is in this sense that the word *jinn* is used in the Holy Quran in the story of Solomon:

> "And of the jinn there were those who worked before him by the command of his Lord. ... They made for him what he pleased of synagogues and images…" — 34:12–13

The description of the *jinn* here as builders shows them to have been men. And they are also spoken of as devils (*shayāṭīn*) in 38:37, where they are called builders and divers, and it is further added that some of them were "fettered in chains". Surely those who built buildings and dived into the sea were not invisible spirits, nor do invisible spirits require to be fettered in chains. These were in fact the strangers whom Solomon had subjected to his rule and forced into service.

In one place in the Holy Quran, jinn and people are addressed as one class or community (*ma'shar*):

> "O community of jinn and people, did not messengers come to you from among you, relating to you My messages and warning you of the meeting of this day of yours?" — 6:130

Now the messengers who are mentioned in the Holy Quran or Hadith all belong to mankind, and the Holy Book does not speak of a single messenger from among the jinn. The jinn in this case, therefore, are either non-Arabs or the iniquitous leaders who mislead others.

In one verse, it is stated:

> "If jinn and people should combine together to bring the like of this Quran, they could not bring the like of it, though they helped one another." — 17:88

while in another verse (2:23), in an exactly similar challenge, the expression "your helpers" or "leaders" has been used instead of jinn.[14]

The jinn mentioned at the beginning of chapter 72 of the Quran are evidently foreign Christians, since they are spoken of as holding the doctrine of sonship.[15] In 72:6, they are called *rijāl* (pl. of *rajul*), which word is applicable to the males of human beings only. Again, in the 46th chapter the word *jinn* has been used in the sense of foreigners when a party of the jinn is stated to have come to the Holy Prophet and listened to the Holy Book and believed in it[16] because all the injunctions contained in the Holy Quran are for human beings, and there is not one for the jinn. This was evidently a party of the Jews of Nisibus as reports show, and the Quran speaks of them as believers in Moses.[17]

At any rate, the Holy Quran and the Hadith do not speak of the jinn as they exist in the popular imagination, interfering in human affairs or controlling the forces of nature or assuming human or any other shape or taking possession of men or women and affecting them with certain diseases.

Notes to Chapter 6

1. *Malā'ika* is derived from *'alk* or *'alūka,* meaning *risāla* or the 'bearing of messages'. Some authorities trace it to the root *malk* or *milk,* meaning 'power'.

2. Muslim, book 55: 'Piety and Softening of hearts', ch. 10, h. 2996 (MDS: book 53, ch. 10, h. 7495).

3. See the Quran, 15:88 and 26:215.

4. The Quran, 11:69–70, 15:51–52, 51:24–25.

5. The Quran, 2:34.

6. Bukhari, book 59: 'Beginning of Creation', ch. 6, h. 3217.

7. *Ibid.,* h. 3208.

8. Muslim, book 52: 'Description of Judgment Day', ch. 16, h. 2814b (MDS: book 50, ch. 16, h.7109). *Editor's Note:* The previous hadith in this chapter (h. 2814a or MDS: h. 7108) mentions only "his associate from among the jinn", while this one adds: "and his associate from among the angels".

9. The Quran, 2:256.

10. "And he [the devil] said: Certainly I will take of Your servants an appointed portion, and certainly I will lead them astray and excite in them vain desires" (the Quran, 4:118–119).

11. The Quran, 2:14, 3:174, 8:48, 15:17, 21:82, etc.

12. Al-Tabrizi's Exposition of *al-Hamāsah* quoted in Lane's Lexicon.

13. *Qāmūs, Tāj al-'Arūs* and Lane's Lexicon.

14. *Editor's Note:* Since in 17:88 it is stated that jinn cannot produce the like of the Quran, this shows that such jinn must have been known to be able to compose books, and that too in Arabic. Thus they were human beings.

15. The Quran, 72:3–4.

16. The Quran, 46:29.

17. The Quran, 46:30.

7. Revealed Books

Revealed books mentioned under three names

Revealed books are mentioned in the Holy Quran under three names. The first name is *kitāb* (pl. *kutub*), meaning a Book. The word *al-Kitāb* has been used in the Holy Quran for the Quran itself, for its chapters, for any previous revelation, for all previous revelations taken together and for all revealed books including the Holy Quran.[1] The word *kitāb* has, however, been used to speak of the revelation of God to prophets whether written or not, while it is also freely used regarding the Divine decrees or ordinances.[2]

Revealed books are also spoken of as *ṣuḥuf* (pl. of *ṣaḥīfah*, meaning 'anything spread out' or written pages). All previous books, particularly the books of Moses and Abraham, have been so called,[3] and the Holy Quran itself has been spoken of as *ṣuḥuf*.[4]

The third name under which revealed books are mentioned is *zubur* (pl. of *zabūr*).[5] The singular form, *zabūr*, occurs only three times in the Holy Quran, twice in connection with the book of David,[6] and on one occasion a quotation is given from *al-Zabūr*.[7] The word *zabūr* means *any writing* or *book,* and particularly *the Book of the Psalms* of David is called *al-Zabūr*.

Revelation to objects and beings other than man

The Arabic word for revelation, *waḥy,* has, in its highest form, come to signify the Divine word which is communicated to prophets, and to saints or righteous servants of God (*auliyā'*) who have not been raised to the dignity of prophethood.[8] According to the Holy Quran, revelation is a universal fact, so much so that it is even spoken of as being granted to inanimate objects:

> "Then He directed Himself to the heaven and it was a vapour, so He said to it and to the earth: Come both willingly or unwillingly. They both said: We come willingly. So He

ordained them seven heavens in two periods, and revealed in every heaven its affair." — 41:11–12

On another occasion there is mention of revelation to the earth:

"When the earth is shaken with her shaking, and the earth brings forth her burdens, and man says: What has happened to her? On that day she will tell her news, as if your Lord had revealed to her." — 99:1–5

In the first instance, God's speaking to the earth and the heavens and His revelation to the heavens shows that there is a kind of revelation through which the Divine laws are made to operate in the universe; in the second, a great revolution that is brought about upon earth — its "bringing forth its burdens", explained as the laying open of its treasures[9] in the form of minerals and other products — is spoken of as a kind of revelation.

There is also a revelation to the lower animals:

"And your Lord revealed to the bee: Make hives in the mountains and in the trees and in what they build, then eat of all the fruits and walk in the ways of your Lord submissively." — 16:68–69

This is really an example of the Divine revelation being granted also to the lower creation, so that what they do by instinct is really a revelation. These two examples show that Divine revelation is intended for the development and perfection of everything within its ordained sphere. Here may also be mentioned the revelation to angels:

"When your Lord revealed to the angels: I am with you, so make firm those who believe." — 8:12

As revelation itself is communicated through angels, it appears that there are various orders of angels; and it is for this reason that Gabriel, the angel who brings revelation to the prophets of God, is regarded as the greatest of them all.

Revelation to *auliya'*

Much misconception prevails as to the sphere of revelation to man. It is generally thought that revelation is limited to the prophets of God. This is not true. On several occasions the Holy Quran speaks of revelation (*waḥy*) having been granted to such righteous servants of

God as were not prophets, men as well as women. The mother of Moses is said to have received a revelation though she was undoubtedly not a prophet, and so are the disciples of Jesus who were not prophets:

> "And We revealed (*auhai-nā*) to Moses' mother, saying: Suckle him; then when you fear for him, cast him into the river, and do not fear, nor grieve; surely We shall bring him back to you and make him a messenger." — 28:7

> "And when I revealed (*auhai-tu*) to the disciples [of Jesus], saying, Believe in Me and My messenger." —5:111

These verses leave not the least doubt that revelation (*wahy*) is granted to those who are not prophets as well as to prophets, and therefore the door to revelation is not closed, even though no prophet at all would come after Prophet Muhammad. It is only authoritative revelation, the form of revelation peculiar to prophets, the revelation through Gabriel as explained in the next paragraph, that has ceased after him.

Revelation to man granted in three ways

Revelation to inanimate objects, to the lower animals and to the angels is of a different nature from revelation to man, and it is the latter with which we are chiefly concerned. Divine revelation to man is stated to be of three kinds:

> "And it is not granted to a mortal that Allah should speak to him, except by revelation (*wahy*) or from behind a veil, or by sending a messenger and revealing by His permission what He pleases." — 42:51

The first of these, which is called *wahy* in the original, is the inspiring of an idea into the heart, for the word *wahy* is used here in its primary significance of a *hasty suggestion* or *infusing into the heart,* as distinguished from a revelation in words. In spite of the fact that this kind of revelation is the "infusing of an idea into the heart," it is called a form of God's speaking to man. This is technically called *wahy khafiyy* or inner revelation, and the sayings of the Holy Prophet touching on religious matters are in this class. Revelation in this form is common to both prophets and those who are not prophets.

The second mode of God's speaking to man is said to be "from behind a veil", and this includes dream (*ru'yā*), vision *(kashf)* and *ilhām* (when voices are heard or uttered in a state of trance, the recipient being neither quite asleep, nor fully awake). This form of revelation is also common both to prophets and those who are not prophets, and in its simplest form, the dream, it is a universal experience of the whole of humanity. The Holy Quran tells us of the vision of a king, who was apparently not a believer in God — a vision which had a deep underlying significance.[10] This shows that, according to the Quran, revelation in its lower forms is the common experience of all mankind, of the unbeliever as well as the believer, of the sinner as well as of the saint.

The third kind, which is peculiar to the prophets of God, is that in which the angel Gabriel, referred to as "messenger" in the above verse, brings the Divine message in words. This is the surest and clearest form of revelation, and such was the revelation of the Quran to the Prophet. This is called *revelation that is recited in words* (*wahy matluww*). It is the highest and most developed form, and it was in this manner that revelation was granted to all the prophets of God in every nation. The revealed books are a record of this highest revelation, and technically the word revelation (*wahy*) is applied to this form as distinguished from the lower forms.

Object of God's revelation to man

Speaking of Adam, the Holy Quran has stated the reason why revelation from God was needed, and the purpose which it fulfilled. Man had two objects before him, to conquer nature and to conquer self, to bring under his control the powers of nature and his own desires. In the story of Adam as the prototype of man, as related in the Quran, we are told that Adam was given the knowledge of things, that is to say that man was endowed with the capacity to obtain knowledge of all things (2:31). He was also gifted with the power to conquer nature, for the angels, the beings controlling the powers of nature, were made to submit to him (2:34). But *Iblīs,* the inciter of lower desires in man, did not submit, and man fell a prey to his evil suggestions (2:34–36). Man was powerful against all, but weak against himself. He could attain perfection in one direction by his own exertions; he could conquer nature by his knowledge of things and the power granted to him; but the greater conquest and the greater perfection lay in the conquest of his inner self, and this conquest could only be brought about by a closer connection with the Divine Being. It was to make this perfection possible for him that revelation was needed.

Thus, we are told, when man proved weak against his own desires and passions, Divine help came to him in the form of certain "words from his Lord" (2:37), that is to say, in the form of Divine revelation which was granted to Adam. And as for his posterity, the Divine law was given:

> "Surely a guidance from Me will come to you, then whoever follows My guidance, no fear shall come upon them, nor shall they grieve." — 2:38

In these words man is told that, with the help of Divine revelation, he shall have no fear of the Devil's temptings, and so the hindrance of his progress and the obstacle to the development of his faculties being removed, he will go on advancing on the road to perfection.

Revelation is a universal fact

It has already been pointed out that revelation in its lower forms, in the form of inspiration or that of dreams or visions, is the universal experience of humanity, but even in its highest form, it is not, according to the Holy Quran, limited to one particular man or to one particular nation. It is, on the other hand, most emphatically stated that just as God has given His physical sustenance to each and every nation, even so He has endowed it with His spiritual sustenance for its moral and spiritual advancement. Two quotations from the Quran will suffice to show that revelation in its highest form has been granted to every nation:

> "There is not a people but a warner has gone among them."
> — 35:24

> "And for every nation there is a messenger." — 10:47

And thus the idea of revelation in Islam is as broad as humanity itself.

Belief in all sacred scriptures is an article of Muslim faith

The religion of Islam, therefore, requires a belief, not in the Holy Quran alone but in all the books of God, granted to all the nations of the world. At its very commencement the Quran lays down in clear words, regarding the Holy Prophet's revelation, that Muslims must:

> "…believe in what has been revealed to you [O Prophet] and what was revealed before you…" — 2:4

And again:

> "The Messenger believes in what has been revealed to him from his Lord, and so do the believers. They all believe in Allah and His angels and His Books and His messengers." — 2:285

A book was granted to every prophet of God:

> "Mankind is a single nation. So Allah raised prophets as bearers of good news and as warners, and He revealed with them the book with truth…" — 2:213

> "But if they reject you, so indeed were rejected before you messengers who came with clear arguments and scriptures and the illuminating Book." — 3:184

Only two books are mentioned by their special names, the *Taurāt* (Torah, or book of Moses) and the *Injīl* (Gospel, or book of Jesus). The giving of a scripture (*zabūr*) to David is also mentioned,[11] and the scriptures *(ṣuḥuf)* of Abraham and Moses are mentioned together.[12] But, as stated above, a Muslim is required to believe, not only in the particular books named but in all the books of all the prophets of God; in other words, in the sacred scriptures of every nation, because every nation had a prophet and every prophet had a book.

Revelation brought to perfection

According to the Holy Quran, revelation is not only universal but also progressive, attaining perfection in the last of the prophets, the Holy Prophet Muhammad. A revelation was granted to each nation according to its requirements, and in each age in accordance with the capacity of the people of that age. And as the human brain became more and more developed, more and yet more light was cast by revelation on matters relating to the unseen, on the existence and attributes of the Divine Being, on the nature of revelation from Him, on the requital of good and evil, on life after death, on Paradise and Hell.

The Quran is called a book "that makes manifest",[13] because it shed complete light on the essentials of religion, and made manifest what had hitherto remained, of necessity, obscure. It is on account of this full resplendence of light which it casts on all religious problems that the Quran claims to have brought religion to perfection:

> "This day have I perfected for you your religion and completed My favour to you and chosen for you Islam as a religion." — 5:3

Six hundred years before this revelation, Jesus Christ said:

> "I still have many things to say to you but you cannot bear them now. However, when he, the spirit of truth, has come, he will guide you into all truth".[14]

This is clearly a reference to the coming of a revelation with which religion will come to perfection, and, among the sacred books of the world, the Holy Quran alone advances the claim that it has brought religion to perfection; and, in keeping with that claim, it has cast the fullest light on all religious questions.

The Quran as guardian and judge of previous revelation

Besides bringing revelation to perfection and making plain what was obscure in the previous scriptures, the Holy Quran claims to be a guardian over those scriptures, guarding the original teachings of the prophets of God, and a judge deciding the differences between them. Thus after speaking of the Torah and the Gospel,[15] it says:

> "And We have revealed to you [O Prophet] the Book with the truth, verifying what is before it of the book and a guardian over it..." — 5:48

It is elsewhere pointed out in the Quran that the teachings of the earlier scriptures had undergone alterations, and therefore only a revelation from God could separate the pure Divine teaching from the mass of error which had grown around it. This the Quran did, and hence it is called a guardian over the earlier scriptures. As for its authority as a judge, we are told:

> "We certainly sent messengers to nations before you [O Prophet]... And We have not revealed to you the Book except that you may make clear to them what they differ about." — 16:63–64

Religious differences had grown to such an extent that religion itself would have lost its hold on humanity had not a revelation from God guided humanity aright. All religions were from God, yet each denounced all others as leading man to perdition; and their basic doctrines had come to differ from one another to such an extent that it had become simply unthinkable that they could have proceeded from the same Divine source; till the Quran pointed out the common ground, namely, the Unity of God, and the universality of revelation.

Defects of earlier scriptures removed

There is much that is common to the Holy Quran and the previous scriptures, especially the Bible. The Quran has repeatedly declared that the basic principles of all religions were the same, only the details differing according to the time and the stage of a people's development. All these principles in a more developed form are taught by the Quran, and occasionally lessons have been drawn from previous history. But it is remarkable that, both in its discussion of religious principles and in its references to history, the Quran has done away with the defects of the earlier books.

Take, for example, the Bible. It mentions many incidents which, so far from conveying any ennobling lesson, are derogatory to the dignity of prophethood and, sometimes, even of an obscene nature. An educated Jew or Christian would prefer that his sacred book did not contain such statements as that Abraham, that great and revered patriarch of all nations, was a liar, that Lot committed incest with his own daughters, that Aaron made the image of a calf and led the Israelites to its worship, that David, whose beautiful Psalms are the texts of sermons in churches and synagogues, committed adultery with Uriah's wife, and that Solomon with all his wisdom worshipped idols to please his wives!

The Holy Quran speaks of all these great men but it accepts none of these statements and rejects most of them in unmistakable words. Again, it speaks of the Devil tempting Adam, but in a language which makes it clear that it is the story of man's everyday experience: there is no image of dust into whose nostrils the breath of life is breathed;[16] no rib of Adam is taken out to make the woman;[17] there is no Divine interdiction against the tree of the knowledge of good and evil;[18] there is no serpent to beguile the woman, nor does the woman tempt the man;[19] the Lord God does not walk in the garden in the cool of the day;[20] no punishment is meted out to the serpent that he shall go on his belly and eat dust, the bringing forth of children is not a punishment for the woman, nor is labouring in the fields a punishment for the man.[21] Similarly, the Quran relates the history of Noah several times, but not once does it state that there was a deluge which covered the whole earth and destroyed all living creatures on the face of the earth.[22] It only speaks of a flood that destroyed Noah's people.[23] There are many other examples[24] which show that, though the Quran relates the histories of some of the prophets of yore in order to draw lessons therefrom, yet it does not borrow from the Bible. It is from the Divine source that its knowledge is drawn, and hence it is that when referring to those histories, it removes all their defects.

Alterations of the text of previous scriptures

The examples given above show that the old scriptures, though revealed by God, have undergone considerable changes; and this is not only true of the Bible but applies with equal truth to all the ancient revealed books. Modern criticism of the Bible, together with the accessibility of ancient manuscripts, has now established the fact that many alterations were made in it. It was in the seventh century C.E. that the Quran charged the followers of the Bible with altering its text, and that at a time when nobody knew that such alterations had been made in its text. Only one quotation may be given in this connection:

> "Do you then hope that they would believe in you, and a party from among them indeed used to hear the word of Allah, then altered it after they had understood it, and they know [this]... Woe, then, to those who write the book with their hands and then say, This is from Allah; so that they may take for it a small price!" — 2:75, 79

Hence it should be borne in mind that though the Holy Quran speaks again and again of "verifying" what is before it, yet it does not and cannot mean that there have been no alterations in them. On the other hand, it condemns many of the doctrines taught by the followers of the earlier scriptures, and this shows that while their origin is admitted to be Divine, it is at the same time pointed out that these books have not come down to us in their original purity, and that the truth revealed in them has been mixed up with errors due to alterations effected by human hands.

Door to revelation is not closed

In almost every great religion, Divine revelation is considered to be the peculiar experience of a particular race or nation, and even in that nation the door to revelation is looked upon as having been closed after some great personage or after a certain time. But Islam, while making revelation the universal experience of humanity, also considers its door as standing open for all time. There is an erroneous idea in some minds that, in Islam, the door to revelation was closed with Prophet Muhammad, because it is stated in the Holy Quran that he is the last of the prophets. Why there shall be no prophet after him will be discussed in the next chapter, but it is an error to confuse the discontinuance of prophethood with the discontinuation of revelation. It has been shown that, of the three kinds of revelation, two are common to both prophets and those who are not prophets, while only one form of revelation, the highest, in which the angel Gabriel is sent with a message in words, is peculiar to the prophets. Therefore, when it is said that no prophet shall appear after Prophet Muhammad, the only conclusion that can be drawn from it is that the door has been closed on that highest form of revelation, but by no stretch of words can revelation itself be said to have come to an end.

The granting of revelation to those who are not prophets being an admitted fact, as shown before on the basis of clear Quranic verses, revelation remains, and humanity will always have access to this great Divine blessing, though prophethood, having reached its perfection, has naturally come to an end. The doctrine of the continuance of revelation is clearly upheld in the Quran and the Hadith. The former says:

> "Those who believe and keep their duty, for them is good news (*bushrā*) in this world's life and in the Hereafter." — 10:63 – 64

The *bushrā* granted in this world's life are "good visions which the Muslim sees or which are shown to him," according to a saying of the Holy Prophet.[25] And according to one of the most reliable hadith, *bushrā* or *mubashshirāt* — both words having the same significance — are a part of prophethood. Thus the Holy Prophet is reported to have said:

> "Nothing remains of prophethood but *mubashshirāt* ".

Being asked what was meant by *mubashshirāt,* he replied, "good (or true) visions".[26] According to another hadith, he is reported to have said:

> "The vision of the believer is one of the forty-six parts of prophethood." [27]

In another version of the same report, instead of the "vision of the believer", the words are "good (or true) visions" — *ru'yā ṣāliḥah.*[28] The word *vision* is used here in a wide sense, and includes the inspiration which is granted to the righteous. For we are told in yet another hadith:

> "There used to be among those who were before you persons who were spoken to [by God] though they were not prophets; if there is such a one among my people, it is Umar." [29]

The Holy Quran also says:

> "Those who say, Our Lord is Allah, then continue in the right way, the angels descend upon them saying: Do not fear, nor grieve, and receive good news of the Garden which you were promised." — 41:30

All these Hadith reports and the Quranic verses quoted above afford proof enough that revelation in some of its lower forms is continued after the Holy Prophet, and it is only the highest form of revelation — that brought by Gabriel — which has been discontinued with the termination of prophethood.

Kalām (speaking) is an attribute of the Divine Being

It is thus one of the basic principles of Islam that God speaks as He hears and sees. The attribute *kalām* of the Divine Being is mentioned frequently in the Holy Quran. God "spoke to" (*kallama*) Moses,[30] He "spoke to" (*kallama*) other prophets,[31] He speaks to those who are not prophets.[32] This leaves no doubt that speaking is an attribute of God according to the Holy Quran, just as seeing and hearing are His attributes. Hence, though no prophet will come after the Holy Prophet Muhammad, yet God still speaks to His righteous servants, because it is one of His attributes, and because His attributes cannot cease to function.

Notes to Chapter 7

1. The Quran, 2:2, 13:43, 98:3, 3:119.

2. See the Quran, 8:68, 9:36, 13:38, etc.

3. The Quran, 87:18–19.

4. The Quran, 80:13 and 98:2.

5. The Quran, 3:184, 16:44, 26:196, 35:25, 54:43.

6. The Quran, 4:163, 17:55.

7. "My righteous servants will inherit the land" — the Quran, 21:105.

8. Raghib's *Mufradāt*.

9. *Ibid.*

10. The Quran, 12:43.

11. The Quran, 17:55.

12. The Quran, 53:36–37 and 87:19.

13. The word for "makes manifest" is *mubīn;* see 12:1 etc.

14. John, 16:12–13.

15. The Quran, 5:44, 5:47.

16. Genesis, 2:7.

17. *Ibid.,* 2:22.

18. *Ibid.,* 2:17.

19. *Ibid.,* 3:1–6.

20. *Ibid.,* 3:8.

21. *Ibid.,* 3:14–19.

22. *Ibid.,* 7:17–23.

23. The Quran, 7:64.

24. *Editor's Note:* Maulana Muhammad Ali has noted these and other differences between the Quran and the Bible in the notes to his Translation of the Quran, to which the reader should refer for further information on this point.

25. Razi, Fakhr-ud-Din, *Al-Tafsīr al-Kabīr.*

26. Bukhari, book 91: 'Interpretation of Dreams', ch. 5, h. 6990.

27. *Ibid.,* ch. 4, h. 6987.

28. *Ibid.,* ch. 4, h. 6989.

29. Bukhari, book 62: 'Virtues of the Companions of the Prophet', ch. 6, h. 3689. See also Bukhari, book 60: 'Prophets', ch. 54, h. 3469.

30. The Quran, 4:164, 7:143.

31. The Quran, 2:253.

32. The Quran, 42:51.

8. Prophets

Nabī and *Rasūl*

The next article of faith in Islam is belief in the prophets. The Arabic word for prophet is *nabī,* which is derived from *naba',* meaning 'an announcement of great utility imparting knowledge of a thing', and the word *naba'* is applied only to such information as is free from any liability to untruth.[1] A *nabī* is the man who gives information about God.[2] This has been further explained as "the man to whom God gives information concerning His Unity and to whom He reveals secrets of the future and imparts the knowledge that he is His prophet".[3]

A *nabī* is also called a *rasūl,* which means 'a messenger' (lit., 'one sent'). The two words *nabī* and *rasūl* are used interchangeably in the Holy Quran, the same person being sometimes called *nabī* and sometimes *rasūl;* while occasionally both names are combined. The reason seems to be that the prophet has two capacities: he receives information from God, and he imparts the message to mankind. He is called a *nabī* in his first, and a *rasūl* in his second capacity, but there is one difference. The word *rasūl* has a wider significance, being applicable to every messenger in a literal sense;[4] and the angels are called Divine "messengers" (*rusul,* plural of *rasūl*)[5] because they are also bearers of Divine messages to carry out the Divine will.

Faith in Divine messengers

It has already been stated that a faith in Divine revelation is one of the essentials of Islam, and since revelation must be communicated through a man, faith in the messenger is a natural sequence, and is mentioned in the Quran along with faith in the revealed books.[6] In fact, there is a deeper significance underlying faith in the prophets, and hence the greater stress is laid upon this article of faith. The prophet is not only the bearer of the Divine message but he also shows how that message is to be interpreted in practical life; and therefore he is the model to be followed. It is the prophet's example that inspires a living faith in the hearts of his followers and brings about a real transformation in their lives. That is why the Holy Quran lays special stress on the fact that the prophet must be a human being:

> "Their messengers said to them: We are nothing but mortals like yourselves..." — 14:11

and the Holy Prophet Muhammad is told to say to people:

> "I am only a mortal like you." — 18:110, 41:6

The reformation of human beings can only be accomplished through human prophets. God incarnate would serve no purpose in the reformation of man, even if it were possible that He should come in the flesh, considering that man has to face temptations at every step, but there is no temptation for God.

Universality of the institution of prophethood

Just as God has granted His gifts of physical sustenance to all alike, so His spiritual gift of prophethood, through which a spiritual life is awakened in man, is also a free gift to all the nations of the world. It is not among the Israelites alone that prophets were raised as would appear from the Bible. According to the Holy Quran, there is not one nation in the world in which a prophet has not appeared:

> "There is not a people but a warner has gone among them." — 35:24

> "For every nation there is a messenger." — 10:47

The Holy Prophet was further told that there had been prophets besides those mentioned in the Quran:

> "And We sent messengers We have mentioned to you before, and messengers We have not mentioned to you." — 4:164

It is, in fact, stated in a hadith that there have been 124,000 prophets, while the Quran contains only about twenty-five names, among them being several non-Biblical prophets, Hud and Salih in Arabia, Luqman in Ethiopia, a contemporary of Moses (generally known as Khidr) in Sudan, and Dhu-l-Qarnain (Darius I, who was also a king) in Persia; all of which is quite in accordance with the theory of the universality of prophethood. And as the Holy Book has plainly said that prophets have appeared in all nations and that it has not named all of them, which in fact was unnecessary, a Muslim may accept the great luminaries who are accepted by other nations as having brought light to them, as the prophets of those nations.

A Muslim must believe in all the prophets

The Quran, however, not only establishes the theory that prophets have appeared in all nations; it goes further and renders it necessary that a Muslim should believe in all those prophets. In the very beginning we are told that a Muslim must:

> "believe in what has been revealed to you [O Prophet] and what was revealed before you" — 2:4

Further on, Muslims are made to declare:

> "We believe in Allah and in what has been revealed to us and in what was revealed to Abraham and Ishmael and Isaac and Jacob and the tribes, and in what was given to Moses and Jesus, and in what was given to the prophets from their Lord; we do not make any distinction between any of them and to Him we submit." — 2:136

Here the word *prophets* clearly refers to the prophets of other nations. And again, the Holy Quran speaks of Muslims as believing in all the prophets of God and not in Prophet Muhammad alone:

> "…but righteous is the one who believes in Allah and the Last Day and the angels and the Book and the prophets." — 2:177

> "The Messenger believes in what has been revealed to him from his Lord, and so do the believers; they all believe in Allah and His angels and His Books and His messengers; [they say] we make no distinction between any of His messengers." — 2:285

In fact, to believe in some prophets and reject others is condemned as unbelief (*kufr*):

> "Those who disbelieve in Allah and His messengers, and desire to make a distinction between Allah and His messengers and say: We believe in some and disbelieve in others,

and desire to take a course in between — these are truly disbelievers." — 4:150–151

A belief in all the prophets of the world is thus an essential principle of the religion of Islam, and though the faith of Islam is summed up in two brief sentences, *There is no god but Allah and Muhammad is His Messenger,* yet the one who confesses belief in the Prophet Muhammad, in so doing, accepts all the prophets of the world, whether their names are mentioned in the Quran or not. Islam claims a universality to which no other religion can aspire, and lays the foundation of a brotherhood as vast as humanity itself.

National Prophets

The Divine scheme whereby prophets were raised for the regeneration of the world, as disclosed in the Holy Quran, may be briefly summed up as follows. Prophets appeared in every nation but their message was limited to that particular nation and in some cases to one or a few generations. All these prophets were, so to speak, national prophets, and their work was limited to the moral upliftment and spiritual regeneration of one nation only. But while national growth was of necessity the first step, when each nation lived almost an exclusive life and the means of communication were wanting, the grand aim which the Divine scheme had in view was the upliftment and unification of the whole human race. Humanity could not remain forever divided into water-tight compartments of nationality, formed on the basis of blood or geographical limitations. In fact these divisions had, through jealousy, become the means of discord and hatred among different nations, each looking upon itself as the only chosen nation, and despising the rest. Such views tended to extinguish any faint glimmerings of aspirations for the unity of the human race. The final step, therefore, in the institution of prophethood was the coming of one prophet for all the nations, so that the consciousness of being one whole might be brought to the human race. The day of the national prophet was ended; it had served the purpose for which it was meant, and the day of the world-prophet dawned upon humanity in the person of the Holy Prophet Muhammad.

The world-prophet

The idea of the world-prophet is not based on a solitary passage occurring in the Holy Quran, as to the extent of the mission of this or that prophet; but is a fully developed Divine scheme. When mentioning the earlier prophets the Quran says that Noah was sent "to his people", and so were Hud, Salih and Shuaib — everyone of them was sent to *his* people.[7] It speaks of Moses as being commanded to "bring forth *your* people from darkness into light" (14:5), it speaks of Jesus as "a messenger to the children of Israel" (3:49) but in speaking of Holy Prophet Muhammad it says in unequivocal words:

> "We have not sent you but as a bearer of good news and as a warner *to all mankind...*" — 34:28

The Arabic words for "all mankind" are *kāffat-an li-l-nās,* where even *al-nās* carries the idea of *all people,* and the addition of *kāffah* is meant to emphasize further that not a single nation was excluded from the heavenly ministration of the Prophet Muhammad.

On another occasion also, the universality of the Holy Prophet's mission is thus stressed:

> "Say: O mankind, surely I am the Messenger of Allah to you all,[8] of Him Whose is the kingdom of the heavens and the earth." — 7:158

One thing is sure, that no other prophet is spoken of either in the Quran or in any other scripture as having been sent to the whole of humanity or to all people or all nations;[9] nor is Prophet Muhammad ever spoken of in the Quran as having been sent to *his people* only. The Quran itself is repeatedly termed "a Reminder for the nations".[10] And the Holy Prophet is called not only "a warner to all the nations" (25:1) but a mercy to all of them as well:

> "And We have not sent you but as a mercy to the nations." — 21:107

The idea that a world-prophet must follow the national prophets is further developed in the Holy Quran. It is in a Madinah revelation that the whole proposition, the appearance of a world-prophet, the distinguishing feature of his religion and the necessity for believing in him is laid down in clear words. The complete passage is as follows:

> "And when Allah made a covenant through the prophets: Certainly what I have given you of Book and wisdom — then a Messenger comes to you verifying what is [already]

with you, you shall believe in him, and you shall aid him. He said: Do you affirm and accept My compact in this matter? They said: We do affirm. He said: Then bear witness, and I too am a bearer of witness with you. Whoever then turns back after this, these are the transgressors. Do they then seek other than Allah's religion? And to Him submits whoever is in the heavens and the earth, willingly or unwillingly, and to Him they will be returned. Say: We believe in Allah and in what is revealed to us, and in what was revealed to Abraham and Ishmael and Isaac and Jacob and the tribes, and in what was given to Moses and Jesus and to the prophets from their Lord; we make no distinction between any of them, and to Him we submit. And whoever seeks a religion other than Islam, it will not be accepted from him, and in the Hereafter he will be one of the losers." — 3:81–85

That a world-prophet is spoken of here is evident from the fact that his acceptance — "you shall believe in him and you shall aid him" —is made obligatory on the followers of all the prophets that had passed away before him. As prophets had been sent, according to the teachings of the Holy Quran, to every nation, the conclusion is obvious that the followers of every prophet are required to believe in this, the final Prophet. The distinguishing feature of the world-prophet as mentioned here is that he will "verify what is with you," in other words, that he will bear testimony to the truth of all the prophets of the world. One may turn the pages of all the sacred books and search the sacred history of every nation, and it would be found that there was but One Prophet who verified the scriptures of *all* religions and bore testimony to the truth of the prophets of every nation. In fact, no one could aspire to the dignity of world-prophet who did not treat the whole humanity as one; and Muhammad is the only man who did so by declaring that prophets of God had appeared in every nation and that everyone who believed in him must also believe in *all* the prophets of the world. Hence it is that the verse requiring a belief in all the prophets of God — a belief in Abraham, in Ishmael, in Isaac, in Jacob, in Moses, in Jesus, and finally and comprehensively in *the prophets* — which occurs several times in the Quran, is repeated here again, and followed by the clear statement that Islam, or *belief in all the prophets of God,* is the only religion with God, and whosoever desires a religion *other than Islam* — a belief only in one prophet while rejecting all others — it shall not be accepted from him, because belief in *one* prophet is, after all, only acceptance of partial truth, and tantamount to the rejection of the whole truth, i.e., that there have been prophets in every nation.

Muhammad (peace be on him), therefore, does not only claim to have been sent to the whole world, to be a warner to all peoples and a mercy to all nations, but lays the foundations of a world-religion by making a belief in the prophet of every nation the basic principle of his faith. It is the only principle on which the whole of humanity can agree, the only basis of equal treatment for all nations.

The idea of a world-prophet is not a stray idea met with in the Quran; it is not based simply on one or two passages, stating that he had been raised for the regeneration of all nations; but the idea is here developed at length, and all the principles which can form the basis of a world-religion are fully enunciated. The whole of humanity is declared to be one nation;[11] God is said to be the *Rabb* (lit., 'the Nourisher unto perfection') of all nations;[12] prophets are declared to have been raised in all the nations for their uplift;[13] all prejudices of colour, race and language are demolished;[14] and a vast brotherhood, extending over all the world, has been established, every member of which is bound to accept the prophets of all nations, and to treat all nations equally. Thus not only is the Prophet Muhammad a world-prophet who takes the place of the national prophets but he has also established a world-religion wherein the idea of nationality is super-seded by the consciousness of the unity of the human race.

All prophets are one community

All prophets, being from God, are as it were brethren. This doctrine of the brotherhood of all prophets is not only taught in the interdiction against making distinctions between the prophets of God, as stated above, but is laid down in the plainest words in both the Holy Quran and Hadith. Thus, after speaking of various prophets in the chapter *Prophets,* we are told:

> "Surely this your community is a single community, and I am your Lord, so serve Me." — 21:92

And again:

"O messengers, eat of the good things and do good. Surely I am Knower of what you do. And surely this your community is one community, and I am your Lord, so keep your duty to Me." — 23:51–52

Every prophet may have some special characteristic of his own, but, generally, what is said of one in the Quran, of his high morals or sublime character or noble teachings or trust in God, is true of all. Thus of Abraham we are told that he was "a truthful man" (19:41); of Moses that he was "one purified" (19:51); of Noah, Hud, Salih, and Lot that they were "faithful" (26:107, 125, 143, 162); of Jesus that he was "worthy of regard in this world and the Hereafter, and one of those who are drawn near to Allah" (3:45); of John the Baptist that he was "honourable and chaste" (3:39). It is the gravest mistake to think that the high qualities attributed to one prophet may be wanting in others. The prophets are all one community: they were all raised for one purpose, the teachings of all were essentially the same, they were all truthful, all faithful, all worthy of regard, all were made near to God, all were pure, all were honourable and chaste.

Why prophets are raised

The prophets are raised for the uplift of humanity and for freeing people from the bondage of sin. It has been shown in the last chapter that Divine revelation was needed to enable man to subdue the devil, who would, otherwise, be a great hindrance in his moral and spiritual progress. Man was commanded to live in a spiritual paradise, but since he was unable to withstand the temptations of the devil, the Divine revelation came to his aid; and a rule for all time was laid down for the guidance of all people:

"Surely a guidance from Me will come to you, then whoever follows My guidance, no fear shall come upon them, nor shall they grieve." — 2:38

The negation of fear refers to the fear of the devil's temptation, and as a remedy against this, Divine revelation was first granted to mankind.

Again, every prophet brings the message of the Unity of God, and the significance underlying this message has already been shown to be the all-round advancement of man, physical as well as spiritual and moral (see page 77). And every prophet is called a *giver of good news* and a *warner;*[15] the good news relating to man's advancement and elevation, the warning to the retarding of or interference with his progress.

The four works entrusted to the Prophet, as mentioned several times in the Quran, are stated thus:

> "We have sent among you a Messenger from among you, who recites to you Our messages and purifies you and teaches you the Book and the Wisdom…" — 2:151, etc.

The Arabic word for "purifies" is *yuzakkī* which is derived from *zakā,* originally meaning the *progress attained by Divine blessing,*[16] i.e., by the development of the faculties placed by God within man, and relates to the affairs of this world as well as the Hereafter, that is to say, to man's physical as well as spiritual advancement. The Holy Prophet's message of *purification,* therefore, signifies not only purification from sin but also man's setting forth on the road to physical and moral advancement.

All these references to the Holy Book show that the object of sending prophets was no other than the uplift of man, to enable him to subjugate his animal passions, to inspire him with nobler and higher sentiments, and to imbue him with Divine morals.

Sinlessness of prophets

The men who are commissioned for the high office of prophethood must themselves be free from the bondage of sin, and more than that, they must be the possessors of high morals if they are to fulfil the mission entrusted to them. The doctrine of the sinlessness of prophets has therefore always been an admitted principle among Muslims. The Holy Quran not only speaks of individual prophets in terms of the highest praise, but also lays down clearly in general terms that the prophets cannot go, either in word or in deed, against any commandment of God:

> "They are honoured servants; they do not speak before He speaks and according to His command they act." — 21:26–27

> "And it is not for a prophet to act dishonestly." — 3 : 161

These two verses set out in general words the principle of the sinlessness of prophets, while it has already been shown how each individual prophet has been spoken of in terms of the highest praise: one called "truthful", another said to have been "purified" by God's hand, yet another mentioned as "honourable and chaste"; and many of them, including Prophet Muhammad,[17] are described as being *amīn,* which means *one who is completely faithful to God.* The Quran, therefore, leaves not the least doubt as to the sinlessness of the prophets.

Certain words misunderstood

There are, however, certain words which have been misunderstood by some critics, who have straightaway rushed to the erroneous conclusion that the Quran gives no support to the doctrine of the sinlessness of prophets.

The most important of these words is *istighfār* which is generally taken as meaning *asking for forgiveness of sins.* It, however, carries a wide significance, being derived from the root *ghafr* which means 'the covering of a thing with that which will protect it from dirt'.[18] Therefore s*eeking of protection from sin* is as much a meaning of *istighfār* as *seeking of protection from the punishment of sin.* When it is established that, according to the teachings of the Quran, the prophets are sinless, *istighfār* can, in their case, only be taken as meaning the *seeking of protection from the sins to which man is liable,* for it is through Divine protection alone that they can remain sinless. Hence the Holy Prophet is spoken of in a hadith as saying *istighfār* a hundred times a day; that is to say, he was every moment seeking the protection of God, and praying to Him, that he may not go against His will. *Istighfār* or the prayer for protection (*ghafr*) is in fact a prayer for Divine help in the advancement to higher and higher stages of spiritual perfection. Thus, even those who have been admitted into Paradise are described in the Quran as praying to God for His *ghafr.*[19] Forgiveness, in the narrow sense of pardoning of sins, is meaningless here, because none can be admitted into Paradise unless his sins are pardoned. *Ghafr* or forgiveness, therefore, stands here for Divine help in the spiritual advancement of man, which will continue even after death.

Another misunderstood word is *dhanb* which is generally translated as meaning sin; but *dhanb* also is a word with a very wide significance. It is as much applicable to sins as to inadvertent shortcomings. A righteous man, without in the least departing from the course of righteousness, would always feel that he had fallen short in doing some good to humanity or in doing his duty to God; and thus, even though he is engaged in doing some good, he feels that there is something lacking in him. Between the shortcoming of such a one and that of the sinner is a world of difference. The sinner's shortcoming or _dhanb_ is that he has set himself against the will of God deliberately and done evil, while the righteous man's shortcoming lies in the fact that he is not satisfied that he has done all the good that it was in his power to do.

Christian criticism — individual cases of prophets

Christian criticism of Islam has been particularly directed against the doctrine of the sinlessness of the prophets, and this is due to the Christian doctrine of Atonement which falls _ipso facto_ the moment anyone else is regarded as sharing with Jesus Christ the honour of sinlessness. This criticism is, however, based, not on any principle enunciated in the Holy Quran, but on certain cases of individual prophets. Most of this misdirected criticism is due to a wrong conception of the words explained above. For example, it is said that Noah was a sinner because he prayed to God, saying: "…unless You forgive me and have mercy on me, I shall be among the losers" (11:47). The word used for 'forgiving' is from _ghafr,_ which, as shown above, also means the granting of protection and the prayer is not a confession of sin on the part of Noah. Similarly, Abraham is a sinner according to the critics because he is spoken of as expressing the hope that God "will forgive me my mistake on the Day of Judgment" (26:82). It is one thing to commit a mistake and quite a different thing to go against the Divine commandments, and no sensible person would consider these words to be a confession of sin. Moses is also said to have committed a sin by killing a Copt, but the Holy Quran makes it clear that he simply used his fist to ward off an attack against an Israelite who was being ill-treated (28:15), and thus death was only accidental. Concerning Adam, it is undoubtedly said that "Adam disobeyed his Lord" (20:121), but even here there is no commission of sin, for as a preliminary to that incident, it is clearly stated: "And certainly We gave a commandment to Adam before, but he forgot; and We found in him no resolve [to disobey]" (20:115). There was no intention on the part of Adam to disobey the Divine commandment; it was simply forgetfulness that brought about the disobedience.

In 2:36 the word used, instead of *disobedience,* is a derivation of *zalla* which means a *slip* or *mistake.*

Prophet Muhammad

The Holy Prophet Muhammad is said by these critics of Islam to be a sinner because he is commanded to seek Divine protection (*istighfār*) for his _dhanb_.[20] Now to seek protection against sin does not mean that sin has been committed — he who seeks Divine protection rather guards himself against the commission of sin; and, moreover, the word used here is _dhanb_ which means any human shortcoming. The following verses about the Holy Prophet may also be considered:

> "Surely We have granted you a clear victory, that Allah may cover for you your _dhanb_ in the past and those to come…"
> — 48:1–2

There is no imputation of sin here in any case, but only of human shortcomings, for, as has been already shown, _dhanb_ carries that wider significance. But as a matter of fact, "your _dhanb_" here means the _dhanb attributed to you,_ that is to say, "alleged shortcomings".[21] The "victory" spoken of here was the Hudaibiyah truce. Before that, during a prolonged state of hostilities between the Muslims and their opponents, the latter had drawn a dark picture of the Holy Prophet as their enemy. The truce put a stop to hostilities, and with peace being established in the country, non-Muslims freely mixed with Muslims, and the good points of Islam together with the high morality of the Prophet made their impression. Misunderstandings were removed, and this is how that "victory" became a means of covering (_ghafr_) the shortcomings alleged against the Holy Prophet in the past. The reference in "those to come" is to the later fault-finding of the critics of Islam, and means that evil things will be said about the Holy Prophet at a later date as well, and that all such misrepresentations and misunderstandings will, in their turn, be swept away.

Conception of miracles in Islam

The word employed in the Holy Quran for miracle is *āyat,* the primary meaning of which is 'an apparent sign or mark by which a thing is known'.[22] As used there, it generally carries one of two significations: *an indication, evidence* or *proof,* and a *Divine message* or *communication.* In the first sense, it includes the miracle in its meaning, and in the second, a verse of the Holy Quran. The adoption of the same word to indicate a Divine message and its proof is noteworthy. It shows that the Divine message itself is first and foremost proof of its own truth, and hence it is that the Holy Quran has always been looked upon by all Muslims as the greatest miracle of the Holy Prophet. And it is indeed the greatest miracle ever vouchsafed to a prophet because it stands in need of no other evidence whatever, but is itself a living proof of its own truth for all time.

The conception of miracles, as given by the Holy Quran, is quite different from that in other religions and in popular thinking. Here the supreme object before the Prophet is to effect a moral and spiritual transformation; the means adopted are an appeal to the reasoning faculty, an appeal to the heart of man to convince him that the Divine message is meant for his own uplift, and lessons drawn from previous history showing how the acceptance of truth has always benefited man, and its rejection has worked to his own undoing. The miracle has its own place in the Divine scheme; something great and beyond human power and comprehension is wrought now and again to show that the source of the great Message of Truth is supernatural, Divine. Thus the Holy Quran makes it clear that the bringing about of a transformation is the real object for which prophets are raised, that this object is attained by several means, each of which, therefore, has but a secondary value, and that among these evidences of the truth of the Prophet, the miracle does not occupy the highest place.

Thus it is that, while the Holy Quran is full of arguments, makes frequent appeals to human nature, and repeatedly refers to the histories of previous peoples, the mention of miracles in it is very rare. But still they are not denied:

> "And they swear their strongest oaths by Allah that if a sign comes to them they would certainly believe in it. Say: Signs are with Allah. And what should make you know that when they come they do not believe?" — 6:109

The words "signs are with Allah" clearly imply, as do those that follow, that extraordinary signs will be shown as an evidence of the Divine mission of the Prophet. Strange it is that there are critics of Islam who see in this verse a denial of signs, only because it is said that signs are with God. It is true that the Holy Quran does not represent Prophet Muhammad as a wonder-worker, as the Gospels represent Jesus Christ. Signs were shown, not when the Prophet so desired, or when his opponents demanded, but when it was the will of God; hence, whenever an extraordinary sign of the Prophet's truth was demanded, the reply was that such a sign would come when God willed it.

The miracles of Islam

As already stated, the greatest miracle of Islam is the Holy Quran. Nor is this an after-thought on the part of Muslims, for the Holy Book itself claims to be a miracle and has challenged the world to produce its like:

> "If people and jinn should combine together to bring the like of this Quran, they could not bring the like of it, though they helped one another." — 17:88

> "Or, say they: He has forged it. Say: Then bring ten forged chapters like it, and call upon whom you can besides Allah, if you are truthful." — 11:13

> Or, say they: He has forged it? Say: Then bring a chapter like it and call upon whom you can besides Allah, if you are truthful." — 10:38

> "And if you are in doubt as to that which We have revealed to Our servant, then produce a chapter like it, and call on your helpers besides Allah, if you are truthful." — 2:23

The proof of this claim lies in the result achieved — a miraculous transformation — which has been acknowledged alike by friends and critics of Islam. The Quran is a miracle because it brought about the greatest transformation that the world has ever witnessed — a transformation of the individual, of the family, of society, of the nation, of the country, an awakening material as well as moral, intellectual as well as spiritual. It produced an effect far greater than that of any other miracle recorded of any prophet; hence its claim to be the greatest of all miracles is incontestable and uncontested.

Prophecy

Of all miracles, the Holy Quran gives the first place to prophecy, and, in fact, prophecy does, in some respects, enjoy a distinction beyond that attributed to other miracles. Miracles generally are manifestations of the powers of God, and prophecy gives prominence to God's infinite knowledge which comprehends the future as well as the past and present. But there is one great disadvantage attaching to all miracles which are merely manifestations of power. It is very difficult to secure reliable evidence for them under all circumstances. Certain people may have witnessed the performance of such a miracle and their evidence may satisfy their contemporaries, but, with the lapse of time, their testimony loses much of its value. Therefore a miracle stands in need of being proved up to the hilt before it may be used as evidence of a prophet's claim, and in most cases it is very hard, if not impossible, to adduce any proof that the miracle ever actually took place. Another difficulty in the matter of miracles generally is to be found in the fact that, however wonderful a performance, it may be explained scientifically, and thus lose all value as a sign of the Divine mission of its worker.

Such doubts, however, do not exist in the case of prophecy, which can stand the test of scientific investigation. Moreover, the evidence in such a case rests on a firmer basis altogether, and its fulfilment generally comes to pass after a long time. A prophecy which proceeds from a Divine source must, of course, disclose some event which is beyond the scope of human knowledge and which cannot possibly be discovered by human foresight. It must also be connected with some deep Divine purpose in relation to the elevation of humanity, for prophecies are not meant merely to satisfy human curiosity. Lastly, it must have behind it the force of conviction, so that it is not only uttered with the utmost certainty but even in circumstances which apparently conflict with what is disclosed in the prophecy. A prophecy that fulfils these three conditions is one of the greatest miracles, a miracle which by an appeal to reason shows that there is a God Who reveals deep secrets to man and with Whom man can hold communion.

Prophecy of the triumph of Islam

The prophecies mentioned in the Holy Quran and those uttered by the Holy Prophet, of which Hadith literature is full, cover so vast a ground and relate to a future so distant that they require separate treatment. But one example may be given in illustration of what has been said above.

The Holy Quran gives prominence to the great prophecy of the triumph of Islam, and its earlier revealed chapters are full of such prophecies uttered in various forms. Now these chapters were revealed, and these prophecies announced, at a time when the Holy Prophet was quite alone and helpless, beset on all sides by enemies plotting to put an end to his life. The few adherents to his cause had been forced by cruel persecution to leave their homes and to take shelter in a foreign land. There was not the remotest prospect of Islam ever making any headway against the mighty forces of polytheism and idolatry, the mass of superstition and evil of every kind ranged against it. Previous attempts at the regeneration of Arabia, those of the Jewish nation which had settled down in various parts of Arabia, of the Christian missionaries who had the backing of the powerful Roman empire on the north and of Abyssinia in the south and west, the indigenous Arab attempt known as Hanifism, had all proved utter failures, and thus the fate of each previous attempt was only a symbol of despair for any fresh reform movement. Yet under these adverse circumstances, amidst nothing but despair on every side, we find prophecy after prophecy announced in the surest and most certain terms to the effect that the great forces of opposition would be brought to naught, that the enemies of Islam would be put to shame and perish, that Islam would become the religion of the whole of Arabia, that the rule of Islam would be established and battles be fought in which the Muslims would be victorious and the enemy brought low, that Islam would spread to the farthest corners of the earth and that it would ultimately be triumphant over the religions of the world. A few such prophecies from the Quran are quoted here.[23]

All this has been stated in the Holy Quran in plain words, and at a time when there was not the least prospect of Islam gaining ground, and all this was brought to fulfilment, against all expectations, in the lifetime of the Holy Prophet. No one who has the slightest acquaintance with the Quran and the history of Islam can have any hesitation in affirming these facts.

The value of prophecy as a miracle of Islam is, however, much more extensive. There are great and wonderful prophecies in the Book, and more still in Hadith, extending into the far future, many of which have been fulfilled in our own age, and almost every generation of Muslims sees with its own eyes the fulfilment of one or more of these great prophecies, and needs not to turn the pages of history to find out what miracles were performed by the Holy Prophet in a previous age.

Another feature of this miracle is that it has been granted even to the righteous followers of the Holy Prophet in every age. Thus it is not only the Prophet's own prophecies that are witnessed in every age, for prophecy is also a heritage to his devout and faithful followers.[24]

Finality of prophethood

In the Holy Quran, the Prophet Muhammad is spoken of as the last of the prophets:

> "Muhammad is not the father of any of your men, but he is the Messenger of Allah and the *Khātam al-nabiyyīn*, and Allah is ever Knower of all things." — 33:40

The word *khātam* means 'a seal' or 'the last part' of a thing. The words *khātam al-nabiyyīn* and *khātim al-nabiyyīn* mean *the last of the prophets,* for both the words *khātam* and *khātim* mean *the last portion of anything.*[25] The best Arabic lexicologists are agreed that *khātam al-qaum* means *the last of a people.*[26] The doctrine of the finality of prophethood in Muhammad (peace be upon him), therefore, rests on the clear words of the Holy Quran.

Hadith is even clearer on this point. The meaning of *khātam al-nabiyyīn* was thus explained by the Holy Prophet himself:

> "My example and the example of the prophets before me is the example of a man who built a house and he made it very good and very beautiful with the exception of a stone in the corner, so people began to go round it and to wonder at it and to say, Why has not this stone been placed? He [the Prophet] said: I am this stone and I am *khātam al-nabiyyīn.*"[27]

This hadith, in which the Holy Prophet speaks of himself as the corner-stone of prophethood and the last of the prophets, is related by Muslim and Tirmidhi as well, and also by Ahmad ibn Hanbal in his *Musnad* in more than ten places. Another report in which the Holy Prophet speaks of himself as the last of the prophets is contained in the following words:

> "The Israelites were led by prophets; whenever a prophet died, another came after him; surely there is no prophet after me, but there will be successors, many of them."[28]

This is also narrated by Muslim and Ahmad in several places. According to another hadith, the Holy Prophet is reported to have said to Ali, when on the occasion of the Tabuk expedition he left him in Madinah in his place:

> "Are you not pleased that you should stand to me in the same relation as Aaron stood to Moses except that there is no prophet after me." [29]

Similar reports in which the Holy Prophet has made it clear that no prophet would appear after him abound in other books of Hadith.

A Prophet for all peoples and all ages

The idea that prophethood came to a close in the person of the Holy Prophet Muhammad is not a stray idea. On the other hand, it is the natural conclusion of the universalization of the theory of revelation which is the basic principle of the religion of Islam. Revelation, according to the Holy Quran, is not the solitary experience of this or that nation but the spiritual experience of the whole of the human race. Allah is spoken of in the very opening verse as the *Rabb* of all the nations of the world, the *Nourisher unto perfection,* physically as well as spiritually, of the whole human race. Starting from that broad basis, the Holy Quran develops the theory that prophets were sent to every nation:

> "There is not a people but a warner has gone among them." — 35:24

> "And for every nation there is a messenger." — 10:47

At the same time it is stated that every prophet was sent to a single nation and, therefore, though prophethood was in one sense a universal fact, it was more or less a national institution, the scope of the preaching of every prophet being limited to his own nation. The advent of the Holy Prophet Muhammad universalized the institution of prophethood in a real sense. The day of the national prophet was over, and one prophet was raised for the whole world, for all nations and for all ages:

> "Blessed is He Who sent down the *Furqān*[30] upon His servant that he might be a warner to [all] the nations." — 25:1

"Say: O mankind, surely I am the Messenger of Allah to you all, of Him Whose is the kingdom of the heavens and the earth." — 7:158

"And We have not sent you but as a bearer of good news and as a warner to all mankind, but most people do not know." — 34:28

Unification of human race based on finality of prophethood

The world-prophet therefore took the place of the national prophets, and the grand idea of unifying the whole human race, and gathering it together under one banner, was thus brought to perfection. All geographical limitations were swept away as were all bars of colour and race, and the basis of the unity of the human race was laid upon the grand principle that the whole human race was one, and that all people, wherever they may be found, were a single nation.[31] Such unity could not be accomplished unless the finality of prophethood was established, for if prophets continued to appear after the world-prophet, they would undoubtedly demand the allegiance of this or that section, and shatter the very foundations of the unity at which Islam aimed by giving a single prophet to the whole world.

Significance underlying finality

It may, however, be further added that by bringing prophethood to a close, Islam has not deprived the world of a blessing which was available to previous generations. The object of sending a prophet to a people was to make known the Divine will, and point out the ways by walking in which human beings could hold communion with God. That object was also brought to perfection through the great World-Prophet, whose message was so perfect that it met the requirements not only of all contemporary nations but of all future generations as well. This is plainly claimed by the Holy Quran, a claim not put forward by any other heavenly book or any other religion:

"This day have I perfected for you your religion and completed My favour to you and chosen for you Islam as a religion." — 5:3

The perfection of religion and the completion of the blessing of prophethood thus go hand in hand, and the blessing of prophethood being made complete in the person of the Holy Prophet Muhammad, it is a distortion of facts to say that, if no more prophets appeared, the Muslims would be without the blessing of prophethood, since they possess that blessing in its most complete form. Religion being made perfect, and prophethood being made complete, there remained no need for another religion after Islam or for another prophet after Prophet Muhammad.

Appearance of the Messiah

There is a prophecy in books of Hadith which states that the Messiah, "son of Mary", would appear among the Muslims.[32] This prophecy has given rise to a more or less general misconception that the Israelite prophet Jesus Christ would appear among the Muslims, a misconception due to not giving proper attention to the doctrine of finality of prophethood, for if there is *no need* for a prophet, as clearly set forth in the Holy Quran, neither a new nor an old prophet can appear. In fact, the appearance of an old prophet would be as much subversive of the doctrine of the finality of prophethood, and as derogatory to the dignity of the *last* prophet of the world, as would the appearance of a new prophet. The words of the prophecy are so clear that, if due attention had been paid to them, there could never have been a misconception. The son of Mary spoken of in the prophecy is clearly called "your Imam *from among yourselves*", and therefore the Israelite prophet Jesus Christ, who was from among the Israelites, could *not* be meant.[33]

Of Jesus Christ it is nowhere said in the Holy Quran that he went up into heaven. On the other hand, it is plainly stated that he died a natural death:

> "When Allah said: O Jesus, I will cause you to die and exalt you in My presence and clear you of those who disbelieve and make those who follow you above those who disbelieve to the Day of Resurrection." — 3:55

> "And when Allah will say: O Jesus, son of Mary, did you say to people, Take me and my mother for two gods besides Allah? He will say… I said to them nothing but what You commanded me: Serve Allah, my Lord and your Lord; and I was a witness of them so long as I was among them, but when You caused me to die You were the Watcher over them. And You are witness of all things." — 5:116–117

The words *mutawaffī-ka* and *tawaffaita-nī,* which have been translated as "I will cause you to die" and "You caused me to die" respectively in the above verses, carry exactly this significance and nothing else: that Allah took his soul or caused him to die. In the first verse the *raf'* of Jesus Christ to Allah is spoken of ("exalt you in My presence"). *Raf'* signifies *raising* or *elevating* and also *exalting* and *making honourable.* But wherever the *raf'* of a human being to God is spoken of in the Holy Quran, or in the religious literature of Islam, it is always in the latter sense, for raising someone in his body to Himself would mean that God is limited to a particular place.

Therefore there is not the least basis for supposing that Jesus Christ is alive in heavens and would appear again in the world. In addition, there is the clearly defined and strongly established fact of the finality of prophethood which bars the advent of any prophet, old or new, after the Holy Prophet Muhammad.

Appearance of reformers

It must however be borne in mind that, as shown in the last chapter (see page 111), Divine revelation is granted to prophets as well as to those who are not prophets, and that, therefore, though prophethood, being no more needed, has been brought to a close, the gift of Divine revelation to the righteous servants of God is still granted as before. People do not stand in need of a new prophet because they have a perfect law in the Holy Quran, but they do stand in need of Divine blessings, and Divine revelation is the highest of all blessings. Moreover, speaking is an attribute of the Divine Being, just as hearing and seeing are His attributes also, and Divine attributes never cease to function.

It has also been shown in the last chapter that, according to a most reliable hadith in Bukhari, a part of prophethood called *mubash-shirāt* (lit., *good visions*) remains after prophethood has ceased, and according to another, God speaks to the righteous in this Muslim *Ummah* though they are not prophets. There is another hadith showing that *mujaddids* (reformers) will appear among the Muslims: "Surely Allah will raise for this community [of Muslims], at the commencement of every century, one who will reform their religion".[34] A *mujaddid* is a reformer commissioned to remove errors that have crept in among the Muslims, and to shed new light on the great religious truths of Islam in the new circumstances which the Muslim community will be called upon to face.

Notes to Chapter 8

1. Raghib's *Mufradāt*.

2. Dictionary *Qāmūs*.

3. Dictionary *Tāj al-'Arūs*.

4. *Editor's Note:* In the Quran, the word *rasūl* is also applied to a man who was a messenger, not from Allah, but from a king (12:50).

    The following examples are found in Bukhari. A man sent by the Holy Prophet Muhammad to Abu Bakr, with the message to lead people in prayers in his place, has been called *rasūl* (book 10: 'Call to prayer', ch. 46, h. 678 and ch. 51, h. 687). In another case, a man sent by the Holy Prophet to a Companion has been described as *rasūl* of the *rasūl* of Allah (book 64: 'Military expeditions', ch. 79, h. 4418). A man appeared before the Holy Prophet to inform him of his acceptance of Islam and called himself a *rasūl* of the people he had left behind (book 3: 'Knowledge', ch. 6, h. 63). When the Holy Prophet called various clans of the Quraish to gather to listen to him, it is reported that those clans who could not come sent a *rasūl* to see what it was about (book 65: 'Commentary on the Quran', under *Sūrah* 26, h. 4770). A man sent to someone by Uthman is called the *rasūl* of Uthman (book 62: 'Virtues of the Companions', ch. 7, h. 3696).

    A hadith in Abu Dawud has been quoted earlier (see page 44) according to which the Holy Prophet said: "Praise be to Allah Who has granted the messenger (*rasūl*) of His Messenger (*rasūl*) what pleases the Messenger of Allah".

5. The Quran, 35:1. See also 7:37, 22:75 etc.

6. The Quran, 2:177, 2:285.

7. The Quran, 7:59, 7:65, 7:73, 7:85.

8. The word for "all" here is *jamī'-an.*

9. Jesus Christ was the last of these national prophets; and though the message of Christianity has now been conveyed to all the nations of the world, yet that was never Christ's own idea. He was perfectly sure that he was "not sent except to the lost sheep of the house of Israel" (Matthew, 15:24); so sure indeed that he did not hesitate to call those who were not Israelites "dogs" in comparison with the "children" who were the Israelites (Matthew, 15:26), and the bread of the children could not be cast to the dogs.

10. The Quran, 68:52, 81:27, 38:87, 12:104.

11. The Quran, 2:213.

12. The Quran, 1:1.

13. The Quran, 35:24.

14. The Quran, 30:22, 49:13.

15. The Quran, 2:213.

16. Raghib's *Mufradāt*.

17. *Editor's Note:* The Holy Prophet Muhammad is called *amīn* in 81:21.

18. Raghib's *Mufradāt*.

19. The Quran, 66:8.

20. The Quran, 40:55.

21. Such usage is common in the Arabic language. Again and again the Holy Quran speaks of "associates of God", though the meaning is that they are the associates *attributed* to the Divine Being by polytheists. Similarly in 5:29 the word *ithmī*, uttered by one son of Adam to the other, does not mean *my sin*, but *the sin committed against me:* "I would rather that you should bear the sin against me (*ithmī*) and your own sin".

22. Raghib's *Mufradāt*.

23. "Or do they say: We are an army allied together to help each other? Soon shall the armies be routed, and they will show their backs." — 54:44–45

    "And you dwell in the abodes of those who wronged themselves, and it is clear to you how We dealt with them and We made them examples for you. And they have indeed planned their plan, and their plan is with Allah, though their plan is such that the mountains should be moved by it. So do not think that Allah will fail in His promise to His messengers. Surely Allah is Mighty, the Lord of retribution." — 14:45–47

    "Those who disbelieve, neither their wealth nor their children shall avail them at all against Allah... as was the case of the people of Pharaoh, and those before them. They rejected Our messages, so Allah destroyed them on account of their sins." — 3:10–11

    "And certainly We wrote in the Book after the reminder that My righteous servants will inherit the land." — 21:105

    "Allah has promised to those of you who believe and do good that He will surely make them rulers in the earth as He made those before them rulers, and that He will surely establish for them their religion which He has chosen for them, and that He will surely give them security in exchange after their fear." — 24:55

    "He it is Who has sent His Messenger with the guidance and the Religion of Truth that He may make it prevail over all the religions..." — 9:33, 48:28, 61:9.

24. *Editor's Note:* See page 111 on continuity of revelation among Muslims.

25. Lane's Lexicon.

    The Quran has adopted the word *khātam* and not *khatim*, because a deeper significance is carried in the phrase *Seal of the prophets* than mere *finality*. In fact, it indicates *finality* combined with *perfection of prophethood*, along with *a continuance* among his followers of certain *blessings of prophethood*.

Through the Holy Prophet a perfect law was given, suiting the requirements of all ages and all countries, and this law was guarded against all corruption, and the office of the prophet was therefore no more required. But people still stood in need of receiving Divine favours, and the highest of these favours is Divine inspiration. It is recognized by Islam that God speaks to His chosen ones among Muslims, but such people are not *prophets*. (See page 111.)

26. *Tāj al-'Arūs.*

27. Bukhari, book 61: 'Virtues (of the Prophet and his Companions)', ch. 18, h. 3535.

28. Bukhari, book 60: 'Prophets', ch. 50, h. 3455. The original Arabic words for "there is no prophet after me" here are: *Lā nabiyya ba'dī.*

29. Bukhari, book 64: 'Military Expeditions', ch. 78, h. 4416. The original Arabic words for "there is no prophet after me" here are: *Laisa nabiyy-un ba'dī.*

30. *Furqān* is a name for the Quran, meaning criterion or distinction, used in the Quran here and in 2:185 and 3:4.

31. The Quran, 2:213.

32. Bukhari, book 60: 'Prophets', ch. 49, h. 3448, h. 3449. Muslim, book 1: 'Faith', ch. 71.

33. *Editor's Note:* In the Muhsin Khan translation of Bukhari, in h. 3449 (cited in the note above), instead of translating the words *imāmu-kum min-kum* as "he will be your imam from among yourselves", the translation given is "he will judge people by the law of the Quran and not by the law of Gospel", and *Fath al-Bārī,* a commentary on Bukhari, is cited for these meanings. However, it is grievously misleading to represent this interpretation as being the translation itself.

34. Abu Dawud, book 39: 'Battles' (*Al-Malāḥim*), ch. 1, h. 4291 (MDS: b. 36).

9. Life after death

Al-Ākhirah

A faith in a life after death is the last of the basic principles of Islam. The word generally used in the Holy Quran to indicate this life is *al-ākhirah,* which signifies 'that which comes after', or 'the future', or 'the last'. *Al-yaum al-ākhir* or 'the last day' is also used instead of *al-ākhirah.*[1]

Death, according to the Quran, is not the end of a human's life; it only opens the door to another, a higher, form of life:

> "We have ordained death among you and We are not to be overcome, that We may change your state and make you grow into what you do not know." — 56:60–61

Just as from the small life-germ grows a human being, and he does not lose his individuality for all the changes which he undergoes, so from this human is made the higher man, his state being changed, and he himself being made to grow into what he cannot conceive at present. That this new life is a higher form of life is also made clear by the Quran. After speaking of "this transitory life" (17:18), it says:

> "And certainly the Hereafter is greater in degrees and greater in excellence." —17:21

Importance of faith in Future Life

The Holy Quran accords to faith in the Future Life an importance which is next only to faith in God. Very often all the doctrines of faith are summed up as amounting to belief in God and the Future Life:

> "And there are some people who say, We believe in Allah and the Last Day, and they are not believers." — 2:8 (see also 2:62, 2:126, 2:228, etc.)

The opening chapter of the Holy Quran plays the greatest part in creating a true Muslim mentality, for the Muslim must recite it in the five daily prayers. In this chapter God is spoken of as the "Master of the Day of Requital" (or Day of Recompense), and thus the idea that every deed must be requited is brought before the mind of the Muslim continually. It undoubtedly impresses on the mind the reality of a future life, when every deed shall find its full reward. The greater the faith in the good or bad consequences of a deed, the greater is the incentive which urges a person to, or withholds him from, that deed. Therefore this belief is both the greatest impetus towards good and noble deeds, and the greatest restraint upon evil or irresponsible deeds. But more than this, such a belief purifies the motives with which a deed is done. It makes a man work with the most selfless of motives, for he seeks no reward for what he does; his work is for higher and nobler ends relating to the life beyond the grave.

Connection between the two lives

The Quran not only speaks of a life after death which opens out for us a new world of advancement, it also shows that the basis of that life is laid in this our life on earth. For the good, the heavenly life, and for the wicked, a life in hell, begin even here, though the limitations of this life do not allow most people to realize that other life:

> "[O man] you were indeed heedless of this, but now We have removed from you your veil, so your sight is sharp this day." — 50:22

This shows that the spiritual life which is hidden from the human eye by reason of material limitations, will become manifest in the Resurrection; because human perception will then be clearer, the veil of material limitations having been removed.

The Holy Quran clearly speaks of two paradises for the righteous and two punishments for the wicked, and as clearly of a heavenly and hellish life, each beginning here:

> "And for him who fears to stand before his Lord are two Gardens." — 55:46

> "O soul who is at rest! Return to your Lord, well pleased [with Him], well pleasing [Him]. So enter among My servants and enter My Garden!" — 89:27–30

> "No indeed, if only you knew with a certain knowledge, you will certainly see hell." — 102:5–6

"It is the fire kindled by Allah which rises over the hearts."
— 104:6–7

"And whoever is blind in this [life], he will be blind in the
Hereafter…" — 17:72

"Such is the punishment. And certainly the punishment of
the Hereafter is greater, if only they knew!" — 68:33

State between death and Resurrection

The state between death and Resurrection is called *barzakh* which
literally means 'a thing that intervenes between two things', or a
barrier. As signifying the state between death and Resurrection, it
occurs in the following verses:

> "Until when death catches up with one of them, he says: My
> Lord, send me back, that I may do good in that which I have
> left. By no means! It is only a word that he speaks. And
> before them is a barrier (*barzakh*), until the day they are
> raised." — 23:99–100

This intervening state is also known by the name of *qabr,* which,
although meaning *grave,* has also been used in the wider sense of the
state which follows death. The three states, namely, death, the grave
and Resurrection, are spoken of as follows, where the *grave* undoubtedly stands for the state of *barzakh:*

> "Then He causes him to die, then assigns to him a grave, then,
> when He will, He raises him to life again." — 80:21–22

The raising to life on the Day of Resurrection is spoken of as the
raising of those who are in their graves, as in 100:9 and 22:7, where
all people are meant, whether actually buried or not.

Second stage of the higher life

Since the Holy Quran speaks of the growth of a higher life even in
the life of this world, the spiritual experience of man is the first stage
of the higher life. Ordinarily, man is neglectful of this higher experience, and it is only persons of a very high spiritual development
that are in any way conscious of that higher life. *Barzakh* is really the
second stage in the development of this higher life, and it appears that
everyone has a certain consciousness of the higher life at this stage,
though full development has not yet taken place.

In the Quran, even the development of the physical life is mentioned as passing through three stages. The first stage of that life is the state of being in the earth; the second, that of being in the mother's womb; and the third, that in which the child is born.[2] Corresponding to these three stages in the physical development of man, the Quran speaks of three stages in his spiritual development.

The first is the growth of a spiritual life which begins in this very life, but it is a stage at which ordinarily there is no consciousness of this life, like the dust stage in the physical development of man. Then there comes death, and with it is entered the second stage of a higher or spiritual life, the *barzakh* or the *qabr* stage, corresponding to the embryo stage in the physical development of man. At this stage, life has taken a definite form, and a certain consciousness of that life has grown up, but it is not yet the full consciousness of the final development which takes place with the Resurrection, the third stage, which may therefore be compared to the actual birth of man, to his setting forth on the road to real advancement, to a full awakening of the great truth. The development of the higher life in *barzakh* is as necessary a stage in the spiritual world as is the development of physical life in the embryonic state. The two thus stand on a par.

That there is some kind of awakening to a new spiritual experience immediately after death is abundantly evident from various Quranic statements. For example, the verses in which *barzakh* is spoken of,[3] set forth the spiritual experience of the evil-doer, who immediately becomes conscious of the fact that, in his first life, he has been doing something which is now detrimental to the growth of the higher life in him, and hence desires to go back, so that he may do good deeds which may help the development of the higher life. On another occasion, we are told that evil-doers, the people of Pharaoh, are made to taste of the evil consequences of their deeds in this state of *barzakh,* the consciousness of the chastisement becoming clear on the Resurrection Day.[4] While in the Holy Quran the guilty are spoken of as receiving chastisement in the state of *barzakh,* in Hadith this punishment is spoken of as the punishment meted out in the grave. These two punishments are one and the same, and the "grave" and *barzakh* are identical.

Similarly, the righteous are spoken of as tasting the fruits of good deeds immediately after death:

> "And do not think of those who are killed in Allah's way as dead. Rather, they are alive, being provided sustenance from their Lord, rejoicing in what Allah has given them out of His grace; and they rejoice for the sake of those who, being left behind them, have not yet joined them, that they have no fear nor shall they grieve." — 3:169–170

These verses show that the departed ones are even conscious of what they have left behind, and this establishes some sort of connection between this world and the next.

Duration of *barzakh*

All questions connected with the life of the other world are of an intricate nature, inasmuch as they are not things that can be perceived by human senses; they are "secrets" that shall be made known only after death, according to the Holy Quran,[5] and according to a saying of the Holy Prophet: "what no eye has seen, and no ear has heard, and what the mind of man has not conceived".[6] As will be shown later on, the very ideas of time and space as relating to the next world are different from those here, and therefore we cannot conceive of the duration of *barzakh* in terms of this world. Moreover, the full awakening to the higher life will take place in the Resurrection, and the state of *barzakh* is therefore a state, as it were, of semi-consciousness. Hence it is that it is sometimes likened to a state of sleep as compared with the great awakening of the Resurrection, for the unbelievers are made to say:

> "O woe to us! Who has raised us up from our sleeping-place?" — 36:52

The state of *barzakh,* as regards those who have wasted their opportunities in this life, lasts till the Day of Resurrection according to the Holy Quran (see 23:100 above). As regards those in whom the life spiritual has been awakened during the life on earth, consciousness in the *barzakh* state will undoubtedly be more vivid, and there is a hadith which speaks of the righteous being exalted to a higher state after forty days, and thus making progress even in that state.

Various names of Resurrection

The Resurrection is spoken of under various names, the most frequent of which is *yaum al-qiyāmah* or 'the Day of the Great Rising', which occurs seventy times in the Quran. Next to it is *al-sā'ah* which means 'the Hour', and occurs forty times; *yaum al-ākhir* or 'the Last Day' occurs twenty-six times, while *al-ākhirah* as meaning 'the Future Life' occurs over a hundred times. Next in importance is *yaum al-dīn* which means 'the Day of Requital'. Other names, each prefixed by *yaum* or 'Day', are as follows: The Day of Decision, of Reckoning, of Judgment, of Meeting, of Gathering, of Abiding, of Coming Forth, of being Raised to Life, of Regret, of Calling Forth, of Manifestation of Losses, and the Day that draws near. Some other names are: The Striking Calamity, the Overwhelming Calamity, the Deafening Calamity, the Predominating Calamity, the Great Truth, and the Great Event.

A general destruction and a general awakening

It will be seen that most of these names refer either to a destruction or an awakening and rising to a new life; they relate to the sweeping off of an old order and the establishment of a new one. A few quotations descriptive of the Resurrection will make the point clearer:

> "He [man] asks: When is the Day of Resurrection? So when the sight is confused, and the moon becomes dark, and the sun and the moon are brought together — man will say on that day: Where to flee? No! There is no refuge! With your Lord on that day is the place of rest. Man will that day be informed of what he sent on ahead and what he put off. ... No, but you love the present life, and neglect the Hereafter. [Some] faces that day will be bright, looking to their Lord. And [other] faces that day will be gloomy, knowing that a great disaster will be made to befall them." — 75:6–13, 20–25

> "So when the stars are made to disappear, and when the heaven is torn apart, and when the mountains are carried away as dust". — 77:8–10

> "Surely the day of Decision is appointed — the day when the trumpet is blown, so you come forth in companies, and the heaven is opened so it becomes as doors, and the mountains are moved off so that they remain a mere semblance." — 78:17–20

> "The day when the quaking one shall quake — the consequence will follow it. Hearts that day will palpitate, their

> eyes downcast. … It is only a single cry, when lo! they will be awakened." — 79:6–9, 13–14

> "When the earth is shaken with her shaking, and the earth brings forth her burdens… On that day people will come forth, in diverse bodies, that they may be shown their works." — 99:1–2, 6

> "The day when they come forth from the graves in haste, as if racing to a goal". — 70:43

> "So when the trumpet is blown with a single blast, and the earth and the mountains are borne away and crushed with one crash — on that day will the Event come to pass… On that day you will be exposed to view — no secret of yours will remain hidden." — 69:13–15, 18

> "On the day when the earth will be changed into a different earth, and the heavens [as well]…" — 14:48

Three Resurrections

The two words used most frequently regarding the Resurrection are *al-qiyāmah* and *al-sā'ah*. The first of these refers, apparently, to the *rising,* which is its literal significance, the second to destruction, being *the hour of doom.* The word *al-sā'ah* is used in a wider sense, and indicates, besides the Doomsday, sometimes the death of an individual and sometimes the passing of a generation. The Quran says:

> "They are losers indeed who reject the meeting with Allah, until when the hour comes upon them suddenly…" — 6:31

Here "the hour" (*al-sā'ah*) clearly stands for the death of the person who rejects.

As regards the use of *al-sā'ah* in the sense of the end of a generation, the Holy Prophet is reported to have said about a boy: "If the life of this boy is lengthened, he will not die till the hour (*al-sā'ah*) comes to pass",[7] and it is related that he was the last to die from among the Companions of the Prophet; "the hour" in this case signifying the passing away of the generation of the Companions. There are examples of similar use in the Holy Quran also:

> "The hour (*al-sā'ah*) drew near and the moon was split
> apart." — 54:1

"The hour", in this case, stands for the doom of the opponents of the
Holy Prophet. And again:

> "Or do they say: We are an army allied together to help each
> other? Soon shall the armies be routed and they will show
> their backs. Indeed, the hour (*al-sā'ah*) is their promised time,
> and the hour is most grievous and bitter." — 54:44–46

When the Holy Prophet was faced with a most serious situation on
the day of the battle of Badr, the Muslims being in danger of utter
annihilation at the hands of their powerful opponents, and was praying for their safety, he was reminded of this prophecy, and comforted
his Companions by reciting these verses aloud, showing that "the
hour" here meant the hour of the enemy's defeat.[8]

Spiritual resurrection and the greater resurrection

Just as the word *al-sā'ah* is used in a wider sense, so do the words
qiyāmah (rising) and *ba'th* (raising the dead to life) sometimes occur
in a wider sense. On many occasions when the Holy Quran speaks of
the dead, it means those who are spiritually dead, and by giving life
to them it means the bringing about of a spiritual awakening in them,
as for example:

> "Is he who was dead, then We raised him to life and made
> for him a light by which he walks among the people, like
> him whose likeness is that of one in darkness from which he
> cannot come forth?" — 6:122

Here, clearly, the dead one is he who is spiritually dead, and God's
raising him to life is giving him the life spiritual. On one occasion
even, by "those in the graves" are meant those who are dead spiritually, who cannot hear the Prophet's call:

> "Neither are the living and the dead alike. Surely Allah
> makes him whom He pleases hear, and you cannot make
> those hear who are in the graves. You are only a warner." —
> 35:22–23

The context shows that by "those in the graves" are meant those
whom death has overtaken spiritually, whom the Prophet would warn
but they would not listen.

On another occasion, where those in the graves are mentioned, the words convey a double significance, referring to the spiritual awakening brought about by the Holy Prophet as well as to the new life in the Resurrection:

> "And you see the earth barren, but when We send down water upon it, it stirs and swells and brings forth a beautiful growth of every kind. This is because Allah, He is the Truth, and He gives life to the dead and He is Powerful over all things, and the Hour is coming, there is no doubt about it; and Allah will raise up those who are in the graves." — 22:5–7

The first part of this passage, describing the giving of life to dead soil by means of rain, shows that the second part refers to the giving of spiritual life by means of Divine revelation, a comparison between rain and revelation being of frequent occurrence in the Quran. "The Hour" here, as in so many other places, refers to the doom of the opponents of the Holy Prophet, and "the dead" and "those in the graves" are evidently the spiritually dead. But, though speaking primarily of the spiritual resurrection, there is also a reference to the great Resurrection of the dead. In fact, not only here but in many other places in the Holy Quran, the spiritual resurrection, to be brought about by the Holy Prophet, and the greater Resurrection of the dead are mentioned together, the one being as it were an evidence of the other, because an awakening to spiritual life shows the existence of a higher life, the development of which is the real aim of the greater resurrection.

This is the first great argument running throughout the pages of the Holy Quran as to the truth of the greater Resurrection. The spiritual resurrection brought about by the Holy Prophet, the awakening to a spiritual life, makes the higher life an experience of humanity, and thus clears the way for a development of that life in a higher sphere, above the limitations of this material world.

Life has an aim

That the whole of creation on this earth is for the service of humanity, and that human life has some great aim and purpose to fulfil, is yet another argument for Resurrection advanced by the Holy Quran:

> "Does man think that he will be left aimless?" — 75:36

> "Do you then think that We have created you in vain and that you will not be returned to Us?" — 23:115

Just as belief in God ennobles man's life, and endows it with the purest and highest impulses, so does belief in the Resurrection introduce a seriousness into man's life which cannot be otherwise attained. It will be taking too low a view of human nature to imagine that with all those vast capacities for ruling nature and its wonderful forces, human life itself has no aim. If everything in nature is intended for the service of man, human life itself could not be without purpose. The Holy Quran refers to this argument in the following verses:

> "Certainly We have created man in the best make, then We render him the lowest of the low, except those who believe and do good, so theirs is a reward never to be cut off." — 95:4–6

The last words clearly refer to the higher life which is never to be cut off, and this argument is followed by the conclusion: "So who can belie you after this about the Judgment?" (95:7).

It cannot be that the whole of creation should serve a purpose and that man alone, who is lord of it and endowed with capabilities for ruling the universe, should have a purposeless existence. It is the Resurrection alone that solves this difficulty. Man has a higher object to fulfill, he has a higher life to live beyond this world; which is the aim of human life in this world.

Good and evil must have their reward

Another argument adduced by the Holy Quran in support of the Resurrection is that good and evil must have their reward. Of the whole living creation, man alone has the power to discriminate between good and evil. And so acute is his perception of good and evil that he strives with all his might to promote good and to eradicate evil. He makes laws for this purpose, and uses the whole machinery of power at his disposal to enforce them. Yet what do we see in practical life? Good is often neglected and starves, while evil prospers. That is not as it should be.

> "Allah does not waste the reward of the doers of good." — 11:115, 12:90, etc.

"We do not waste the reward of him who does a good work."
— 18:30

"I will not let the work of any worker among you to be lost, whether male or female, each of you is as the other." — 3:195

"So whoever does an atom's weight of good will see it. And whoever does an atom's weight of evil will see it." — 99:7–8

Such are some of the plain declarations made by the Holy Quran. And when we look at nature around us, we find the same law at work. Every cause has its effect, and everything done must bear a fruit. Even that which man does in the physical world must bear a fruit. Why should man's good or evil deeds be an exception to this general rule working in the whole universe? And if they are not an exception, as they should not be, the conclusion is evident that good and evil must bear their full fruit in another life, which indicates the continuity of the life of man in another world, when death has put an end to it in this.

Resurrection as a workable principle of life

It will be seen from the above that the Resurrection is not a dogma in which a person is required to believe for his salvation in another life; rather it is a principle of human life, a principle which makes that life more serious and more useful, while at the same time awakening in him the consciousness of a life that is higher. The one who sincerely believes in the Resurrection will try his utmost to take advantage of every opportunity that is offered him to live his life to the best purpose; he will try hard to do any good that he possibly can to the creatures of God, and he will shun every evil deed as far as he can. Thus a belief in the Resurrection is needed in the first place to make this lower life worth living. Without such a belief, life loses not only its meaning, leaving man without any real or abiding aim, but also all incentive to do good and eschew evil.

Resurrection is quite consistent with present scientific knowledge

The idea of a life after death is so strange to the average mind that the Holy Quran has, again and again, to answer the question: How will it be? And the answer given in all cases is that the great Author of all existence, Who made this vast universe out of nothing, could also bring about a new creation.

> "And they say: 'When we are bones and decayed particles, shall we then be raised up as a new creation?... Who will return us?' Say: He Who created you at first." — 17:49–51

> "And they say: 'When we are bones and decayed particles, shall we then be raised up into a new creation?' Do they not see that Allah, Who created the heavens and the earth, is able to create the like of them?" — 17:98–99

> "Do you not see that Allah created the heavens and the earth with truth? If He please, He will take you away and bring a new creation. And that is not difficult for Allah. And they will all come forth to Allah..." — 14:19–21

The Quran reverts to this subject too often to enable all the verses bearing on it to be reproduced, but the one underlying idea running through them all is that this old creation, the earth and its heaven, and the rest of the universe, would give place to a new creation. The old order would be changed into an entirely new one. It shall be a day "when the earth will be changed into a different earth and the heavens as well" (14:48). Just as this universe has grown out of chaos and a nebulous mass into its present state of systems of galaxies and stars and their families, it will, in its turn, give place to a higher order which will be evolved from it. The idea is quite consistent with the scientific knowledge of the universe to which man has attained at the present day — the idea of evolution, order out of chaos, a higher order out of a lower order, and with this order of the universe, a higher order of human life of which our present senses cannot conceive.

Will the Resurrection be corporeal?

There is nothing in the Holy Quran to show that the body which the soul left at death will be restored to it. On the other hand, there are statements to show that it will be a new creation altogether. If, as the quotations given above show, the very earth and heaven have changed at the Resurrection, how can the human body remain the same? And in fact the Quran has stated clearly that it shall be a new body altogether. In one place, the human beings at the Resurrection are called the likes of the present race:

> "Do they not see that Allah, Who created the heavens and the earth, is able to create the like of them?" — 17:99

Here the Arabic words for "the like of them" are *mithla-hum,* the personal pronoun *hum* referring to people, not to heaven and earth. In another place, the statement that the bodies would be changed is even clearer. There, the question of the unbelievers is first mentioned:

> "When we die and become dust and bones, shall we then indeed be raised?" — 56:47

And the reply is given

> "Do you see that which you emit [i.e., the semen]? Is it you that create it or are We the Creator? We have ordained death among you and We are not to be overcome, that We may change your state and make you grow into what you do not know. And certainly you know the first growth, why do you not then be mindful?" — 56:58–62

After human beings have become dust and bones, they shall be raised up again but their "state" will be entirely "changed", and the new growth will be one which "you do not know", while "you know the first growth". The human body at the Resurrection is therefore a new growth which, with our present senses, we cannot even know. And this is as true of the human body as of all things of the next life, of the blessings of Paradise as well as of the chastisement of Hell, that they are things which, according to a saying of the Holy Prophet, "no eye has seen, and no ear has heard", and which "the mind of man has not conceived".[9] The body after resurrection has therefore nothing in common with the body of this world except the name or the form which preserves the individuality.

A body prepared from the good and evil deeds of man

To understand how, what may be called the spiritual body of the life after death, is prepared, one must turn again to the Holy Quran. There it is stated that angels have been appointed to record the good and evil deeds of man. Thus at the beginning of the 13th chapter, a denial of the Resurrection — "When we are dust, shall we then be in a new creation?" (13:5) — is followed by the answer:

> "Alike [to Him] among you is he who conceals the word and he who speaks openly, and he who hides himself by night

and who goes forth by day. For him are angels guarding the consequences[10] [of his deeds], before him and behind him, who guard him by Allah's command." — 13:10–11

It is first stated that to God all are alike, those who conceal their words and those who speak them openly, and those that do a good or evil deed in the darkness of the night and those who do it in the light of the day; and it is then added that there are angels before and behind man that guard him. The guarding of the man and the guarding of his deeds are thus one and the same thing. In fact, this has been made clear in an earlier chapter — earlier in point of revelation:

> "No, but you call the Judgment a lie, and surely there are keepers [or, guardians][11] over you, honourable recorders, they know what you do." — 82:9–12

Here the angels that are called "keepers over you", being un-doubtedly the guarding angels (13:11), are plainly described as the recording angels who know what man does. Thus both these verses show that an inner self of man is being developed, all along, through his deeds, and that is what is meant by *guarding man* in one case and *guarding his deeds* in the other. It is the inner self that assumes a shape after death and forms first the body in *barzakh* and is then developed into the body in Resurrection.

Elsewhere, a similar denial of the Resurrection — "When we die and become dust — that is a far return" (50:3) — is rebutted by saying:

> "We know indeed what the earth diminishes of them and with Us is a book that preserves." — 50:4

It is here admitted that the body does indeed become dust but there is with God a writing that preserves what is essential to growth in the next life. That *preserving writing* is the record of good and evil deeds kept by the guardian angels, so that, here again, we are told that while the outer garb of the soul, the body, becomes dust and goes back to the earth, the inner self is preserved and forms the basis of the higher life — life in the Resurrection.

Spiritualities materialized

This materialization of spiritualities — not a materialization in the sense in which it is accepted in this life, but a materialization of the new world to be evolved from the present world — is spoken of frequently in the Holy Quran as well as in Hadith. For instance, those who are guided by the light of faith in this life shall have a light running before them and behind them on the Day of Resurrection:

> "Is he who was dead, then We raised him to life and made for him a light by which he walks among the people, like him whose likeness is that of one in darkness from which he cannot come forth?" — 6:122

> "On that day you will see the believers, men and women, their light gleaming before them and on their right hand." — 57:12

And the fruits of good deeds are spoken of as fruits of Paradise:

> "And give good news to those who believe and do good deeds, that for them are gardens in which rivers flow. Whenever they are given a portion of the fruit of these [gardens], they will say: This is what was given to us before; and they are given the like of it." — 2:25

Similarly, the fire which burns within the heart of man in this life, by reason of inordinate love of wealth, becomes the fire of Hell in the next life:

> "It is the Fire kindled by Allah, which rises over the hearts." — 104:6–7

And the spiritual blindness of this life turns into blindness in the next life:

> "And whoever is blind in this [world], he will be blind in the Hereafter..." — 17:72

The seventy years of evil-doing — seventy being the average span of human life — are turned into a chain of "seventy lengths long" (69:32). The person who acts according to the Book of God, or takes it in his right hand here, shall be given his book in the right hand on the Day of Resurrection, and the one who will have none of it, and throws it behind his back, shall be given his book behind his back or in his left hand.[12]

Hadith also is full of examples of this. The spiritualities of this life take an actual shape in the Hereafter. This is the truth underlying all the blessings of Paradise and the torments of Hell.

The book of deeds

The *guarding* of the good and evil deeds of man, which form the basis of the higher life, is spoken of as *writing them down;* and a book of good and evil deeds is repeatedly mentioned, as for example:

> "This is Our record (*kitāb*) that speaks against you with truth. Surely We wrote what you did." — 45:29

> "And the book (*kitāb*) is placed, and you see the guilty fearing for what is in it, and they say: O woe to us! what a book is this! It leaves out neither a small thing nor a great one, but numbers them all." — 18:49

> "So whoever does good deeds and is a believer, there is no rejection of his effort, and We surely write it down for him." — 21:94

Not only has every individual his book of deeds, but even nations are spoken of as having their books of deeds:

> "Every nation will be called to its record (*kitāb*). This day you are recompensed for what you did." — 45:28

It is not meant, of course, that there will be a physical book, a collection of pages written with pen and ink. The word *kitāb* does not always mean a book as such; sometimes it signifies the knowledge of God. A study of the verses in which the recording of actions, or the books of deeds, is referred to, leads to the conclusion that it is the *effect produced by those actions* that is meant. For instance:

> "And We have made every human being's actions to cling to his neck, and We shall bring forth to him on the Day of Resurrection a book which he will find wide open." — 17:13

Making the actions cling to the doer's neck is clearly to cause the effect of the actions to appear on the person concerned; in other words, all actions, good or bad, have their impress on the man. This is in accordance with what has been already stated, namely that an inner self of man is being prepared in this life. That inner self is really his book of deeds, a book in which is noted down the effect of every deed done. It is to this that the concluding words of the verse allude where it is said that this book of deeds, the inner self, which here is hidden from the human eye, will become an open book on the Day of Resurrection. And, quite in consonance with this, the next verse goes on to say:

> "Read your book. Your own soul is sufficient as a reckoner against you this day." — 17:14

In other words, the effect of a one's deeds becomes so manifest on the Day of Resurrection that no outside reckoning is needed. It is the person himself who reads his own book, that is to say, sees all his actions in the impress left on him, and judges himself because the reckoning has already appeared in his own self.

In agreement with this are two other verses of an earlier chapter:

> "No, surely the record (*kitāb*) of the wicked is in the prison." — 83:7

> "No, surely the record (*kitāb*) of the righteous is in the highest places." — 83:18

As opposed to the righteous who are in the highest places, the wicked should have been spoken of as being in the lowest places, but instead of that they are stated to be in prison, which means that a bar is placed against their advancement; hence they are mentioned further on as being "debarred from their Lord" (83:15), while the righteous go on advancing to higher and higher places. The word "record" or "book" here plainly stands for the inner self of man; in any other sense, the placing of the book in a prison is meaningless. Thus it is clear from the various descriptions of the book, or record, of deeds that it is the effect of good or evil deeds accelerating or retarding a person's spiritual progress, as the case may be, that is meant, and that the writing is nothing but the impress that is left on a person when he does a good or bad deed — an impress which no human eye can see, but whose reality cannot be doubted by any conscientious thinker.

Balance

A "balance" (*mīzān*) is also spoken of in connection with the good and evil deeds of man. It is true that the measure of material things is judged by a pair of scales or by some other implement, but the deeds of man need no scales for their measurement. In connection with the deeds of human beings, it means the doing of justice in their reckoning.[13] The following verses illustrates what is meant:

> "And We will set up a just balance (*mawāzīn,* pl. of *mīzān*) on the Day of Resurrection, so no soul will be wronged in the least." — 21:47

The meaning is made clear by the addition of the words "no soul will be wronged in the least".

The *mīzān* or "measure" of human beings is clearly spoken of elsewhere as having been sent down by God:

> "Certainly We sent Our messengers with clear arguments, and sent down with them the Book and the measure (*mīzān*) that people may conduct themselves with equity." — 57:25

Revelation, or the Book, is sent down by God to awaken the spiritual life in man, and therefore the measure, which is spoken of as having been sent down along with revelation, must also relate to the spiritual life of man. The book contains the directions in principle, to do good and shun evil, and the balance or measure is there to weigh the good and the evil, so that the spiritual life awakened in man takes a good or bad turn, a higher or lower form, according to the preponderance of good or evil. Thus not only do good and evil deeds leave their effect behind but also there is a balance which gives shape to that effect and makes the spiritual growth possible, or has a retarding effect on that growth if evil preponderates.

The "balance" of the Hereafter, therefore, differs not at all from the "balance" of this life, except that there it takes a more palpable form. The general principle is laid down in the following verses:

> "And We will set up a just balance on the Day of Resurrection, so no soul will be wronged in the least. And if there were the weight of a grain of mustard seed, We will bring it, and sufficient are We to take account." — 21:47

> "And the judging (*wazn*) on that day will be just, so as for those whose good deeds are heavy, they are the successful. And as for those whose good deeds are light, those are they who ruined their souls..." — 7:8–9

Jannah or **Paradise**

The life after death takes two forms: a life in Paradise for those in whom the good preponderates over the evil, and a life in Hell for those in whom the evil preponderates over the good. It is the word *garden (jannah)* or its plural *(jannāt)* that is generally used to indicate the abiding place of the righteous. This word is derived from a root which signifies *the concealing of a thing so that it is not perceived by the senses,* and *jannah,* in the ordinary usage, means 'a garden' because its ground is covered by trees. The use of this name for the abode of bliss has a deeper significance, since of Paradise it is plainly stated that its blessings are such as cannot be perceived by the physical senses. The description of Paradise usually given is "gardens in which rivers flow", corresponding to which the description of the righteous generally is "those who believe and do good". These two descriptions, read in the light of what has gone before as to the materialization in the next world of the spiritualities of this life, are an indication of the fact that faith, which is the water of spiritual life, is converted into rivers, and good deeds, which spring from faith, are the seeds from which grow the trees of the next life.

Blessings of Paradise

The description of Paradise as a garden, with rivers flowing in it, is clearly stated to be a parable or a likeness, not an actuality, in terms of this life:

> "A parable of the Garden which is promised to those who keep their duty: In it flow rivers. Its fruits are perpetual and [so is] its plenty *(ẓill)*." — 13 : 35

> "A parable of the Garden which the dutiful are promised: In it are rivers of water not altering for the worse…" — 47 : 15

And quite in keeping with this description is the statement made elsewhere, that the blessings of Paradise cannot be conceived of in this life, not being things of this world:

> "So no soul knows what joy of the eyes is hidden for them: a reward for what they did." — 32 : 17

An explanation of these words was given by the Holy Prophet himself when he said:

> "Allah says: I have prepared for My righteous servants what no eye has seen, and no ear has heard, and what the mind of man has not conceived." [14]

A few examples may be added. *Zill,* which means *a shadow,* is spoken of, in some places, as one of the blessings of Paradise:

> "The dutiful are amid shades and fountains". — 77:41

Zill does not in any of these cases bear the significance of *shade;* the name is there but its import is quite different. In fact we are plainly told in the Holy Quran that there is no sun in Paradise:

> "They will see therein neither sun nor intense cold." — 76:13

Hence in the case of Paradise, it signifies *protection* or *plenty,* as being the idea underlying the word *shade*. Note that the same word has also been used in connection with the rigours of Hell:

> "And shadow (*zill*) of black smoke, neither cool nor refreshing." — 56:43–44

Zill is *every covering whether good or bad;* and hence it is also spoken of as one of the severities of Hell.[15]

Those in Paradise are spoken of as being given *sustenance* (*rizq*). But it cannot mean what sustains the body here. It is the sustenance that is needed for the inner self of man, and it is for this reason that prayer is also called sustenance in 20:131. The fruits of Paradise, whether mentioned under a particular name or generally, are not the fruits of this life, but of deeds done. The name is the same, but the significance is quite different. Thus we are told:

> "Whenever they are given a portion of the fruit of these [gardens], they will say: This is what was given to us before." — 2:25

Evidently the fruits of good deeds are meant here, and not the fruits that the earth grows, because the latter are not given to all the true believers here while the former are. Similar is the case with the rivers of water, milk and honey, all of which are plainly spoken of as a parable;[16] the thrones, the cushions and carpets,[17] the ornaments, the bracelets, the silk robes[18] — all these are not things of this life, but are mentioned simply to show that whatever may serve to perfect the picture of the happiness of human beings, will be there. As for the exact form they will take, that cannot be made known to man, because his senses are incapable of perceiving it. All descriptions of the blessing of the next life are only *a likeness* or *a parable* (*mathal*) as is explained in the Holy Quran.[19]

Even our ideas of space and time are inapplicable to the next life. Paradise extends over the whole of the heavens and the earth, that is to say, the whole of this universe:

> "And hasten to forgiveness from your Lord and a Garden, as wide as the heavens and the earth." — 3:133, 57:21

And when the Holy Prophet was asked where was Hell, if Paradise extended over the whole of the heavens and the earth, he replied: "Where is the night when the day comes?"[20] This shows that Paradise and Hell are more like two conditions than two places. Again, despite the fact that the two are poles asunder, the one being the highest of the high and the other the lowest of the low, they are separated only by a wall:

> "Then a wall, with a door in it, will be raised between them. Within it shall be mercy, and outside of it punishment." — 57:13

And elsewhere, speaking of the inmates of Paradise and the inmates of Hell, it is said:

> "And between them is a veil." — 7:46

It is impossible, with our present ideas of space, to conceive of these two things at one and the same time. Again, a "vehement raging and roaring" of hell-fire is repeatedly mentioned,[21] but those in Paradise shall "not hear its faintest sound"[22] while they will hear the call of the inmates of that fire:

> "And the companions of the Fire call out to the owners of the Garden: Pour on us some water or some of what Allah has provided for you. They say: Surely Allah has prohibited them both to the disbelievers". — 7:50

Thus those in Paradise shall hear the talk of those in Hell, but they shall not hear the roaring of the fire of Hell. This shows that the change that will come over man in the Resurrection will be so thorough that even his present senses will be changed into others, of which it is impossible for him to conceive in this life, senses which would hear the lowest tones of one kind, but not the most terrible sounds of another.

Women in Paradise

The things mentioned among the blessings of Paradise are, therefore, not the things of this world but things which we have neither seen nor heard of in this life; nor, with our present senses, can we even conceive of them. All descriptions given are simply to show that the life of the righteous will be perfect in the Resurrection. It is with the same end in view that mention is made of the company of men and women in that state, to which sensually minded people have attached a sensual significance. As sexual relationship, as understood in this life, is a requirement of nature to help the act of procreation, it is clear that the relationship of sexes or the company of men and women in the Resurrection has quite a different significance.

The mention of women in Paradise in the Holy Quran is, in the first place, to show that men and women are both equal in the sight of God, and that both will enjoy the higher life in the Resurrection. That women, in general, shall have access to Paradise, like men, is made clear in many places:

> "So their Lord accepted their prayer [saying]: I will not let the work of any worker among you to be lost, *whether male or female;* each of you is as the other ... I shall truly remove their evil and make them enter Gardens in which rivers flow — a reward from Allah." — 3:195

> "Allah has promised to *the believers, men and women,* Gardens, in which rivers flow, to abide in them, and goodly dwellings in Gardens of perpetual abode. And greatest of all is Allah's goodly pleasure. That is the mighty achievement." — 9:72

> "...and whoever does good, *whether male or female,* and is a believer, these shall enter the Garden, to be given sustenance in it without measure." — 40:40 (see also 4:124)

> "On that day you will see *the believers, men and women,* their light gleaming before them and on their right hand. Good news for you this day! — Gardens in which rivers flow, to abide in them! That is the mighty achievement." — 57:12

The wives of the righteous are mentioned particularly as accompanying their husbands in Paradise:

> "Gardens of perpetuity, which they will enter along with those who do good from among their fathers and their wives and their offspring…" — 13:23

> "They and their wives are in shades, reclining on raised couches." — 36:56

> "Our Lord! make them enter the Gardens of perpetuity, which You have promised them and such of their fathers and their wives and their offspring as are good." — 40:8

> "Enter the garden, you and your wives, being made happy." — 43:70

Ḥūr

Among the various descriptions of women in Paradise is the word *ḥūr,* which occurs four times in the Holy Quran, as in:

> "The dutiful will be surely in Gardens and bliss… and We shall join them to pure (*ḥūr*), beautiful ones." [23] — 52:17, 20

Purity is the prevailing idea in the root meaning of *ḥūr;* hence "pure ones" is its nearest rendering in English.[24] The word *ḥawārī,* which is derived from the same root, means *a pure and sincere friend,* and has been particularly applied in the Quran to the chosen disciples of Jesus.

Are *ḥūr* the women that go to Paradise, the wives of the righteous? A hint to this effect is given in a hadith. The last of the occasions on which the *ḥūr* are spoken of is 56:22, and in continuation of the subject there occur the words:

> "Surely We have created them as a [new] creation, so We have made them virgins, loving, equals in age". — 56:35–37

In connection with their being a new creation, the Holy Prophet is reported to have said that by this are meant women who have grown old here.[25] The meaning, therefore, is that all good women will be in a new creation in the life of the Resurrection so that they shall all be virgins, equals in age. The Prophet's explanation shows that the word *ḥūr* is used to describe the new growth into which women of the world will grow. An anecdote is also related that an old woman came to the Holy Prophet when he was sitting with his Companions, and asked him if she would go to Paradise. In a spirit of mirth, the Holy Prophet remarked that there would be no old woman in Paradise. She was about to turn away rather sorrowfully, when the Holy Prophet comforted her with the words that all women shall be made to grow into a new growth, so that there shall be no old woman in Paradise, and recited the verses quoted above.[26]

Even if the *ḥūr* are taken to be a blessing of Paradise, and not the women of this world, it is a blessing as well for men as for women. Just as the gardens, rivers, milk, honey, fruits, and numerous other things of Paradise are both for men and women, even so are *ḥūr*. What these blessings actually are, no one knows, but the whole picture of Paradise drawn in the Holy Quran strongly condemns the association of any sensual idea with them. As to why these blessings are described in words which apply to women, the fact is that the reward spoken of here has special reference to the purity and beauty of character, and if there is an emblem of purity and beauty, it is womanhood, not manhood.

Children in Paradise

What is true of women is also true of children. The Holy Quran speaks, on one occasion, of the presence in Paradise of *ghilmān,* plural of *ghulām* meaning 'a boy', and on two occasions of *wildān,* plural of *walad* meaning 'a son' or 'a child':

> "And round them go boys (*ghilmān*) of theirs as if they were hidden pearls." — 52:24

> "Round about them will go youths (*wildān*), never altering in age". — 56:17, 76:19

In the first case, there is a double indication showing that these boys are the offspring of the faithful; they are called "their boys", and it is clearly stated only three verses earlier that God will:

> "unite with them [i.e., with the righteous] their offspring". — 52:21

To the same effect, it is elsewhere said that the "offspring" of the faithful will be made to enter Paradise with them.[27] Hence the "boys" and the "youth" are the young children who have died in childhood. There is, however, a possibility that these boys are only a blessing of Paradise, as boyhood is, like womanhood, an emblem of purity and beauty.

Paradise is the abode of peace

The picture of Paradise as portrayed in the Holy Quran has no implication whatsoever of any sensual pleasure. Some of the verses which reveal the true nature of Paradise are quoted below:

> "Allah has promised to the believers, men and women, Gardens in which rivers flow, to abide in them, and goodly dwellings in Gardens of perpetual abode. And greatest of all is Allah's goodly pleasure. That is the mighty achievement." — 9:72

> "Those who believe and do good, their Lord guides them by their faith; rivers will flow beneath them in Gardens of bliss. Their cry therein will be, Glory be to You, O Allah! and their greeting, Peace! And the last of their cry will be: Praise be to Allah, the Lord of the worlds!" — 10:9–10

> "Surely those who keep their duty are in Gardens and fountains: Enter them in peace, secure. And We shall remove whatever of bitterness is in their hearts — as brothers, on raised couches, face to face. Toil does not afflict them therein, nor will they be ejected from there." — 15:45–48

> "And they say: Praise be to Allah, Who has removed grief from us! Surely our Lord is Forgiving, Multiplier of reward, Who out of His grace has settled us in a house abiding forever; therein toil does not touch us nor does fatigue afflict us therein." — 35:34–35

> "In it they have fruits and they have whatever they desire. Peace! a word from the Merciful Lord." — 36:57–58

> "Enter it in peace. That is the day of abiding. They shall have in it all they wish, and with Us is yet more." — 50:34

> "They hear therein no idle or sinful talk, but only the saying, Peace! Peace!" — 56:25–26

Quite in accordance with this description of Paradise, one of the names by which Paradise is mentioned in the Quran is the *abode of peace (dār al-salām)*.[28]

The meeting with God

The ultimate object of the life of man is described as *liqā' Allāh* which means *the meeting with God.* In one of the earliest chapters of the Holy Quran we are told:

> "O man! You must strive a hard striving [to attain] to your Lord until you meet Him." — 84:6

But this object cannot be fully attained in this life; it is only in the life after death, the higher life, that a human being is able to reach this stage. Hence it is that those who deny the life after death are said to be deniers of the meeting with God:

> "And they say: When we are lost in the earth, shall we then be in a new creation? Indeed, they are disbelievers in the meeting with their Lord." — 32:10

To be content with this life, and not to look forward to a higher goal and a higher life, is repeatedly condemned:

> "Those who do not expect the meeting with Us, and are pleased with this world's life and are satisfied with it, and those who are heedless of Our messages — these, their abode is the Fire because of what they earned... We leave those alone, who have no hope of meeting with Us, in their inordinacy, blindly wandering on." — 10:7–8, 11. [29]

Only those who are sure that they will meet their Lord work on patiently for this great object:

> "And seek assistance through patience and prayer, and this is hard except for the humble ones, who know that they will meet their Lord and that to Him they will return." — 2:45–46

The meeting with the Lord is the great goal to attain, for which all good deeds are done:

> "So whoever hopes to meet his Lord, he should do good deeds, and make no one a partner [with God] in the service of his Lord." — 18:110

And what is Hell itself but being debarred from the Divine presence:

> "No, rather, what they earned is rust upon their hearts.
> No, surely they are that day debarred from their Lord.
> Then they will surely enter the burning Fire." — 83:14–16

Paradise is therefore the place of meeting with God, and life in Paradise is above all bodily conceptions.

Advancement in the higher life

That, however, is only the beginning of the higher life. The goal has been attained, but it only opens out wide fields for further advancement. If man has been granted such vast capabilities even in this physical life that his advancement knows no bounds, that advancement could not cease with the attainment of the higher life. In accordance with the idea of the Resurrection as the birth into a higher life, the Holy Quran speaks of an unending progress in that life, of the righteous ever rising to higher and higher stages:

> "O you who believe, turn to Allah with sincere repentance.
> It may be your Lord will remove from you your evil and
> make you enter Gardens in which rivers flow, on the day on
> which Allah will not disgrace the Prophet and those who
> believe with him. Their light will gleam before them and on
> their right hands — they will say: Our Lord, make perfect
> for us our light and grant us protection; surely You are
> powerful over all things." — 66:8

It is clear from the first part of this verse that all evil is removed from those who enter into Paradise, and as clear from the concluding portion that the soul of the righteous shall still be animated by a desire for more and more light, which evidently indicates a desire to attain to higher and ever higher stages of spiritual life. And there shall be means of fulfilment of every desire in Paradise:

> "In it they have fruits and they have whatever they desire."
> — 36:57

So the desire to attain to higher and higher stages cannot remain unfulfilled:

> "But those who keep their duty to their Lord, for them are
> high places, above which are yet higher places, built for
> them…" — 39:20

The new life granted to the righteous in Paradise is thus the starting-point for a new advancement, in which man shall continue to rise to higher and higher places. The joys of Paradise are thus really the true joys of advancement.

Hell, a manifestation of spiritualities

In the Holy Quran, the most frequently occurring name of Hell is *Jahannam,* which is, as it were, a proper name for Hell. Its meaning signifies *a great depth.* Another name for Hell which bears a similar significance, but which occurs only once, is *hāwiya,*[30] meaning *an abyss* or *a deep place of which the bottom cannot be reached,*[31] hence indicating low desires.[32] Four names of Hell are taken from the analogy of fire: *jahīm, sa'īr, saqar* and *lazā.* The seventh name of hell is *hutamah,* occurring only twice in the same context,[33] whose root means *the breaking of a thing,* also *making it infirm* or *weak with age,* while *hutamah* means *a vehement fire.*[34] The word *hutām* is used for *dried up and broken down* vegetation.[35]

It will be seen from the above that the different names of Hell convey three different ideas: the idea of falling down to a great depth, the idea of burning and the idea of being broken down. Thus as the idea of rising higher and higher is connected with Paradise, that of *falling down to abysmal depth* is essentially connected with Hell; and as the ideas of contentment and happiness are associated with Paradise, the idea of burning is associated with Hell which is itself but *the result of burning with passion in this life;* and lastly, as the idea of a fruitful life is associated with Paradise, life in Hell is represented as *an unfruitful life.* All this is the result of man's own deeds. Because he follows his low desires and baser passions, he makes himself fall into the depths; the burning caused by worldly desires and passions changes into a flaming fire after death; and since the only end in view is some sort of gain in this life, such deeds can bear no fruit after death. Just as the blessings of Paradise are a manifestation of the hidden realities of this life, so are the depths, the fire and unfruitfulness of hell, and the Day of Resurrection is, according to the Quran, the day of the manifestation of hidden realities[36] when the veil shall be removed from the eyes of man so that he shall see clearly the consequences of the deeds of which he took no heed in this life.[37]

In other words, the spiritual torments and mental pangs, that are generally felt almost imperceptibly in this life, assume a palpable shape in the life after death. The answer to the question, what is Hell, is unequivocally given as:

> "It is the Fire kindled by Allah which rises over the hearts."
> — 104:6–7

Now the fire which consumes the hearts is that caused by inordinate passions. Regret for the evil done is also spoken of as fire:

> "Thus will Allah show them their deeds to be intense regret to them, and they will not escape from the fire." — 2:167

The low desires of this life (*ahwā'*), that are so often a hindrance in man's awakening to a higher life and nobler aims, become the abysmal depth (*hāwiyah* or *jahannam*), to which the evil-doer makes himself fall. Accordingly, in the Holy Quran we are told:

> "So shun the filth of the idols and shun false words, being upright for Allah, not setting up partners with Him; and whoever sets up partners with Allah, it is as if he had fallen from on high…" — 22:30–31

And of the people whose exertions are all limited in this world's life, it is said:

> "Those whose effort is lost in this world's life, and they think that they are making good manufactures. Those are they who disbelieve in the messages of their Lord and meeting with Him, so their deeds are fruitless." — 18:104–105

Remedial nature of Hell

Hell, therefore, only represents the evil consequences of evil deeds, but still it is not a place merely for undergoing the consequences of what has been done; it is also a remedial plan. In other words, its chastisement is not for the purpose of torture but for purification; so that man, rid of the evil consequences which he has brought about with his own hands, may be made fit for spiritual advancement. The Holy Quran has clearly laid down the same law even for those punishments which are inflicted on man here on earth:

> "And We did not send a prophet to a town but We seized its people with distress and affliction that they might humble themselves." — 7:94

It is clear from this that God brings down His punishment upon a sinning people in order that they may turn to Him, in other words, that they may be awakened to a higher life. The same must therefore be the object of punishment in Hell.

In fact, a little consideration would show that good is enjoined because it helps the progress of man, and evil is prohibited because it retards that progress. If a person does good, he himself gets the advantage of it; if he does evil, it is to his own detriment. It is a subject to which the Quran returns over and over again:

> "Your striving is surely for diverse ends. Then as for him who gives [in charity] and keeps his duty, and accepts what is good — We facilitate for him [the way to] ease. And as for him who is miserly and considers himself self-sufficient, and rejects what is good — We facilitate for him [the way to] distress." — 92:4–10

> "If you do good, you do good for your own souls. And if you do evil, it is for them." — 17:7

> "Whoever does good, it is for the good of his own soul; and whoever does evil, it is to its detriment. And your Lord is not in the least unjust to the servants." — 41:46

Purification being the great object, the man who has wasted his opportunity here must undergo the ordeal of Hell in order to obtain it. Various other considerations lead to the same conclusion. In the first place, such great prominence is given in the Quran to the attribute of mercy in God that He is spoken of as having "ordained mercy on Himself";[38] the Divine mercy is described as encompassing all things,[39] so that even those who have acted extravagantly, against their own souls, should not despair of the mercy of God;[40] and finally it is laid down that for mercy did He create all human beings.[41] Such a merciful Being could not chastise man unless for some great purpose, which is to set him again on the road to the higher life, after purifying him from evil. It is like a hospital where different operations are performed only to save life.

The ultimate object of the life of man is that he shall live in the service of God:

> "And I have not created the jinn and the people except that they should serve Me." — 51:56

The man who lives in sin is debarred from the Divine presence,[42] but, being purified by fire, is again made fit for Divine service. Hence Hell is called, in one place, the "friend" (*maulā*) of the sinners, and their "mother" (*umm*) in another.[43] Both descriptions are a clear indication that Hell is intended to raise up man by purifying him from the dross of evil, just as fire purifies gold of dross. The faithful are purified through their suffering, in the way of God, in this life; and the evil-doers shall be purified by hell-fire. Hell is called a "friend" of sinners, because through suffering it will fit them for spiritual progress, and it is called their "mother", because in its bosom they will be brought up, so that they may be able to tread the path of a new life.

Punishment of Hell not everlasting

Another consideration which shows that this punishment is of a remedial nature is that, according to the teachings of the Holy Quran and the Sayings of the Holy Prophet, all those who are in Hell shall ultimately, when they are fit for a new life, be released from it. This is a point on which great misunderstanding prevails even among Muslim theologians. They make a distinction between the Muslim sinners and the non-Muslim sinners, holding that all Muslim sinners shall be ultimately taken out of Hell, but not the non-Muslim sinners. Neither the Quran nor the Hadith upholds this view. There are two words, *khulūd* and *abad,* used in connection with the abiding in Hell or Paradise, and both these words, while, no doubt, indicating *eternity,* also bear the significance of *a long time.* Not only do all authorities on Arabic lexicology agree on this, but the use of these words in the Quran also makes it quite clear.

The word *khulūd* has been freely used regarding the punishment in Hell of Muslim as well as of non-Muslim sinners. One example of its use for Muslim sinners is that after stating the law of inheritance, it is said:

> "These are Allah's limits. … And whoever disobeys Allah and His Messenger and goes beyond His limits, He will make him enter fire, to abide (*khālid-an*) in it, and for him is a humiliating punishment." — 4:13–14

Here clearly Muslim sinners are spoken of, and yet their abiding in Hell is called *khulūd.*

The other word *abad* occurs three times in the Holy Quran, in connection with the abiding of sinners in Hell. Ordinarily, it is taken as meaning *forever* or *eternally,* but that it sometimes signifies only *a long time,* is abundantly clear from the fact that both its dual and plural forms are in use. This significance of *abad* is fully recognized in Arabic lexicology.[44] That in the case of those in Hell, it signifies *a long time* and not *forever,* is clear from the fact that the abiding in Hell of even the unbelievers is elsewhere stated to be for *ahqāb,*[45] which is the plural of *huqbah,* meaning *a year* or *many years.*[46] At all events it indicates a definite period of time, and hence serves as a clear indication that even *abad,* in the case of abiding in Hell, means *a long time.*

We now consider the statements in the Quran which are generally taken as meaning that those in Hell shall forever and ever suffer its endless tortures:

> "…they will not escape from the fire." — 2 : 167

> "They would desire to come forth from the fire, and they will not come forth from it, and theirs is a lasting punishment." — 5 : 37

> "Whenever they desire to go out from it, from grief, they are turned back into it." — 22 : 22

> "Whenever they desire to go forth from it, they are brought back into it, and it is said to them: Taste the punishment of the fire, which you called a lie." — 32 : 20

These verses are self-explanatory. Those in Hell shall desire to escape from it but shall not be able to do so. The evil consequences of sin cannot be avoided, howsoever one may desire, and even so is the fire of Hell. None can escape from it. But not a word is there in any of these verses to show that God will not take them out of it, or that the tortures of Hell are endless. They only show that every sinner must suffer the consequences of what he has done, and that he cannot escape them; but that he may be set free when he has undergone the necessary chastisement, or that God may, of His boundless mercy, deliver the sinners when He pleases, is not denied here.

The following two verses clearly indicate the ultimate deliverance of those in Hell:

> "He will say: The Fire is your abode — you shall abide in it, *except as Allah please.* Surely your Lord is Wise, Knowing." — 6:128

> "Then as for those who are unhappy, they will be in the Fire; for them there will be in it sighing and groaning — abiding in it so long as the heavens and the earth endure, *except as your Lord please.* Surely your Lord is Doer[47] of what He intends." — 11:106–107

Both these verses show that the abiding in Hell must come to an end. To make this conclusion clearer still, the Quran has used in the very next verse a similar expression for those in Paradise but with quite a different ending:

> "And as for those who are made happy, they will be in the Garden, abiding in it so long as the heavens and the earth endure, except as your Lord please — a gift never to be cut off." — 11:108

The two expressions are similar; those in Hell and those in Paradise abide, each in his place, as long as the heavens and the earth endure, with an exception added in each case — "except as your Lord please" — showing that they may be taken out of that condition. But the concluding statements are different. In the case of Paradise, the idea that those in it may be taken out of it, if God pleases, is immediately followed by the statement that it is a gift that shall never be cut off, showing that they shall not be taken out of Paradise; while in the case of Hell, the idea that those in it will be taken out is confirmed by the concluding statement, that God is the mighty Doer of what He intends.

This conclusion is corroborated by Hadith. The Holy Prophet is reported to have said:

> "Then Allah will say: The angels have interceded and the prophets have interceded and the faithful have interceded and none remains but the most Merciful of all merciful ones. So He will take out a handful from the fire and bring out a people who have never done any good." [48]

Three kinds of intercession are spoken of in this hadith — of the faithful, of prophets and of the angels — and the intercession of each class is undoubtedly meant for people who have some sort of close relation with that class. The faithful will intercede for people who have come into contact with them personally; the prophets will intercede for their followers; the angels, who move people to do good, will intercede for people who are not followers of a prophet, but who have done some good. And the report adds that the most Merciful of all still remains, so He will bring out from the fire even people who have never done any good. It follows that, thereafter, none can remain in Hell, and in fact the handful of God cannot leave anything behind.

Other Hadith reports state even more explicitly that everyone shall be ultimately taken out of Hell: "Surely a day will come over Hell when there shall not be a single human being in it". And a saying of Umar, the second Caliph, is recorded as follows: "Even if the dwellers in Hell may be numberless as the sands of the desert, a day will come when they will be taken out of it". A similar saying is recorded from Ibn Masud: "Surely a time will come over Hell when its gates shall be blown by wind, there shall be none in it, and this shall be after they have remained therein for many years". Similar sayings are reported from many other Companions and also from the learned men of the next generation. And later Imams, such as Ibn Arabi, Ibn Taimiyah, Ibn Qayyim, and many others, have held similar views.[49]

Thus there can be but little doubt left that Hell is a temporary place for the sinner, whether Muslim or non-Muslim, and this also supports the view that the chastisement of Hell is not for torture but as a remedy, to heal the spiritual diseases which a person has incurred by his own negligence, and to enable him to start again on the road to the higher life. The truth of this has already been established from the Holy Quran, but a hadith also may be quoted here which expressly speaks of inmates of the fire as being set on the road to the higher life:

> "Then will Allah say, 'Bring out [of the Fire] everyone in whose heart there is faith or goodness to the extent of a mustard seed,' so they will be taken out having become quite black; then they will be thrown into the river of life and they will grow as grows a seed by the side of the river." [50]

This report is conclusive as to the remedial nature of Hell and establishes beyond a doubt that all human beings will ultimately be set on the way to the higher life.

Notes to Chapter 9

1. The Quran, 2:8, 2:62, etc.

2. The Quran, 53:32, 32:7–9, 23:12–14.

3. The Quran, 23:99–100.

4. The Quran, 40:45–46.

5. The Quran, 32:17.

6. Bukhari, book 59: 'Beginning of Creation', ch. 8, h. 3244.

7. Raghib's *Mufradāt. Editor's Note:* There are similar reports in Muslim, book 54: 'Tribulations and Signs of the Last Hour', ch. 27, h. 2952 to h. 2953 (MDS: book 52, ch. 27, h. 7409–7412).

8. Bukhari, book 65: 'Commentary on the Quran', h. 4875 on *Surah* 54:45 and h. 4877 on *Surah* 54:45–46. See also Bukhari, book 56: '*Jihād*', ch. 89, h. 2915.

9. Bukhari, book 59: 'Beginning of Creation', ch. 8, h. 3244.

10. *Editor's Note:* The Arabic word here in 13:11 translated as "angels guarding the consequences" is *mu'aqqibāt.*

11. *Editor's Note:* The Arabic word here in 82:10 is *ḥāfiẓīn,* meaning "keepers" or "guardians". This is the same word which is used as a verb in 13:11 to mean "who guard him" (*yaḥfaẓūna-hū*).

12. The Quran, 69:19, 69:25, 84:7, 84:10.

13. See Raghib's *Mufradāt* under the word *wazn.*

14. Bukhari, book 59: 'Beginning of Creation', ch. 8, h. 3244.

15. Raghib's *Mufradāt.*

16. The Quran, 47:15.

17. The Quran, 88:13–16.

18. The Quran, 18:31.

19. The Quran, 13:35, 47:15.

20. *Rūḥ al-Ma'ānī,* Commentary of the Quran, vol. 1, p. 670.

21. The Quran, 25:12, 67:7.

22. The Quran, 21:102.

23. The other three places are 44:54, 55:72 and 56:22.

24. *Ḥūr* is a plural of *aḥwar,* applied to a man, and of *ḥaurā',* applied to a woman, signifying 'one having eyes characterized by [the quality termed] *ḥawar'* — Lane's Lexicon.

    Ḥawar means *originally* 'whiteness', which is a symbol of purity, and the word *ḥaurā'* is applied to *a woman who is of a white colour and whose white of the eye is intensely white and the black thereof intensely black* — *Lisān al-'Arab.*

Aḥwar, besides *being* applied to a man of a similar description, also signifies *pure* or *clear intellect* — Lane's Lexicon.

25. Tirmidhi, book 47: 'Commentary on the Quran', hadith 3296 (MDS: book 44, ch. 56).

26. *Shama'il Tirmidhi,* ch. 'Joking of the Messenger of Allah'. See *Shama'il Muhammadiyya* at Sunnah.com, book 36, hadith 240.

27. The Quran, 40:8.

28. The Quran, 6:128, 10:25.

29. See also 29:23 and 30:7–8.

30. The Quran, 101:9.

31. *Lisān al-'Arab.*

32. Raghib's *Mufradāt.*

33. The Quran, 104:4–5.

34. Lane's Lexicon.
35. In 57:20 and elsewhere.

36. The Quran, 86:9.

37. The Quran, 50:22.

38. The Quran, 6:12, 54.

39. The Quran, 6:147, 7:156, 40:7.

40. The Quran, 39:53.

41. The Quran, 11:119.

42. The Quran, 83:15.

43. The Quran, 57:15 and 101:9.

44. See Raghib's *Mufradāt.*

45. The Quran, 78:23.

46. See *Lisān al-'Arab* and Raghib's *Mufradāt.*

47. The word translated here as "Doer" is *fa''āl,* which is an intensive form of *fā'il,* the latter word meaning *doer.* As a Divine attribute, the intensive form indicates that God does even those things which seem impossible to others. (From footnote to 11:107 in Maulana Muhammad Ali's English Translation of the Holy Quran.)

48. Muslim, book 1: 'Faith', ch. 81, h. 183a (MDS: h. 454).

Editor's Note: See also Bukhari, book 97: 'Oneness of God', ch. 24: 'Faces that day will be bright, looking to their Lord', h. 7439, narrated by Abu Sa'id Al-Khudri. In this hadith, the very last people to be taken out of hell are called as "emancipated by the Beneficent" (*'utaqā'-ur-Raḥmān*) near the end of the hadith.

49. For all the references in this paragraph, see the commentary of the Quran entitled *Fath al-Bayān fī maqāṣid al-Qur'ān* by Siddiq ibn Hasan ibn Ali al-Bukhari (d. 1890).

50. Bukhari, book 2: 'Faith', ch. 15, h 22.

10. *Taqdīr* or 'Predestination'

Predestination (*taqdīr* or *qadar*) is not among articles of faith

The Holy Quran speaks of *qadar* or *taqdīr* but these words by no means carry the significance of predestination or of a decree of good and evil for man, as popularly supposed. Moreover, there is no mention at all, in the Quran or in the most reliable Hadith collection of Bukhari, of faith (*īmān*) in *qadar* or *taqdīr* as being one of the fundamentals of religion like faith in God and His angels and His books and His messengers and a life after death.

Significance of *qadar* and *taqdīr*

Qadar and *taqdīr* mean 'the making manifest of the measure of a thing', or simply 'measure'. God's *taqdīr* of things is in two ways, by granting *qudra,* i.e., *power,* or by making them in a particular measure and in a particular manner, as wisdom requires.[1] An example of this is given in the *taqdīr* of the date-stone, out of which it is the palm only that grows, not an apple or olive tree. *Taqdīr* is therefore the law or the ordinance or the measure which is working throughout the creation; and this is exactly the sense in which the word is used in the Holy Quran. For example, it speaks of a *taqdīr* for each and everything that has been created:

> "Blessed is He … Who created everything, then ordained for it a measure (*taqdīr*)." — 25:1–2

> "Surely We have created everything according to a measure (*qadar*)." — 54:49

The law according to which foods, provisions and other things are provided in the earth is also called a *taqdīr* of God, and so also the law according to which rain falls on the earth, and that according to which night and day follow each other.[2] Though man is included in the creation, and his *taqdīr* is therefore the same as that of the whole creation, he is also separately spoken of as having a *taqdīr* similar to the law of growth and development in other things:

> "Of what thing did He create him? Of a small life-germ. He creates him, then *proportions him (qaddara-hū)*". — 80:18 – 19

All these verses go to show that, as according to lexicologists, *taqdīr* in the language of the Holy Quran is the universal law of God, operating as much in the case of man as in the rest of nature — a law extending to everything in the universe. The *taqdīr* of a thing is the law or the measure of its growth and development, and the *taqdīr* of man is not different in nature from the *taqdīr* of other things.

Creation of good and evil

Taqdīr as meaning the *absolute decree of good and evil for man by God,* or the doctrine of man's predestination, is an idea unsupported by the Holy Quran, and is of later growth. It probably arose due to a misunderstanding of the nature of good and evil, in discussions as to whether or not God was the creator of evil. God created man with certain powers which he could exercise under certain limitations, and it is the exercise of these powers in one way or another that produces good or evil. The same act may be a virtue on one occasion and evil on another.

The Quran, therefore, has not dealt with the question of the creation of good and evil at all. It speaks of the creation of heavens and earth and all that is in them; it speaks of the creation of man; it speaks of endowing him with certain faculties and granting him certain powers; it tells us that he can use these powers and faculties within certain limitations, just as all other created things are placed within certain limitations — and the limitations of each kind are its *taqdīr*. But in the Quran there is no mention of a *taqdīr* to mean either the creation of good and evil deeds of man by God, or an absolute decree of good and evil by God.

It may, however, be added that God is recognized by the Quran as the first and ultimate cause of all things; but this does not mean that He is the Creator of the deeds of man. He has, of course, created man; He has also created the circumstances under which he lives and acts; but still He has endowed man with a discretion to choose how to act, which he can exercise under certain limitations, just as all his other powers and faculties are exercised under limitations and only in accordance with certain laws. Thus it is said in the Quran:

> "The truth is from your Lord; so whoever wishes, let him
> believe, and whoever wishes, let him disbelieve." – 18:29

And as he can exercise his discretion or his will in doing a thing or not doing it, he is responsible for his own deeds and is made to suffer the consequences.

The will of God and the will of man

Man's will stands in the same relation to the Divine will as his other attributes to the attributes of the Divine Being. He can exercise it under limitations and laws, and there is a very large variety of circumstances which may determine his choice in each case. Yet it is not true that the choice to exercise it has been taken away from him; and the fact is that, despite all the limitations, he is free to exercise his will. Of course he is not responsible to the same extent for everything and in all cases, because a variety of circumstances must determine the extent of his responsibility, which may be very small, almost negligible, in some cases, and very great in others. Nonetheless, he is a free agent and responsible for what he does.

We now look at the Quranic verses bearing on this subject. The argument that man does an evil deed because God wills it so, is put into the mouth of the opponents of the Holy Prophet on several occasions. For instance:

> "Those who set up partners [with Allah] say: If Allah had
> pleased, we would not have set up partners [with Him], nor
> our fathers, nor would we have made anything unlawful.
> Thus did those before them reject [the truth] until they tasted
> Our punishment. Say: Have you any knowledge so you
> would bring it forth to us? You only follow a conjecture and
> you only tell lies. Say: Then Allah's is the conclusive argu-
> ment; so if He had pleased, He would have guided you all."
> — 6:148–149

The contention of the polytheists here is that what they do, i.e., worship others besides God as His partners, is in accordance with the will of God. This is condemned as a mere conjecture and a lie, and against it, two arguments are adduced. The first is that previous people were punished when they persisted in their evil courses; if what they did was because God had so willed it, He would not have punished them for it. The second is that God had never said so through any of His prophets: "Have you any knowledge so you would bring it forth to us?" And in the verse that follows, the argument is carried further by saying: "If He had pleased, He would have guided you all". The conclusion is clear. If it were the Divine will that people should be compelled to one course, that would have been the course of guidance. But human beings are not compelled to accept even the right way; much less could they be compelled to follow the wrong course. This is clearly laid down:

> "We have truly shown him the way; he may be thankful or unthankful." — 76:3

> "Clear proofs have indeed come to you from your Lord: so whoever sees, it is for his own good; and whoever is blind, it is to his own harm." — 6 : 104

> "The truth is from your Lord; so whoever wishes, let him believe, and whoever wishes, let him disbelieve." – 18:29

The Divine will is therefore exercised in the raising up of prophets, and in the pointing out of the courses of good and evil, and human will is exercised in the choice of one course or the other.

It is this very law that is expressed at the end of chapter 76:

> "Surely this is a Reminder; so whoever wishes, let him take a way to his Lord. And you do not wish, unless Allah please." — 76:29–30

And again to the same effect:

> "It is nothing but a Reminder for the nations, for whomever among you who wishes to go straight. And you do not wish, unless Allah please, the Lord of the worlds." — 81:27–29

In both these places, the Quran is spoken of as having been revealed for the upliftment of man, yet, it is added, only he will derive benefit from it who chooses to go straight or takes a way to his Lord, that is, exercises his will in the right direction. Thus man is left to make his choice after God has sent down a revelation, and the will of man to make a choice is thus exercised only after the will of God has been exercised in the sending down of a revelation. If God had not pleased to reveal the reminder, man would have had no choice. Thus the words "you do not wish, unless Allah please" mean only this, that if

God had not pleased to send a revelation, man would not have been able to make his choice of good or evil.

God does not lead astray

A great misconception regarding the teachings of the Holy Quran is that it ascribes to God the attribute of leading astray. Nothing could be further from the truth. While *al-Hādī,* or the *One Who guides,* is one of the names of Allah, as accepted by all Muslims, *al-Muḍill,* or *the One Who leads astray,* has never been recognized as such. The sinners' own confession, as repeatedly mentioned in the Quran, is that their great leaders misled them, or that the Devil misled them. Not once do they put forward the excuse that it was God Himself Who misled them:

> "And none but the guilty led us astray." — 26:99

> "And they say: Our Lord, surely we only obeyed our leaders and our great men, so they led us astray from the path. Our Lord! Give them a double punishment and curse them with a great curse." — 33:67–68

If God had really led people astray, their best excuse on the Day of Judgment would have been that they did not deserve to be punished because it was God Himself Who led them astray. But not once is that excuse advanced, and it is always the guilty leaders who are denounced by the followers as having misled them.

Again, the Quran is full of statements to the effect that God sends His prophets and grants revelation for the guidance of the people. The general rule laid down with regard to Divine dealing with humanity is thus made clear in the very beginning:

> "Surely a guidance from Me will come to you, then whoever follows My guidance, no fear shall come upon them, nor shall they grieve." — 2:38

Guiding and leading astray are two contradictions which could not be gathered together in one being. The Quran itself draws attention to this point:

> "And it is not attributable to Allah that He should lead a people astray after He has guided them, so far so that He

makes clear to them what they should guard against." —
9:115

The mistaken idea that God leads people astray arises out of a misconception of the meaning of the word *iḍlāl* when it is ascribed to God. This word carries a variety of meanings besides *leading someone astray.* It should be noted that wherever this act is attributed to God, it is only in connection with the transgressors, the unjust, and the extravagant,[3] not people generally. The word *iḍlāl*, as used in the Holy Quran with reference to God, means *judging* or *finding someone to be in error.* This was a recognized use of the word among the Arabs. In fact, this sense of the word is recognized by all lexicologists.[4]

God's sealing of hearts

Another misconception is that it is thought that God has created some people with their hearts sealed and closed, while others have been created with free and open hearts. No trace of any such distinction is met with anywhere either in the Holy Quran or in Hadith. All are created sinless, all are created pure, that is the express teaching of Islam. The Quran says:

> "So set yourself for religion, being upright, the nature
> (*fiṭrah*) made by Allah in which He has created mankind.
> There is no altering Allah's creation. That is the right reli-
> gion." — 30:30

According to this verse all humans have been created in pure nature, and a hadith of the Holy Prophet, which is really an explanation of this verse, says:

> "Every child that is born conforms to *fiṭrah* (human nature),
> and it is his parents who make him a Jew or a Christian or a
> Magian." [5]

The Quran does speak of God setting seals on some hearts, but it says expressly that seals are set on the hearts of the reprobate, the hardened sinners who pay no heed to the call of the Prophet. In the very beginning of the Quran, it is stated:

> "Those who disbelieve — to whom it is the same whether
> you warn them or do not warn them — they will not believe.

> Allah has sealed their hearts and their hearing; and there is a covering on their eyes." — 2:6–7

The sealing spoken of here is in connection with those who have so hardened their hearts that they do not pay any heed to the Prophet's warning. They refuse to open their hearts to receive the truth, and do not lend their ears to listen to it, nor use their eyes to discern the truth from falsehood. As is elsewhere stated:

> "They have hearts with which they do not understand, and they have eyes with which they do not see, and they have ears with which they do not hear. They are as cattle..." — 7:179

It is always the reprobate whose heart is said to be sealed:

> "Thus does Allah seal every heart, of a proud, insolent one." — 40:35

The fact that the cause of the seal is the sinner's own act of not heeding the warning, is made clear on another occasion also, where it is stated in the Quran:

> "And some of them seek to listen to you, till, when they go forth from you, they say to those who have been given knowledge: What was it that he said just now? These are they whose hearts Allah has sealed and they follow their low desires." — 47:16

All these verses show that God sets a seal upon the hearts of certain people as a result of their own actions. Those who themselves close the doors of their hearts are visited with the natural consequence of this, the setting of a seal. The seal, therefore, being the consequence of a man's own deeds, has nothing to do with the doctrine of predestination.

Hadith and predestination

As regards Hadith reports from which predestination is concluded, it has to be borne in mind clearly that Hadith must be read subject to the broad principles established in the Holy Quran, and must be so interpreted as not to clash with the Book of God, and that in case of a clash it is the Hadith report that must be rejected; for its words are often the words of narrators, and in such metaphysical subjects there has been a good deal of mixing up of the ideas of the narrators through a long chain of transmitters.

Taking Bukhari, the most reliable collection of Hadith, in the first place it does not relate a single report speaking of faith in *qadar*, and thus the question that such a faith is one of the fundamentals of Islam is disposed of, for faith in *qadar* is unknown both to the Quran and to the most reliable collection of Hadith. Coming to the actual reports which Bukhari has related in his Collection in the book entitled *Qadar*, one finds that not a single report in it lends any support to the theory that a good or an evil course has been chalked out beforehand and is forced upon man. The reports related here, as well as in other collections, generally speak either of the Divine knowledge of things or of the Divine command prevailing over all.

The most well-known report from which predestination is concluded is that speaking of an angel being in charge of the embryo — "an angel is sent to the embryo, and he is commanded with four things: his sustenance and his term of life and whether he is unhappy or happy".[6] These words can be interpreted in consonance with the teachings of the Quran to mean that the Divine knowledge of things is all-comprehensive, so much so that God knows all about a person even in the embryonic state. As the properties of the seed are all in the seed, so even the embryo shows what the man will develop into. No human eye can see these hidden potentialities; but nothing is hidden from God.

We cannot go into details of the rest of the reports of Bukhari. Many of them are wrongly interpreted. For example, in one hadith the Holy Prophet is reported to have remarked in a certain company that there was not a man but his place in fire or in Paradise was written down. Thereupon a man said:

> "Shall we not rely then [i.e., rely on what is written, and give up the doing of deeds], O Messenger of Allah?"

The Holy Prophet said:

> "No. Do work, for to everyone it is made easy."[7]

Then the Holy Prophet recited the following verses:

> "Then as for him who gives [charitably] and keeps his duty and accepts what is good — We facilitate for him [the way

to] ease. And as for him who is miserly and considers himself self-sufficient and rejects what is good — We facilitate for him [the way to] distress." — 92:5–10.

If any conclusion of predestination could be drawn from the words of this report, the verses quoted by the Holy Prophet, in support of what he said, negative such a conclusion, for they speak of two different ends for two different kinds of workers. The words of the Holy Prophet himself lead to the same conclusion, for he laid stress on works. Nor do his concluding words — "to everyone it is made easy" — lead to any other conclusion, for the meaning is that to the worker of good, the good end, and to the worker of evil, the evil end, is made easy, as stated in the Quranic verses quoted in support of his assertion.

Faith in *qadar* finds no place in the Quran and Bukhari

It must be clearly understood that the fundamentals of religion are all fully explained in the Quran itself; and a thing cannot be accepted as a fundamental of Islam of which there is no mention in the Holy Book. Hadith is only a secondary source of the religion of Islam and, as a matter of fact, it deals only with secondary matters of religion or its details. The great principles, the basic doctrines, must all be sought from the Quran, which neither mentions *qadar* among the fundamentals of Islam, nor even speaks of a faith in it. It is only in Hadith that we find mention of *qadar,* and even here the most reliable of all collections, the Bukhari, does not contain any report mentioning *qadar* as an article of faith.

Faith in *qadar* is a doctrine of later growth

There is indeed one hadith which shows that faith in *qadar* is of later growth. In his second book, the book of *Faith,* Bukhari relates the following report from Abu Hurairah:

> "The Holy Prophet was one day sitting outside among a number of people when there came to him a man and said: What is faith? He replied: Faith is this that you believe in Allah and His angels and the meeting with Him, and His messengers, and that you believe in life after death." [8]

The report is a lengthy one and only the first portion relating to the subject of discussion has been quoted here. This same report is also related in Sahih Muslim through three different channels. In the first channel, the four narrators are the same as in Bukhari, and the words reported from the Holy Prophet as to what is faith are also almost the same:

> "That you believe in Allah and His angels and His Book and the meeting with Him, and His messengers, and that you believe in the life after death." [9]

In his second channel, the first three narrators are again the same as in Bukhari and the report is narrated as above.[10] In his third channel, only the first two narrators are the same, the rest being different, and a change is introduced into the words, the portion relating to the Holy Prophet's reply now having added to it the words:

> "and that you believe in *qadar,* in the whole of it." [11]

This shows beyond the shadow of a doubt that the words referring to faith in *qadar* were added by the third narrator, and that the inclusion of faith in *qadar* among the fundamentals of faith, is an addition of about the end of the first century of *Hijrah*. There is no doubt that discussions about *qadar* arose later, and it was during these discussions that, through inadvertence or otherwise, some narrator put these words into the mouth of Abu Hurairah.

Significance of faith in *qadar*

It is difficult to say what meaning *faith* in *qadar* carried. This much is certain that belief in *qadar* does not mean belief in predestination. A strict predestinarian, who believes that man has no control at all over his actions, would deny the very basic principle of religion, that is, the responsibility of man for his actions. The orthodox position has always been the middle one. Man has a free will, but that will is exercised under certain limitations. It is only the Divine will that can be called an absolutely free will, a will under no limitations; but everything created, and therefore everything human, is subject to *qadar,* to a Divine measure of things, to limitations imposed upon it by a Higher controlling Power. Human knowledge, human power and human will are all subject to limitations, and these limitations are placed upon man by the Divine measure which is called *qadar.* It is only in this sense that a Muslim can be said to have faith in *qadar.*

Notes to Chapter 10

1. Raghib's *Mufradāt*.

2. See the Quran, 41:10, 15:21, 23:18, 43:11, and 73:20.

3. The Quran, 2:26, 14:27 and 40:34.

4. According to the dictionary *Lisān al-'Arab,* the words *aḍallanī ṣadīqī* mean 'my friend judged me to be in error', not 'my friend led me astray'. Lane in his Lexicon says that *aḍalla-hū* means 'he found him to be erring, straying', quoting this from *Tāj al-'Arūs.*

5. Bukhari, book 23: 'Funerals', ch. 79, h. 1358, h. 1359.

6. Bukhari, book 82: '*Qadar*', ch. 1, h. 6594.

7. *Ibid.,* ch. 4, h. 6605. See also Bukhari, book 23: 'Funerals', ch. 82, h. 1362.

8. Bukhari, book 2: 'Faith', ch. 37, h. 50.

9. Muslim, book 1: 'Faith', ch. 'What is *Īmān* (Faith)?', h. 8e (MDS: h. 97).

10. *Ibid.,* h. 9 (MDS: h. 98).

11. *Ibid.,* ch. 'What is Islam?', h. 10 (MDS: h. 99).

11. Prayer

Section 1: *The Value of Prayer*

Importance of prayer in Islam

The fundamental religious duties recognized by Islam for the individual are: prayer, charity, fasting and pilgrimage. Among these, prayer undoubtedly occupies the most important position, and is given the greatest prominence in the Holy Quran, charity coming next to it. It was the first duty enjoined on the Holy Prophet, and though prayer and charity are often mentioned together in the Holy Quran, prayer always takes precedence. The keeping up of prayer is the frequently repeated injunction of the Quran and it has also been generally recognized as the first and foremost duty of a Muslim.

There are several reasons why prayer has been given this importance. It is really the first step in the onward progress of man, and yet it is also his highest spiritual ascent (*mi'rāj*). Prayer keeps man away from evil; it helps him to realize the Divine in him, and that realization not only urges him to do disinterested service for humanity but also makes him attain the highest degree of moral and spiritual perfection. Prayer is also the means of levelling all differences of rank, colour and nationality, and the means of bringing about a cohesion and unity among people which is the necessary basis of a living civilization.

Self-development through prayer

What prayer really aims at is stated in the very beginning of the Quran. There we are told that a Muslim, who would tread the road to self-development, must accept certain principles and carry out certain duties:

> "This Book, in which there is no doubt, is a guide to those who keep their duty, who believe in the Unseen and keep up prayer and spend [on good works] out of what We have given them, and who believe in what has been revealed to you [O Prophet] and what was revealed before you, and of

> the Hereafter they are sure. These are on a right course from
> their Lord and these it is that are successful (*muflihūn*)."
> 2:2–5

The word *falāh* means 'success', and from it *muflihūn* means 'those
who are successful'. This word, whether relating to this life or to the
next, carries with it the idea of the complete development of the inner
faculties of man, and the achievement of both material and moral
greatness; what, in other words, may be called the full self-development of man. This self-development is reached, according to the
Quran, by the acceptance of three principles, the existence of God,
His revealing Himself to man, and the Hereafter; and by the exercise
of two duties, the keeping up of prayer, or seeking communion with
God, and the spending of one's wealth for others or the service of
humanity. The place of prayer in the self-development of man is given
such a prominence in Islam that in the call to prayer the words "come
to prayer" are immediately followed by the words "come to success
(*falāh*)", showing that self-development is attained through prayer.
On another occasion, using the same word, the Quran says clearly:

> "Successful (*aflaha*) indeed are the believers, who are humble
> in their prayers". — 23:1–2

Prayer as the means of realizing the Divine in man

Belief in God is the fundamental principle of every religion; nevertheless the object of religion is not simply to preach the doctrine of
the existence of God as a theory; it goes far beyond that. Religion
seeks to instil the conviction that God is a living force in the life of
man; and prayer is the means by which it is sought to achieve this
great end. The real conviction that *God is* comes to man, not by the
belief that there is a God in the outer world, but by the realization of
the Divine within himself; and that this realization is attained through
prayer is made clear by what is stated in the beginning of the Quran,
as quoted above. The three requisites of a true Muslim are there given
in their natural order. The first is a belief in the Unseen, which means
a belief in God, the great *Unseen* Who cannot be perceived by the
physical eye of man. The second, which follows immediately the
belief in the Unseen, is the keeping up of prayer, thus showing that
belief in the Unseen is turned into a certainty of the Divine existence,
a realization of the Divine within man, by means of prayer; and it is
with reference to this realization that we are told, a little further on:

> "And seek assistance through patience and prayer, and this
> is hard except for the humble, who know that they will meet
> their Lord and that to Him they will return." — 2:45–46

The third requisite, spending out of what God has given, is the
natural sequel of the second, and shows that the realization of the
Divine in man leads to the service of humanity. In one of the earliest
revealed chapters of the Quran, it is stated that prayer is useless unless
it leads to the service of humanity:

> "So woe to the praying ones, who are unmindful of their
> prayer, who do good to be seen, and refrain from acts of
> kindness." — 107:4–7

Prayer, a means of attaining to moral greatness

Prayer to God is the natural sequel of the acceptance, in theory, of the
existence of God. The aspiration to rise to moral greatness is
implanted in human nature more deeply than even the aspiration to
rise to material greatness; but the only way in which the former can
be realized is to be in touch with the All-Pervading Spirit, the
fountain-head of purity and the source of the highest morality. "All
the perfect attributes are Allah's", says the Quran (7:180). But man
stands in need of perfect attributes as well for there is implanted in
him the unquenchable desire to rise higher and higher. How can he
do so except by being in touch with the Being that possesses the
perfect attributes, the Being that is free from all defects? And prayer
is but an attempt to be in touch with Him. And the only way to
become imbued with Divine morals is to get in touch with the Divine
Spirit, to be drawn away from all worldly hindrances for a while, and
to drink deep at that source, which is prayer to God. In many sayings
of the Holy Prophet, prayer is spoken of as *munājāt* or *confidential
relations* with the Lord.[1] In one it is related that man should pray to
God as if he were seeing Him.[2] Such descriptions of prayer show its
real nature to be that of being in actual intercourse with the Divine
Being and intercourse means nothing but becoming imbued with
Divine morals.

Prayer as the means of purification of heart

The right development of human faculties depends upon the purification of man's inner self and the suppression of evil tendencies.
Referring to the soul, the Holy Quran says:

"He is indeed successful who purifies it." —91:9

Prayer is spoken of as a means of purification for the heart:

> "Recite what has been revealed to you of the Book and keep up prayer. Surely prayer keeps one away from indecency and evil." — 29:45

> "And keep up prayer at the two ends of the day and in the first hours of the night. Surely good deeds take away evil deeds." — 11:114

In a hadith, the saying of prayers is compared to washing oneself in a river:

> "Abu Hurairah says that he heard the Prophet say: If one of you has a river at his door in which he washes himself five times a day, what do you think? Would it leave any dirt on him? The Companions said: It would not leave any dirt on him [and he would be perfectly clean]. The Prophet said: This is an example of the five prayers, with which Allah blots off all the evils of a man." [3]

There are many other Hadith reports in which it is stated that prayer is a means of suppressing the evil tendencies of man. The reason is plain. In the Quran, "the remembrance of Allah" is stated to be the object of keeping up prayer (20:14), while it is also stated that "the remembrance of Allah is the greatest" restraint upon sin (29:45). A law generally requires a sanction behind it, and behind all Divine laws which relate to the development of man and to his moral betterment, the only sanction is a belief in the great Author of those laws. The more often, therefore, a person reverts to prayer, to that state in which, disengaging himself from all worldly attractions, he feels the Divine presence as an actual fact, the greater is his certainty about the existence of God, and the greater the restraint upon the tendency to break that law. Prayer, thus, by checking the evil tendencies of man, purifies his heart of all evil, and sets him on the right road to the development of his inner faculties.

Unification of the human race through Divine service

The service of prayer is divided into two parts, one to be said in private and the other to be performed in congregation, preferably in a mosque. While the private prayer is meant simply for the development of the inner self of man, the public one has other ends as well in view, ends, indeed, that make the Islamic prayer a mighty force in the unification of the human race. In the first place, this gathering of all people living in the same vicinity five times daily in the mosque is a help to the establishment of healthy social relations. In the daily prayer services these relations are limited to a narrow circle, i.e., only to members of the same neighbourhood, but the circle becomes wider in the weekly Friday service which gathers together all Muslim members of a particular locality, and still wider in the two great *'Īd* gatherings.

Far more important than this, however, is the levelling of social differences brought about by means of congregational prayer. Once within the doors of the mosque, every Muslim finds himself in an atmosphere of equality and love. Before their Maker they all stand shoulder to shoulder, the ruler along with his poorest subject, the rich with the beggar, the white man with the black. Differences of rank, wealth and colour vanish within the mosque, and an atmosphere of brotherhood, equality and love, totally differing from the outside world, prevails within the holy precincts. Man has to work amidst inequalities, amidst strife and struggle, amidst scenes of hatred and enmity, and yet he is drawn out of these five times a day, and made to realize that equality, fraternity and love are the real sources of human happiness. The time spent on prayer is not, therefore, wasted even from the point of view of active humanitarianism; on the contrary, the best use of it is made in learning those great lessons which make life worth living.

Regulation of prayer
Prayer in Islam thus not only enables man to realize the Divine in him, not only makes him drink deep at the fountain of Divine morals, purifies his heart and sets him on the right road to the development of human faculties; but it goes a step further and, levelling all differences, brings about love, concord and a true union of humanity. This last object cannot be achieved without a regularly instituted form of prayer, so that everyone should gather together in mosques at the stated times and should stand up reverently, bow down and prostrate themselves before their great Maker as one. But even apart from that consideration, the grand idea of holding communion with God or realizing the Divine within man, which is so essential to the

moral elevation of man, could not have been kept alive unless there was an outward form to which all people should try to conform.

In the first place, no idea can live unless there is an institution to keep it alive. Secondly, the masses in any community, even though it may be educated, can be awakened to the recognition of a truth only through some outward form, which reminds them of the underlying idea. And thirdly, there can be no uniformity without a form, and without uniformity the community or nation, as a whole, cannot make any progress, the end in view being the moral elevation of the community as a whole and not the elevation of particular individuals.

It must be added that prayer in Islam is not so rigid as it is generally thought to be. It is true that all Muslims are required to assemble at particular times in the mosques, and to follow the lead of the *Imām,* but every prayer is divided into two parts, one to be performed in congregation, the other alone. Even in the congregational part there is ample scope for the individual to give expression to the soul's sincerest desire before its Maker, and for an outpouring of the true sentiments of the heart. But in the private part of the prayer, it is not only left to the individual to select the portions of the Quran which he likes, but he can also give vent to his own feelings by making any supplications that he likes and in any language that he chooses, in any of the four postures, the posture of standing, bowing, prostration and sitting.

Times of prayer

In Islam there is no Sabbath or a day set apart for worship. Prayer is made a part of the everyday affairs of man. There is a prayer in the morning before sunrise upon rising from bed, another just after midday, a third in the afternoon, a fourth at sunset, and a fifth before going to bed. Prayer is thus the first daily act of a Muslim and it is also his last act of the day, and between these two there are other prayers during hours of business or recreation. Thus Islam requires that, in all the varying conditions through which man has to pass, his spirit should be in touch with the Divine Spirit. Even when busiest, he should still be able to disengage himself from all worldly occupations for a short while and resort to prayer. The object in view in this arrangement is clearly that man should feel the Divine presence under all conditions, so that while he is doing his work, God should still be nearest to his heart. Such an arrangement enhances the value of prayer as a moral force in the transaction of everyday affairs.

Mode of worship

The Islamic mode of worship is calculated to concentrate attention on one object, the realization of the Divine presence. The ablution preceding prayer, the reverential attitude in standing, the bowing down, the kneeling with the forehead placed on the ground, and the reverent sitting posture — all help the mind to realize the Divine presence as a fact; and the worshipper, as it were, finds his heart's joy in doing honour to the Great Master, not only with his tongue but with his whole body, adopting a reverent attitude. There is not the least doubt that the spirit of humility in man finds particular expression in the reverential postures which must be adopted in prayer. The whole prayer is a most solemn and serious affair during which the worshipper does not turn his attention to anything else, nor does he indulge in any movement which should distract his attention or disturb his prayerful attitude. The prayer is thus an undisturbed meditation on the Divine, and it is for this reason that in Islam it is not accompanied with music but by recitations from the Quran speaking of Divine love, mercy, power and knowledge.

In cases of sickness, or when one is on a journey, the worshipper is permitted to say his prayers in any posture which he finds convenient. In such a case he is willing to humble himself in any position, but since his bodily condition does not allow him to assume the prescribed posture, a departure from regular procedure in that case does not affect the sincerity of him who prays or the efficacy of his prayer.

Language of prayer

Naturally a person would like to unfold his heart before his Maker by praying in the language in which he can most readily express his feelings, and this is fully recognized in Islam. Not only in private prayer but in the course of the public service as well, the worshipper is at liberty to pray to God in his own tongue, after or during the recitation of portions of the Holy Quran in a standing posture, or after utterance of words of Divine glory in that of bowing down or prostration. In the public service such prayers would undoubtedly be limited since the worshipper must follow the Imam, but in the private portion they may be of any length.

The question, however, assumes a different aspect when the public service itself is considered, for, unless the public service is conducted in a language which is common to all Muslims, there must again be a failure in achieving the great end for which prayer is instituted. As already stated, the unification of Muslims through prayer is as much an end and object of prayer as to bring man into communion with God. It is prayer that daily gathers together persons of different callings and different ranks and positions in society, under one roof, and on a perfect status of equality, and these homogeneous units are again united by the more extensive gathering for the Friday prayers, or the still larger assemblies at *'Id* prayers, culminating in that mighty assemblage at Makkah of all nations and all races on the most perfect status of equality. Now all these various gatherings are expressly for Divine worship, and if there were a babel of languages prevailing in these gatherings, the object of unification of the human race through Divine service — an idea unique to Islam — would fail altogether. The bond of a common language is one of the greatest factors towards unification, and this bond Islam has established by the use of a common language at the Divine service. This language, it is evident, could be none other than Arabic, the language of the Quran.

Some people think that a service held in any other language than that of the congregation will not fulfil the purpose of worship. In the first place, the Islamic prayer does not consist of mere words of praise of the Divine glory and majesty, or the mere expression, in words, of the inner feelings of the heart. There is also the attitude of mind, the inner feeling itself, of which the words are meant to be an expression. Now this attitude of mind is produced, in the first place, by the atmosphere about the worshipper and by the particular postures of reverence which he adopts. The mood, more than words, generates a true spirit of humility, and the first condition of a prayerful mind is humility, as the Quran itself lays down: "Successful indeed are the believers, who are humble in their prayers" (23:1–2).

If there is a person who takes part in a public service without understanding a word of Arabic, it would still be entirely wrong to say that prayer does not benefit him, for there are the movements of his body, the raising of the hands to the ears, the standing up with folded hands, the bowing down, the placing of the forehead on the ground, the sitting down in a particular attitude of reverence, all of which go a long way towards producing in him humility and consciousness of the Divine presence. In fact, his whole self is expressive of what the words convey. It will indeed be highly more beneficial if he understands the spoken language also, but it is absurd to say that the language of movements has no meaning for him.

As regards the language of words, the most often repeated expressions and the seven short sentences of the opening chapter of the Quran, called *al-Fātiḥah,* can be learnt, along with their meanings, in a short time and with very little effort. Even if the Divine service were held in one's own language, still he would have to spend some time in learning it, and the learning of the significance of the Arabic words would only require a little additional time. Keeping in view the grand object of unifying the human race through Divine service, the time thus spent would be well worthwhile.

There are two other considerations which make it necessary to maintain the Arabic language in Divine service. Firstly, the Holy Quran, parts of which are recited in the service, was revealed in the Arabic language, and a translation can never fully express the ideas of the original. And when the original is the word of God, and the ideas expressed are those relating to God's majesty and glory, it is still more difficult to convey the full significance in a translation. Secondly, there is a music in the original which no translation can possibly render. The music of the Quran is not only in its rhythm but also in its diction, and the recitation of the Quran serves the purpose of communicating grand and beautiful ideas to the accompaniment of music.

Prayer as index of Muslim mentality — *Al-Fātiḥah*

The opening chapter of the Holy Quran, the *Fātiḥah,* is the most essential part of the Islamic prayer, being the only portion of the Quran which must be repeated in every *rak'ah* of a prayer. It is the guiding principle of a Muslim's life and a true index of his mentality. The main principles underlying the *Fātiḥah* may be considered briefly here.

These are, firstly, the desire to give praise to the Divine Being under all circumstances, for the chapter opens with the words "All praise is due to Allah". The Muslim has to come to prayer five times a day whatever the circumstances may be. There may be occasions when he is in distress, has suffered a reverse or a defeat, has a friend or near relative in distress, when someone very dear to him has just passed away and he is under the burden of a great bereavement, yet in all these conditions he is required to give praise to God Who brings about all these conditions, just as he would do had he received a blessing or some great benefit from God. The attitude of mind thus produced is to live in perfect peace with one's environment, neither to be carried away by joy, nor give way to dejection or depression. It is an attitude of mind which keeps one steadfast in pleasure as well as pain, in joy as well as sorrow.

The second and third main ideas which determine a Muslim's mental attitude towards things are contained in the words *Rabb al-'ālamīn* ("Lord of the worlds"), the Nourisher unto perfection of all the worlds or all the nations. This attribute of God brings to man the comfort of knowing that whatever may happen to him, whether he receives a blessing or faces disaster, he must still be sure that he is being led on to perfection through these different stages. The addition of the words *al-'ālamīn,* all worlds or all nations, opens up his mind and widens the sphere of his love and sympathy not only towards all human beings, to whatever nation or creed they may belong, but also to the whole of God's creation. The person who recognizes that God is the Nourisher unto perfection of all human beings cannot bear hatred towards them. He must recognize, in fact, that God is much more to all people than is a father to his sons.

The fourth main idea is carried in the words *Raḥmān* and *Raḥīm.* God is "Beneficent" and "Merciful" — Loving. He has provided man with everything necessary for his development, physical as well as moral and spiritual; but still that development depends on the right use of outward things as well as of the inner faculties which are meant for this object. The choice is man's whether he takes advantage of those means and reaches the goal, or rejects or ignores them and suffers the evil consequences thereof.

The fifth and sixth great ideas contained in the *Fātiḥah* are those conveyed in the words *Māliki yaum-id-dīn* or Master of the Day of Recompense or Requital. God is here called the *Mālik* or the Master, and not *Malik* or King. The two words are almost alike; but there is this vast difference between a *Mālik* and a *Malik,* that the latter is bound to give to each what he deserves, but the former may, if he likes, forgive an offender altogether. There are some religions that lay so much stress on Divine justice that they refuse to recognize a God who can forgive offenders without having some compensation. Such a narrow view of Divine justice has a corresponding effect on man's morals. The word *Mālik* rejects this idea, and shows God to be a Master, Who can forgive if He likes, however great the offence may be. The addition of the words *yaum al-dīn,* the Day of Requital, is by way of reminder that man must face the consequence of his own deeds. There is no deed, good or bad, that is without a consequence, and if these consequences are not seen in this life, there is still a Day of Requital, even after death.

The seventh idea is contained in the words *iyyā-ka na'budu* ("You do we serve"), the idea of rendering obedience to God with entire submission. This is meant to create in man the mentality of obedience to the Divine commandments, even when these are opposed to the commandments of some temporal authority or to his own wishes. These words also give man the strength to carry out the Divine commandments.

The eighth idea is contained in the words *iyyā-ka nasta'īn* ("You do we beseech for help"). The mental attitude which it is sought to create by these words is that of entire dependence on God and never despairing of the attainment of an object, for even if outward means have failed, there is God, the Controller of all means, Whose help will not fail the one who depends on Him.

The ninth idea is contained in the words *ihdi-nā:* "Guide us" (on the right path). This signifies the soul's inner desire — prayer being nothing but the expression of the soul's inmost desire — of being led on and on to the goal, such being the significance of *hidāyah* (guidance). These words also show that the mentality of being content to live in perfect peace with one's environment is not a negation of action. The Muslim attitude towards the world comprises both the desire to remain in peace with his environment, and the desire to move on and on so as to reach the great goal. He gives praise to God at every step, yet his is not a stationary condition; he is not the slave of his environment, but forever struggling and striving to master it.

The tenth idea ruling the Muslim mentality, as disclosed in the *Fātiḥah* ("the path of those upon whom You have bestowed favours") is the longing to walk in the footsteps of those who have received Divine blessings of any kind, temporal or spiritual, and the desire to be able to avoid the errors of those who have been the objects of Divine displeasure or those who have gone astray ("not those upon whom wrath is brought down, nor those who go astray"). The latter are the followers of the two extremes, while those who have received the Divine favours are those who keep to the middle path — which is the straight path.

With these ten ideas ruling the mind — and this is what is aimed at by the frequent repetition of the *Fātiḥah* in prayer — the Muslim is armed with the best weapons both for happiness and success.

Prayer, an incentive to action

Prayer to God does not mean that one has simply to entreat the Divine Being to grant him this or that favour and do nothing himself towards attaining it. Prayer is, in fact, a search for means and is thus an incentive to action. The central idea of the *Fātiḥah,* as already shown, is one of action or being led on to action, for here the supplicator does not ask for certain favours but only to be guided on the right path. The prayer is: *guide us on the right path,* or, as shown with reference to the meaning of *hidāyah* (guidance), *lead on to the goal by keeping us on the right path.* Prayer is thus only the means of leading a Muslim onwards and discovering the path by walking whereon he may attain the goal. It is a mistake to suppose that prayer for any object negatives the adoption of human means to gain it. Elsewhere in the Quran the acceptance of prayer is spoken of as rewarding men and women for the hard work they have done:

> "So their Lord accepted their prayer, [saying] I will not let the work of any worker among you to be lost, whether male or female, each of you is as the other." — 3:195

The rule has been laid down in the Quran in several places that no end can be gained without making a hard struggle for it, for example:

> "And that man can have nothing but what he strives for, and that his striving will soon be seen, then he will be rewarded for it with the fullest reward." [4] — 53:39–41

It may however be asked, what is the need for prayer if man must work for an end and avail himself of the means to gain it? Here, again, is a misconception as to the capabilities of man. It often happens that, despite the hardest struggle, a person is unable to gain an end, and finds himself quite helpless. In such a case prayer is a help, a source of strength, to the worker. He does not lose heart nor does he despair, because he believes that, though the means at his disposal have failed, though all around there are difficulties and darkness, though his own strength is failing, yet there is a Higher Power with Whom nothing is impossible, Who can still bring a ray of light to dispel the darkness and Who remains a perpetual source of strength for him in his help-lessness, and that by praying to Him he can still achieve what seems otherwise quite unattainable. That is the function of prayer, and it is thus one of the means to gain an end when all other means have failed, and a source of strength to a person at all times, but especially in moments of utter weakness and despair.

That such is the true function of prayer, and that it is only a source of greater energy and greater strength to enable man to face difficulties and achieve an end, is shown by the early history of Islam. The Holy Prophet Muhammad and his Companions were undoubtedly the greatest believers in prayer — they are spoken of in the Quran as spending two-thirds of the night, half the night or one-third of the night in prayer[5] — and yet this was the very band of men whose love for work knew no bounds, whose energy was inexhaustible and who faced extreme difficulties with an iron determination. Those who, in ten years, with the scantiest of resources, conquered two of the most powerful empires of the world, cannot be said to have been idle and inefficient. Prayer, in fact, transformed the neglected race of the Arabs into the most distinguished nation, turning an idle and ineffi-cient people into the most zealous and untiring workers for the pro-gress of humanity, in all phases of its advancement.

Section 2: *The Mosque*

No consecration is necessary

The Arabic word for mosque is *masjid,* which means 'a place where one prostrates oneself,' or 'a place of worship'. It should be borne in mind, in the first place, that prayer can be performed anywhere. No particularly consecrated place is necessary for the holding of the Divine service. To this effect there is an express saying of the Holy Prophet, who, speaking of some of his distinctions, is reported to have said:

"The whole of the earth has been made a mosque for me." [6]

A Muslim may, therefore, say his prayers anywhere he likes. The mere fact that he does so elsewhere than in a mosque detracts in no way from the efficacy of the prayer; nor does a building when constructed for the express purpose of prayer stand in need of consecration. All that is required is that the builder should declare his intention to have that building used as a place of prayer.

The mosque as a religious centre

In spite of what has been stated above, the mosque plays a more important part in Islam than does any other house of worship in any other religion. All religious buildings are resorted to generally once a week, but the mosque is visited five times a day for the remembrance of God's name. The whole atmosphere of the mosque is charged with the electricity of the Divine name. There is the call to prayer five times a day; there is the individual service, carried on in silence, but with God's name on the lips of every individual worshipper; there is the public service in which the Imam recites aloud portions of the Quran, that tell of Divine grandeur and glory, with the refrain of *Allāhu Akbar* repeated at every change of movement; and when the prayer is finished, there is again a chorus of voices speaking of Divine greatness, making the mosque echo and re-echo with the remembrance of God. It is true that God does not dwell in the mosque, but surely one feels His presence there.

A training ground of equality

Being a meeting-place of Muslims five times daily, the mosque serves as a training ground where the doctrine of the equality and fraternity of mankind is put into practical working. The mosque enables Muslims to meet five times a day, on terms of perfect equality and in a spirit of true brotherhood, all standing in a row before their great Maker, knowing no difference of colour or rank, all following the lead of one man. All differences and distinctions are, for the time being, obliterated. Without the mosque, the mere teaching of the brotherhood of man would have remained a dead letter as it is in so many other religions.

The mosque as a national centre

Besides being its religious centre, the mosque is also the cultural centre of the Muslim community. Here the Muslim community is educated on all questions of its welfare. The Friday sermon is a regular weekly lecture on all such questions, but, besides that, whenever in the time of the Holy Prophet and his early successors it became necessary to inform the Muslim community on any matter of importance, a sermon or a lecture was delivered in the mosque. It was the centre of all kinds of Muslim activities. Here all important national questions were settled. Deputations from Muslim as well as non-Muslim tribes were received in the mosque, and some of the more important deputations were also lodged there, as in the case of the famous Christian deputation from Najrān, and the deputation of Thaqīf, a polytheist tribe; and for this purpose tents were set up in the yard of the mosque.

Indeed, once on the occasion of a festival, the Prophet even allowed certain Abyssinians to give a display with shield and lance in the mosque.[7] Hassan ibn Thabit used to recite in the mosque his verses in defence of the Prophet against the abuse of his enemies.[8] Juridical affairs were also settled in the mosque,[9] and it was used in a number of other ways.[10] The mosque was thus not only the spiritual centre of the Muslims but also their political, educational and social centre — in fact, their national centre.

Respect for mosques

The fact, however, that the mosque may be used for other objects than the saying of prayer, does not in any way detract from its sacred character. It is primarily a place for Divine worship and must be treated as such. Nor are any proceedings allowed in the mosque, except such as related to the welfare of the Muslim community or have a national importance. The carrying on of any business or trade in the mosque is expressly forbidden.[11] Due respect must be shown to the house of God; thus even the raising of loud voices is denounced,[12] and spitting is expressly prohibited.[13] Saying prayers, with shoes on, is permitted[14] but the shoes must be clean and not dirty. The general practice is, however, to remove one's shoes at the door of the mosque as a mark of respect to the mosque and to ensure cleanliness. Keeping the mosque clean and neat is an act of great merit.[15]

Building of the mosque

The only requirement of the law of Islam regarding the building of a mosque is that it should face the Ka'bah, the Sacred Mosque of

Makkah. According to the Holy Quran, the Ka'bah was the first house for the worship of God that was ever built on this earth:

"Certainly the first house appointed for mankind is the one at Bakkah,[16] blessed and a guidance for nations." — 3:96

The Ka'bah, being thus the first mosque on earth, all mosques are built to face it. This practice is based on an express injunction contained in the Quran:

"And from whatsoever place you come forth, turn your face towards the Sacred Mosque. And wherever you are, turn your faces towards it…" — 2:150

The underlying purpose is stated just prior to this:

"And everyone has a goal to which he turns himself, so vie with one another in good works. Wherever you are, Allah will bring you all together." — 2:148

The *bringing of all together* clearly means *the making of all as one people,* so that beneath the ostensible unity of direction lies the real unity of purpose. Just as they have all one centre to turn to, they must set one goal before themselves. Thus the unity of the *Qiblah,* the direction of prayer, among Muslims stands for their unity of purpose, and forms the basis on which rests the brotherhood of Islam. Hence the Holy Prophet's saying:

"Do not call those who follow your *Qiblah* (*ahl Qiblah*) disbelievers (*kafir*)." [17]

Hadith recommends that the mosque should be as simple as possible. All adornments are generally avoided, in accordance with a saying of the Holy Prophet:

"I have not been commanded to raise the mosques high."[18]

According to another hadith, the Holy Prophet is reported to have said:

"The hour of doom (*al-sā'ah*) will not come till people vie with one another in [the building of] mosques." [19]

As shown earlier (see page 144), *al-sā'ah* in this case means the time of downfall of a nation.

The mosque built by the Holy Prophet himself at Madinah, called the Prophet's Mosque, was a simple structure in a vast court-yard in which tents could be pitched in time of need. The building was made of bricks baked in the sun, and the roofed portion, resting on columns consisting of the stems of palm-trees, was covered with palm-leaves and clay. The great mosques of Islam erected in the time of Umar were all simple structures like the Prophet's Mosque at Madinah, built either of reeds or bricks baked in the sun, with vast courtyards, large enough to accommodate congregations of even 40,000, the floors being generally strewn with pebbles. The custom of building mosques with domes and having one or more minarets grew up later, but even these are, notwithstanding their grandeur, monuments of simplicity, their chief adornment being the writing on theirs walls, in mosaic, of verses from the Quran.

A name may be given to any mosque, either that of the founder or of the people who resort to it, or any other name. In later times, Muslims belonging to different sects had their own mosques, the Ka'bah, the Central Mosque, gathering all together at the time of the pilgrimage. But when a mosque has once been built it is open to Muslims of all persuasions and no one has the right to prohibit Muslims of a certain persuasion or sect from entering it. This is a point on which the Quran contains a clear injunction:

> "And who is more unjust than he who prevents [people from entering] the mosques of Allah, from His name being remembered in them, and strives to ruin them?"
> — 2:114

Admission of women to mosques

There was no question in the Holy Prophet's time as to whether women may go to mosques. Women freely took part in religious services. There is indeed a hadith which tells us that on a certain night the Holy Prophet was very late in coming out to lead the night prayers, when the people had assembled in the mosque; and he came only on hearing Umar call out: "The women and the children are going to sleep".[20] This shows that women were in the mosque even at such a late hour. According to another hadith narrated by Aishah, women used to be present at the morning prayer, which was said at an hour so early that they returned to their houses while it was still dark.[21] Yet another hadith shows that even women who had children to suckle would come to the mosque, and that when the Prophet heard a baby crying, he would shorten his prayer lest the mother should feel inconvenienced;[22] while in one hadith it is stated that when the Holy Prophet had finished his prayers, he used to stay a little and did not rise until the women had left the mosque.[23] All these Hadith reports afford overwhelming evidence of the fact that women, just in the same way as men, used to frequent the mosques and that there was not the least restriction in this matter.

There are other reports which show that the Holy Prophet had given orders not to prohibit women from going to the mosque. For instance, there is one which quotes the Holy Prophet as saying:

> "Do not prohibit the handmaids of Allah from going to the mosques of Allah." [24]

According to another, the Holy Prophet is reported to have said that if a woman wanted to go to the mosque at night she should not be prohibited from doing so.[25] The words of a third hadith are more general:

> "When the wife of one of you asks permission to go out, she should not be prohibited from doing so." [26]

There was an express injunction that on the occasion of the *'Īd* festival women should go out to the place where prayers were said; women in a state of menstruation were also to be present, though they would not join the prayers.[27]

The practice for women to be present in the mosques at the time of prayer seems to have continued long enough after the Holy Prophet's time. Within the mosque they were not separated from men by any screen or curtain; only they formed into a line behind the men;[28] and though they were covered decently with an over-garment, they did not wear a veil. On the occasion of the great gathering of the pilgrimage (*hajj*), a woman is expressly forbidden to wear a veil.[29] Many other reports show that women formed themselves into a back row and that the men retained their seats until they had gone out of the mosque.[30] This practice seems to have existed for a very long time. Thus we read of women calling out *Allāhu Akbar* along with men in the mosque during the three days following *'Īd al-Aḍhā* as late as the time of Umar ibn Abdul Aziz, the Umayyad Caliph who ruled about the end of the first century.[31] In the year 256 A.H., the

Governor of Makkah is said to have tied ropes between the columns to make a separate place for women.[32] Later on, the practice grew up of erecting a wooden barrier in the mosque to form a separate enclosure for women, but by and by women were altogether shut out from mosques.

Another question connected with this subject relates to the entrance of women into mosques during their menstruation. It must be borne in mind, in the first place, that in Islam a state of menstruation is not looked upon as a state of impurity, as in many other religions. All that the Holy Quran says about menstruation is that conjugal relations should be discontinued during the state of menstruation.[33] According to Hadith, a woman is exempted from saying her prayers, or keeping the fast, as long as menstruation lasts. As regards pilgrimage, she may perform all obligations except making the circuits of the Ka'bah *(tawāf)*, but there is no idea of impurity attaching to her in this condition. There is a very large number of reports showing that all kinds of social relations with women in this condition were permitted, that the husband and wife could occupy the same bed, that the Holy Prophet used to recite the Quran when sitting in close contact with his wife who had her courses on, and that a woman in this condition was allowed to handle the Quran.[34] There is not the least idea of defilement in a menstruating woman. Even the very clothes which she wears need not be washed if they are not actually defiled.[35]

The Imam

The most important office-bearer in the mosque[36] is the *Imām,* the man who leads the prayers and delivers the sermon (*khuṭbah*) on Friday. The honour of leading the prayers was, in the time of the Holy Prophet, and also for a long time after that, given to the best man in the community. Bukhari has the following heading for one of his chapters: "Those who are well-grounded in knowledge and possess the greatest excellence are most entitled to lead prayer".[37] Abu Dawud narrates sayings of the Holy Prophet requiring the honour of leading the prayer to be conferred on the man who was most learned in the Quran, or in a case where two men were equal in that respect, other considerations were to be applied.[38]

The Holy Prophet himself was the Imam in the central mosque at Madinah and after him his successors, the respective caliphs, Abu Bakr, Umar and Uthman. A governor appointed to a province was also appointed as Imam to lead the prayers. The office of the spiritual leader and that of the temporal leader were combined in one person for a long time. The priest and the present-day *mulla* had no place in early Islam. Nor does the Imam, like the mosque, stand in need of consecration, because everyone is consecrated by entering into the fold of Islam. Anyone can lead the prayers in the absence of the Imam, and anyone may act as Imam when several people are gathered together. A woman is also spoken of as acting as an Imam, while men followed her, though it was in her own house.[39]

Section 3: *Purification*

Outward purification as a prelude to prayer

Prayer, according to the Holy Quran and Hadith, is the means for the purification of the soul, and also of the body and the garments one wears which is declared to be necessary as a preparation for prayer. The 74th chapter of the Quran is the second revelation which the Holy Prophet received, and its first five verses may here be quoted to show the importance of outward cleanliness in the religion of Islam:

> "O you who wrap yourself up! Arise and warn, and your Lord do magnify, and your garments do purify, and uncleanliness do shun". — 74 : 1–5

Thus warning the people, magnifying the Lord which is done through prayer, and purifying the garments and the body, are laid down here as three fundamental duties. The two ideas, the purification of the body and of the soul, are very often mentioned together in the Quran, for example:

> "Surely Allah loves those who turn much to Him, and He loves those who purify themselves." — 2 : 222

Hadith also lays special stress on outward purification. According to one, "purification is the key to prayer";[40] and according to another, "purification is one-half of faith".[41] Inward purity is the real aim, but outward purity is a necessary preparation.

The Holy Quran recommends good clothing generally and in case of prayer. It is stated that clothes are meant as a covering and also as a beauty:

> "O children of Adam, we have indeed sent down to you
> clothing to cover your shame and for beauty; and clothing
> that guards against evil — that is the best." —7:26

The *clothing that guards against evil* indicates that, as virtue is an embellishment of the mind, when man has seen the good of embellishing his person, he should be aware of the necessity of embellishing his mind.

Further on, it says:

> "O children of Adam, attend to your adornment at every
> time [or place] of prayer". — 7:31

This shows that when assembling in mosques for prayer, attention must be paid to outward appearance and purity as well. One who is dirty in clothing or person would undoubtedly be offensive to others. Hence it is specially laid down that, in the larger gatherings on Fridays, everyone must take a bath before coming to prayer, and use scent if possible. But what is specially aimed at is adornment in a spiritual sense. A Muslim must attend to inner beautification, for prayer is really meant as an aid to the beauty of the soul. He must come to prayer with a heart free from all impurities and full of the highest aspirations and noblest sentiments.

Wuḍū

Wuḍū, in the terminology of Islamic law, means the washing of certain parts of the body before prayers. The necessary details of *wuḍū* are given in the Holy Quran:

> "O you who believe, when you rise up for prayer, wash your
> faces, and your hands up to the elbows, and wipe your heads,
> and [wash] your feet up to the ankles." — 5:6

The practice of the Holy Prophet, as recorded in Hadith, contains substantially the same details. Briefly these may be described as follows:

1. The hands are first washed up to the wrists.
2. The mouth is then cleaned with water, or by rinsing with a toothbrush and by gargling if necessary.
3. The nostrils are then cleaned by snuffing a little water into them and blowing the nose if necessary.

4.   The face is then washed from the forehead to the chin and from one ear to the other.

5.   Then the right arm, and after that the left, is washed from the wrist to the elbow.

6.   The head is then wiped over with wet hands, and the inner side of the ears wiped with forefingers and its outer side with thumbs.

7.   The feet are then washed up to the ankles, the right foot being washed first. If socks or stockings are being worn, and they have been put on after performing *wuḍū*, it is not necessary to take them off; the three fingers of the wet hand may be passed over them. The same practice may be resorted to in the case of shoes. If the socks or the shoes are then taken off, the *wuḍū* remains. It is, however, necessary that the feet should be washed once in every twenty-four hours.

Wuḍū may be performed before every prayer, but the necessity for it arises only when there has been passing of urine, stools or wind, or when one has been fast asleep.

Taking a bath

The taking of a bath is rendered necessary in certain cases before prayer can be performed. It becomes necessary after nocturnal emission of seminal fluid, sexual intercourse, the period of menstruation, and the period of post-natal bleeding. It undoubtedly promotes habits of cleanliness and is conducive to health. The direction is contained in the Holy Quran itself:

> "And if you are under an obligation to perform a total ablution (*junub*),[42] then wash yourselves." — 5:6

Bathing is also enjoined in Hadith on occasions of large gatherings, such as the Friday prayers and the *'Īd* prayers, when clean clothes must also be put on and scent used if available. These directions serve as a preparation for going before a higher Presence, and help to wrest one's attention from lower objects and divert it to the higher, and they also make the atmosphere in which gatherings of people take place, purer and healthier.

Tayammum

When water is not available, still it is necessary to perform an act which diverts attention from bodily purification to the purity of the soul, which is the aim of prayer. The direction is thus laid down in the Holy Quran:

> "And if you are sick, or on a journey, or one of you comes from the toilet, or you have had [sexual] contact with women, and you cannot find water, then resort (*tayammamū*) to pure earth and wipe your faces and your hands with it. Allah does not desire to place a burden on you but He wishes to purify you, and that He may complete His favour on you, so that you may give thanks." — 5:6

The word *tayammum* means 'resorting', or 'betaking oneself', to something, and since the word is used here in connection with betaking oneself to pure earth, *tayammum* has come technically to mean this particular practice.

Thus when a person is unable to find water, or when the use of water or the taking of a bath is harmful, he is enjoined to avail himself of pure earth, which is stated to be a means of purification. Now, wiping of the face and the hands with earth does not serve the purpose of bodily purification; therefore it is the purification of the soul which is intended here. By the order of *tayammum* attention is thus drawn to the inner purpose underlying *wuḍū* and the bath.

As stated in the Holy Quran, and amplified in Hadith, *tayammum* consists of striking both hands on pure earth or anything containing pure dust, then blowing off the excess of dust from the hands, and passing the hands over the face and the backs of the two hands, the left over the right and the right over the left.[43]

Section 4: *The Call to Prayer*

The origin of the call to prayer (*adhān*)

The word *adhān* means an 'announcement', or an announcement *of prayer* and *of its time*— the *call to prayer*.[44] Regarding its origin, Bukhari tells us that when Muslims came to Madinah, they used, at first, to have a time appointed for prayer, at which they all gathered together. This arrangement being unsatisfactory, a consultation was held at which, suggestions for ringing a bell or blowing a horn having been rejected, Umar proposed that a man should be appointed who should call out for prayer. At this the Holy Prophet ordered Bilal to call out for prayers in the words of *adhān* as we now have it.[45] The need for the call to prayer was felt after the emigration of the Muslims to Madinah because at Makkah the unbelievers did not allow them to say their prayers openly.

The delivery of the Call to Prayer

The Call to Prayer is delivered in every mosque, or wherever there is a gathering for congregational prayer,[46] five times a day. The call is given out from a minaret or some raised platform in a loud voice. The man giving the call stands with his face to the *Qiblah,* i.e., towards Makkah, with both hands raised to the ears, chanting the following sentences in the order given:

Allāhu Akbar, Allāhu Akbar, Allāhu Akbar, Allāhu Akbar.	Allah is the Greatest (repeated four times).
Ashhadu an lā ilāha ill-Allāh, Ashhadu an lā ilāha ill-Allāh.	I bear witness there is no god but Allah (repeated twice).
Ashhadu anna Muḥammad-ar Rasūl-ullah, Ashhadu anna Muḥammad-ar Rasūl-ullah.	I bear witness that Muhammad is the Messenger of Allah (repeated twice).
Ḥayya ‘al-aṣ-ṣalāh, Ḥayya ‘al-aṣ-ṣalāh.	Come to prayer (repeated twice, turning the face to the right).
Ḥayya ‘al-al-falāḥ, Ḥayya ‘al-al- falāḥ.	Come to success (repeated twice, turning the face to the left).
Allāhu Akbar, Allāhu Akbar.	Allah is the Greatest (repeated twice).
Lā ilāha ill-Allāh.	There is no god but Allah.

The following sentence is added in the call to the morning (*fajr*) prayer after *Ḥayya ‘ala-l- falāḥ* ('Come to success'):

Aṣ-ṣalātu khair-un min-annaum, Aṣ-ṣalātu khair-un min-an-naum.	Prayer is better than sleep (repeated twice).

Significance of *adhān*

The *adhān* is not only an announcement of the time of prayer, but also of the great principles of Islam and of the significance underlying them. It is an announcement, made five times daily, of the Unity of God and of the prophethood of Muhammad, which are the two fundamental principles of Islam. But it goes further and carries also the real significance of the Unity of God which is contained in the words *Allāhu Akbar* or Allah is the Greatest, so that man must bow only before Him, and before none else. And the real message of religion, the realization of the Divine in man, is declared with equal force, "Come to prayer", and immediately thereafter, "Come to success". Coming to prayer is the attainment of success in life because it is only through the realization of the Divine in man that complete self-development (*falāḥ*) is attained. The meaningless ringing of a bell or blowing of a trumpet is replaced by an announcement of the principles of Islam and a declaration that anyone may attain to success in life through prayer.

Section 5: *Times of Prayer*

Regularization of prayer

The institution of prayer in Islam is a perfectly regularized institution, and it is the first lesson which a Muslim learns in the organization of things. Without divesting the individual of the liberty to pray to God at whatsoever place and time and in whatsoever manner he or she likes, Islam has thoroughly organized the institution of prayer. As stated earlier, prayer brings about not only the development of the individual but also a perfect development of society, being a means for the unification of humanity. This latter object cannot be obtained without a properly organized institution of prayer with a fixed place and fixed times and a uniform method, so that through it individuals may be brought together. Hence it is that the Holy Quran requires prayer to be said at appointed times:

> "Prayer indeed has been enjoined on the believers at fixed times." — 4:103

Times of prayer

The Quran does not explicitly state the times of prayer, but it does give indications of these times. For example, it is stated:

> "Keep up prayer from the declining of the sun till the darkness of the night, and the recital of the Quran at dawn. Surely the recital of the Quran at dawn is witnessed." — 17:78

Now, as the practice of the Holy Prophet shows, there are four prayers which follow one another successively: the early afternoon prayer, the late afternoon prayer, the sunset prayer and the night prayer; and the time of each of the first three extends till the starting time of the next prayer (except for a very short interval, when the sun is actually setting, between the late afternoon and the sunset prayer). These four prayers are, therefore, spoken of together in the words "from the declining of the sun till the darkness of the night", the times of the first and last of these being clearly mentioned. The morning prayer is mentioned separately as "the recital of the Quran at dawn".

In another verse it is stated:

> "And celebrate the praise of your Lord[*] before the rising of the sun and before its setting, and glorify Him during the hours of the night and parts of the day, that you may be well-pleased." — 20:130

Here the morning prayer ("before the rising of the sun") and the late afternoon prayer ("before its setting") are indicated while the two evening prayers are spoken of together as being "during the hours of the night". A third verse of the later Makkah period throws further light on the times of the prayers:

> "And keep up prayer at the two ends of the day and in the first hours of the night." — 11:114

The addition of the words "first hours" of the night here makes it clear that, apart from a prayer in the darkness of the night, which is spoken of in 17:78, there is also a prayer in the "first hours", that is to say, immediately after sunset.[47] Thus, in an explicit way, the morning prayer, the early afternoon and the night prayer are referred to in 17:78, the late afternoon prayer in 20:130, and the sunset prayer in 11:114.

Five obligatory prayers

The five times of prayer are thus mentioned in the Quran, not in one place but in many, as if by way of reference to something which already existed. As a matter of fact, the Quran only enjoins the organization (*iqāmah*) of prayer and the details of that organization were given by the Holy Prophet guided by the Holy Spirit[48] or by his inner revelation. The following are the times of the five obligatory prayers, and their names, according to the practice of the Holy Prophet:

---

[*] This refers to prayer as shown by the context, since 20:132 says: "And enjoin prayer on your people and steadily adhere to it."

1. *Fajr,* or the early morning prayer, is said after dawn and before sunrise. It is mentioned by this name in the Quran in 17:78 and 24:58. If the time is missed, then the prayer may still be said even though the sun may have risen.[49]

2. *Ẓuhr,* or the early afternoon prayer, is said when the sun begins to decline, and its time extends until the next prayer. In the summer it is better to delay it till the severity of the sun is mitigated a little.[50]

3. *'Aṣr,* or the late afternoon prayer, is said when the sun is about midway on its course to setting, and its time extends till the sun begins to set.[51]

4. *Maghrib,* or the sunset prayer, is said immediately after the sun sets, and its time extends till the red glow in the west disappears.

5. *'Ishā',* or the night prayer, is said when the red glow in the west disappears, and its time extends till midnight. It is mentioned by name in the Quran in 24:58.

Combining prayers

The two afternoons prayers, *Ẓuhr* and *'Aṣr,* may be combined when one is on a journey, and so may the two night prayers, *Maghrib* and *Ishā'.*[52] Such a combination is also allowed when it is raining, and according to one hadith this combination may be effected even when there is neither journey nor rain.[53] The Holy Prophet is said to have combined prayers "so that his followers may not be in difficulty".[54] When two prayers are thus combined, their time is from the starting time of the earlier prayer to the ending time of the later prayer.

Voluntary prayers

The only voluntary prayer spoken of in the Quran is *Tahajjud:*

> "And during a part of the night, keep awake by it, beyond what is incumbent on you; maybe your Lord will raise you to a position of great glory." — 17:79

While it is voluntary for Muslims generally, the Holy Prophet, in one of the earliest revelations in chapter 73, was commanded to observe it and in the same chapter, we are told further on, that this prayer was regularly observed by the Prophet and even by his Companions.[55] It is said after midnight, after one has had some sleep. In some Hadith reports, another voluntary prayer called *Ḍuḥā* is mentioned. *Ḍuḥā* is the time before noon when the sun is high.

Section 6: *The Service*

The form and spirit of the prayer

The Arabic word for prayer is *ṣalāt,* which originally means 'praying' or 'the making of a supplication', and was employed in this sense before Islam. In the Holy Quran, the word is used both in the technical sense of Divine service as established by Islam, and in the general sense of simply *praying* as in "surely your prayer is a relief to them" (9:103), i.e., that the prayer of the Holy Prophet for his followers brings comfort to them.

In the technical sense it is almost always used with one of the derivatives of the word *iqāmah,* which means 'keeping a thing in a right state'. Hence the *iqāmah* of *ṣalāt* would mean the *keeping of the prayer in a right state,* which includes both the proper observance of the outward form and maintaining its true spirit. The purification before prayer, the mosque, the fixing of times and finally the settling of the form, are all parts of the outward organization, without which the spirit could not have been kept alive. Hence a form has been fixed for the institution of the Islamic prayer, the individual having, in addition, liberty to pray to God in accordance with the desire of his own soul, when and where and as he or she likes. Like the times of prayer, the form was revealed to the Holy Prophet by the Holy Spirit or Gabriel.

The outward form is not, however, the end; it is only a help. Thus in the Holy Quran, the observance of the form of the prayer is spoken of as being meant to free a person from evil:

> "And keep up prayer at the two ends of the day and in the first hours of the night. Surely good deeds take away evil deeds. This is a reminder for the mindful." — 11:114

And only they are said to attain self-development, or success, who are true to the spirit of the prayer:

> "Successful indeed are the believers, who are humble in their prayers". — 23:1–2

And mere form without the spirit is condemned in one of the earliest revelations:

"So woe to the praying ones, who are unmindful of [the spirit of] their prayers, who do good to be seen, and refrain from acts of kindness." — 107:4–7

It is a great mistake to think that Islam only requires the form to be observed; it no doubt enjoins a form, but only a form with a spirit in it.

Parts of the Divine service

Each service has two parts, the congregational, which is called *farḍ* (obligatory), and individual, which is called *sunnah* (the Holy Prophet's practice). Both are made up of a number of sections, each called a *rak'ah,* varying from two to four. Literally the *rak'ah* is an act of bowing down before God, but technically it indicates one complete act of devotion which includes standing, bowing down, prostration and sitting reverentially, and is thus a kind of a unit in the Divine service. The order in which these different postures are adopted is a natural order. The worshipper first stands reverentially and offers certain prayers; then he bows down and glorifies God; then he stands up again praising God; then falls prostrate placing his forehead on the ground and glorifying God; then he sits down in a reverential position and makes a petition; then again falls down in prostration. Each change of posture (except as mentioned later) is performed with the utterance of the words *Allāhu Akbar,* "Allah is the Greatest", known as *takbīr.*

The obligatory part of the prayer which, in a congregation, is performed after the Imam, contains the following number of *rak'ahs:*

> *Fajr* or morning prayer 2
> *Ẓuhr* or early afternoon prayer 4
> *'Aṣr* or late afternoon prayer 4
> *Maghrib* or sunset prayer 3
> *'Ishā'* or night prayer 4

The individual parts (*sunnah*) contain the following number of *rak'ahs,* which are said before or after the obligatory part as indicated:

> *Fajr* .... 2 *rak'ahs* before.
> *Ẓuhr* .... 4 *rak'ahs* before, 2 *rak'ahs* after.
> *Maghrib* .... 2 *rak'ahs* after.
> *'Ishā'* .... 2 *rak'ahs* after, followed by 3 *rak'ahs* called *witr.*
>   *Witr* is really part of the *tahajjud* prayer (see later).

Postures of prayer

The prayer is started with the standing position (*qiyām*). The worshipper, turning his face in the direction of the Ka'bah, the Central Mosque of the world, raises both hands to his ears and utters the *Allāhu Akbar* ("Allah is the Greatest"). With this utterance, attention to everything but prayer is prohibited. As a sign of reverence for the Holy Presence, before Whom the worshipper stands, the hands are thereafter folded on the breast. That is the preferable position, but they may as well be folded lower below the navel, or they may be left quite free in the natural position. These are small matters in which people may differ according to their tastes. The essential factor is that the worshipper should stand in a reverential position, having the feeling that he is standing before the Holy and Majestic Presence. In this standing position, the Divine Being is praised and prayers are addressed to Him and certain portions of the Holy Quran are recited, as will be explained later on.

This is followed by the posture known as *rukū'*, which means 'bowing down'. The change of posture is marked by the utterance of *Allāhu Akbar*. In this posture the worshipper, while standing, bows forward and places both his hands on his knees and utters words declaring Divine glory.

Next comes the *sajdah,* or prostration, but before falling down in *sajdah* the worshipper rises up from the *rukū',* so that he again assumes the standing position with both hands hanging down freely, and along with the assumption of this position the following words are uttered: *Sami' Allāhu li-man ḥamidah,* meaning, "Allah listens to him who praises Him". And, with this, words of Divine praise are uttered, *Rabba-nā wa la-k-al-ḥamd,* that is, "Our Lord! all praise is due to You". After thus standing up, the worshipper prostrates himself with *Allāhu Akbar* on his lips. In this state, the toes of both feet, both knees, both hands and the forehead touch the ground, and thus a posture of the utmost humility is assumed, while words declaring the Divine glory and Divine greatness are on the lips of the worshipper. This posture is assumed twice, the worshipper in between raising his head with *Allāhu Akbar* on his lips and briefly assuming the sitting position.

After the first *rak'ah,* the worshipper stands up, while uttering *Allāhu Akbar,* and performs the second *rak'ah* in exactly the same manner as the first. After the second *rak'ah* the sitting position (*qa'dah*) is assumed, with the open hands placed on the knees. This position is kept so long as the necessary recitals are made.

If the prayer consists of two *rak'ahs,* it ends in this position. In the case of three or four *rak'ahs* the standing position is again assumed, while uttering *Allāhu Akbar,* and the required number of *rak'ahs* (one or two) is performed in the same manner. The last position, with which the prayer comes to an end, is in all cases the sitting position and the prayer concludes with the utterance of the words *as-salāmu 'alai-kum wa raḥmat-ullāh,* meaning 'Peace be on you and the mercy of Allah'.

Departure from these postures

The different postures are sufficient to inspire the heart of the worshipper with true awe of the Divine Being, and to bring before his mind a picture of the great majesty and glory of God, as he stands up, then bows down, then places his forehead on the ground. It cannot be denied that the different postures of the body have a corresponding effect on the mind, and Islam seeks to make the spiritual experience of the Muslim perfect by making him assume one position of reverential humility after another, so that he may pass from one experience to another.

The law allows modifications in certain cases; as, for instance, when a person is sick, he may say his prayers in a sitting position, or if unable to sit down, he may say them while lying down, dispensing with even bowing down and prostration if necessary.[56] So, on a journey, a person is allowed to say his prayers while riding a horse or a camel, and though this is expressly allowed only in the case of voluntary prayers, the obligatory (*farḍ*) prayer, while one is travelling in any vehicle, would follow the same rule. The postures adopted in all such cases must be subject to the exigencies of the situation. Even the direction of prayer may not be towards the *Qiblah.*[57] However, when there is no exigency, one may not make a departure from the form prescribed by the Holy Prophet.

Remembrance of God (*dhikr*)

Corresponding to the different postures of humility which the worshipper assumes in saying his prayers, he is enjoined to give expression to the praise and glory of God, to His great attributes of love, mercy, forgiveness, etc., to confess his own weakness, to pray for Divine help to support him in his weakness and for Divine guidance to lead him aright and make him achieve the goal of his existence. All such expressions are known in Arabic by the one name *dhikr,* which is generally translated as *remembrance.* The whole of prayer is called in the Holy Quran *dhikr Allāh,* or the remembrance of Allah.[58] The Quran itself is also frequently referred to as *dhikr.* Hence, whether a portion of the Quran is recited in prayer, or words giving expression to Divine glory and greatness are uttered, as taught by the Holy Prophet, all goes by the name of *dhikr.*

Dhikr in standing posture (*qiyām*)

The standing posture starts with the utterance of *Allāhu Akbar,* known as *takbīr.* Nothing besides the *takbīr* must be said to open the prayers. Between the first *takbīr* and the recital of the opening chapter of the Holy Quran, which is the most essential part of the prayer, several kinds of *dhikr* are reported from the Holy Prophet. The best known is as follows:[*]

> *Subhāna-k-Allāhumma wa bi-hamdi-ka wa tabārak-asmu-ka wa taʿāla jaddu-ka wa lā ilāha ghairu-ka.*
>
> Glory be to You, O Allah, and Yours is the praise, and blessed is Your name, and exalted is Your majesty, and there is none to be served besides You.

These *dhikr* are uttered in a low voice not heard by others. This is followed by the words:

> *A ʿūdhu bi-llāhi min ash-shaitān-ir-rajīm.*
>
> I seek the refuge of Allah from the accursed devil.

The prayer actually opens with the first chapter of the Holy Quran, the *Fātihah,* prefixed by the well-known *Bismillāh,* as follows:

> *Bismillāh-ir-Rahmān-ir-Rahīm.*
>
> In the name of Allah, the Beneficent, the Merciful.

---

[*]*Editor's Note:* Many of the *dhikr* and prayers reproduced by Maulana Muhammad Ali in the *The Religion of Islam* have been omitted in this Handbook. These are also given in his book *The Muslim Prayer Book.* The reader should refer to those two books for further details.

<table>
<tr><td>1. Al-ḥamdu li-llāhi Rabb-il-'ālamīn.</td><td>Praise be to Allah, the Lord of the worlds.</td></tr>
<tr><td>2. Ar-Raḥmān-ir-Raḥīm.</td><td>The Beneficent, the Merciful.</td></tr>
<tr><td>3. Māliki yaum-id-dīn.</td><td>Master of the Day of Recompense.</td></tr>
<tr><td>4. Iyyā-ka na'budu wa iyyā-ka nasta'īn.</td><td>You do we serve and You do we beseech for help.</td></tr>
<tr><td>5. Ihdi-n-aṣ-ṣirāt-al-mustaqīm.</td><td>Guide us on the right path.</td></tr>
<tr><td>6. Ṣirāt-alladhīna an'amta 'alai-him.</td><td>The path of those upon whom You have bestowed favours.</td></tr>
<tr><td>7. <u>Ghair-il-maghdūbi</u> 'alai-him wa l-aḍ-ḍāllīn.</td><td>Not those upon whom wrath is brought down, nor those who go astray.</td></tr>
</table>

At the close of the above is said *Āmīn,* which means "Be it so!"

The recital of the *Fātiḥah* is followed by any other portion of the Quran, which may be a short or a long chapter or it may be verses selected from anywhere. Often, chapter 112, entitled *al-Ikhlāṣ* or 'The Unity', is recited, which is a chapter of four very short verses containing the doctrine of the Unity of the Divine Being in its perfection.

The standing position in the second *rak'ah* is commenced with the *Fātiḥah* (verses 1 to 7 as above), followed by some recitation from the Quran as in the first *rak'ah*. In the third and fourth *rak'ahs*, only the *Fātiḥah* is essential.

Dhikr in bowing (*rukū'*) and prostration (*sajdah*)

The *dhikr* during bowing down is as follows:

Subḥāna Rabbiy-al-'Aẓīm.	Glory be to my Lord, the Great.

During prostration it is similar:

Subḥāna Rabbiy-al-A'lā.	Glory be to my Lord, the Most High.

In each case it is repeated three times.

The *sajdah,* in particular, is the most fitting position for addressing any prayer in any language to the Almighty. There are reports showing that the Holy Prophet used to pray in the *sajdah* in both forms: in the form of glorifying and praising the Divine Being and in the form of petition or asking the Divine Being for His favours.[59] Numerous forms of these prayers are given in Hadith, and all of them show an outpouring of the soul in a state of true submission, which is what, in fact, every worshipper needs, and therefore he is free to express the yearning of his soul before his great Maker in any way that he likes.

Dhikr in sitting posture

There are two sitting postures, the first being the *jalsah,* the short sitting between the two *sajdahs.* A prayer which may be addressed in this position is as follows:

Allāhumm-aghfir-lī w-arham-nī w-ahdi-nī wa ʻāfi-nī w-arzuq-nī.	O Allah! grant me protection and have mercy on me and guide me and grant me security and grant me sustenance.

The second sitting position, the *qaʻdah,* is assumed after the first two *rakʻahs* have been offered. During this the following prayer is offered:

At-tahyyātu li-llāhi w-assalawātu w-at-tayyibātu. Assalāmu ʻalai-ka ayyuh-annabiyyu wa rahmat-ullāhi wa barakātu-hū. As-salāmu ʻalai-nā wa ʻala ʻibādi-llāh-iṣ-ṣāliḥīn. Ashhadu an lā ilāha ill-Allāhu wa ashhadu anna Muhammad-an ʻabdu-hū wa rasūluh.	All services rendered by words and bodily actions and sacrifice of wealth are due to Allah. Peace be on you, O Prophet, and the mercy of Allah and His blessings. Peace be on us and on the righteous servants of Allah. I bear witness that there is no god but Allah, and I bear witness that Muhammad is His servant and His Messenger.

In a prayer of two *rakʻahs,* the worshipper continues in this sitting position reciting other *dhikr* as explained below, and then concludes the prayer. In a prayer of three or four *rakʻahs,* the worshipper now stands up to complete the remaining one or two *rakʻahs,* till reaching again this point in the *qaʻdah,* where the *dhikr* above has been recited, and carries on as follows in the next paragraph.

Continuing in the sitting position, the following *dhikr,* called *al-ṣalā ʻala-l-Nabiyy,* is added:

Allāhumma ṣalli ʿalā Muḥammad-in wa ʿalā āli Muḥammad-in kamā ṣallaita ʿalā Ibrāhīma wa ʿalā āli Ibrāhīma; inna-ka Ḥamīd-un Majīd.	O Allah! exalt Muhammad and the true followers of Muhammad as You exalted Abraham and the true followers of Abraham; surely You are Praised, Magnified.
Allāhumma bārik ʿalā Muḥammad-in wa ʿalā āli Muḥammad-in kamā bārakta ʿalā Ibrāhīma wa ʿalā āli Ibrāhīma; inna-ka Ḥamīd-un Majīd.	O Allah! bless Muhammad and the true followers of Muhammad as You blessed Abraham and the true followers of Abraham; surely You are Praised, Magnified.

Abraham's prayer for himself and his progeny from the Holy Quran, 14:40–41, is often added at this point. This may be followed by any other prayers which the worshipper may wish to offer.

The concluding *dhikr* in the sitting position is *taslīm,* or the utterance of the following words:

As-salāmu ʿalai-kum wa raḥmat-ullāh.	Peace be on you and the mercy of Allah.

These words are uttered turning the face to the right and then uttered again turning the face to the left. This concludes the prayer.

Dhikr after finishing prayer

There is no reference in any hadith to the Holy Prophet raising up hands for supplication after offering prayers, as has become the general practice, but some kinds of *dhikr* are recommended. In addition to these, the recital of verse 2:255 of the Quran, known as *āyat al-kursiyy* (the verse of Divine knowledge), is also recommended, as well as that of the words *subḥān-Allāh* (glory be to Allah), *al-ḥamdu li-llāh* (praise be to Allah), and *Allāhu Akbar* (Allah is the Greatest), several times each.

The congregation

As already noted, the essential part of the obligatory prayers called *farḍ* is said in congregation.* The very form of the different prayers

---

* When an individual is unable to join a congregation, he or she says the obligatory part in the same manner as the *sunnah* part is said individually.

to be recited shows that Islam has laid special stress on prayer in congregation. The whole Muslim body that can assemble in one place, both men and women, must gather at the appointed time, praise and glorify God, and address their petitions to Him in a body. All people stand shoulder to shoulder in a row, or in several rows, as the case may be, their feet being in one line, and one person, chosen from among them and called the Imam, which means *leader,* leads the prayer and stands in front, with the rows behind him. If, however, there are women in the congregation, they form a row by themselves at the back, and after the congregational prayer is over the men are not allowed to leave their places until the women have gone out. The distance between the Imam and the first row, or between the different rows, is such that the persons in each row may be able to prostrate themselves, so that their heads may be almost at the feet of the front row. The smallest number of people that can form a congregation is two, one leading the prayer and the other following, and these two stand together, the Imam a little ahead, say about six inches (fifteen centimetres), and standing to the left while the follower stands on the Imam's right. If a third person joins while the prayer is thus being led, either the Imam moves forward or the person following moves backward, so that the two who follow form a row.

The discipline is so perfect that the followers are bound to obey the Imam, even though he may make a mistake, though they have the right to point out the mistake, by pronouncing the words *subḥān-Allāh* (glory be to Allah). This amounts to a hint that God alone is free from all defects, such being the meaning of the word *subḥāna.* It is, however, the judgment of the Imam which is the decisive factor, and the followers, after giving the hint, must still obey him.

Prayer announcement (*iqāmah*)

To announce that the congregational prayer is ready, the *iqāmah* (which means 'causing to stand') is pronounced in a loud voice, though not so loud as the call to prayer (*adhān*). The sentences of the *adhān* (see page 209) are also the sentences which form the *iqāmah,* but with the difference that the sentences which are repeated in the *adhān* may be uttered only once, and the following sentence is uttered twice after *Ḥayya ʿala-l- falāḥ:*

Qad qāmati-ṣ-ṣalāh.   Prayer is ready.

The additional words of the morning *adhān* also do not find a place in the *iqāmah,* which is generally recited by the person who calls out the *adhān,* though in his absence anyone else standing in the row behind the Imam may do so.

Congregational prayer

When the *iqāmah* has been called out, the followers do not begin the prayer until the Imam starts it by saying *Allāhu Akbar* in a loud voice. With the utterance of these words by the Imam, the whole congregation, like the Imam, raises hands to ears while uttering the same words in a low voice. Both the Imam and the followers then recite, still in a low voice, some introductory *dhikr,* as stated above (see page 217).

After this, in the two *rak'ahs* of the morning prayer (*Fajr*) and the first two *rak'ahs* of the sunset and early night prayers (*Maghrib* and *'Ishā*), the Imam recites the opening chapter of the Holy Quran (*Fātiḥah*) in a loud voice. He ought to pause slightly after every verse, so that during the interval the followers may silently repeat each sentence.[60] After the Imam has recited the *Fātiḥah,* the whole congregation says *Āmīn,* either in a loud or a low voice, the former, no doubt, having the greater effect. After this, the Imam recites in a loud voice any portion of the Holy Quran, the followers listening in silence, occasionally glorifying God or praising Him or addressing some petition to Him in accordance with the subject-matter of the verses that are being recited.

In the case of the first two *rak'ahs* of the other prayers (*Ẓuhr* and *Aṣr*), prayer is more in the nature of a meditation, like the private prayer, and the Imam and the followers individually recite the *Fāti-ḥah* and a portion of the Quran inaudibly. In the last two *rak'ahs* of both these prayers and the early night prayer (*'Ishā*), as well as in the last *rak'ah* of the sunset prayer (*Maghrib*), the *Fātiḥah* is recited in a similar manner, individually and inaudibly.

The utterance of *Allāhu Akbar* at the changes of posture, and of the final *taslīm* (the words *As-salāmu 'alai-kum wa raḥmat-ullāh*) ending the prayer, are, however, done by the Imam in a loud voice in all congregational prayers, and so is the *dhikr Sami' Allāhu li-man ḥamidah* recited on rising from the bowing position while the followers in this last case say in a low voice, *Rabba-nā wa la-k-al-*

ḥamd (see page 215). The various *dhikr* during bowing down and prostration and the sitting posture are repeated in a low voice by the Imam, as well as those who follow him.

Mistake in prayer

If a mistake is made in prayer, or the worshipper is doubtful about the number of *rak'ahs,* he adds, what is called *sajdah sahw* (*sahw* meaning 'mistake'), at the close of prayer, just before the *taslīm.* It consists of performing a double prostration like the ordinary prostration in prayer. If the Imam has made a similar mistake, he, along with the whole congregation, performs *sajdah sahw.*

Late-comers

A person who comes in late joins the congregational service at the point it has reached. If he has missed one or more *rak'ahs,* he must complete the missing number after the Imam has finished. A *rak'ah* is deemed to have been completed behind the Imam if a person joins the bowing position (*rukū'*), though he may have missed the standing position.

Prayer in the case of one who is on a journey

If one is on a journey, the prayers are shortened. There is some difference of opinion as to whether it is necessary that the journey should extend over a certain specified distance or a certain specified time. But the best judge on this matter is the person concerned. A time-limit of a day and a night as the minimum is favoured. The *sunnahs* are all dropped with the exception of the two of the morning prayer. The number of obligatory *rak'ahs* in the *Ẓuhr, 'Aṣr* and *'Ishā'* is reduced from four to two, while the three *rak'ahs* of the *Maghrib* remain unchanged. In addition to this, the person who is journeying is allowed to combine the *Ẓuhr* and *'Aṣr* prayers and also the *Maghrib* and *'Ishā'* prayers. The *witr* of the *'Ishā'* prayer are also retained.

Section 7: *The Friday Service*

Friday service specially ordained

There is no sabbath in Islam, and the number of prayers on Friday is the same as on any other day, with this difference, that the specially ordained Friday service takes the place of the early afternoon (*Ẓuhr*) prayer. It is the greater congregation of the Muslims at which the people of a place must all gather together, as the very name of the day *yaum al-jumu'ah* ('the day of gathering') indicates. Though all prayers are equally obligatory, yet the Holy Quran has specially ordained the Friday service, and there it enjoins all Muslims to gather together:

> "O you who believe, when the call is sounded for prayer on Friday, hasten to the remembrance of Allah and leave off business. That is better for you if you know." — 62:9

Any other prayer may be said singly under special circumstances, but not so the Friday service which is essentially a congregational service. The practice has been for all Muslims, who can do so, to gather together at a central mosque, because the underlying idea is, undoubtedly, to enable Muslims to meet together once a week in as large a number as possible.

Preparations for the Friday service

The importance of the occasion and the greater number of persons assembled have made it necessary to issue further instructions regarding cleanliness in preparation for the Friday service. For example, it is recommended that a bath be taken before attending, scent be used, and the best clothes available be worn; also that the mouth be well-cleaned with a tooth-brush.[61]

The Sermon

A special feature of the Friday service is the sermon (*khuṭbah*) by the Imam, before the prayer service is held. After the people have assembled in the mosque, following the call to prayer, the call for prayer is given for a second time while the Imam is sitting. When the *adhān* is finished, the Imam stands up facing the audience and delivers the sermon. He begins with the *kalimah shahādah* — the Arabic sentence meaning "I bear witness that there is none to be worshipped but Allah, and I bear witness that Muhammad is His servant and Messenger" — or words speaking of the praise and glory of God, and then goes on to recite a text of the Quran which he expounds to the audience, who are specially enjoined to remain sitting and silent during the sermon.[62] This is delivered in two parts, the Imam taking a little rest by assuming the sitting position in the middle of the sermon, and then continuing.

Any subject relating to the welfare of the community may be dealt with in the sermon. The Holy Prophet's practice shows that the sermon is for the education of the masses, to awaken them to a general sense of duty, to lead them to the ways of their welfare and prosperity and warn them against that which is a source of loss or ruin to them. Therefore it must be delivered in a language which the people understand, and there is no sense in delivering it in Arabic to an audience which does not know the language. Prayer service is quite different, as it consists of a number of stated sentences, the meaning of which can be fully learnt in a short period. It is of the utmost importance that the masses should know what the preacher is saying in the Friday sermon which is the best means of education for the masses and for maintaining the vitality of the Muslim community as a whole.

The Friday service

After the sermon is over, the *iqāmah* is pronounced and a congregational service of two *rak'ahs* is held, in which the Imam recites the opening chapter and a portion of the Holy Quran in a loud voice, as he does in the morning and evening prayers. This is the only obligatory service, but two *rak'ahs sunnah* are said as soon as a person enters the mosque; even if he comes late and the Imam has already started the sermon, the late-comer must still perform these two *rak'ahs*.[63] Two *rak'ahs sunnah* are also said after the service has ended.[64]

As already stated, there is in Islam no sabbath, or seventh day for Divine worship. Hence the Quran plainly speaks of daily business being done before the Friday service (62:9), leaving it only for the sake of the service, and again it speaks of business being done after the service has been held:

> "But when the prayer is ended, disperse in the land and seek of Allah's grace..." — 62:10

Section 8: *The 'Īd Prayers*

Festivals of Islam

There are, in Islam, two great festivals having a religious sanction, and in connection with both of them a congregational service of two *rak'ahs* is held, followed by a sermon. Both these festivals go under the name of *'Īd,* which means 'a recurring happiness'.[65] The first of these is called *'Īd al-Fiṭr* and takes place immediately after the month of fasting.[66] The other is called *'Īd al-Aḍhā*.[67] Both these festivals are connected with the performance of some duty, in the first case the duty of fasting, and in the second the duty of sacrifice. A day of happiness following the performance of duty is intended to show that true happiness lies in the performance of duty. In the moment of their greatest joy, Muslims gather in as vast a congregation as possible and fall prostrate before their great Maker, giving thanks to Him that He has enabled them to perform their duty or to make a sacrifice. The spiritual significance of both festivals is thus brought out in the Divine service which is the chief feature of the day of festival.

Gathering for the *'Īd*

The preparation for *'Īd* is similar to the preparation for the Friday service. One must take a bath, put on one's best clothes, use scent, and do everything possible to appear neat and tidy. Though women take part in all the prayers and in the Friday service, they are specially enjoined to be present at the *'Īd* gatherings, for the Holy Prophet is reported to have said that "the young girls and those that have taken to seclusion and those that have their menses on, should all go out [for the *'Īd*] and be present at the prayers of the Muslims".[68] The time of *'Īd* prayers is any time after sunrise and before noon.

The *'Īd* service

The *'Īd* service consists only of two *rak'ahs* in congregation. No *adhān* is called out for the *'Īd* prayers, nor an *iqāmah* for the arranging of the lines.[69] The Imam recites the *Fātiḥah* and a portion of the Holy Quran in a loud voice, as in the Friday service. There is a number of *takbīrs* (saying *Allāhu Akbar*) in addition to those that are meant to indicate the changes of position. On the best authority, the number of these additional *takbīrs* is seven in the first *rak'ah* and five in the second, before the recital of the *Fātiḥah* in both *rak'ahs*.[70] A difference of opinion does, however, exist as to their number. The *takbīrs* are uttered aloud by the Imam, one after another, as he raises both hands to the ears and then leaves them free in the natural position. Those who stand behind him raise and lower their hands similarly.

The *'Īd* sermon

The *'Īd* sermon is delivered after Divine service is over. As regards the manner and the subjects dealt with, it is similar to the Friday sermon, except that it is not necessary to break it up into two parts by assuming the sitting posture in the middle of it. It was the Holy Prophet's practice to address the women separately, who were all required to be present whether they joined in the service or not.

The *'Īd* charity

While celebrating the great *'Īd* festivals, a Muslim not only remembers God by attending the Divine service but he is also enjoined to remember his poorer brethren. The institution of a charitable fund is associated with both occasions. On the occasion of the *'Īd al-Fiṭr,* every Muslim is required to give *ṣadaqa al-Fiṭr* (lit., the *Fiṭr charity*). A monetary level is fixed by the Muslim community per family member, including the old as well as the youngest members, males as well as females. The payment is to be made before the service is held, and it is obligatory. It is meant to be an organized institution according to Hadith.[71]

'Īd al-Aḍhā also furnishes an occasion for the exercise of charity. The sacrifice of an animal on that day (for which see under the next heading) not only makes the poorest members of the community enjoy the festival with a good feast of meat but national funds for the amelioration of the poor or the welfare of the community can be considerably strengthened if the skins of the sacrificed animals are devoted to this purpose. In addition to this, in places where the number of sacrificed animals is in excess of the needs of the population, the surplus meat may be preserved and sold, and the proceeds thereof used for some charitable object. Islam does not allow the wastage of natural resources, and it has organized all its charities in such a manner that they can be turned to the best use.

The Sacrifice

At the *'Īd al-Aḍhā,* every Muslim who can afford to do sacrifices an animal. In the case of a goat or a sheep, one animal suffices for one household, while in the case of a cow or a camel, seven men may be partners.[72] The animal is sacrificed after the *'Īd* prayers are over. It may be sacrificed on the day of *'Īd* or during the two or three days that follow, called the *tashrīq* days, the time during which pilgrims stop in Mina.[73]

As regards the meat of the slaughtered animals, the Holy Quran says:

> "Eat of them and feed the contented one and the beggar."
> — 22:36

There is no harm if it is dried and sold and the proceeds used for the feeding of the poor. The idea that the meat of the sacrifices should not be stored or eaten for more than three days is contradicted by a saying of the Holy Prophet.[74] The giving of one-third, or more, or less, to the poor is simply optional. No hard and fast rules have been laid down. The skin of the animal must, however, be disposed of in charity.[75]

Can sacrifice be replaced by charity?

It is sometimes asked: May not a Muslim, instead of sacrificing an animal, give away its price in charity? The answer to this question, in the light of the Islamic law, is in the negative. The sacrifice by Muslims throughout the world on the *'Īd* day is intended to make Muslim hearts, throughout the world, beat in unison with the hearts of the unparalleled assemblage at Makkah, the centre of Islam. Millions of people assemble there from all parts of the world, people who have sacrificed all comforts of life for no object except to develop the idea of sacrifice, a sacrifice selfless beyond all measure, because it has no personal or even national end in view, a sacrifice for the sake of God alone. However grand that idea, it receives a greater grandeur from the fact that the people who have been unable to make that sacrifice actually, are made to share the same desire and show their willingness to make the same sacrifice by the ostensible act of the sacrifice of an animal, which is the final act of the pilgrimage. One desire moves the hearts of the whole Muslim world from one end to the other at one moment, and this is made possible only by the institution of sacrifice. This institution also, of course, serves the purpose of charity as Islam does not allow its rich members to forget their poorer brethren in the hour of their joy at a time of festival.

The idea underlying sacrifice

The sacrifice does not consist in the act of shedding the blood of an animal or consuming its meat. This is made clear by the Holy Quran:

"Not their flesh, nor their blood, reaches Allah, but to Him is acceptable the observance of duty on your part." — 22:37

The underlying significance is made clearer still in the following verse:

"And for every nation We appointed acts of devotion that they might mention the name of Allah on the cattle quadrupeds that He has given them. So your God is One God, therefore to Him should you submit. And give good news to the humble, whose hearts tremble when Allah is mentioned, and who are patient in their afflictions..." — 22:34–35

The act of the sacrifice of an animal is thus in some way connected with righteousness, with submission to One God, with humbleness of heart, with patience under sufferings; and the sacrifice of the animal is plainly regarded as affecting the heart, as making it tremble at the mention of Allah's name. Taking away the life of an animal and shedding its blood does not make them ferocious but creates humbleness in their hearts. The institution of sacrifice has been accepted in one form or another by all the nations of the world. Like all other religious principles which are universally recognized, the principle of sacrifice finds a deeper meaning in Islam. The outward act is still there but it no longer conveys the meaning attached to it in some ancient religions, namely that of appeasing an offended deity or serving as an atonement for sin. In Islam it signifies the sacrifice of the sacrificer himself. The animal that is sacrificed really stands for the animal within him. And one day, and one particular moment on that day, is chosen so that all Muslim hearts from one end of the world to the other may pulsate with one idea at a particular moment, and thus lead to the development of the idea of self-sacrifice in the community as a whole.

Section 9: *Service on the dead*

Preparatory to service

A Divine service is held over the dead body of every Muslim, young or old, even of infants who have lived only for a few minutes or seconds. It is called *ṣalāt al-janā'iz*. When a person dies, the body is washed with soap or some other disinfectant and cleansed of all impurities which may be due to disease. In washing the dead body, the parts which are washed in ablution for prayer are taken first, and then the whole body is washed.[76] It is then wrapped in one or more white sheets and scent is also added.[77] The dead body is then placed on a bier, or, if necessary, in a coffin, and carried on the shoulders, as a mark of respect, to its last resting-place, though the carrying of the body by any other means is not prohibited. The Holy Prophet stood up when he saw the bier of a Jew pass by. He did this to show respect to the dead, and then enjoined his followers to stand up as a mark of respect when a bier passed by, whether that of a Muslim or a non-Muslim.[78]

The service

Following the dead body to the grave and taking part in the Divine service held over it is regarded as a duty which a Muslim owes to a Muslim, and so is also the visiting of the sick.[79] Women are not prohibited from going with the bier, though their presence is not considered desirable, because being more emotional and tender-hearted than men they may break down. The service may be held anywhere, in a mosque or in an open space or even in the graveyard if sufficient ground is available there. All those who take part in the service must perform the ablution for prayer.

The bier is placed in front, the Imam stands facing the middle of the bier, and people form lines behind him, facing the *Qiblah*. The service starts with the *takbīr* (utterance of *Allāhu Akbar*), with the pronouncement of which hands are raised to the ears and placed in the same position as in prayer. Four *takbīrs* in all are pronounced loudly by the Imam.[80] After the first *takbīr,* the same *dhikr* relating to the praise and glory of God is repeated quietly by the Imam as well as those who follow, as in the first *rak‘ah* of the daily service, followed by the opening chapter of the Quran (*Fātiḥah*) only.[81] The second *takbīr* is then pronounced without raising the hands to the ears, and the *dhikr* known as *al-ṣalā ‘ala-l-Nabiyy* is recited quietly (see p. 219–220). After the third *takbīr,* a prayer for the forgiveness of the deceased is addressed to God, again quietly. Different forms of this prayer are reported as having been offered by the Prophet, and it seems that prayer in any form is permissible. After the fourth *takbīr,* the *taslīm* (i.e., *As-salāmu ‘alai-kum wa raḥmat-ullāh*) is pronounced loudly by the Imam, as at the close of prayer. The entire service is held in the standing position. A similar Divine service may be held in the case of a deceased when the dead body is not present.[82]

When the service is over, the bier is taken to the grave and buried. The grave is dug in such a manner that the dead body may be laid in it facing Makkah. After burial, a prayer is again offered for the deceased and the people then depart.

Patience enjoined under afflictions

Islam forbids indulgence in intemperate grief for the dead. It requires that all affliction be borne patiently, as the Holy Quran says:

> "And We shall certainly try you with something of fear and hunger and loss of property and lives and fruits. And give good news to the patient, who, when a misfortune befalls them, say: Surely we are Allah's and to Him we shall return." — 2:155–156

On hearing of the death of a relative or a friend or of any other affliction, a Muslim is enjoined to say *Innā li-llāhi wa innā ilai-hi rāji'ūn:* "Surely we are Allah's and to Him we shall return". These words are a source of unlimited solace and comfort in bereavement. Allah has taken away His own; all of us come from God and must return to Him. Hence it is forbidden that one should indulge in excessive mourning or ostentatious grief.

A very large number of innovations has grown up about what may be done for the benefit of the dead. There is no mention in any hadith of distributing charity at the grave, or having the Quran recited at the grave or elsewhere for the benefit of the dead. There are reports speaking of the Quran being read to the dying person,[83] but there is no mention at all of its being read over the dead body or over the grave. Neither is there any mention of saying the *Fātiḥah,* or a prayer for the dead, when people come to console the relatives of the departed. The Holy Prophet is, however, reported as having prayed for the dead when visiting their graves, and the simple act of asking forgiveness for the deceased is not forbidden. The preparing of food on the third or tenth or fortieth day after death is also an innovation. There is no mention of it in any hadith. Instead of the family of the deceased preparing food for others, it is recommended that food should be prepared and sent to the family of the deceased by others.[84]

Alms may, however, be given on behalf of the deceased, and doing deeds of charity is the only thing allowed. It is stated in a hadith that "a man came to the Messenger of Allah and said that his mother had died suddenly, and he was sure that if she could speak, she would give something in charity, and enquired whether she would get any reward if he gave charity on her behalf." The Holy Prophet is reported to have replied in the affirmative.[85]

Section 10: *Tahajjud and Tarāwīḥ*

Tahajjud prayer is voluntary

The word *tahajjud* literally signifies the 'giving up of sleep'. The *Tahajjud* prayer is so called because it is said after one has had some sleep, and sleep is then given up for the sake of prayer. It is specially mentioned, even enjoined, in the Holy Quran itself in the very earliest revelations, but it is expressly stated to be voluntary.[86]

As the Holy Quran shows, the Holy Prophet used to pass half or even two-thirds of the night in prayer (see 73:20). His practice was to go to sleep immediately after the *'Ishā'* prayers, and then he generally woke up after midnight and passed almost all this latter half of the night in *Tahajjud* prayers, sometimes taking a short nap, which would give him a little rest, just before the morning prayer. This practice he kept up to the last. While in the congregational prayers the recitation of the Holy Quran was generally short, in consideration of the children, women and aged people among the audience, the recitation in the *Tahajjud* prayers was generally long.

The *Tahajjud* prayer consists of eight *rak'ahs,* divided into a service of two at a time, followed by three *rak'ahs* of *witr.* To make it easier for the common people the *witr* prayer, which is really a part of *Tahajjud,* has been made a part of the voluntary portion of *'Ishā'* or night prayer, and therefore, if the *witr* prayer has been said with *'Ishā', Tahajjud* would consist of only eight *rak'ahs.* But if there is not sufficient time, one may stop after any two *rak'ahs.*[87] The Companions of the Holy Prophet were very particular about *Tahajjud* prayer, though they knew it was not obligatory. The Holy Prophet laid special stress on *Tahajjud* in the month of Ramadan, and it was the *Tahajjud* prayer that ultimately took the form of *Tarāwīḥ* in that month.

Tahajjud was an individual prayer, but later on, Umar introduced a change whereby this prayer in Ramadan became a congregational prayer during the early part of the night, and was said after the *'Ishā'* prayer. He himself is reported to have said that it was an innovation, though the latter part of night during which people kept on sleeping was preferable to the early part in which they said this prayer.[88] While for the average person the change introduced by Umar is welcome, nevertheless in the month of Ramadan *Tahajjud* in the latter part of the night and as an individual prayer is preferable.

Tarāwīḥ

The origin of the word *Tarāwīḥ* means 'the act of taking rest'. The name *Tarāwīḥ* seems to have been given to this prayer because the worshippers take a brief rest after every two *rak'ahs*. It is now the practice that the whole of the Holy Quran is recited in the *Tarāwīḥ* prayers in the month of Ramadan. The number of *rak'ahs* in the *Tarāwīḥ* prayers seems, at first, to have been eleven, being exactly the number of *rak'ahs* in the *Tahajjud* prayers (including of course three *witr rak'ahs*). Later on, the number seems to have been increased to twenty, with three *rak'ahs* of *witr*, now making a total of twenty-three. And this practice is now generally maintained throughout the Muslim world, the Ahl Hadith and Ahmadis being almost the only exception.

Notes to Chapter 11

1. Bukhari, book 8: 'Prayer', ch. 38, h. 416 and ch. 39, h. 417; book 9: 'Times of prayers', ch. 8, h. 531 and h. 532; book 21: 'Actions while praying', ch. 12, h. 1214.

2. Bukhari, book 2: 'Faith', ch. 37, h. 50.

3. Bukhari, book 9: 'Times of prayers', ch. 6, h. 528.

4. See also in the Quran 39:39, 90:4.

5. The Quran, 73:20.

6. Bukhari, book 8: 'Prayer', ch. 56, h. 438.

7. *Ibid.,* book 8, ch. 69, h. 454–455.

8. *Ibid.,* book 8, ch. 68, h. 453.

9. Bukhari, book 8: 'Prayer', ch. 44, h. 423; book 92: 'Tribulations (*Fitan*)', ch. 18, h. 7100 and h. 7101.

10. See, for example, Bukhari, book 8: 'Prayer', ch. 57, h. 439; ch. 77, h. 463; and ch. 78, heading.

11. Abu Dawud, book 2: 'Prayer', ch. 'Gathering on Friday before prayer', h. 1079.

12. Bukhari, book 8: 'Prayer', ch. 83, h. 470.

13. *Ibid.,* book 8, ch. 37, h. 415.

14. *Ibid.,* book 8, ch. 24, h. 386.

15. *Ibid.,* book 8, ch. 72, h. 458.

16. Bakkah is the same as Makkah, being from *tabākk* meaning *the crowding together* of people. See Raghib's *Mufradāt* and Rāzī's commentary.

17. *Al-Nihāyah* under *Kufr.*

18. Abu Dawud, book 2: 'Prayer', ch. 'Building of Mosques', h. 448.

19. *Ibid.,* h. 449.

20. Bukhari, book 9: 'Times of the prayers', ch. 22, h. 566.

21. Bukhari, book 8: 'Prayer', ch. 13, h. 372; see also book 10: 'Call to Prayer', h. 867 and h. 872.

22. Bukhari, book 10: 'Call to prayer', ch. 65, h. 707–710.

23. *Ibid.,* book 10, ch. 152, h. 837; see also h. 849, h. 850 and h. 870.

24. Bukhari, book 11: 'Friday Prayer', ch. 13, h. 900; see also h. 899.

25. Bukhari, book 10: 'Call to prayer', ch. 162, h. 865.

26. *Ibid.,* book 10, ch. 166, h. 873.

27. Bukhari, book 13: 'The two *'Īds'*, ch. 15, h. 974; ch. 21, h. 981; and ch. 12, h. 971. See also book 6: 'Menstruation', ch. 23, h. 324.

28. Bukhari, book 10: 'Call to prayer', ch. 164, h. 870, h. 871.

29. Bukhari, book 25: 'Pilgrimage (*manāsik*)', ch. 23, saying of Aishah in the chapter heading.

30. Bukhari, book 10: 'Call to prayer', ch. 163, h. 866, h. 867.

31. Bukhari, book 13: 'The two *'Īds'*, ch. 12, the chapter heading.

32. *Encyclopaedia of Islam,* first edition, art. *Masjid,* v. 3, p. 326, col. 2.

33. The Quran, 2:222.

34. Bukhari, book 6: 'Menstruation', chs. 2–5.

35. *Ibid.,* book 6, ch. 11, h. 312.

36. Every mosque will ordinarily have a *mutawallī* (lit., *guardian*), who is charged with its management by those who have built it. The *mutawallī* has the right to appoint the imam, but he has no right to prohibit Muslims, on account of sectarian differences, from entering the mosque. Every mosque has also generally a *mu'adhdhin* who gives the call for prayers, and may also look after the mosque.

37. Bukhari, book 10: 'Call to prayer', ch. 46.

38. Abu Dawud, book 2: 'Prayer', ch. 'Who is more entitled to be Imam', h. 582–584, h. 589.

39. *Ibid.,* ch: 'Women acting as Imam', h. 591–592.

40. Tirmidhi, book 1: 'Purification', ch. 3, h. 3.

41. Muslim, book 2: 'Purification', ch. 1, h. 223 (MDS: h. 534).

42. The word *junub* is a technical term and means 'one who is under an obligation to perform a total ablution', i.e., to take a bath. To call this a state of
pollution or defilement is not correct.

43. Bukhari, book 7: '*Tayammum*', ch. 4, h. 338, and ch. 5, h. 339–343.

44. Lane's Lexicon.

45. Bukhari, book 10: 'Call to prayer', ch. 1, h. 604.

46. *Ibid.,* book 10, ch. 18, h. 630–631.

47. *Editor's Note:* Prayer at "the two ends of the day" in 11:114 indicates the
morning prayer, *Fajr,* at one end and the two afternoon prayers, *Ẓuhr* and
'Aṣr, at the other.

48. Bukhari, book 9: 'Times of the prayers', ch. 1, h. 521–522.

49. *Ibid.,* ch. 35, h. 595.

50. *Ibid.,* ch. 9, h. 533–538.

51. *Ibid.,* ch. 11, h. 541.

52. Bukhari, book 18: 'Shortening the prayers', chs. 13 – 15, h. 1106–1111.

53. Bukhari, book 9: 'Times of the prayers', ch. 12, h. 543.

54. Muslim, book 6: 'Prayer of Travellers and its Shortening', ch. 6, h. 705b,
705c, 706b, 705d (MDS: h. 1629, 1630, 1632, 1633).

55. The Quran, 73 : 1 – 4 and 73 : 20.

56. Bukhari, book 18: 'Shortening the prayers', ch. 19, h. 1117.

57. *Ibid.,* ch. 7, h. 1093, 1094, 1095, and ch. 8, h. 1096.

58. The Quran, 29 : 45, 62 : 9, 63 : 9 etc.

59. *Zād al-Ma'ād,* vol. I, p. 60.

60. The Hanafis, however, hold that the Imam's recitation is sufficient, and that
the followers need not recite the sentences of the *Fātiḥah.*

61. Bukhari, book 11: 'Friday Prayer', ch. 2, h. 877–879, ch. 3, h. 880, and chs.
7–8, h. 886–888.

62. *Ibid.,* ch. 6, h. 883, and ch. 19, h. 910.

63. *Ibid.,* ch. 32, h. 930, and ch. 33, h. 931.

64. *Ibid.,* ch. 39, h. 937.

65. *Editor's Note:* The word *'Īd* is often spelt in English as Eid to indicate the
pronunciation to the general reader.

66. The word *fiṭr* means 'to begin', from which is also derived *fiṭrah* meaning
'nature'. *Ifṭār* means 'the breaking of the fast', as if the faster had returned to
a natural course, and it is from this that the name *'Īd al-Fiṭr* seems to have
been taken, because it immediately follows the month of fasts.

67. *Aḍḥā* is the plural of *aḍhāt,* meaning 'a sacrifice'.

68. Bukhari, book 13: 'The two *'Īds*', ch. 15, h. 974; book 6: 'Menstruation', ch. 23, h. 324.

69. Bukhari, book 13: 'The two *'Īds*', ch. 7, h. 959–960.

70. Tirmidhi, book 5: 'The two *'Īds*', ch. 34, h. 536.

71. Bukhari, book 24: '*Zakāt*', ch. 77, h. 1511; book 40: 'Representation, Proxy (*Wakāla*)', ch. 10, h. 2311.

72. Tirmidhi, book 19: 'Sacrifices', ch. 8, h. 1502 (MDS: book 17).

73. Mishkat, book 4: 'Prayer', ch. 49, sec. 3, h. 1388 (v. 1, p. 313).

74. Bukhari, book 25: 'Pilgrimage', ch. 124, h. 1719.

75. *Ibid.,* ch. 121, h. 1717.

76. Bukhari, book 23: 'Funerals', chs. 9–11, h. 1254–1256.

77. *Ibid.,* chs. 19–21, h. 1265–1267, and ch. 26, h. 1275.

78. *Ibid.,* ch. 49, h. 1311–1312.

79. *Ibid.,* ch. 2, h. 1239–1240.

80. *Ibid.,* ch. 64, h. 1333–1334.

81. *Ibid.,* ch. 65, h. 1335.

82. *Ibid.,* ch. 4, h. 1245.

83. Abu Dawud, book 21: 'Funerals', ch. 24, h. 3121 (MDS: book 20).

84. Bukhari, book 70: 'Food', ch. 24, h. 5417. Abu Dawud, book 21: 'Funerals', ch. 30, h. 3132 (MDS: book 20).

85. Bukhari, book 23: 'Funerals', ch. 95, h. 1388; book 55: 'Wills', ch. 15, h. 2756.

86. The Quran, 73 : 1–6, 73 : 20 and 17 : 79.

87. Bukhari, book 19: '*Tahajjud*', ch. 10, h. 1137.

88. Bukhari, book 31: '*Tarawīḥ*', ch. 1, h. 2010.

12. Charity

Charity as one of the two principal duties

Charity towards fellow human beings, in its widest sense, is laid down in the Holy Quran as the second great pillar on which the structure of Islam stands. This is made plain in the very beginning of the Holy Book (2:3–4) where the main principles of Islam, three theoretical and two practical, are laid down. The three theoretical essentials are belief in God, in Divine revelation and in the Hereafter; and the two practical are keeping up prayer and spending out of what God has given to man. Muslims are described there as those:

> "who believe in the Unseen and keep up prayer and spend out of what We have given them." — 2:3

Prayer, which has already been discussed in the last chapter, is the means of the realization of the Divine in man, while spending out of whatever has been given to man, stands for charity in a broad sense, i.e., for all acts of benevolence and doing good to humanity in general. For what God has given to man is not only the wealth which he possesses but all the faculties and powers with which he has been gifted.

That benevolence, or the doing of good to man, is one of the two mainstays of religion, is a constant theme of the Holy Quran. For example, rejecting the Jewish and Christian claims to salvation on the basis of certain dogmas, the Holy Book says:

> "No, whoever submits himself entirely to Allah and he is the doer of good to others, he has his reward from his Lord, and there is no fear for such nor shall they grieve." — 2:112

In this verse submission to Allah takes the place of keeping up prayer, and the doing of good to humanity is spoken of in place of spending out of what has been given to man. The numerous ordinances relating to various aspects of life, whether contained in the Quran or in the practice and sayings of the Holy Prophet, are only offshoots of these two practical essentials of religion.

Prayer is useless if it does not lead to charity

The relation in which prayer stands to charity is made clear by the order in which the two are mentioned. When prayer and charity are spoken of together, and this combination is of frequent occurrence in the Quran, prayer always takes precedence over charity, but this is only because prayer prepares a man for the service of humanity. Verse 3 of chapter 2, which we quoted above, begins with mention of belief in God, the Unseen, and this is immediately followed by an injunction to keep up prayer, and this again by another to do acts of benevolence. This is to show the natural order. Belief in the Unseen is the starting point of man's spiritual progress. But this would lead to no good if the next step, the seeking of communion with the Unseen through prayer, does not follow. And this again is meaningless if it does not lead to acts of benevolence. Prayer, therefore, is the first step because it leads to the second, that is, charity. This is elsewhere made plain:

> "Woe to the praying ones, who are unmindful of their prayers, who do good to be seen, and refrain from [small] acts of kindness." — 107:4–7

Conception of charity in Islam

The most frequently recurring words for charity are *infāq* which means 'spending benevolently', *iḥsān* which means 'the doing of good', *zakāt* which means 'growth' or 'purification', and *ṣadaqah* which is derived from the root *ṣidq,* meaning 'truth', and comes to signify a 'charitable deed'. The very words used to denote charitable deeds are an indication of the broadness of its conception. The Holy Quran not only lays stress on such great deeds of charity as the emancipation of slaves,[1] the feeding of the poor,[2] taking care of orphans[3] and doing good to humanity in general, but gives equal emphasis to smaller acts of benevolence. It is for this reason that, in 107:7 quoted above, the withholding of *small acts of kindness and charity* is stated to be against the spirit of prayer. And in a similar strain, the speaking of a kind word to parents is referred to as *iḥsān* in 17:23, and generally the use of kind words is recommended as in itself a charitable deed in many places, for example 2:83 and 4:8.

Hadith is much more explicit. To remove from the road anything which may cause hurt is called a *ṣadaqah* or a charitable deed.[4] According to another hadith, "there is a *ṣadaqah* (charity) due on every limb with every new sun, and to do justice among people is also a charity".[5] Another report gives yet more detail:

> "On every limb there is a charity due every day; a man helps another to ride his animal, it is a charity; or he helps him to load his animal, this is also a charity; and so is a good word; and every step, which a man takes in going to pray, is a charity; and to show [someone] the way is a charity." [6]

Examples of other charitable deeds are "your salutation to people," "your enjoining what is right and forbidding what is wrong," "refraining from doing evil to anyone" and so on.[7] The circle of those towards whom an act of charity may be done is equally wide. The Holy Prophet said:

> "Whatever you feed yourself with is a charity, and whatever you feed your children with is a charity, and whatever you feed your wife with is a charity, and whatever you feed your servant with is a charity."

> "Whoever tills a field and birds and beasts eat of it, it is a charity." [8]

The Quran also speaks of extending charity not only to all people including believers and unbelievers[9] but also to the dumb creation.[10]

Voluntary charity

Charity, in the sense of giving away one's wealth, is of two kinds, voluntary and obligatory. Voluntary charity is generally mentioned in the Holy Quran as *infāq* or *iḥsān* or *ṣadaqah,* and though the Holy Book is full of injunctions on this subject, and hardly a leaf is turned which does not bring to the mind the grand object of the service of humanity as the goal of man's life, the subject is specially dealt with in verses 261 to 273 of the second chapter. The reward of charity is first spoken of:

> "The parable of those who spend their wealth in the way of Allah is as the parable of a grain growing seven ears, in every ear a hundred grains. And Allah multiplies further for whom He pleases." — 2:261

A charitable deed must be done as a duty which man owes to man, so that it conveys no idea of the superiority of the giver or the inferiority of the receiver:

> "Those who spend their wealth in the way of Allah, then do not follow up what they have spent with reproach or injury, their reward is with their Lord. … A kind word with forgiveness is better than charity followed by injury. … O you who believe, do not make your charity worthless by reproach and injury, like him who spends his wealth to be seen by people and does not believe in Allah and the Last Day." — 2:262–264

Love of God should be the motive in all charitable deeds, so that the very doing of them fosters the feeling that all mankind is but a single family:

> "And they give food, out of love for Him, to the poor and the orphan and the captive." — 76:8

> "…but righteous is the one who… gives away wealth out of love for Him to the near of kin and the orphans and the needy and the traveller and to those who ask and to set slaves free." — 2:177

> "And the parable of those who spend their wealth to seek Allah's pleasure and for the strengthening of their souls is as the parable of a garden on elevated ground…" — 2:265

Only good things and well-earned wealth should be given in charity:

> "O you who believe, spend out of the good things that you earn and of what We bring forth for you from the earth, and do not aim at the bad to spend from it, while you would not take it yourselves unless you turned a blind eye to it." — 2:267

Charitable deeds may be done openly or secretly:

> "If you manifest charity, how excellent it is! And if you hide it and give it to the poor, it is good for you. And it will do away with some of your evil deeds." — 2:271

Those who do not beg should be the first to receive charity:

"[Charity is] for the poor who are confined in the way of Allah, they cannot go about in the land; the ignorant man thinks them to be rich on account of their abstaining from begging. You can recognize them by their mark — they do not beg of people demandingly." — 2:273

Significance of *zakāt*

Obligatory charity is generally mentioned under the name *zakāt,* but it is sometimes called a *ṣadaqah,* especially in Hadith. The word *zakāt* is derived from *zakā,* which means 'it (a plant) grew'. The other derivatives of this word, as used in the Holy Quran, carry the sense of *purification from sins.* The Holy Prophet is again and again spoken of as *purifying* those who would follow him,[11] and the purification of the soul is repeatedly mentioned as being real success in life.[12] The word *zakāt* is also used in the sense of purity from sin.[13] The idea of purity, and that of the growth of human faculties and success in life, are thus connected together. *Zakāt* is wealth which is taken from the rich and given to the poor, being so called because it makes wealth grow, and because the giving away of wealth is a source of purification. In fact both these reasons hold true. The giving away of wealth to the poorer members of the community increases the wealth of the community as a whole, and at the same time it purifies the giver's heart of the inordinate love of wealth which brings numerous sins in its train. The Holy Prophet himself has described *zakāt* as wealth "which is taken from the rich and returned to the poor".[14]

Importance of *zakāt* in Islam

The two commandments, to keep up prayer and to give *zakāt,* often go together. This combination of the two is met with in the earliest chapters of the Holy Quran, as well as in those which were revealed towards the end of the Holy Prophet's life. Thus in ch.73, which is undoubtedly one of the very earliest revelations, we have:

> "…and keep up prayer and give the *zakāt* and offer to Allah a goodly gift." — 73:20

And in the ninth chapter, which is the latest in revelation, we have:

> "Only he can maintain the mosques of Allah who believes in Allah and the Last Day, and keeps up prayer and gives the *zakāt* and fears none but Allah." — 9:18

Not only are prayer (*ṣalāt*) and *zakāt* mentioned together in a large number of passages but also these two are treated as being the basic ordinances of the religion of Islam, and their carrying into practice is often mentioned as being sufficient indication that one is a believer in the religion of Islam. The two verses quoted above point to the same conclusion.[15]

Zakāt as the basic principle of every religion

Ṣalāt and *zakāt* are also spoken of together as the basic ordinances of the religion of every prophet. Thus of Abraham and his posterity, it is said:

> "And We made them leaders who guided people by Our command, and We revealed to them the doing of good and the keeping up of prayer and the giving of *zakāt*." — 21 : 73

The Israelite law is also said to have contained a similar commandment:

> "And Allah said: Surely I am with you. If you keep up prayer and give the *zakāt* and believe in My messengers and assist them and offer to Allah a goodly gift, I will certainly cover your evil deeds, and make you enter gardens in which rivers flow." — 5 : 12

Ishmael is also spoken of as giving the same commandment to his followers:

> "And he enjoined on his people prayer and *zakāt,* and he was one in whom his Lord was well-pleased." — 19 : 55

Even Jesus is said to have received a similar Divine commandment:

> "…and He has enjoined on me prayer and *zakāt* so long as I live." — 19 : 31

This view of religion shows that, according to the Holy Quran, the service of humanity and the amelioration of the condition of the poor has always been among the principal aims and objects of religion. It is, however, true that the same stress has not been laid on this principle in the previous religions, and, moreover, the institution of *zakāt,* like every other principle of religion, has been brought to perfection, along with the perfection of religion, in Islam.

Problem of the distribution of wealth

One of the greatest problems facing humanity is undoubtedly the problem of the distribution of wealth, with which is also bound up the question of political power. The system of capitalism, which is the foundation-stone, so to speak, of the materialistic civilization of the West, has led to the concentration of wealth in fewer and fewer hands. Political power has followed in the wake of wealth, and at the bidding of the capitalist the politician has to declare war and peace. The insatiable thirst for wealth on the part of the capitalists, who are the real controllers of political power, has reduced many nations of the world to a state of slavery, and regular plunder has been legalized under various high-sounding phrases.

The reaction against capitalism set in towards the middle of the nineteenth century C.E. It came under the name of socialism, or communism, to liberate the people, but it is as much of a bondage as capitalism. The question is, does state-ownership of all means of production finally solve the great problem of the distribution of wealth? The people entrusted with the carrying out of the scheme, the state-agents, would degenerate into an oligarchy similar to the oligarchy of capitalism since human nature is too prone to these tendencies, and hardly any remedy is offered to check such tendencies. But there is more than this. What came as the friend of labour defeats its own end by denying to labour its fruits. The rigid system of doling out the necessaries of life to all alike, to the indolent and the diligent, the stupid and the intelligent, will undoubtedly foster conditions which would soon become unbearable for humanity; for it is going directly against nature and nature's recognized laws. But its evil results cannot be seen in a day.[16]

Islam's solution of wealth problem

To Islam is due the credit of not only solving the wealth problem but, at the same time, developing the higher sentiments and building up character, on which alone can be laid the foundations of a lasting civilization for the human race. Islam accomplishes both objects by its state institution of charity, which goes under the name of *zakāt*. Every possessor of wealth is required to contribute annually one-fortieth of his wealth to a common fund, which is managed by the state, or by the Muslim community where there is no Muslim state, and this fund is utilized by the state or community for the amelioration of the condition of the poor. *Zakāt*, therefore, acts not only as a levelling influence but also as a means of developing the higher sentiments of man, the sentiments of love and sympathy towards his fellow-man; while the rigid system of state ownership and equality of distribution helps to kill man's higher instincts. By this means, too, wealth is made to circulate in the body-politic of Islam, just as blood circulates in a living organism, a fixed portion of the wealth of the richer members being drawn to the centre, from where it is sent forth to those parts of the body-politic which need it most. The institution of *zakāt* thus becomes not only a levelling influence but also one of the means for the uplift of the nation as a whole.

Zakāt is a state institution

It should be borne in mind that *zakāt* is not simply obligatory charity. It is a state institution or, where there is no Muslim state, a national institution. The individual is not at liberty to calculate and spend his *zakāt* as he likes. It must be collected by the state on a national basis, and spent by the state or community. Where the Holy Quran describes the main heads of the expenditure of *zakāt*, it mentions an item of expenditure on officials appointed to collect and distribute the same, which shows clearly that, by the institution of *zakāt*, it contemplated either a department of the state or at least a public fund managed entirely by a public body. The donor is not required to give *zakāt* to deserving persons, but to contribute it to a fund which must be used for the uplift of the community. It was in this sense that the Holy Prophet understood it, and when he assumed control of the government, he made *zakāt* a state institution, appointing officials to collect it and directing his governors to do the same in distant provinces.

Property on which *zakāt* is payable

Though injunctions relating to *zakāt* are met with in very early revelations, the details were given only after Islam was established at Madinah. Silver and gold are the two commodities which man has always loved to hoard, and besides this these are the two precious metals which are the basis of the currencies of the world. These two, therefore, find special mention as being articles on which *zakāt* must be paid. Ornaments made of silver or gold were treated as silver or gold. And cash, whether in the form of coins or notes or bank deposits, would follow the same rule. Precious stones were excepted from *zakāt,* because in taking a part, in this case, the whole would have to be broken up or damaged. Articles of merchandise were also considered as being subject to *zakāt* to whatever class they may belong. Animals used for trade purposes were subject to *zakāt* only if they were kept on pastures belonging to the state. There is no mention of immovable property, such as agricultural lands and house property, among the things on which *zakāt* was levied, but the produce of land, whether cereals or fruits, was subject to a tax called '*ushr,* literally, the tenth part. It has been treated as *zakāt;* actually, however, it falls within the category of land revenue. Since *zakāt* is a tax on property, therefore it is realizable though the property may belong to a minor.

Niṣāb and rate of *zakāt*

Zakāt was an annual charge on property which remained in the possession of a person for a whole year, when its value reached a certain limit, called *niṣāb. Niṣāb* differed with different kinds of property, the most important being the cases of silver and gold. The *niṣāb* of cash was the same as that of silver or gold, according to whether the cash was held in silver or gold. In the case of merchandise of all kinds, the value was calculated on the basis of, and the *niṣāb* was judged by, the silver standard. In the case of ornaments, the *niṣāb* was that of silver or of gold, according to the metal they were made of. But jewels and the like would be excepted, and only the weight of silver or gold would be considered in determining the *niṣāb.* There were also different levels of *niṣāb* in case of animals such as bulls, cows, goats etc. There was also a *niṣāb* in the case of cereals.

With the exception of animals, *zakāt* was levied at almost a uniform rate, being 2½ per cent of the accumulated wealth. In the case of animals, camels and sheep, detailed rules were laid down, and animals of a particular age were taken as *zakāt* when the herd reached a specified number. However, in the main, the rate of 2½ per cent seems to have been kept in view. In case of '*ushr,* as already stated, it is not technically *zakāt;* it is really land revenue. The state takes only one-tenth of the produce of agricultural land when it is grown with the aid of rain-water or natural springs, and one-twentieth when irrigated by wells or other artificial means in which labour is engaged by the owner of the land.

Zakāt under modern conditions

It will thus be seen that *zakāt* proper is only a charge on accumulated wealth, and is intended to do away with the inequalities of capitalism. Wealth has a tendency to accumulate, and *zakāt* aims at its partial redistribution in such a manner that the community, as a whole, may derive advantage from it. A part of the amassed wealth or capital of every individual is taken away annually and distributed among the poor and the needy. *Zakāt* would therefore be payable on all cash hoardings, or hoardings in gold or silver, as well as on any form of capital, whether in the shape of cash or kind. Precious stones, as already stated, are excepted, because the payment of *zakāt* on them would necessitate their sale. Machinery employed in industry must follow the same rule. It should, in fact, be regarded in the same light as the implements of a skilled worker, and its earnings become taxable when the necessary conditions as to the assessment of *zakāt* are fulfilled. Stock-in-trade should be treated in a similar manner; that is to say, only the yearly profit should be taxable, not the stock itself. In the case of all things on which *zakāt* is payable, whether cereals, live-stock or other articles of merchandise, their value should be determined, and *zakāt* levied at the universal rate of 2½ per cent.

Where the Muslims live under non-Muslim governments, and the collection and disbursement of *zakāt* cannot be undertaken by these governments, the duty devolves on the Muslim community as a whole, and the institution of *zakāt* must take the shape of a national Muslim institution in every country where there is a Muslim population.

How *zakāt* should be spent

The items of the expenditure of *zakāt* are thus expressly stated in the Holy Quran:

> "Charity (*ṣadaqāt*) is only for the poor and the needy, and those employed to administer it, and those whose hearts are made to incline to truth, and [to free] the captives, and those in debt, and in the way of Allah, and for the traveller — an ordinance (*farīḍah*) from Allah, and Allah is Knowing, Wise." — 9:60

As already noted, *zakāt* is sometimes mentioned under the name of *ṣadaqah*. That this is the significance here of *ṣadaqāt* (its plural form) is made clear by the concluding words of the verse, where it is called an "ordinance", *farīḍah* or an obligatory duty, this word being applicable to *zakāt* only.

The eight heads of expenditure spoken of here may be divided into three classes. The first relates to those who stand in need of help, including the poor, the needy, those whose hearts are made to incline to truth, captives, debtors and travellers. Secondly, there are the officials appointed for collection and disbursement of the fund. And, thirdly, a part of the *zakāt* is required to be spent in the way of Allah. A few words of explanation may be added as regards each class.

It will be seen that six kinds of people fall under the first head. The first, translated as "poor", are *fuqarā'* (plural of *faqīr*), and the second, translated as "needy", are *masākīn* (plural of *miskīn*). There exists a good deal of difference as to the real distinction between these two words, but keeping their literal significance in view, the real distinction appears to be that *faqīr* is one who is unable to earn on account of some disability, while *miskīn* is one who, though fit to earn sufficient, is unable to do so on account of poverty or lack of resources. The *miskīn* is the needy person who, if given a little help, can earn livelihood for himself. The unemployed would fall in this category.

These are the two chief classes for whose benefit the institution of *zakāt* is maintained, and hence they are separated from others by a mention of the establishment. The other groups falling in this class are also of persons who stand in need of help for some sufficient reason. There are those whose hearts are made to incline to truth, that is, people who are in search of truth but unable to find means to have access to it on account of poverty. In this category would also fall new converts to Islam who are deprived of the means of their subsistence because of their conversion. Then there are the captives, or those who have been deprived of their liberty, and are unable to regain it by their own exertion. The freeing of slaves falls in this category. Then there are the debtors who are unable to pay off their own debts, and, lastly, there are the travellers who are stranded in a foreign country or in a distant place, and are unable to reach their homes.

There are two other heads of expenditure of *zakāt*. The first of these is the maintenance of an establishment and office for the collection of *zakāt*. This shows that *zakāt* was meant to be collected at some central place, and then distributed, and the maintenance of people who did this work was a charge under this head. The Quran, therefore, does not allow the giving away or spending of *zakāt* according to the individual's choice.[17]

Zakāt may be spent in defence and propagation of Islam

The only remaining item of expenditure is what is called *fī sabīl-illāh,* or "in the way of Allah", which is accepted generally as meaning *fighters defending the faith.* While such fighters are a most important national need of a community, it is equally true that they are an exception and not the rule, and hence the significance of the words "in the way of Allah" cannot be limited to them. But there is another paramount need of the Muslim community which is called the great *jihād,* in the Quran:

> "And if We pleased, We could raise a warner in every town. So do not obey the unbelievers, and strive against them a mighty striving (*jihad-an kabīr-an*) with it." — 25:51–52

The personal pronoun *it,* as the context clearly shows, refers to the Quran, and therefore striving with the Quran, or taking the message of the Quran to distant corners of the world, is the greatest *jihād* of Islam. The item of expenditure "in the way of Allah" hence refers to both these paramount needs of national existence: war in self-defence (being the only kind of war allowed to Muslims) and the work of the propagation of Islam. The latter, i.e., the propagation of Islam, is the greatest need of this age. Hence it will be seen that the institution of *zakāt,* while chiefly aiming at the amelioration of the condition of the poor, has also in view the defence and advancement of the Muslim community as a whole.

Other national charitable institutions

Zakāt, though the most important, is not, however, the only national institution of charity set up by Islam. There are two others of a similar nature, both connected with the *'Īd* festivals, whereby into every Muslim heart is instilled the idea that even when in his happiest mood, he must never forget the distress of his poorer brethren. The first of these institutions is the charity connected with the *'Īd al-Fiṭr.* Every Muslim on that occasion is required to give away in charity a certain measure of food, or its equivalent in money. This sum must be collected by every Muslim community and then distributed among those who deserve it. Here too the choice of distribution is not with the individual but with the community (see also p. 227). The second institution is connected with the *'Id al-Aḍḥā* on which occasion not only are the poor members of the community fed with the meat of the sacrificed animals, but the skins of those animals (and also dried or preserved meat, in case the supply is greater than the demand) are sold, and the sum thus realized spent on some charitable object of national value, such as the propagation of Islam (see also pages 227–228).

Notes to Chapter 12

1. The Quran, 90:13, 2:177.

2. The Quran, 69:34, 90:11–16, 107:1–3.

3. The Quran, 17:34, 76:8, 89:17, 90:15, 93:9, 107:2.

4. Bukhari, book 46: 'Oppressions', ch. 24, ch. heading. See also book 56: *'Jihād'*, ch. 128, h. 2989.

5. Bukhari, book 53: 'Peace-making', ch. 11, h. 2707.

6. Bukhari, book 56: *'Jihād'*, ch. 72, h. 2891. See also ch. 128, h. 2989.

7. *Musnad* of Ahmad ibn Hanbal, v. 2, p. 329 and v. 4, p. 395.

8. *Ibid.*, v. 4, p. 131 and v. 4, p. 55.

9. "Their guidance is not your duty, but Allah guides whom He pleases. And whatever good thing you spend, it is to your good. And you do not spend but to seek Allah's pleasure" (The Quran, 2:272).

   Editor's Note: Reports relating to this verse show that it means that a Muslim must also extend his charity to the poor among sinners, non-Muslims and even opponents of Islam, and not let the fact that they are not following true guidance prevent him from helping them. See Commentary of Ibn Kathir under this verse; see also Bukhari, book 24: *'Zakāt'*, ch. 15, h. 1421.

10. "And in their wealth was a due share for the beggar and for one who is deprived" — 51:19. The word *maḥrūm* or 'deprived' is understood as applying both to a poor man who does not beg and to dumb animals as they are not capable of speaking. (See also 70:24–25.)

11. The Quran, 2:129, 2:151, 3:163, 9:103, 62:2.

12. The Quran, 91:9, 92:18.

13. The Quran, 19:12–13, 18:81.

14. Bukhari, book 24: *'Zakāt'*, ch. 1, h. 1395.

15. Some more examples of such verses are: 98:5, 31:2–4 and 9:11.

16. *Editor's Note:* These words were written in the 1930s. In *The Religion of Islam,* in this discussion Maulana Muhammad Ali had, after noting that

communism "holds Russia in its grip", added: "Whether, in Russia, it has come to stay is a question which only the future can decide." Just over fifty years after he wrote these words, communism collapsed in the old Soviet Union.

17. There is a hadith which states that the Holy Prophet allowed up to one-third of the *zakāt* to be spent by an individual for those whom he thought fit to receive the *zakāt*. He is reported to have said: "When you estimate, leave one-third; if you do not leave one-third, then leave one-fourth" (Abu Dawud, book 9: *'Zakāt'*, ch. 15, h. 1605). Explaining this hadith, Imam Shafi'i says that the one-third or one-fourth was to be left so that the person from whom the *zakāt* was taken should spend the portion left on his relatives or neighbours as he desired (see the commentary on Abu Dawud, *'Aun al-Ma'būd 'alā Sunani Abī Dāwūd,* under this hadith).

13. Fasting

Institution of fasting in Islam

The primary signification of the word *ṣaum* is 'abstaining', in an absolute sense. In the technical language of the Islamic law, *ṣaum* and *ṣiyām* signify fasting or abstaining from food and drink and sexual intercourse from dawn till sunset.

The institution of fasting in Islam came after the institution of prayer. It was in Madinah in the second year of Hijrah that fasting was made obligatory, and the month of Ramadan was set apart for this purpose. Before that the Holy Prophet used to fast, as an optional devotion, on the tenth day of the month of Muharram, and he also ordered his followers to fast on that day, it being a fasting day for the Quraish as well.[1] The origin of fasting in Islam may thus be traced to the time when the Holy Prophet was still at Makkah; but it was after his move to Madinah that he saw the Jews fasting on the tenth day of Muharram; and being told that Moses had kept a fast on that day in commemoration of the delivery of the Israelites from Pharaoh, he remarked that they (Muslims) were nearer to Moses than the Jews and ordered that day to be observed as a day of fasting.[2]

A universal institution

In the Holy Quran the subject of fasting is dealt with only in one place, that is, in verses 183 to 188 of the second chapter; though there is mention on other occasions of fasting by way of expiation in certain cases. The first verse on this subject opens with the remark that the institution of fasting is a universal one:

> "O you who believe, fasting is prescribed for you, as it was prescribed for those before you, so that you may guard against evil." —2 : 183

The truth of the statement made here, that fasting "was prescribed for those before you", is borne out by a reference to religious history. The practice of fasting has been recognized almost universally in all the higher, revealed religions, though the same stress is not laid on it in all, and the forms and motives vary. According to the *Encyclopaedia Britannica:*

> "Its modes and motives vary considerably according to climate, race, civilization and other circumstances; but it would be difficult to name any religious system of any description in which it is wholly unrecognized." [3]

Present-day Christianity may not attach much value to religious devotions of this sort, but not only did the Founder of Christianity himself keep a fast for forty days and observe fasting on the Day of Atonement like a true Jew, but also commended fasting to his disciples:

> "Moreover, when you fast, do not be like the hypocrites, with a sad countenance. For they disfigure their faces that they may appear to men to be fasting... But you, when you fast, anoint your head and wash your face, so that you do not appear to men to be fasting." [4]

The early Christians are also spoken of as fasting, and even St. Paul fasted.[5]

New meaning introduced by Islam

In all nations before Islam, fasting was undertaken in times of mourning and afflictions. Among the Jews, generally, fasting was observed as a sign of grief or mourning. Thus, David is mentioned as fasting for seven days during the illness of his infant son;[6] and, as a sign of mourning, fasting is mentioned elsewhere.[7] Besides the Day of Atonement, which was prescribed by the Mosaic law as a day of fasting,[8] various other fast-days came into vogue after the Exile to commemorate certain sad events which had occurred in the downfall of the kingdom of Judah. Thus it was generally some trouble or tragedy of which the memory was kept up by a fast. The fasting by Moses for forty days — which example was later followed by Jesus Christ — seems to be the only exception, and the fast, in this case, was kept preparatory to receiving a revelation.

The idea underlying this voluntary suffering in the form of a fast in times of sorrow and affliction seems to have been to propitiate an angry Deity and excite compassion in Him. The idea that fasting was an act of penitence seems gradually to have developed from this as an affliction or calamity was considered to be due to sin, and fasting thus became an outward expression of the change of heart brought about by repentance. It was in Islam that the practice received a highly developed significance. It rejected *in toto* the idea of appeasing Divine wrath, or exciting Divine compassion through voluntary suffering, and introduced in its place regular and continuous fasting, irrespective of the condition of the individual or the nation, as a means, like prayer, to the development of the human inner faculties.

Though the Holy Quran speaks of expiatory or compensatory fasts in certain cases of violation of the Divine law, yet these are quite distinct from the obligatory fasting in the month of Ramadan, and are mentioned only as an alternative to an act of charity, such as the feeding of the poor or freeing of a slave. Fasting, as an institution, is here made a spiritual, moral and physical discipline of the highest order, and this is made clear by changing both the form and the motive. By making the institution permanent, all ideas of distress, affliction and sin are dissociated from it, while its true object is made plain in the verse quoted earlier, which is "that you may guard against evil (*tattaqūn*)".[9] The Arabic word used here indicates *the guarding of self against that of which the evil consequences may be feared*.[10] But besides this, the word has been freely used in the Quran in the sense of fulfilment of duties and obligations. In fact, in the language of the Quran, to be a *muttaqī*, which is another form of the same word and means "one who guards against evil", is to attain to the highest stage of spiritual development. Allah is called their friend, and it is said that He loves them and is with them;[11] for them is "the good end" and "an excellent destination".[12] These and numerous similar passages show clearly that the *muttaqī*, according to the Quran, is the one who has attained to the highest stage of spiritual development. And as the object of fasting is to be a *muttaqī*, the conclusion is evident that the Quran enjoins fasting with the object of making a person ascend the spiritual heights.

A spiritual discipline

Fasting, according to Islam, is primarily a spiritual discipline. On two occasions in the Holy Quran those who fast are called *sā'iḥ*,[13] or spiritual travellers; and according to one authority, when a person refrains, not only from food and drink but from all kinds of evil, he is called a *sā'iḥ*.[14] While speaking of Ramadan, the month in which fasting is ordained, the Quran specially refers to nearness to God, as if its attainment were an aim in fasting:

> "And when My servants ask you [O Prophet] concerning Me, surely I am near. I answer the prayer of the supplicant when he calls on Me, so they should hear My call [by fasting] and believe in Me, that they may walk in the right way [or, find the way to Me]." — 2:186

In Hadith too, special stress is laid on the fact that the seeking of Divine pleasure should be the ultimate object in fasting:

> "Whoever fasts during Ramadan, having faith [in Allah] and seeking His pleasure…" [15]

> "… he refrains from food and drink and other desires to seek My pleasure: fasting is for Me only." [16]

No temptation is greater than the temptation of satisfying one's thirst and hunger when drink and food are in one's possession, yet this temptation is overcome not once or twice, as if it were by chance, but day after day regularly for a whole month, with a set purpose of drawing closer and closer to the Divine Being. A person can avail himself of food and drink, yet he prefers to remain hungry and parching with thirst; he touches neither food nor drink, simply because he thinks that it is the commandment of God that he should not do so. There is none to see him if he ate or drank, yet there has developed in him the sense of the nearness to God to such an extent that he would not do so. Whenever a new temptation comes before him, he overcomes it, because there is an inner voice, "God is with me," "God sees me". The Divine presence becomes a reality for him, and this is made possible by the spiritual discipline underlying fasting. A new consciousness of a higher life, a life above that which is maintained by eating and drinking, has been awakened in him, and this is the life spiritual.

A moral discipline

There is also a moral discipline underlying fasting, for it is the training ground where man is taught the greatest moral lesson of his life — the lesson that he should be prepared to suffer the greatest privation and undergo the hardest trial rather than indulge in that which is not permitted to him. That lesson is repeated from day to day for a whole month, and just as physical exercise strengthens man physically, moral exercise through fasting, the exercise of abstaining from everything that is not allowed, strengthens the moral side of his life.

Another aspect of human moral development by this means is that he is thus taught to conquer his physical desires. He takes his food at regular intervals and that is no doubt a desirable rule of life, but fasting for one month in the year teaches him the higher lesson that, instead of being the slave of his appetites and desires, he should be their master, being able to change the course of his life if he so wills it. The person who is able to rule his desires is the one who has attained to true moral greatness.

Social value of fasting

In addition to its spiritual and moral values, fasting as prescribed in the Holy Quran has also a social value, more effective than that which is realized through prayer. The commencement of the month of Ramadan is a signal for a mass movement towards equality which is not limited to one vicinity or even one country but affects the whole Muslim world. The rich and the poor may stand shoulder to shoulder in one row in the mosque, but in their homes they live in different environments. The rich sit down on tables laden with dainties, while the poor cannot find sufficient food with which to satisfy their hunger even twice a day. The latter often feel the pangs of hunger to which the former are utter strangers. A great social barrier thus exists between them in their homes, and this barrier is removed only when the rich are made to feel the pangs of hunger like their poorer brethren and go without food throughout the day, and this experience has to be gone through, not for a day or two, but for a whole month. They have perforce to come closer to their poorer brethren. This is why the helping of the poor is specially enjoined in the month of Ramadan.

Physical value of fasting

Refraining from food during stated intervals does no physical harm to a healthy person. On the contrary, the rest given to the digestive organs for a whole month only gives them additional strength, like fallow ground which, by rest, becomes more productive. But fasting has yet another, and a more important, physical value. The person who cannot face the hardships of life, who is not able to live, at times, without his usual comforts, cannot be said to be even physically fit for life on this earth. Fasting accustoms him to face the hardships of life, being in itself a practical lesson to that end, and increases his powers of resistance.

The month of Ramadan

With some exceptions, which will be mentioned later on, Muslims are required to fast for the 29 or 30 days of the month of Ramadan. The exact number depends on the lunar month which is either 29 or 30 days. Fasting commences with the new moon of Ramadan and ends on the new moon of the next month, Shawwal. The Holy Prophet is reported to have said:

> "We are a people who neither write nor do we keep account; the month is thus and thus, showing [by his fingers] once twenty-nine and again thirty." [17]

> "Do not fast until you see the new moon and do not break fasting until you see it [again], and if it is cloudy, calculate its appearance." [18]

Another hadith says that if it is cloudy, thirty days should be completed.[19] To begin and end by the actual appearance of the new moon was the easier method for a people who did not know writing and did not keep account, as stated in the first hadith quoted above. The second hadith quoted above allows that the appearance of the moon may be judged by computation.

Choice of Ramadan

The injunction laid down in the Holy Quran, relating to fasting in the month of Ramadan, runs as follows:

> "The month of Ramadan is that in which the Quran was revealed, a guidance to people and clear proofs of guidance and the Criterion. So whoever of you is present in the month, he shall fast in it." — 2:185

This particular month has been chosen for fasting because it is the month in which the Quran was revealed. It is well-known that the Quran was revealed piecemeal during a period of twenty-three years; therefore by its revelation in the month of Ramadan is meant that its revelation first began in that month. The first revelation came to the Holy Prophet during one of the nights of the month of Ramadan when he was in the cave of Hira, being the 24th of Ramadan according to some.[20] The month which witnessed the greatest spiritual experience of the Holy Prophet was thus considered to be the most suitable month for the spiritual discipline of the Muslim community, which was to be effected through fasting.

If a particular time had not been specified the discipline would have lost all its value. It is due to the choice of a particular month that with its advent the whole Muslim world is, as it were, moved by one current from one end to the other. All sections of Muslim society, from one end of the earth to the other, suddenly change the course of their lives when Ramadan begins. There is no other example of a mass movement on this scale on the face of the earth, and this is due to the specification of a particular month.

Persons who may not fast

People who are exempted from fasting are specially mentioned either in the Holy Quran or in the Hadith. The Quran mentions the sick and those on journey in the following words:

> "But whoever among you is sick or on a journey, [he shall fast] a like number of other days. And those who find it extremely hard[21] may effect redemption by feeding a poor one." — 2:184

This is not an absolute exemption for the sick one and the traveller; they are required to fast afterwards, when the sickness has gone or when the journey ends, but there may be cases of protracted illness or constant journeying, and such people are allowed to effect a redemption by feeding a poor person for every fast missed. Hadith makes a further extension and gives relaxation to certain classes of people who, on account of some physical disability, are not able to fast; for example, those who are old, pregnant women, and women suckling a child, who should feed a poor person instead.[22] It will be seen that the underlying idea is that a burden should not be placed on anyone, which he or she is unable to bear. The case of old people who have become enfeebled by age is very clear, while in the case of pregnant and nursing women the permission to effect a redemption is due to the fact that fasting may cause harm to the unborn baby, or the baby that is being nursed, as well as to the woman herself; and as she is likely to remain in this condition for a sufficiently long time, she is given the benefit of the relaxation. Sickly people and those who are too weak to bear the burden would be dealt with as sick. Ibn Taimiyah further extends the principle that the fast may be deferred in cases of hardship, and holds that those engaged in war may not fast, though they may not be journeying, for, he adds, the hardships of war are greater than the hardships of travel.[23] From this it may be argued that, in unavoidable cases of very hard labour, as in gathering the harvest, the choice of postponing the fast may be given to those who are engaged in such labour.

To define the limits of sickness or travel is rather difficult. There is an opinion that whatever the ailment, great or small, it entitled a person to the benefit of the exception.[24] But generally it has been held that only such sickness as is likely to cause harm comes under the exception. As regards travel, there is nothing on record from the Holy Prophet as to its limit. It has been held that the proposed journey must be one that extends over more than a day, i.e., twenty-four hours; according to others, it must extend over two days; and still others think it necessary that it should extend over three days at least. But when the journey is actually started, the fast may be broken, whatever the distance travelled over may be. The exception relating to sickness and travel may be interpreted as meaning a sickness or journey which causes inconvenience to the subject of it, as the exception is followed by the words: "Allah desires ease for you, and He does not desire hardship for you" (2:185).

The sick person and the traveller have the option of keeping the fast if they do not find it hard, since if the fasts are broken the number of days must be completed afterwards when the sickness or the journey is over. The permissive nature of the words of the Quran is reflected in many of the most reliable Hadith reports. There are reports showing that the Holy Prophet himself kept a fast while on a journey.[25] In one hadith it is stated that on a certain journey on a very hot day, only the Prophet and one other man kept the fast.[26] When questioned by a person whether he should or should not break the fast when on a journey, his own inclination being for fasting, the Holy Prophet replied: "Keep the fast if you like, and break it if you like".[27] When people travelled with the Holy Prophet, those who kept the fast did not find fault with those who broke it, nor did those who broke the fast find fault with those who kept it.[28] There is no doubt a saying of the Holy Prophet to the effect that "it is not a virtue to fast when journeying," but these words were spoken to a person who was in severe distress on account of the fast, and around whom people had gathered to provide shade for him from the heat.[29]

Who is bound to fast?

The commandments of the Holy Quran are meant for those who are full-grown, and so is the injunction relating to fasts. According to Imam Malik, minors should not fast, but the Caliph Umar is quoted as saying: "Even our children are fasting".[30] The object may have been to habituate the children to fasting. From what has been stated above, it would further appear that only such people are bound to fast as are physically fit. Women are bound to fast if they are free from menstruation,[31] but they must make good the fasts not kept due to periods and complete the missed number after Ramadan. The bleeding of childbirth is considered as menstruation with this difference, that if the mother is nursing the baby, she can effect a redemption by feeding a poor person.

In all cases in which fasts have to be recovered, a person is at liberty to do it when he or she likes, before the coming of the next Ramadan.[32]

Voluntary fasts

In all the four principal ordinances of Islam — prayer, charity, fasting and pilgrimage — there is an obligatory part (*fard*) and a voluntary part (*nafl*). But there are some restrictions imposed on voluntary fasting. According to a hadith, what the Holy Prophet recommended to a person, who was intending to undertake voluntary fasting every-day, was voluntary fasting for three days in the month, or at the very most, on that man's insistence, every other day, but on no account should the voluntary fast be continuous. There are Hadith reports in which it is stated that the Holy Prophet especially recommended for voluntary fasting certain days of certain months, or the 13th, 14th and 15th of the lunar month, etc.,[33] but his own practice was that he never specified any particular day or days for voluntary fasting, as the following hadith shows:

> "Aishah was asked: Did the Messenger of Allah, may peace and the blessings of Allah be on him, specify any days [for fasting]. She said: No." [34]

Voluntary fasting is particularly prohibited on the two *'Īd* days.[35] It is also forbidden that Friday should be specially chosen for voluntary fasting.[36] Nor should a day or two before Ramadan be specially selected.[37] Other restrictions are that it should not be resorted to if it is likely to interfere with other duties. There is no asceticism in Islam, and no one is allowed to go to the length of neglecting his worldly duties for the sake of religious exercises. Religion is meant to enable one to live a better life, and voluntary fasting should be undertaken only if the aim is to achieve this objective.

This is made clear in the story of a husband and wife and their guest. The husband used to fast and pray excessively and neglect his wife. When the meal was served, the husband refused to eat because he was fasting. The guest said he would not eat unless his host also ate, so the husband broke the fast. Later the guest restrained him from excessive praying at night, and told him:

> "You owe a duty to your Lord, and you owe a duty to yourself, and you owe a duty to your wife and children."

When this was mentioned to the Holy Prophet, he approved of it.[38] Here the husband was forbidden to fast for the sake of his wife and guest. Similarly the wife should not resort to voluntary fasting without the permission of her husband.[39] And as the host in the story cited above broke the fast on account of his guest, there is a hadith that the guest should not undertake a voluntary fast without the permission of the host.[40]

Limits of the fast

The limits of a fast are clearly laid down in the Holy Quran:

> "And eat and drink until the whiteness of the day becomes distinct from the blackness of the night at dawn, then complete the fast till nightfall." — 2:187

The "night" begins when the sun sets, and hence the fast in the terminology of Islam is kept from the first appearance of dawn, which is generally about an hour and a half before sunrise, till sunset. Continuing the fast throughout the night and then the next day, so that there is no break, is definitely prohibited.[41] But one hadith permits continuity of fast till daybreak.[42] This would mean that one may not, if one chooses, break the fast at sunset but must take the morning meal for fasting for the next day; in other words, one must take a meal at least once in twenty-four hours. It appears, however, that the Holy Prophet himself sometimes kept a continuous fast;[43] but, for how many days, is not definitely known. When he was asked why he forbade it to others, when he himself kept continuous fasts, he replied:

> "I pass the night while my Lord gives me food and makes me drink." [44]

He referred of course to the spiritual food which sometimes makes a man bear hunger and thirst in an extraordinary way, thus, in a sense, taking the place of food and drink. But everyone had not the same spiritual sustenance, and, moreover, continuity of fast, if allowed generally, would have given rise to ascetic practices which Islam does not encourage.

Though the taking of a morning meal is not made obligatory, yet special stress is laid on it, and it is said to be a source of blessing, because it enables a person the better to cope with the hardship of the fast. The Holy Prophet is reported to have said:

> "Take the morning meal, for there is blessing in the morning meal (*suḥūr*)." [45]

This meal was taken very near the break of dawn. One Companion relates that, after taking the morning meal, he hastened to the mosque so that he might be able to join the morning prayer. Another says that the interval between the finishing of the morning meal and the beginning of prayer in congregation was such that hardly fifty verses could be recited in it.[46] It is even recommended that the morning meal should be taken as near the break of dawn as possible.[47] And even if the call to prayer for *Fajr* prayers is sounded when the dawn has fully appeared, and you have a cup in your hand ready to drink, you need not put it away and may drink it up.[48]

As it is recommended in the case of the morning meal that it should be as late as possible, it is recommended that the breaking of the fast should be as early as possible. The Holy Prophet is reported to have said that when the sun is set, the fast should be broken, and according to another hadith:

> "People will have the good so long as they hasten in breaking the fast." [49]

Some wait to break the fast till they see the stars, thinking that the night does not set in till darkness is spread, but there is no authority for this.

An important question arises here regarding countries in which the days are sometimes very long, where it would be beyond the power of ordinary people to abstain from food and drink from the breaking of the dawn to sunset. There is a report according to which the Companions of the Holy Prophet are related to have asked him about their prayers in a day which extended to a year or a month, and the Prophet is related to have answered that they should measure according to the measure of their days.[50] From this it would follow that in countries where the days in the summer are too long the time of fasting may be measured in accordance with the length of an ordinary day, or where practicable postpone the fasts to shorter days of about normal length.[51]

The *niyyah* ('intention')

A good deal of misunderstanding prevails on the question of *niyyah* in the observance of fasts. The *niyyah* really means *intention, aim* or *purpose* in the doing of a thing; but it is wrongly supposed that the *niyyah* consists in the repetition of certain words stating that one intends to do so and so. Bukhari shows the true significance of *niyyah* when he gives as the heading to one of his chapters: "He who fasts during Ramadan having faith [in Allah] and seeking His pleasure and having an aim or purpose (*niyyah*)".[52] And he adds a portion of a hadith in which it is stated that "people will be raised up [on the Day of Judgment] according to their aims (*'alā niyyati-him*)".

The very first hadith with which Bukhari opens his Hadith collection is an example of what *niyyah* means: "[Good] actions shall be judged only by their aims". The example of actions given there is *hijrah,* the flight of a person for the sake of his principles which is an action of the highest value, but as the report tells us, if the *hijrah* is undertaken with a bad aim in view, for worldly purposes, it loses all its value. Hence if a good action is done with a bad aim, it shall not benefit the doer. Exactly the same object is in view in the statement that there must be a *niyyah* in fasting, as Bukhari says; that is, the one who fasts must have an aim or purpose before him. The aim or purpose of fasting has already been stated, being, according to the Quran, to make the fast a spiritual discipline, to attain nearness to God and to seek His pleasure in all one's actions, and to make it a moral discipline, to shun all evil. It is in this sense alone that the *niyyah* is of the essence of fasting, as it is in fact of the essence of all good actions.

"Formulating the *niyyah*", or the expression of one's intention in set words, is unknown to the Quran and the Hadith. Only in the case of voluntary fasting, instances are reported in Hadith of making up the mind in daytime to fast, when nothing had been eaten up to that time, which is understandable. But there is no question of such intention in the month of Ramadan, when people know that they must fast.

What breaks the fast

The three things which a person should abstain from in fasting being eating, drinking and having sexual intercourse, these three, if resorted to of free will and intentionally, between daybreak and sunset, would break the fast, but if done through forgetfulness or inadvertently, the fast remains and must be completed.[53] Rinsing the mouth with water or with a toothbrush, gargling or sniffing the water into the nostrils, even if a little water passes into the throat unintentionally, does not break the fast.[54] Nor does taking a bath or keeping a wet cloth on the head or pouring water on the head break the fast, even though done intentionally to relieve the severity of thirst.[55] Vomiting also does not break the fast, for a fast is broken by that which goes into the body, not by that which comes out.[56] It is also related that the Holy Prophet would kiss his wife when fasting.[57]

There is a difference of opinion regarding the punishment for breaking a fast intentionally before its time. The Holy Quran is silent on this point, while Hadith only shows that it is sufficient that the violator should be sincerely repentant.[58] If fast is broken on a cloudy day, under the impression that the sun has set, and the sun then appears, then the fast should be completed.[59] If one is fasting and then undertakes a journey, the fast may be broken.[60] The same rule may be followed in the case of sickness. In the case of voluntary fast, a person is at liberty to break the fast on account of a guest or the persistence of a friend.[61]

Ethical, moral and spiritual side of fasting

What has been said hitherto relates only to the external side of the fast but, as stated in the beginning, the essence of the fast is its moral and spiritual value, and the Holy Quran and Hadith have laid special stress on this. One hadith says:

> "Whoever does not give up lying and acting falsely, Allah does not stand in need of his giving up food and drink." [62]

This is true of all the Islamic injunctions. One who says his prayers and does not keep in view their inner meaning, the object of prayer, is condemned in clear words:

> "So woe to the praying ones, who are unmindful of [the object of] their prayers". — 107:4–5

In another hadith, the ethical side of the fast is shown in the following words:

> "Fasting is a shield, so let the one who fasts not indulge in any foul speech or do any evil deed, and if anyone fights or quarrels with him or abuses him, he should say, I am fasting. By Him Who holds my soul in His hand, the breath of the one who is fasting is more pleasant with Allah than the scent of musk." [63]

It is not refraining from food that makes the breath of the faster so sweet; it is refraining from foul speech and abuse and evil words and deeds of all kinds, so much so that he does not utter an offensive word even by way of retaliation. Thus a fasting person undergoes not only a physical discipline by curbing his carnal desires, the craving for food and drink, and the sex appetite, but he is actually required to undergo a direct moral discipline by avoiding all kinds of evil words and evil deeds. In the sight of God, as plainly stated in these Hadith reports, the fast loses its value not only by taking food or drink but also by telling a lie, using foul language, acting unfaithfully, or doing an evil deed.

The moral value of the fasting discipline is further enhanced by laying stress on the doing of good to humanity in the month of Ramadan. The example of the Holy Prophet is quoted in this connection in a hadith:

> "The Prophet, may peace and the blessings of Allah be upon him, was the most bountiful of all people, and he exceeded his own bounty in the month of Ramadan." [64]

Another hadith describes the month of Ramadan as "a month in which the sufferings of the poor and the hungry must be attended to".[65]

These injunctions make clear the significance of the hadith which says that, when the month of Ramadan commences, "the doors of Heaven are opened and the doors of Hell are closed and the devils are put into chains".[66] The devils are chained for the one who keeps the fast because he curbs and conquers the lower passions, by exciting which the devil makes a person fall into evil. The doors of Hell are closed on him because he shuns all evil which is man's hell. The doors of Heaven are opened for him because he rises above physical desires and devotes himself to the service of humanity. In one hadith, fasting is described as bringing about a forgiveness of sins "for one who fasts in Ramadan having faith [in Allah] and seeking His pleasure" and having an aim or purpose.[67] There is not the least doubt that fasting, as qualified here, that is, when it is kept having true faith in God and when the person fasting resorts to it as a discipline for seeking the pleasure of God, is practical repentance of the highest value; and when a person sincerely repents of sins, his previous sins are forgiven, because the course of his life has been changed.

There is, however, yet another sense in which the doors of Heaven are opened to a fasting person in the month of Ramadan. It is specially suited for spiritual advancement, for attaining nearness to God. Speaking of Ramadan, the Holy Quran says:

> "And when My servants ask you concerning Me, surely I am near; I answer the prayer of the supplicant when he calls on Me..." — 2:186

The ways of attaining nearness to God are here spoken of as being specially opened in Ramadan, and this nearness is to be sought through prayer. It is for this reason that the Holy Prophet used to have special regard for *Tahajjud* prayers in the month of Ramadan. And he also recommended that his followers should, during this month, rise at night for prayers.[68]

I'tikāf

I'tikāf means literally 'to stay in a place'; technically it is staying in a mosque for a certain number of days, especially the last ten days of the month of Ramadan. An *i'tikāf* may be performed in other days,[69] but the last ten days of Ramadan are specially mentioned in Hadith and *i'tikāf* is spoken of in the Holy Quran in connection with Ramadan.[70] Bukhari has devoted a whole book to *i'tikāf,* showing the practice of the Holy Prophet in this connection. During these days, the person who enters the state of *i'tikāf* dissociates himself from all worldly affairs, and he does not leave the mosque unless there is necessity, such as evacuation, or having a bath, etc.[71] Women are also allowed to enter a state of *i'tikāf.*[72] The person in *i'tikāf* may be visited by other people.[73]

Lailat al-Qadr

One of the last ten nights of the month of Ramadan is called *Lailat al-Qadr, the night of grandeur* or *majesty.* In the Holy Quran, it is spoken of in two places:

> "Surely We revealed it on *Lailat al-Qadr.* And what will make you comprehend what *Lailat al-Qadr is? Lailat al-Qadr* is better than a thousand months. The angels and the Spirit descend in it by the permission of their Lord — for every affair — Peace! it is till the rising of the morning." — chapter 97.

Here this night is spoken of as the night in which the Quran was revealed, and it is further stated that it is the night on which angels and the Spirit descend. It is also mentioned in ch. 44 where it is called "a blessed night" (*lailat-in mubārakat-in*):

> "By the Book that makes manifest [the truth]! We revealed it on a blessed night — truly We are ever-warning. Therein is made clear every affair full of wisdom". — 44:2−5

It will be seen that, in both places, the Holy Quran is spoken of as having been revealed on this night, and in 2:185 it is stated that the Quran was revealed in the month of Ramadan, which shows that this night occurs in the month of Ramadan. The revelation of the Quran on this night means that its revelation began on that night; in other words, the first revelation came to the Holy Prophet on this night. It is called a blessed night or the grand night because in it was laid the basis of a new revelation to the world which contains every matter full of wisdom and knowledge. *Lailat al-Qadr* is, therefore, as it were, the anniversary of the revelation of the Quran.

As shown above, the last ten days of Ramadan are specially observed as days of devotion, so much so that, though Islam discourages asceticism, yet in these ten days, a Muslim is allowed to lead an ascetic life, by keeping himself to the mosque and giving up all worldly affairs. There are various Hadith reports showing that Muslims should look for this night as one of the odd nights in the last ten nights of Ramadan or in the last seven nights.[74] According to some reports it is the twenty-fifth or twenty-seventh or twenty-ninth night of Ramadan. One hadith says that some of the Companions of the Holy Prophet were shown *Lailat al-Qadr* in their dreams in the last seven nights.[75]

It should be borne in mind that *Lailat al-Qadr* is a spiritual experience, as it was the spiritual, not the physical, experience of the Holy Prophet, and as the hadith mentioned just above shows, it was the spiritual experience of the Companions, and therefore it is an error to think that it can be observed as a physical experience, or that any physical change is witnessed on that night. It is the spiritual experience of the one who exerts himself in Ramadan to seek nearness to the Divine Being.

Notes to Chapter 13

1. Bukhari, book 30: 'Fasting', ch. 1, h. 1892–1893.
2. *Ibid.,* ch. 69, h. 2004.
3. *Encyclopaedia Britannica,* 11th edition, art. Fasting.
4. Matthew, 6:16–18. See also Luke, 5:33–35 on this subject.
5. Acts, 13:2–3, 14:23. 2 Cor., 6:5, 11:27.
6. 2 Samuel, 12:16–18.
7. For example, 1 Samuel, 31:13.
8. Leviticus, 16:29.
9. The Quran, 2:183.
10. Raghib's *Mufradāt.*
11. The Quran, 45:19, 3:76, 9:4, 9:7, 2:194, 9:36, 9:123.
12. The Quran, 7:128, 11:49, 28:83, 38:49.
13. The Quran, 9:112, 66:5.
14. Raghib's *Mufradāt.*
15. Bukhari, book 2: 'Faith', ch. 28, h. 38.
16. Bukhari, book 30: 'Fasting', ch. 2, h. 1894.

17. *Ibid.,* ch. 13, h. 1913.

18. *Ibid.,* ch. 11, h. 1906. Muslim, book 13: 'Fasting', ch. 2, h. 1080a (MDS: h. 2498).

19. Bukhari, book 30, ch. 11, h. 1907.

20. Ibn Jarir Tabari's Commentary of the Quran, under 2:185. (*Editor's Note:* By 24th may be meant the night *following* the 24th, i.e., the 25th night.)

21. The Arabic word is *yuṭīqūna-hū,* which is generally interpreted as meaning *those who are able to do it.* If this interpretation is adopted, the significance would be that invalids and travellers may either fast afterwards when they are not under such disability, or they may effect a redemption by feeding a poor man for every day of fasting. But the other interpretation which some commentators have accepted is preferable, i.e., that it means *those who find it hard* to keep the fast even afterwards; only such persons are allowed to effect a redemption by feeding a poor person.

22. Bukhari, book 65: 'Commentary on the Quran', ch. 25 on *Surah* 2, v. 184, ch. heading. Abu Dawud, book 14: 'Fasting', ch. 3, h. 2318.

23. *Zād al-Ma'ād,* vol. 1, pp. 165, 166.

24. Bukhari, book 65: 'Commentary on the Quran', ch. 25 on *Surah* 2, v. 184, ch. heading.

25. Bukhari, book 30: 'Fasting', ch. 33, h. 1941.

26. *Ibid.,* ch. 35, h. 1945.

27. *Ibid.,* ch. 33, h. 1943.

28. *Ibid.,* ch. 37, h. 1947.

29. *Ibid.,* ch. 36, h. 1946.

30. *Ibid.,* ch. 47, ch. heading.

31. *Ibid.,* ch. 41, h. 1951.

32. *Ibid.,* ch. 40, h. 1950; see also ch. heading.

33. *Ibid.,* ch. 62, h. 1983; see also ch. 60, ch. heading and h. 1981.

34. *Ibid.,* ch. 64, h. 1987.

35. *Ibid.,* ch. 66, h. 1990–1992.

36. *Ibid.,* ch. 63, h. 1984–1986.

37. *Ibid.,* ch. 14, h. 1914.

38. *Ibid.,* ch. 51, h. 1968.

39. Bukhari, book 67: 'Marriage', ch. 85, h. 5192.

40. Tirmidhi, book 8: 'Fasting', ch. 70, h. 789 (MDS: book 6).

41. Bukhari, book 30: 'Fasting', chs. 48–49, h. 1961–1966.

42. *Ibid.,* ch. 50, h. 1967.

43. *Ibid.,* chs. 48–49, h. 1961–1966.

44. *Ibid.,* chs. 48–49, h. 1961, 1963, 1965 1966.

45. *Ibid.,* ch. 20, h. 1923.

46. Bukhari, book 9: 'Times of the prayers', ch. 27, h. 576.

47. *Musnad* of Ahmad ibn Hanbal, v. 5, p. 147.

48. Abu Dawud, book 14: 'Fasting', ch. 18, h. 2350.

49. Bukhari, book 30: 'Fasting', ch. 45, h. 1957.

50. Muslim, book 54: 'Tribulations and Portents of the Hour', ch. 20, h. 2937a (MDS: book 52, ch. 20, h. 7373). Abu Dawud, book 39: 'Battles (*Al-Malāḥim*)', ch. 14, h. 4321 (MDS: b. 36).

51. *Editor's Note:* This paragraph is taken from a footnote to 2:187 by Maulana Muhammad Ali in his English Translation of the Holy Quran.

52. Bukhari, book 30: 'Fasting', ch. 6, ch. heading.

53. *Ibid.,* ch. 26, h. 1933.

54. *Ibid.,* see ch. headings of chs. 25, 26, 27, 28.

55. *Ibid.,* ch. 25, ch. heading. Mishkat, book 7: 'Fasting', ch. 3, sec. 2, h. 1913 (v. 1, p. 436).

56. Bukhari, book 30, ch. 32, ch. heading.

57. *Ibid.,* ch. 23, h. 1927.

58. *Ibid.,* ch. 30, h. 1936.

59. *Ibid.,* ch. 46, h. 1959.

60. *Ibid.,* ch. 34, h. 1944.

61. *Ibid.,* ch. 51, h. 1968.

62. *Ibid.,* ch. 8, h. 1903.

63. *Ibid.,* ch. 2, h. 1894.

64. *Ibid.,* ch. 7, h. 1902.

65. Mishkat, book 7: 'Fasting', ch. 1, sec. 3, h. 1868 (v. 1, p. 427).

66. Bukhari, book 30: 'Fasting', ch. 5, h. 1899.

67. *Ibid.,* ch. 6, h. 1901 and ch. heading. See also book 2: 'Faith', ch. 28, h. 38.

68. Bukhari, book 2: 'Faith', ch. 27, h. 37.

69. Bukhari, book 33: *'I'tikāf',* ch. 6, h. 2033–2034. Abu Dawud, book 14: 'Fasting', ch. 78, h. 2464 (MDS: ch. 77).

70. The Quran, 2:187.

71. Bukhari, book 33: *'I'tikāf'*, ch. 3, h. 2029; and ch. 4, ch. heading.

72. *Ibid.,* ch. 6, ch. heading.

73. *Ibid.,* ch. 11, h. 2038.

74. Bukhari, book 32: 'Virtues of *Lailat-ul-Qadr*', ch. 3, h. 2017; and ch. 2, h. 2015.

75. *Ibid.,* ch. 2, h. 2015.

14. Pilgrimage (*Ḥajj*)

Ḥajj

The word *ḥajj* means, literally, 'repairing to a thing for the sake of a visit', and in Islamic law 'repairing to the House of Allah' to observe the necessary devotions.[1] *Bait-Allāh,* or the House of Allah, is one of the names by which the *Kaʿbah* is known. The word *manāsik,* meaning 'acts of worship', is particularly used to signify the acts of devotion prescribed in the pilgrimage to Makkah, and it is generally under the head *manāsik* that injunctions relating to the pilgrimage are mentioned in Hadith collections.

Critics' views on adoption of the pilgrimage by Islam

As an institution *ḥajj* existed before the advent of Islam from a very remote antiquity. Modern Western criticism takes the view that its adoption by Islam, with certain reforms, of course, was due to several causes which sprang up after the Prophet's migration to Madinah. Chief among these causes are said to be the victory won by Islam at Badr which, it is suggested, made the Prophet look forward to the conquest of Makkah, and the final rupture with the Jews, whom the Prophet had, at first, hoped to win over to his cause.[2]

This theory is in flat contradiction to historical facts. The battle of Badr was fought in the month of Ramadan, in the second year of Hijrah, and the final rupture with the Jews came in the third year after the battle of Uhud; while the Kaʿbah was made a *qiblah* sixteen months after the Hijrah,[3] that is to say, about three months before the battle of Badr. The structure which, according to this theory, was built on the victory of Badr and the rupture with the Jews — that is to say, the idea of formulating a doctrine of the religion of Abraham, the father of monotheism, as a prototype of Islam, Judaism and Christianity; of the sacredness of the Kaʿbah and its connection with the names of Abraham and Ishmael; of the Kaʿbah being made a *qiblah* and of the institution of *ḥajj* with prospects of conquering Makkah — all this existed not only long before the battle of Badr but even before the Holy Prophet's move to Madinah. The religion of Abraham as pure monotheism is mentioned in a chapter of the Quran belonging to the middle Makkah period:

> "Then We revealed to you [O Prophet]: Follow the faith of Abraham, the upright one; and he was not of those who set up partners [with Allah]." — 16:123

And again in a chapter belonging to the last Makkah period:

> "My Lord has guided me to the right path — a right religion, the faith of Abraham, the upright one, and he was not of those who set up partners [with Allah]." — 6:161

Sacredness of Makkah and the Ka'bah recognized in earliest revelations

Similarly, the sacredness of Makkah and its connection with the names of Abraham and Ishmael finds clear mention in the early Makkah revelations. In one of the earliest chapters, Makkah is described as "this city made secure" (95:3). In another equally early revelation, it is referred to simply as the City:

> "No, I call to witness this City — and you [O Prophet] will be made free from obligation in this City — and the father and the offspring whom he produced!" —90:1–3.

Here, in the last words, Abraham and Ishmael are referred to. In a revelation of the same period, the Ka'bah is called *al-Bait al-ma'mūr*, meaning "the frequented House" or the House that is visited (52:4), while another revelation of the early Makkah period speaks of *al-Masjid al-Harām* or "the Sacred Mosque" (17:1). The sacredness of Makkah, the names of Abraham and Ishmael in connection with it, and the fact of its being a place of resort for people, are spoken of in still clearer words in revelations of the middle Makkah period:

> "I am commanded only to serve the Lord of this City, Who has made it sacred, and His are all things." — 27:91

> "And when Abraham said: ... Our Lord, I have settled a part of my offspring in a valley unproductive of fruit near Your Sacred House, our Lord, that they may keep up prayer; so make the hearts of some people yearn towards them and provide them with fruits..." — 14:35,37

All these are themes of the earliest as well as the later revelations, and thus the theory built up by the critics of Islam has no foundation whatever.

Why Ka'bah was not made *qiblah* earlier

It is true that the various commandments and prohibitions were revealed gradually, and that the command to make the Ka'bah a *qiblah* was revealed at Madinah, but even this happened before the battle of Badr. Despite even the fact that it was the Prophet's own desire that the Ka'bah should be made his *qiblah*,[4] he continued to follow the *qiblah* of the last prophet that had passed away before him, that is, Jerusalem, and awaited the Divine direction. The Quran recognized the truth of all the prophets, including the prophets of Israel, and as Jesus was the last of those prophets and his *qiblah* the same as that of the Israelite prophets, namely, the temple at Jerusalem, which place was honoured by the Quran (17:1) as *al-Masjid al-Aqṣā* (lit., *the Remote Mosque*), he retained it as his *qiblah* until he received an express revelation to turn towards the Sacred Mosque. Moreover, he did not receive that commandment when he was at Makkah among the idolaters when it might have been said that he was scheming to win over the Arabs; but it was after his coming to Madinah, at a time when relations with the Jews were still friendly, when the prospects of winning over the Arabs were as distant as ever, and when war with the Quraish at Makkah had become inevitable, that the Holy Prophet received a revelation to turn to the Ka'bah as the future *qiblah* of the Muslim world.

When was pilgrimage first instituted

The *hajj* was a recognized institution in the first and second years of Hijrah before the commencement of the battles with the Quraish. The second chapter which was, in the main, revealed in 1–2 A.H., is full of directions relating to *hajj*, the context whereof shows clearly that fighting had not actually taken place, though prospects of a war were in sight. The months in which *hajj* is to be performed are mentioned in 2:189 and again in 2:197. Between these two verses occur the verses by which the Muslims were permitted to resort to fighting to defend themselves against those who attacked them (2:190–193); from which it will be seen that the details of *hajj* were being given when fighting was as yet only permitted, and it was after that that the actual fighting began. The details of *hajj* were, therefore, revealed before the battle of Badr. There is a clear injunction there to accomplish the *hajj:*

> "And accomplish the *hajj* and the *'umrah* [i.e., the visit to the Ka'bah at any time][5] for Allah." — 2:196

The rules of conduct to be observed when proceeding on *hajj* are also stated in the same context:

> "…there shall be no immodest speech, nor abusing, nor altercation in the pilgrimage." — 2:197

Other features and details of the *hajj* are also mentioned in verses 196 to 203, and even in an earlier verse 2:158.

Hence the institution of *hajj* had already been recognized as part of the laws of Islam. In fact, we find a Muslim, here and there, performing the *hajj* in the earliest days when, on account of some alliance, he deemed himself secure, which was impossible, of course, for the generality of the Muslims. It is related of one Muslim that, on account of his friendship with a certain Quraish chief, he went to Makkah to perform an *'umrah* after the Hijrah and before the battle of Badr.[6] Hence it is clear that *hajj* was a recognized institution of Islam in 1 A.H.

In fact, *hajj* was instituted before the Hijrah took place, and while the Holy Prophet was still in Makkah. The chapter entitled *al-Ḥajj* was revealed towards the close of the Holy Prophet's career at Makkah and it was in this chapter that *hajj* was proclaimed to be an institution of Islam:

> "And proclaim to mankind the Pilgrimage:[7] they will come to you on foot and on every lean camel, coming from every remote path". — 22:27

Verses 27 to 29 of this chapter leave not the least doubt that *hajj* was ordained as an Islamic institution before the Hijrah.

Description of the Ka'bah

The root-word *ka'aba* means 'it became prominent' or 'it became high and exalted'.[8] The Ka'bah is a rectangular building, almost in the centre of the Sacred Mosque (*Al-Masjid al-Ḥarām*). Its front and back walls, i.e., north-east and south-west, are each 40 feet (12 metres) in length, and the two side-walls 35 feet (10·5m) each, the height being 50 feet (15m). The four walls of the Ka'bah are covered with a black curtain called Kiswa (lit., *clothing*). The four corners of the Ka'bah are known by different names, being named after Iraq (north corner), Yaman (south), *Shām* or Syria (west), and *Ḥajar al-Aswad,* the Black Stone (east). The door of the Ka'bah is in the north-east wall, about seven feet (two metres) from the ground, not in the middle of the wall but nearer the Black Stone which is in the east corner. When the Ka'bah is opened, a stair-case is placed in front of it to enable the visitors to reach the entrance.

Outside the building is an open space, called *al-Ḥijr* (lit., 'prohibited'), marked by a semi-circular wall three feet (about one metre) high, running opposite the north-west wall of the Ka'bah, the two ends of this wall being about six feet (1·8m) distant from the north and west corners of the Ka'bah, and the central part about 37 feet (11m) from the wall. For the purpose of making circuits, *al-Ḥijr* is included in the building.

In the east corner at the height of about five feet (1·5m) is the *Ḥajar al-Aswad* (meaning 'the Black Stone') built into the wall. It is of a reddish black colour, about eight inches (20cm) in diameter, and is now broken into pieces held together by a silver band.

The *Maqām Ibrāhīm* must also be mentioned in connection with the Ka'bah. It means 'the place of Abraham', and the name is given to a very small building within the Sacred Mosque, about five feet (1·5m) square, supported on six columns eight feet (2·4m) high. This name, handed down from antiquity, is a decided proof of the connection of Abraham with the Ka'bah, and attention is drawn to this in the Quran in 3:97. But in 2:125, it refers to the Sacred House itself.*

History of the Ka'bah

The Ka'bah is stated in the Holy Quran to be "the first House [of Divine worship] appointed for mankind" (3:96). In one place it is

---

* *Editor's Note:* The descriptions of the Ka'bah and various other buildings and locations associated with the pilgrimage given in this chapter, and also the movements of the pilgrims as explained here, are according to how these used to be traditionally. In recent years, these have changed in many ways due to modernization of buildings and introduction of new facilities to cater for the hugely increased number of pilgrims.

called the "Ancient House" (22:29). It is also called the "Sacred House" (5:97, 14:37); in other words, a place whose sanctity must not be violated. There is nothing in the Quran or the Hadith to show when and by whom the Kaʿbah was first built, but it is said to have been rebuilt by Abraham and Ishmael, being already there when Abraham left Ishmael in the wilderness of Arabia,[9] along with the baby's mother Hagar. It appears from this that Ishmael had been purposely left near the Sacred House; it was, in fact, under a Divine commandment that Abraham took this step, as stated in a report in Bukhari.[10] It would seem that the Kaʿbah was then in a demolished condition and was afterwards, when Ishmael grew to manhood, rebuilt by Abraham and Ishmael as stated in the Quran in 2:127. The report cited above narrates these events at length. Besides being in a ruined condition, it seems to have had idols placed in it and Abraham was required to purify it of these, as the Quran tells us.[11]

The Kaʿbah was again rebuilt by the Quraish when the Holy Prophet was a young man, and he personally took part in its building, carrying stones on his shoulders. It remained as it was built by the Quraish until the time of Abdullah ibn Zubair (d. 692 C.E.), when the building having been damaged by the Umayyad army which had besieged Makkah, Abdullah decided to rebuild it, instead of repairing it, including the open space of *Hijr* in the building itself. But after the fall of Abdullah, Hajjaj ibn Yusuf (d. 714 C.E.) again rebuilt it on the foundations of the structure erected by the Quraish. And the building today rests on the same foundations.

Al-Masjid al-Ḥarām

The Kaʿbah stands in the centre of an area known as *al-Masjid al-Ḥarām* or the Sacred Mosque, the famous mosque of Makkah. The name is met with in pre-Islamic literature. In the Holy Quran this name occurs in revelations of the early Makkah period, as in 17:1. The area of the Sacred Mosque contains, besides the Kaʿbah, the *Maqām Ibrāhīm* and the building over the fountain of Zamzam. The Sacred Mosque was the centre of all administrative activities before Islam, as within it was situated the Makkan Council Hall (*Dār al-Nadwah*) where all important matters regarding the welfare of the people were settled. Since the advent of Islam, the Sacred Mosque has been the pivot of the intellectual activities of Makkah, and the whole Muslim world looks upon it as its central point.

Ancient origin of the Ka'bah and the pilgrimage

The sacredness of the territory around Makkah and the fact of the Ka'bah being the centre of pilgrimage can only have come down from time immemorial, for there is no tradition or record showing that it was introduced at any time within historical memory. Some of the ceremonial is undoubtedly due to Abraham, as for instance the running between Safa and Marwah which is in commemoration of Hagar's running to and fro to seek water for the baby Ishmael, or the sacrifice which is in commemoration of Abraham's endeavour to obey the Divine commandment which, he thought, meant the sacrifice of Ishmael. The circumambulation of the Ka'bah, however, must have existed before Abraham. But all the main features of the pilgrimage, as existing at the advent of Prophet Muhammad, were undoubtedly based on the authority of Abraham. According to the statement of the Holy Quran, the order was given to Abraham and Ishmael:

> "And when We pointed to Abraham the place of the House, saying: Do not set up any partner with Me, and purify My House for those who make circuits and stand to pray and bow and prostrate themselves. And proclaim to mankind the Pilgrimage…" — 22:26–27

Thus Abraham not only rebuilt the Ka'bah and purified it of all traces of idolatry, but he also enjoined *hajj* with its main features, which were therefore based on Divine revelation. Abraham and Ishmael are spoken of in 2:128 as praying to God to show them their "ways of devotions (*manāsik*)". And it was by Divine revelation that Prophet Muhammad was led to adopt them.

The only change introduced into the features of the pilgrimage, after Abraham, seems to have been the placing of idols in the Ka'bah and other important places. The Ka'bah itself had within it 360 idols, all of which were thrown out by the Holy Prophet at the conquest of Makkah. Some other reforms were also made. For instance, the tribes of Quraish and Kananah used to think it beneath their dignity to join other pilgrims in going forth to the plain of Arafat. This distinction was evidently an innovation on the part of the more powerful tribes; and as Islam tolerated no distinctions, they were ordered to go forth to Arafat along with the others. Another change was the prohibition to go naked while making circuits round the Ka'bah.[12]

Asceticism combined with secularism

Islam discourages asceticism in all its aspects. Yet it lays the greatest stress upon the spiritual development of man, and in its four main institutions, i.e., prayer, *zakāt,* fasting and *hajj,* it introduces workable ascetic formulae into daily life — an asceticism which is quite in keeping with the secular side of life. The five daily prayers require the sacrifice of a small part of a person's time and, without in any way interfering with his everyday life, enable him to realize the Divine that is within him. The institution of *zakāt* demands the giving up of a small portion of his wealth without interfering with his right to property. Fasting requires the giving up of food and drink but not in such a manner as to make one unfit for carrying on regular work or business. It is only in *hajj* that asceticism assumes a marked form, for the pilgrim is required not only to give up his regular work for a number of days for the sake of the journey to Makkah, but he must, in addition, give up many other amenities of life, and live more or less, the life of an ascetic. The *hajj* is, however, a function which generally comes only once in a lifetime, and, therefore, while leading a person through the highest spiritual experience, it does not interfere in any appreciable degree with the regular course of his life.

Levelling influence of the pilgrimage

No other institution in the world has the wonderful influence of the *hajj* in levelling all distinctions of race, colour and rank. Not only do people of all races and all countries meet together before the Holy House of God as His servants, as members of one Divine family, but they are clad in one dress — in two white sheets — and there remains nothing to distinguish the high from the low. There is a vast concourse of human beings, all clad in one dress, all moving in one way, all having but one word to speak, *labbaika Allāhumma labbaika,* meaning *here are we, O Allah! here are we in Your august presence.* It is *hajj* alone that brings into the domain of practicality what would otherwise seem impossible, namely, that all people, to whatever class or country they belong, should speak one language and wear one dress. Thus is every Muslim made to pass once in his life through that narrow gate of equality which leads to broad brotherhood. All human beings are equal in birth and death; they all come into life in one and the same way, and all pass out of it in one and the same way, but *hajj* is the only occasion on which they are taught how to live alike, how to act alike and how to feel alike.

A higher spiritual experience

The description of *ḥajj* usually takes notice only of its outward actions, without trying to discover their real significance and inner value. The details of *ḥajj* will be discussed later on, but looking broadly at the scene at Makkah during the days of the pilgrimage, one is struck in the first place by the unity which is achieved among the discordant elements of humanity. Deeper than that, however, lies another value of *ḥajj,* and this is the higher spiritual experience which is made possible by this unique assemblage of human beings, the experience of drawing nearer and nearer to God till man feels that all those veils which keep him away from God are entirely removed and he is standing in the Divine presence.

It is true that God does not live in Makkah, nor is the Ka'bah the House of God in a material sense; true, too, that a Muslim is taught to hold communion with God in a remote corner, in solitude, in the dead of nights, and thus all alone he goes through the experience of drawing nearer to God; but there is yet a higher spiritual experience to which he can attain in that vast concourse of people assembled in the plain of Arafat. Every member of this great assemblage sets out from his home with that object in view. He discards all those comforts of life which act as a veil against the inner sight. He is required to put on the simplest dress, to avoid all talk of an amorous nature and all kinds of disputes, and to undergo all the privations entailed by an arduous journey to a distant place like Arabia, so that he may be able to concentrate all his meditation on the Divine Being. The comforts of life are undoubtedly a veil which shut out the other world from human sight, and sufferings and privations certainly make a person turn to God.

To concentrate all one's ideas on God, not in solitude but in the company of others, is thus the object of *ḥajj*. A man may have the company of his wife and yet he must not have amorous talk with her; he may be in the company of his adversary, yet he is not allowed to have any quarrel with him; and all this that he may have a higher spiritual experience, the spiritual experience not of the hermit who is cut off from the world, not of the devotee holding communion with God in the corner of solitude, but of the man living in the world, in the company of his wife, his friends and his foes.

The higher significance of one's spiritual experience in an assemblage is evident from another point of view as well. The company of a person who is inspired by similar feelings and who is undergoing a similar experience would undoubtedly give additional force to the spiritual experience of each one of such companions. Take the case of hundreds of thousands of people, all inspired by the one idea of feeling the presence of the Divine Being, all concentrating their minds on the One Supreme Being Who for the time is their sole object; and add to this the mighty effect of the outward unity of them all, clad in the same two sheets, crying in one language what is understood by all, *labbaika Allāhumma labbaika* — "Here are we, O Allah! here are we in Your august presence" (known as the *talbiyah*). Their appearance, as well as the words which are on their lips, show that they are standing in the Divine presence, and are so engrossed in the contemplation of the Divine Being that they have lost all ideas of self and the Divine presence is all in all to them. God is surely not in Makkah to the exclusion of other places, yet that vast assemblage at Makkah sees Him and feels His presence as if He is actually there in their very midst. Such is the higher experience of the pilgrims, gathered together in one place.

On whom is pilgrimage obligatory?

Hajj is obligatory on every adult, only once in his life, and its performance more often is voluntary.[13] The obligation to perform the *hajj* is further subject to the condition that one is able to undertake a journey to Makkah:

> "And pilgrimage to the House is a duty which people owe to Allah — whoever can find a way to it." — 3:97

The ability to undertake the journey depends on various circumstances. There may be a physical disability rendering one unable to bear the hardships of the long journey. For instance, a very aged man was deemed to be exempt from the obligation.[14] Or, the disability may be due to financial reasons, as when a person has not got sufficient provisions for the journey as well as for the dependents whom he leaves behind. The condition of taking sufficient provisions for the journey is laid down in the Holy Quran:

> "And make provision for yourselves, the best provision being to keep one's duty." — 2:197

Danger to life may also be a reason for freeing a person from the obligation of *hajj*. The Holy Prophet himself and many of his Companions could not perform a pilgrimage after the flight to Madinah, because their lives would not have been safe at Makkah. And when ultimately the Prophet undertook a pilgrimage (*'umrah*) with about 1,400 Companions in 6 A.H., he was not allowed by the Quraish to proceed beyond Hudaibiyah and had to come back without performing it.

'Umrah

The word *'umrah* means 'paying a visit' to a place, and in the terminology of Islam it means a visit to the Ka'bah. It differs from *hajj* in two respects. In the first place, *hajj* can only be performed at the fixed time, while *'umrah* may be performed at any time. The months of *Shawwāl, Dhī-qa'd* and ten days of *Dhi-l-Ḥijjah,* these being the 10th, 11th and 12th months of the Muslim calendar, are particularly spoken of as months of *hajj,*[15] so that one can enter into the state of *iḥrām* for *hajj* only in these months, while the actual devotions of *hajj* are limited from the 8th to the 13th of *Dhi-l-Ḥijjah.* Secondly, the going to Arafat and the assembling there is dispensed with in the case of *'umrah,* while it is an essential part of *hajj.* Another difference is that the sacrifice of an animal as the concluding act is essential to *hajj* but not so in the case of *'umrah.* The *'umrah* may be performed separately, or along with *hajj,* when it is like a parallel devotion to the latter. Though *hajj* is spoken of more often in the Holy Quran, yet there is an express injunction to accomplish both:

> "And accomplish the pilgrimage (*hajj*) and the visit (*'umrah*) for Allah." — 2:196

Hadith also speaks of the obligatory nature of the *'umrah.*[16]

There are two ways in which *hajj* may be combined with *'umrah.* One is that the pilgrim should enter a state of *iḥrām* in the months of *hajj* and get out of that state after the performance of the *'umrah,* again entering into a state of *iḥrām* in the days of *hajj.* This is known as *tamattu'* or 'profiting' because between the *'umrah* and the *hajj* the pilgrim profits by living in his ordinary condition and is not bound by the strict rules of *iḥrām.* For this he is required to make a sacrifice, or fast for three days in the *hajj* and seven days after returning from *hajj,* as laid down in the Quran, 2:196. The other way, known as *qirān* or 'uniting together', is to enter a state of *iḥrām* in the months of *ḥajj* and remain in the same state until both *'umrah* and *ḥajj* have been performed.

With the two differences pointed out earlier, whatever is said below concerning *ḥajj* applies also to *'umrah*.

Iḥrām

The state into which the pilgrims are required to put themselves on the occasion of *ḥajj* or *'umrah* is called *iḥrām* (from *ḥaram* meaning 'prevention' or 'forbidding'), or entering upon a state in which a particular dress is put on and certain acts, ordinarily lawful, are forbidden. The *iḥrām* dress, according to Hadith reports,[17] consists of two seamless sheets, a sheet reaching from the navel to below the knees and a sheet which covers the upper part of the body. Both these sheets must preferably be white. As regards women, they can wear their ordinary clothes, and Aishah, wife of the Holy Prophet, held that there was no harm if a woman pilgrim wore cloth dyed black or red or wore boots. She further held that a woman should not cover her face or wear a veil in *iḥrām*.[18] Change of clothes during *iḥrām* is not forbidden. But even women must wear simple dress. The object is to remove all distinctions of rank, and this is done in the case of men by making them all wear two seamless sheets, and in the case of women by requiring them to give up the veil which was a sign of rank. It also gives a practical lesson in simple living.

Before donning the *iḥrām* dress, the pilgrim must take a bath and utter *talbiyah* (see below), facing the *Qiblah*. The practice is also to say two *rak'ahs* of prayer, but all that is related of the Holy Prophet is that he entered a state of *iḥrām* after saying two *rak'ahs* of the early afternoon prayer. During the state of *iḥrām,* and even before that, from the beginning of the journey to Makkah, no amorous talk is allowed:

> "So whoever determines to perform pilgrimage in them [i.e., in the months of the *ḥajj*], there shall be no amorous speech, nor abusing nor altercation in the pilgrimage." — 2 : 197

Sexual intercourse is therefore also forbidden; nor is the use of scent allowed in the state of *iḥrām,* nor shaving, nor the paring of nails. The cares of the body are sacrificed for a few days to devote greater attention to the cares of the soul, and this is a practical lesson which serves a useful purpose on many occasions in one's life.

Mīqāt or *muhill*

The state of *iḥrām* may be entered upon at any time during the months of *hajj*, after the journey is undertaken; but as it would be too inconvenient to remain in this state for a long time, the law has fixed certain places on the different routes to Makkah, on reaching which the pilgrims enter upon a state of *iḥrām*. Such a place is called *mīqāt* meaning 'an appointed time', or 'a place in which a certain action is appointed to be performed'. It is also called a *muhill* which signifies 'the place of raising voices with *talbiyah*'. The *talbiyah* consists in saying aloud *labbaika Allāhumma labbaika,* meaning "Here am I, O Allah! here am I in Your august presence".[19] The full *talbiyah* runs thus:

> *Labbaika Allāhumma labbaika, lā sharīka la-ka labbaika; inn-al-ḥamda w-al-ni'mata la-ka w-al-mulka la-ka, la sharīka la-ka.*

which means: "Here am I, O Allah, here am I in Your august presence; there is no associate with You, here am I; surely all praise is Yours and all favours are Yours and the kingdom is Yours, there is no associate with You".[20]

As soon as the state of *iḥrām* is entered upon, with the determination to devote as little attention to the cares of the body as possible, the spiritual aspect of *hajj* is brought to mind by all the pilgrims crying aloud that they are in the august Divine presence. The place where *iḥrām* is entered upon is, therefore, also the place where voices are raised aloud for the remembrance of God, and the *mīqāt,* is, for that reason, also called the *muhill.*

Ṭawāf

The word *ṭawāf,* in the technical language of Islam, means making circumambulation of the Ka'bah. The command to perform it is contained in the Holy Quran in a Makkah revelation:

> "…and let them go round the Ancient House." — 22:29

In the devotional acts of the pilgrimage, *ṭawāf* occupies the most important place, being the first act of the pilgrim on his arrival at Makkah and his last act when he leaves the holy place. It is reported that the Holy Prophet "made circumambulations on his first arrival in *hajj* and *'umrah,* then offered two *rak'ahs,* then went to and fro between Safa and Marwah".[21] The *tawāf* is performed by going round the Ka'bah, as near the walls of the sacred building as possible, but on the north-western side keeping close to the small semicircular wall bounding the *Hijr.* Before the *tawāf,* it is necessary to make ablution,[22] if possible to take a bath. Men and women perform *tawāf* together, the women keeping apart from the men, but women are not allowed to go inside the Ka'bah until it is emptied of men.[23]

The obligatory *tawāf* is made on the day of sacrifices, the 10th of *Dhi-i-Hijjah,*[24] though generally a *tawāf* is also made on arrival and on departure. The *tawāf* begins at the Black Stone, which is kissed,[25] but even the making of a sign over it is sufficient.[26] In going round, the Ka'bah is kept to the left, and seven rounds are made in all. The first three rounds are made at a fast pace and the remaining four at an ordinary pace.[27] But, if necessary, the *tawāf* may be performed while one is riding on the back of an animal.[28] The doing of an act or speaking, if there is necessity for it, is not forbidden.[29] Prayers or supplications may be addressed to God in the course of *tawāf.* Menstruating women should postpone the *tawāf,* and the running between Safa and Marwah, for the duration of the menses.

The Black Stone

Reference has already been made to the *Hajar al-Aswad* or *the Black Stone.* There is not the least indication to show where this stone came from and when it was placed there, but as it was there before the advent of Islam and was even kissed, it must have been there at least from the time of Abraham, as the main features of the *hajj* are traceable to that patriarch. Yet it is remarkable that though the Ka'bah had 360 idols within its walls before the coming of Islam, the Black Stone was never regarded as an idol by the pre-Islamic Arabs, nor was it ever worshipped by them like the idols of the Ka'bah. Among the innumerable objects which were taken for gods by the pre-Islamic Arabs, the Ka'bah and the Black Stone are the only two which are conspicuous by their absence, notwithstanding the reverence which the Arab mind had for them before Islam. The Ka'bah was known by the name *Bait Allah* or House of God, and there was a belief prevalent among them that no enemy could destroy it. Yet, despite all this reverence, the Ka'bah was never worshipped. It was the idols that were worshipped, and not the Ka'bah; and the same is true of the Black Stone. It was kissed but it was never taken for a god. And Muslims were so averse to idolatry that when they saw two idols, one on each hill of the Safa and the Marwah, they refused to make the run between these two mountains, until a verse was revealed saying: "there is no blame on him [i.e., the pilgrim]" for going between them (2:158). Evidently they had not the same scruples about the Ka'bah as the idols in the Ka'bah were shut up in the building, while those on the Safa and the Marwah were not only exposed to view but even touched by the pilgrims.

If the idea of idolatry had been connected in the least with the circuits round the Ka'bah and the kissing of the Black Stone, Muslims would never have resorted to those practices. The Holy Prophet once made circuits of the Ka'bah on the back of a camel; he also touched the Black Stone with the rod in his hand; all of which goes to show that Muslims never entertained the idea of the worship of these things, nor was their attitude towards them at any time that of the worshipper towards the object of his worship. This shows the absurdity of the criticism that the *ṭawāf* or the kissing of the Black Stone are remnants of pre-Islamic idolatry which were retained in Islam.

Significance underlying *ṭawāf* of the Ka'bah

During the *ṭawāf* of the Ka'bah, a Muslim feels himself in the presence of the One God, crying aloud: *labbaika Allāhumma labbaika, lā sharīka la-ka, labbaika* — "Here am I, O Allah! here am I in Your presence, there is no associate with You, here am I". And *ṭawāf* itself is going round about the House which is an emblem of Divine Unity, the place from which sprang the idea of Divine Unity, the place which would always be the centre for all believers in Divine Unity. All ideas of the pilgrim at that time are concentrated upon one theme, the theme of Divine Unity. The pilgrim forgets everything and remembers only the One God. To him the august Divine presence is all in all. That is the *ṭawāf*.

Significance underlying kissing of the Black Stone

That the Ka'bah was rebuilt by Abraham is an historical fact. That the Black Stone has been there ever since the Ka'bah has been known to exist, there is not the least reason to doubt. That it was a stone sent down from Paradise, or that it was originally white and became black on account of the sins of men, there is no reliable hadith to indicate. The Black Stone is, in fact, the corner-stone of the Ka'bah, and stands there only as an emblem, a token that that part of the progeny of Abraham which was rejected by the Israelites was to become the corner-stone of the Kingdom of God. The Psalms contain a clear reference to it:

> "The stone which the builders rejected has become the chief corner-stone." [30]

Ishmael was looked upon as rejected and the Divine covenant was considered to have been made with the children of Isaac only. That was the Jewish view, and it was due to the fact that Ishmael was placed by Abraham near the Ka'bah. And again while prophet after prophet appeared among the Israelites, no prophet appeared of the progeny of Ishmael, and hence the Jewish belief that Ishmael was rejected became stronger. Yet it was from the progeny of Ishmael that the Last Prophet, "chief corner-stone" in the words of the Psalmist, was to arise, and the Black Stone, from wherever it was brought, was placed as the corner-stone of the Ka'bah, as a sign that the rejected Ishmaelites were the real inheritors of the Divine Kingdom. And while David referred to it as "the stone which the builders rejected", Jesus spoke of it more plainly in the parable of the owner of the vineyard, telling the Israelites that the vineyard, which in the parable stands for the Kingdom of God, would be taken away from them and given to other tenants, that is, to a non-Israelite people:

> "Have you never read in the Scriptures: 'The stone which the builders rejected has become the chief cornerstone....' ... Therefore I say to you, the kingdom of God will be taken from you and given to a nation bearing the fruits of it." [31]

That by the rejected stone in the prophecy was meant a rejected nation is made clear by Jesus Christ. That that rejected nation was no other than the Ishmaelites is borne out by history. And in the whole world there is only this unhewn stone, the stone described in the Bible as "cut out of the mountain without hands",[32] that is the corner-stone of a building which in point of importance stands unique in the world.

The *Sa'y*

Sa'y means 'running', and in the Islamic terminology it signifies the running of the pilgrims between the two little hills situated near

Makkah, called the Safa (*Ṣafā*) and the Marwah. In the devotional acts of *hajj,* it occupies a place next to the *ṭawāf.* In fact, in the case of *'umrah,* the minor pilgrimage as it is called, *ṭawāf* and *sa'y* are the only functions of importance, and the *'umrah* therefore ends with the *sa'y* unless of course there is an animal to be sacrificed when *'umrah* alone is to be performed. The *sa'y* is spoken of in the Holy Quran:

> "The Safa and the Marwah are truly among the signs of Allah; so whoever makes a pilgrimage to the House or pays a visit to it, there is no blame on him if he goes round them."
> — 2:158

The word used in the Quran for "he goes round" is not *sa'y* but a derivative of *ṭawāf.* These two hills were the scene of Hagar's running to and fro in quest of water for her baby Ishmael, when she was left there by Abraham.[33] They have thus become monuments of patience under the hardest trials, and it is in connection with the teaching of patience that the *ṭawāf* of Safa and Marwah is spoken of in the Quran, as the preceding verses 2:153–157 show.

The *ḥajj* proper — march to Mina

Ṭawāf and *sa'y* are the individual acts of every pilgrim when he first arrives at Makkah, whether he intends to perform the *'umrah* or the *hajj.* In case it is simply an *'umrah,* or *'umrah* to be followed by a break before the *hajj,* the pilgrim then emerges from the state of *iḥrām.* The *hajj* proper begins on the 8th of <u>Dhi-l-Ḥijjah</u> when the whole body of pilgrims moves together. The pilgrims who had got out of the state of *iḥrām* after *'umrah* again enter into this state on the morning of the 8th, and so also do the residents of Makkah who wish to perform the pilgrimage.[34] The whole body of pilgrims then moves to Mina, a plain which is midway between Arafat and Makkah, about four miles (6·5 km) distant from the Holy City. During the *hajj* proper, the pilgrims' longest, and in fact the only, stay is in Mina. Mina must be reached before noon, so that the early afternoon prayer, *Ẓuhr,* may be said there. The night is also passed in Mina, and next day, the 9th <u>Dhi-l-Ḥijjah,</u> at midday the pilgrims move to the plain of Arafat.

Staying in Arafat

'Arafa or *'Arafāt* is the name of the plain which is situated to the east of Makkah at a distance of about nine miles (14 km). It is derived from *'arf* or *ma'rifah,* which means 'knowledge of a thing', and

ma'rifah especially means *the knowledge of God.* The name given to this plain seems to be based on the fact that here people assembled together, as equals in all respects, are best able to *know* their God. The *Jabal al-Raḥmah* (lit., the mountain of mercy), on which is the pulpit from which the sermon is delivered, is situated to the east, sixty steps of stone leading to the top. Leaving Mina at noon on the 9th <u>*Dh*</u>*i-l-Ḥijjah,* the pilgrims reach Arafat in time to say the early and late afternoon prayers combined, after which the Imam delivers a sermon from the pulpit on the *Jabal al-Raḥmah.* The pilgrims' stay in Arafat lasts only from afternoon till sunset, but so important is the place it occupies in the devotional acts of *ḥajj,* that *ḥajj* is considered to have been performed if the pilgrim reaches Arafat in time on the 9th <u>*Dh*</u>*i-l-Ḥijjah,* but if he is unable to join, the *ḥajj* is not performed. The whole time of the pilgrims, from afternoon till sunset, is passed in glorifying God and crying aloud *labbaika Allāhumma labbaika.*

Muzdalifah

After sunset the pilgrims leave Arafat, and stop at Muzdalifah (from *zalf* meaning 'nearness'), which is so called because by staying there nearness to God is sought. In the Holy Quran it is called the Sacred, or Holy, Monument (*al-Ma*<u>*sh*</u>*'ar al-Ḥarām*) and the remembrance of God at that place is specially enjoined:

> "So when you press on from Arafat, remember Allah near the Holy Monument, and remember Him as He has guided you, though before that you were certainly in error." — 2:198

On reaching Muzdalifah, the pilgrims say their sunset and night prayers, combining the two.[35] There the night is passed, and then after saying the morning prayer at an early hour the pilgrims leave for Mina. Those who are infirm are allowed to leave even before the morning prayer.[36]

Yaum al-naḥr in Mina

Thus the pilgrims again reach Mina on the morning of 10th <u>*Dh*</u>*i-l-Ḥijjah,* which is called *yaum al-naḥr,* 'the day of sacrifices', being the day which is celebrated as the *'Īd al-Aḍhā* all over the Muslim world. After saying the *'Īd* prayers in Mina, the animals are sacrificed, the pilgrims then return and perform the *ṭawāf* of the Ka'bah. With this, the pilgrim emerges from the state of *iḥrām,* by having his head shaven or his hair clipped. But before the sacrifice there is another small act of devotion called the *ramy al-jimār,* which will be described presently. Though the pilgrim leaves the state of *iḥrām,* yet he must return to Mina again, for it is in Mina that the *hajj* ends.

Days of *tashrīq* (*Ayyām al-tashrīq*)

The pilgrims are required to stay in Mina for three or at least two days after the *yaum al-nahr,* that is, on the 11th, 12th and 13th *Dhi-l-Hijjah*. This stay is required by an express injunction of the Quran, where the ending of the devotional acts of *hajj* is thus spoken of:

> "And remember Allah during the appointed days. Then whoever hastens off in two days, it is no sin for him; and whoever stays behind, it is no sin for him, for one who keeps his duty. And keep your duty to Allah, and know that you shall be gathered together to Him." — 2:203

The "appointed days" referred to here are the two or three days that are spent in Mina after the *yaum al-nahr,* and they are known as the days of *tashrīq*. They may have been so named because the animals were sacrificed after the rising of the sun, which is one of the meanings of *tashrīq*.[37] It may be because *tashrīq* also means 'going east', and Mina lies to the east of Makkah; or it may have a deeper spiritual significance in that it also means *being beautiful and shining in the face*.[38]

Casting of stones

During the last day of *hajj,* the 10th *Dhi-l-Hijjah,* and the three *tashrīq* days the pilgrims are required to cast stones at certain fixed places. This is known as *ramy al-jimār,* 'throwing of (small) stones'. Each of the three places in Mina, where stones are thrown, is also called *Jamrah,* because of the *throwing* or the *collection of stones* there. The practice of the Holy Prophet is thus described. On the *yaum al-nahr* he threw stones in the forenoon, and in *tashrīq* days in the afternoon.[39] The number of stones thrown at each Jamrah was seven, and every stone thrown was accompanied by saying of *Allāhu Akbar*.[40]

In the *hajj* many pre-Islamic practices were retained, but as has been shown above, the origin of these practices is traceable to Abraham, and every one of them carries with it a spiritual significance. The whole atmosphere of *hajj* is a demonstration of the greatness of God and the equality of man. The *hajj* is, as it were, the final stage in man's spiritual progress. Yet in spiritual advancement the temptations of real life must not be forgotten, and the throwing of stones draws attention to the temptations of the Evil one. It teaches the lesson that man must learn to hate evil and that the Evil one should be kept distant a stone's throw. The nearer a person gets to temptations, the more likely he is to yield, and the best way of avoiding them is to keep them at a distance. The throwing of stones is, moreover, a reminder of the spiritual fight which man must wage against evil.

Other activities allowed in pilgrimage

Though *hajj* is meant to bring about an ascetic experience in man's practical life, yet so closely combined are the ascetic and secular experiences in Islam that the utilizing of the pilgrimage to Makkah for secular purposes is not excluded. The Holy Quran, while enjoining the making of sufficient provision for the *hajj* journey, adds:

> "It is no sin for you that you seek the bounty of your Lord."
> — 2:198

The seeking of bounty is accepted here by all commentators as meaning the seeking of increase in one's wealth by means of trade in the pilgrimage season. The Quran thus not only allows the carrying on of trade in the pilgrimage season, but in a way recommends it by calling it a "bounty of your Lord".

If even trading is allowed in the pilgrimage season, this great assemblage of Muslims from all quarters of the world may also be made the occasion of other advantages of a material or cultural nature, and it should serve the purpose of unifying the Muslim world and removing misunderstanding between nation and nation. World-wide conferences are held on many occasions, and this should, in the new conditions of the world, be a regular feature of the *hajj,* and the best minds among the various nations should on this occasion discuss all problems affecting the Muslim world, not the least important of which is the advancement of Islam itself.

Notes to Chapter 14

1. Raghib's *Mufradāt*.

2. *A Dictionary of Islam* by T.P. Hughes under the entry *Ka'bah*, p. 258, col. 2, and the *Encyclopaedia of Islam,* first edition, article on *Hadjdj* by A.J. Wensinck, v. 2, p. 199, col. 1.

3. Bukhari, book 8: 'Prayer', ch. 31, h. 399.

4. Bukhari, book 2: 'Faith', ch. 30, h. 40; book 8: 'Prayer', ch. 31, h. 399; book 65: 'Commentary on the Quran', ch. 12, h. 4486 (on *Surah* 2, v. 144).

5. For *'umrah* see pages 280–281.

6. Bukhari, book 64: 'Military expeditions', ch. 2, h. 3950.

7. The previous verse contains an address to Abraham: "And when We pointed to Abraham the place of the House..." (22:26). Therefore, the words "Proclaim to mankind the Pilgrimage" are generally understood to have been addressed to Abraham. Even if this view is accepted, it is equally an address to the Holy Prophet, for, as the context shows, the mention of Abraham is only by way of parenthesis; and inasmuch as the pilgrimage is an ordinance common to both the Abrahamic and the Islamic faiths, the address is equally to both prophets.

8. Lane's Lexicon and *Nihāyah* of Ibn Athir.

9. The Quran, 2:127 and 14:37.

10. Bukhari, book 60: 'Prophets', ch. 9, h. 3364.

11. The Quran 2:125 and 22:26.

12. Bukhari, book 25: 'Pilgrimage', ch. 67, h. 1622.

13. Abu Dawud, book 11: 'Rites of Pilgrimage (*Manāsik*)', ch. 1, h. 1721.

14. Bukhari, book 25: 'Pilgrimage', ch. 1, h. 1513.

15. See the Quran 2:197 and Bukhari, book 25: 'Pilgrimage', ch. 33, ch. heading.

16. Bukhari, book 26: '*'Umrah*', ch. 1, h. 1773 and ch. 4, h. 1782. According to one hadith, *'umrah* is not obligatory; see Tirmidhi, book 9: 'Pilgrimage', ch. 88, h. 931 (MDS: book 7). But anyone who performs the *hajj* can easily perform the *'umrah.*

17. See Bukhari, book 3: 'Knowledge', ch. 53, h. 134; and book 25: 'Pilgrimage', ch. 23, h. 1545.

18. Bukhari, book 25: 'Pilgrimage', ch. 23, ch. heading.

19. *Editor's Note:* This expression does not indicate whether the speaker is singular or plural, and thus it can mean "here are we" or "here am I".

20. Bukhari, book 25: 'Pilgrimage', ch. 26, h. 1549.

21. *Ibid.,* ch. 63, h. 1614–1617.

22. *Ibid.,* ch. 78, h. 1641–1642.

23. *Ibid.,* ch. 64, h. 1618.

24. *Ibid.,* ch. 129, h. 1732–1733.

25. *Ibid.,* ch. 56, h. 1603.

26. *Ibid.,* ch. 61, h. 1612.

27. *Ibid.,* ch. 63, h. 1616–1617.

28. *Ibid.,* ch. 74, h. 1632–1633.

29. *Ibid.,* chs. 65 and 66, h. 1620–1621.

30. Psalms, 118:22.

31. Matthew, 21:42,43.

32. Daniel, 2:45.

33. Bukhari, book 60: 'Prophets', ch. 9, h. 3364–3365.

34. Bukhari, book 25: 'Pilgrimage', ch. 82, ch. heading.

35. *Ibid.,* ch. 96, h. 1973–1674.

36. *Ibid.,* ch. 98, h. 1676–1681.

37. *Nihāyah* of Ibn Athīr.

38. Lane's Lexicon.

39. Bukhari, book 25: 'Pilgrimage', ch. 134, ch. heading.

40. *Ibid.,* ch. 138, h. 1750.

15. *Jihād*

Significance of *Jihād*

A very great misconception prevails with regard to the duty of *jihād* in Islam, by assuming that the word *jihād* is synonymous with *war* or even *war undertaken for the propagation of Islam*. This is a glaring misstatement. Even some of the greatest Western research scholars of Islam have not taken the pains to find out the true meaning of the word. According to Raghib's classical Arabic dictionary, the word *jihād* is derived from *jahd* or *juhd* meaning 'ability', 'exertion' or 'power', and *jihād* and *mujāhida* mean 'the exerting of one's power in repelling the enemy'.[1] It goes on to say:

> "*Jihād* is of three kinds; namely, the carrying on of a struggle: 1. against a visible enemy, 2. against the devil, and 3. against self (*nafs*)."

Another authority gives the following significance:

> "*Jihād*, inf. n. of *jahada*, properly signifies *the using* or *exerting of one's utmost power, efforts, endeavours* or *ability, in contending with an object of disapprobation;* and this is of three kinds, namely a visible enemy, the devil, and one's self; all of which are included in the term as used in the Kur. xxii. 77 [the Quran, 22:77]." [2]

Jihād is therefore far from being synonymous with *war,* while the meaning of "war undertaken for the propagation of Islam" is unknown equally to the Arabic language and the teachings of the Holy Quran.

Use of the word *jihād* in Makkah revelations

Just as important, or even more so, is the consideration of the sense in which the word is used in the Holy Quran. It is an admitted fact that permission to fight was given to Muslims when they had moved to Madinah, or, at the earliest, when they were on the eve of leaving Makkah. But the injunction relating to *jihād* is contained in the earlier as well as in the later Makkah revelations. Chapter 29 of the Quran was undoubtedly revealed in the fifth and sixth years of the Call of the Prophet; yet there the word *jihād* is freely used in the sense of *exerting one's power and ability,* without implying any war. In one place it is said:

> "And those who strive hard *(jāhadū)* for Us, We shall certainly guide them in Our ways. And Allah is surely with the doers of good." — 29:69

The addition of the words "for Us" shows, if anything further is needed to show it, that the *jihād,* in this case, is the spiritual striving to attain nearness to God, and the result of this *jihād* is stated to be God's guidance of those striving in His ways. The word is used precisely in the same sense twice in a previous verse in the same chapter:

> "And whoever strives hard *(jāhada),* strives *(yujāhidu)* for himself [i.e., for his own benefit]. Surely Allah is above need of His creatures." — 29:6

In the same chapter, and in chapter 31, the word is used in the sense of a contention carried on in words:

> "And We have enjoined on man goodness to his parents. But if they strive *(jāhadā)*[3] to make you set up partners with Me, of which you have no knowledge, do not obey them." — 29:8 (see also 31:15)

Among the later revelations at Makkah may be mentioned the 16th chapter, where it is said, towards the close:

> "Then surely your Lord, to those who flee after they are persecuted, then struggle hard *(jāhadū)* and are patient, surely your Lord after that is Protecting, Merciful." — 16:110

Another prevalent misconception is that at Makkah the Quran enjoined patience (*ṣabr*) and at Madinah it enjoined *jihād,* as if these were two contradictory things. The error of this view is shown by the verse quoted, since it enjoins *jihād* and patience in one breath.

Two more examples may be quoted of the use of the word *jihād* in Makkah revelations:

> "And strive hard *(jāhidū)* for Allah with due striving *(jihād)*." — 22:78

> "So do not obey the disbelievers, and strive *(jāhid)* against
> them a mighty striving *(jihād)* with it." — 25:52

The last word of the second verse above, "it", refers clearly to the
Quran, as the context shows. In the first verse it is a *jihād* to attain
nearness to God, and in the second it is a *jihād* which is to be carried
on against the unbelievers, not of the sword but of the Quran. The
struggle made to attain nearness to God and to subdue one's passions,
and the struggle made to win over the unbelievers, not with the sword
but with the Quran is, therefore, a *jihād* in the terminology of the
Quran, and the injunctions to carry on these two kinds of *jihād* were
given long before the command to fight in self-defence.

Jihād in Madinah revelations

A struggle for national existence was forced on the Muslims when
they reached Madinah, and they had to take up the sword in self-
defence. This struggle also went, and rightly so, under the name of
jihād; but even in the Madinah chapters the word is used in the wider
sense of a struggle carried on by words or deeds of any kind. The
following verse may be quoted which occurs twice:

> "O Prophet, Strive hard *(jāhid)* against the disbelievers and
> the hypocrites, and be firm against them."
> — 9:73 and 66:9

Here the Prophet is commanded to carry on a *jihād* against both
unbelievers and hypocrites. The hypocrites were those who were
outwardly Muslims and lived among, and were treated like, Muslims
in all respects. They came to the mosque and prayed with the Muslims. They even paid the *zakāt.* A war against them was unthinkable,
and none was ever undertaken. On the other hand, they sometimes
fought along with the Muslims against the unbelievers. Therefore the
injunction to carry on a *jihād* against both unbelievers and hypocrites
could not mean the waging of war against them. It was a *jihād* carried
on by means of the Quran as expressly stated in 25:52, a striving hard
to win them over to Islam. In fact, the word is almost always used in
the general sense of striving hard, including fighting where the context so requires. The following description:

> "Those who believe and those who fled [their homes] and
> strove hard *(jāhadū)* in Allah's way" — 2:218, 8:74

applies as much to the fighters as to those who carry on the struggle against unbelief and evil in other ways.

Again, a Madinah revelation speaks together of those who exercise *ṣabr*, i.e., are steadfast or patient, and those who undertake *jihād*, as they are spoken of in a Makkah revelation:

> "Do you think that you will enter the Garden while Allah has not yet known those from among you who strive hard *(jāhadū)* nor known the steadfast?" — 3:142

Jihād in Hadith

Even in Hadith literature, the word *jihād* is not used exclusively for *fighting*. For example, *ḥajj* is called by the Holy Prophet as "the most excellent of all *jihāds*".[4] Of all the collections of Hadith, Bukhari is the most explicit on this point. In his collection, in the book entitled "Holding fast by the Quran and the *Sunnah*", the 10th chapter is thus headed:

> "The saying of the Prophet, A party of my community *(ummah)* shall not cease to be triumphant being upholders of Truth, and these are the people of learning *(ahl al-'ilm)*." [5]

Thus Bukhari's view is that the triumphant party of the Prophet's community does not consist of fighters, but of the men of learning who disseminate the truth and are engaged in the propagation of Islam. Again, in his *Book of Jihād* Bukhari has several chapters the headings of which speak of simple invitation to Islam; for instance, "May the Muslim guide the followers of the Book to a right course, or may he teach them the Book", "To pray for the guidance of the polytheists so as to develop relations of friendship with them", "The excellence of him at whose hands another man accepts Islam", "The excellence of him who accepts Islam from among the followers of the Book", and "How should Islam be presented to a child".[6] These headings show that up to the time of Bukhari, the word *jihād* was used in the wider sense in which it is used in the Quran, a simple invitation to Islam being looked upon as *jihād*.

Other books of Hadith contain similar references. Thus Abu Dawud quotes, under the heading "The continuity of *jihād*", a hadith to the effect that "a party of my community will not cease fighting for truth and it will be triumphant over its opponents",[7] and these words are thus explained in a commentary of Abu Dawud:

> "This party consists of different classes of the faithful, of them being the brave fighters, and the jurists, and the collectors of Hadith, and those who abstain from worldly pleasures and devote themselves to the service of God, and those who command the doing of good and prohibit evil, and a variety of other people who do other good deeds." [8]

This shows that *jihād* in Hadith includes the service of Islam in any form.

Use of the word *jihād* by jurists

It is only among the jurists that the word *jihād* lost its original wider significance and began to be used in the narrower sense of fighting or *qitāl*. The reason is not far to seek. The books of jurisprudence (*fiqh*) codified the Muslim law, and in the classification of the various subjects with which the law dealt, *qitāl* (fighting) found a necessary place, but invitation to Islam, though a primary meaning of the word *jihād,* being a matter of free individual choice, did not form part of the law. The jurists who had to deal with *qitāl,* therefore, used the word *jihād* as synonymous with *qitāl,* and, by and by, the wider significance of *jihād* was lost sight of, though the commentators of the Quran accepted this significance when dealing with verses such as 25:52 ("and strive against them a mighty striving with it"). But that was not the only misuse of the word. Together with this narrowing of the significance of *jihād,* the further idea was developed that Muslims were to carry on a war against all unbelieving nations and countries, whether they were attacked or not, an idea quite foreign to the Quran.

The spread of Islam by force

The propagation of Islam is no doubt a religious duty of every true Muslim, who must follow the example of the Holy Prophet, but the spread of Islam by force is a thing of which no trace can be found in the Holy Quran. In fact, the Holy Book lays down the opposite doctrine in clear words:

> "There is no compulsion in religion — the right way is clearly distinct from error." — 2:256

The reason why there is no compulsion in religion is added here, that the right way is clearly distinct from error. This verse was revealed *after* the permission for war in self-defence had been given, and it is therefore certain that the permission to fight has no connection with the preaching of religion. That the Quran never taught such a doctrine, nor did the Holy Prophet ever think of it, is a fact which is now being gradually appreciated by Western scholars of Islam. And if the Quran and the Prophet never taught such a doctrine, how could it be said to be the religious duty of Muslims?

Circumstances under which war was permitted

It is a mis-statement of facts to say that patience under attack was taught at Makkah, because there was no alternative, and that the right to repel attack came at Madinah. The attitude was no doubt changed but that change was due to the change of circumstances. At Makkah there was individual persecution, and patience was taught. If the conditions had remained the same at Madinah, the Muslim attitude would have been the same. But at Madinah individual persecution could no more be resorted to by the Quraish of Makkah, as the Muslims were living out of their reach. This very circumstance fanned the fire of their wrath, and they now planned the extinction of the Muslims as a nation. They took up the sword to annihilate the Muslim community or to compel it to return to unbelief. That was the challenge thrown at the Muslims, and the Holy Prophet had to meet it.

The Holy Quran bears the clearest testimony to it. The earliest permission to repel attack is conveyed in words which show that the enemy had already taken up the sword or decided to do so:

> "Permission [to fight] is given to those on whom war is made, because they are oppressed. And surely Allah is able to assist them — those who are driven from their homes without a just cause except that they say: Our Lord is Allah. And if Allah did not repel some people by others, surely cloisters and churches and synagogues and mosques in which Allah's name is much remembered, would have been pulled down. And surely Allah will help him who helps His cause." — 22:39–40

The very words of this verse show that it is the earliest on the subject of fighting, as it speaks of a permission being given now which evidently had not been given up to this time. This permission was given to a people upon whom war was made by their enemies, and it was not a permission to make war against others in general but only against those who made war on them, and the reason is stated plainly "because they are oppressed" and have been expelled from their homes "without a just cause". It was clearly an aggressive war on the part of the enemies of Islam who thus sought to exterminate the Muslims or to compel them to forsake their religion, as the Quran says:

> "And they will not cease fighting you until they turn you back from your religion, if they can." — 2:217

It was a holy war in the truest sense because, as stated further on, if war had not been allowed under these circumstances, there would be no peace on earth, no religious liberty, and all houses for the worship of God would be destroyed. Indeed there could be no war holier than the one which was needed as much for the religious liberty of Muslims as for the principle of religious liberty itself, as much to save mosques as to save cloisters and synagogues and churches. If there had ever been a just cause for war in this world, it was for the war that had been permitted to Muslims. And undoubtedly war with such pure motives was a *jihād,* a struggle carried on simply with the object that truth may prosper and that freedom of conscience may be maintained.

The second verse giving to Muslims permission to fight runs as follows:

> "And fight in the way of Allah against those who fight against you, and do not be aggressive. Surely Allah does not love the aggressors." — 2:190

Here again the condition is plainly laid down that Muslims shall not be the first to attack. They had to fight — it had now become a duty — but only against those who fought against them; aggression was expressly prohibited. And this fighting in self-defence is called fighting "in the way of Allah" *(fī sabīl-illāh)* because fighting in defence is the most noble and just of all causes. The words *fī sabīl-illāh* are misinterpreted by the critics of Islam as meaning the *propagation of Islam.* Nothing could be farther from the truth. Muslims were not fighting to force Islam on others; rather they were being fought to force them to renounce Islam, as shown by 2:217 above.

It is sometimes asserted that these injunctions, relating to defensive fighting, were abrogated by a later revelation in chapter 9. Yet that chapter does not make the slightest change in the principles laid down earlier. Fighting with idolaters is enjoined in the ninth chapter, but not with all of them. In the very first verse of that chapter, the declaration of immunity is directed towards only "those of the idolaters with whom you made an agreement", not all idolaters — and even in their case an exception is made:

> "Except those of the idolaters with whom you made an agreement, then they have not failed you in anything and have not backed up anyone against you; so fulfil their agreement to the end of their terms. Surely Allah loves those who keep their duty." — 9:4

This shows that there were idolatrous tribes on friendly terms with Muslims, and Muslims were not allowed to fight with them; it was only the hostile tribes who broke their agreements and attacked the Muslims that were to be fought against. And individual idolaters, even if belonging to hostile tribes, could still have safety, if they wanted to enquire about Islam, and were given a safe conduct back home even if they did not accept Islam:

> "And if anyone of the idolaters seek your protection, protect him till he hears the word of Allah, then convey him to his place of safety. This is because they are a people who do not know." — 9:6

The idolater who stood in need of protection evidently belonged to a hostile tribe, because the friendly tribes, being in alliance with the Muslims, had no need of seeking protection of the Muslim government. Thus even a hostile idolater was to be sent back safely to his own tribe and not molested in any way, as the words of the verse show.

The idolaters with whom fighting was enjoined were those who had violated treaties and were foremost in attacking the Muslims, as the words that follow show:

> "If they prevail against you, they respect neither ties of relationship, nor covenant in your case." — 9:8

> "Will you not fight a people who broke their oaths and aimed at the expulsion of the Messenger, and they attacked you first?" — 9:13

Thus chapter 9, which is supposed to abrogate the earlier verses, still speaks of fighting only against those idolaters who "attacked you first", and this is the very condition laid down in earlier verses, such as 2:190.

So-called "verse of the sword"

Even though chapter 9, as shown above, does not go beyond what is contained in the earliest revelations on the subject of war, the fifth verse of that chapter is called by some people "the verse of the sword", as if it inculcated the indiscriminate massacre of all idolaters or unbelievers. The misconception is due to the fact that the words are taken out of their context, and a significance is forced on them which the context cannot bear. The following words occur in the 5th verse:

> "So when the sacred months have passed, kill the idolaters, wherever you find them…" — 9:5

But similar words occur also in the earliest revelation on the subject: "And kill them wherever you find them" (2:191). In both places it is the context which makes it clear as to the identity of the persons regarding whom the order is given. In both cases those against whom the order is given are the people who have taken up the sword and attacked the Muslims first.

It has already been shown that the injunction to fight against the idolaters, as contained in the opening verses of the 9th chapter, relates only to such idolatrous tribes as had made agreements with the Muslims and then broken them and had attacked the Muslims, and not to all idolatrous people, wherever they may be found in the world. If only we read the verse that precedes the fifth verse, not the shadow of a doubt will remain that *all* idolaters are not spoken of here. For the fourth verse, as quoted already, states that those idolaters were not within the purview of the order who had remained faithful to their agreements. The order was therefore directed against specified idolatrous tribes, the tribes that had made agreements with the Muslims and broken them repeatedly, as expressly stated in 8:56 — "those with whom you make an agreement, then they break their agreement every time".

It is a mistake to regard the order as including all idolatrous people living anywhere in the world or even in Arabia. And if the verse preceding the so-called "verse of the sword" makes a clear exception in case of all friendly idolatrous tribes, that following it immediately makes a clear exception in favour of such members of idolatrous hostile tribes as ask the protection of the Muslims (see 9:6, quoted earlier). And then continuing the subject, it is further laid down that the order relates only to people "who broke their oaths and aimed at the expulsion of the Messenger, and they attacked you first" (9:13). With such a clear explanation of the fifth verse contained in the preceding and following verses, no sane person would interpret it as meaning the killing of all idolaters or the carrying on of unprovoked war against all idolatrous tribes.

When shall war cease

It is thus clear that Muslims were allowed to fight only in self-defence, to preserve their national existence. They were forbidden to be aggressive. The Quran nowhere gives them permission to enter on an unprovoked war against the whole world. Conditions were also laid down as to when war should cease:

> "And fight them until there is no persecution, and religion is only for Allah. But if they cease, then there should be no hostility except against the oppressors." — 2:193

The words *religion is only for Allah* are sometimes misinterpreted as meaning that all people should accept Islam, a significance utterly opposed to the very next words: "But if they *cease,* there should be no hostility except against the oppressors". The *ceasing* plainly refers to desisting from persecution. Similar words occur in another early Madinah revelation:

> "And fight them until there is no more persecution, and all religions are for Allah. But if they cease, then surely Allah is Seer of what they do." — 8:39

Both expressions, "religion is only for Allah" and "all religions are for Allah", carry one and the same significance, namely that religion is treated as a matter between man and his God, a matter of conscience, in which nobody has a right to interfere.

It may be added that, if the words had the meaning which it is sought to give them, the Holy Prophet would have been the first man to translate that teaching into practice, while as a matter of fact he made peace with the enemy on numerous occasions, and stopped fighting with idolatrous tribes when they wanted peace. Even when he subjugated a people, he gave them full liberty in their religion, as it happened in the conquest of Makkah.

Peace recommended

Notwithstanding what has been said above, the Holy Prophet was told in the Quran to accept peace in the middle of war if the enemy wanted peace:

> "And if they incline to peace, you must incline to it also, and trust in Allah. Surely He is the Hearer, the Knower. And if they intend to deceive you — then surely Allah is sufficient for you." — 8:61–62

It should be noted that peace is here recommended even though the enemy's sincerity may be doubtful. The Holy Prophet was so prone to make peace, whenever the enemy showed the least desire towards it, that on the occasion of the Hudaibiyah truce he did not hesitate to accept the position of the defeated party, though he had never been defeated on the field of battle, and his Companions had sworn to lay down their lives, one and all, if the worst had come to the worst. Yet he made peace and accepted terms which his own followers looked upon as humiliating for Islam. He accepted the condition that he would go back without performing a pilgrimage and also that if a resident of Makkah embraced Islam and came to him for protection, he would not give him protection. Thus the injunction contained in the Quran to make peace with the idolaters if they desired peace, combined with the practice of the Holy Prophet in concluding peace on any terms, is a clear proof that the theory of preaching Islam by the sword is a pure myth so far as the teachings of the Holy Quran and the Holy Prophet are concerned.

To sum up, neither in the earlier revelations, nor in the later, is there the slightest indication of any injunction to propagate Islam by the sword. On the other hand, war was clearly allowed as a defensive measure up to the last. It was to be continued only so long as religious persecution lasted, and when that ceased, war was to cease *ipso facto.* And there was the additional condition that if a tribe, against whom Muslims were fighting because of its aggressive and repeated viola-tion of treaties, embraced Islam, it then and there became a part of the Muslim body politic, and its subjugation by arms was therefore foregone, and war with it came to an end. Such remained the practice of the Holy Prophet during his lifetime. And there is not a single instance in history in which he offered the alternative of the sword or Islam to any tribe or individual, nor did he ever lead an aggressive attack.

The last of his expeditions was that of Tabuk, in which he led an army of thirty thousand against the Roman Empire, but when he found, on reaching the frontier, after a very long and arduous journey, that the Romans did not contemplate an offensive, he returned without attacking them. His action on this occasion also throws light on the fact that the permission to fight against the Christians, contained in 9:29, was also subject to the condition laid down in 2:190 that Muslims must not be aggressive in war.

Wars of conquest after the Holy Prophet's time

It is held by some Western critics of Islam that, though the Prophet did not make use of force in the propagation of Islam, nor lead an aggressive attack against an enemy, in the whole of his life, yet this position was adopted by his immediate successors, and was therefore a natural development of his teaching. This opinion is also due to a misconception of the historical facts which led to the wars of the early Caliphate with the Persian and Roman empires. After the death of the Holy Prophet, when Arabia rose in insurrection and Abu Bakr, the first Caliph, was engaged in suppressing the revolt, both Persia and Rome openly helped the insurgents with men and money. It is difficult to go into details of the history in this book, and this subject has been dealt with fully by this author in the book *The Early Caliphate*.[9] In brief, Persia and Rome were the aggressors, and Muslims, in sheer self-defence, came into conflict with those mighty empires. The idea of spreading Islam by the sword was as far away from their minds as it was from that of the great Master whom they followed. We may quote here Sir William Muir, a writer in no way friendly to Islam:

> "The thought of a world-wide mission was yet in embryo; obligation to enforce Islam by a universal Crusade had not yet dawned upon the Muslim mind." [10]

This remark, which occurs under Muir's heading *Omar refuses an advance on Persia,* relates to the year 16 A.H., when more than half the battles of the early Caliphate had already been fought. According to Muir, even the conquest of the whole of Persia was a measure of self-defence, and not of aggression, on the part of the Muslims:

> "The truth began to dawn on Omar that necessity was laid upon him to withdraw the ban against advance. In self-defence, nothing was left but to crush the Chosroes [Persian emperor] and take entire possession of his realm." [11]

And if the wars with the Persian and Roman empires were begun and carried on for five years without any idea of the propagation of Islam by arms, surely there was no occasion for the idea to creep in at a subsequent stage.

Hadith on the object of war

As already stated in this book, Hadith cannot go against the Holy Quran. Being only an explanation of the Holy Book, it must be rejected if it contains anything against the plain teachings of the Quran. The propagation of Islam by force is neither contained in the Quran nor did the Holy Prophet ever entertain such an idea. There is one hadith, however, which has sometimes been misconstrued as meaning that the Prophet was fighting people to make them believe in the Unity of God. It runs thus:

> "It is reported from Ibn Umar that the Messenger of Allah said: I have been commanded to fight people until they bear witness that there is no god but Allah and that Muhammad is the messenger of Allah and keep up prayer and pay the *zakāt*. When they have done this, their lives and their properties are protected unless there is an obligation of Islam, and their account is with Allah." [12]

This report begins with the words *I am commanded to fight,* and surely the commandments to the Prophet were given through Divine revelation and are therefore all of them contained in the Quran. The reference in the report is thus undoubtedly to a Quranic verse. In fact, such a verse is met with in the 9th chapter:

> "But if they repent and keep up prayer and pay the *zakāt,* they are your brethren in faith." — 9:11

The subject-matter of the report is exactly the same, and clearly the commandment referred to in it is that contained in this verse. One has only to read the context to find out the purport of these words. Some of these verses have already been quoted but, on account of the importance of the subject, four of these are repeated below:

9:10   "They respect neither ties of relationship nor covenant in the case of a believer. And these are they who go beyond the limits."

9:11   "But if they repent and keep up prayer and pay the *zakāt*, they are your brethren in faith."

9:12   "And if they break their oaths after their agreement and openly revile your religion, then fight the leaders of disbelief — surely their oaths are nothing — so that they may cease."

9:13   "Will you not fight a people who broke their oaths and aimed at the expulsion of the Messenger and they attacked you first? "

The context clearly shows that there were certain tribes that had no regard for ties of relationships or for agreements entered into, and they were the first to attack the Muslims and made plans to expel the Prophet. These were the people to be fought against. The 9th chapter was revealed in the year 9 A.H. and this was the time when tribe after tribe was coming over to Islam, and so the condition was laid down that if one of the tribes, that had been hostile to Islam, and had broken its agreements, and was at war with the Muslims, came over to Islam, all hostilities against it were to be stopped immediately, because those people became brethren in faith with Muslims. Old wrongs and iniquities had to be forgotten and not one individual of it was to be harmed, however guilty he may have been, unless, in the words of the hadith, an obligation of Islam rendered punishment necessary. The hadith does not mean that the Holy Prophet was commanded to *wage* war against people until they accepted Islam; it simply means, as a reference to the Quran shows, that he was commanded to *cease* fighting with people who were at war with the Muslims if they of their own accord embraced Islam. Even people who had been guilty of the murder of a Muslim were not to be put to death if they accepted Islam afterwards, and examples of this are mentioned in Hadith.[13]

One such case may be cited here:

"Miqdad ibn Amr al-Kindi... said to the Messenger of Allah: 'I meet in battle a man from among the unbelievers and we two fight against each other; he cuts off one of my hands with his sword, then he takes the shelter of a tree and says, I submit to Allah; can I kill him, O Messenger of Allah, after he has spoken those words?' The Messenger of Allah said: 'Do not kill him'. But he said: 'He has cut off one of my hands, O Messenger of Allah, and then he says this after he has cut it off'. The Messenger of Allah said: 'Do not kill him, for if you kill him, he would be what you were before you killed him, and you would be what he was before he uttered those words which he spoke'." [14]

This shows that the Holy Prophet had given definite orders, which were known to his Companions, that fighting should immediately cease when the person or tribe fighting declared Islam. It is in this light that the hadith under discussion has to be read, namely, that the Holy Prophet had been commanded to *cease* war when an enemy at war with him professed Islam. Numerous examples of this are met with in the history of the Prophet's wars, but there is not a single instance in which he declared war against a peaceful neighbour because that neighbour was not a believer in Islam. The fact that treaties and agreements were entered into by the Holy Prophet with the Arab idolaters and the Jews and the Christians is proof that this hadith refers to particular tribes which, as the Quran shows, violated their treaties again and again.

There are many Hadith reports which speak of the excellence of *jihād* or of the excellence of fighting, and these are sometimes misconstrued as showing that a Muslim must always be fighting with other people. War is undoubtedly a necessity of life, and there are times when fighting becomes the highest of duties. Fighting in the cause of justice, fighting to help the oppressed, fighting in self-defence, fighting for national existence are all truly the highest and noblest of deeds, because in all these cases a man lays down his life in the cause of truth and justice, and that is, no doubt, the highest sacrifice that a man can make.

The question is simply this, What was the object for which the Prophet fought? There is not the least doubt about it, as the Quran is clear on the point, as already shown: "Permission to fight is given to those on whom war is made, because they are oppressed" (22:39), "Will you not fight a people who broke their oaths and aimed at the expulsion of the Messenger, and they attacked you first" (9:13); and so on. If then there are Hadith reports which speak of the excellence of keeping horses ready on the frontier of the enemy, or recommending practising with implements of war, or speaking of swords and shields and armour and so on, they show, not that Muslims were spreading Islam by force of arms, not even that they were waging aggressive war against peaceful neighbours, but that they were compelled to fight, and hence all deeds done to carry on a successful war are praised.

Jurists' wrong notion of *jihād*

The wrong notion of *jihād,* as being the obligation upon Muslims to wage unprovoked war against unbelievers, was introduced by the jurists of Islam. It was based on a misconception of certain verses of the Holy Quran due, in the first place, to the fact that no regard had been paid to the context, and, in the second place, to a disregard of the circumstances under which the Prophet fought.

It is, however, also found that the jurists themselves have challenged the accuracy of the principle on which their wrong notion of *jihād* is based. Giving the reason for *jihād* being obligatory, they acknowledge that it is for the repelling of evil (*daf' al-sharr*).[15] This shows that *jihād* in its origin is only for repelling evil and is therefore defensive, not offensive. Again, when discussing the reasons for the prohibition of killing women, children, the old, the blind, and those who refrain from fighting, it is stated that what makes the killing of a man lawful is his fighting.[16] Thus it is not his unbelief which makes the killing of a man lawful, but his fighting in war (*ḥirāb*), for, if people could be killed for unbelief, even women, children, and old and incapacitated men would not be spared. And if it is unlawful to kill anyone merely on account of unbelief, it is also unlawful to undertake war against a people because they are unbelievers. Also, the jurists recognize the making of peace with unbelievers:

> "… [if] it is in the interests of the Muslims, there is no harm in peace, on account of what Allah says, 'And if they incline to peace, you must incline to it also, and trust in Allah' [the Quran, 8:61], and the Holy Prophet entered into agreement with the people of Makkah in the year of Hudaibiyah, that

there shall be no war between him and them for ten years; and because entering into agreement is *jihād* in spirit, when it is for the good of the Muslims, as the object, which is the repelling of mischief, is attained thereby." [17]

The above references show that even the jurists felt that their exposition of *jihād* was opposed to its basic principles laid down in the Quran. Probably the new doctrine grew up slowly. It is clear that the earlier jurists did not go as far as their later annotators. Notwithstanding the wrong conception which was introduced into the meaning of *jihād,* they still recognized that the basic principle of *jihād* was the repelling of the enemy's mischief, and that hence peace with the unbelievers was *jihād* in spirit. But the later generation would not tolerate even this much.

With the new notion introduced into the word *jihad,* the jurists artificially divided the whole world into two domains: *dār al-ḥarb,* 'the abode of war', and *dār al-Islām,* 'the abode of Islam'. The words are not used in the Holy Quran, nor are they traceable in any hadith. Bukhari uses the word *dār al-ḥarb* in the heading of one of his chapters,[18] but it does not occur in the reports under this heading. *Dār al-Islām* is evidently a place where the laws of Islam prevail and which is under a Muslim ruler. The jurists apply the word *dār al-ḥarb* to all states and countries which are not *dār al-Islām,* though they may not be at war with Muslims, and thus look upon a Muslim state as being always in a state of war with the whole of the non-Muslim world. This position is not only inconsistent with the very basic principles of Islam but actually it has never been accepted by any Muslim state that has ever existed in the world. The difficulty has been met by some jurists by bringing a third class, called *dār al-ṣulḥ* or *dār al-'ahd,* or a country which has an agreement with Muslims. But even this does not exhaust the whole world. Many of the laws framed by the Muslim jurists relating to war are based on this fictitious division of the world, for which there is not the least authority either in the Quran or in Hadith.

Jizyah

The word *jizyah* is explained as meaning "the tax that is taken from the free non-Muslim subjects of a Muslim government, whereby they ratify the compact that ensures them protection", or "a tax that is paid by the owner of land", being derived from *jazā* which means to give satisfaction or to compensate someone for a certain thing or for what he had done.[19] In the Holy Quran, *jizyah* is spoken of only in one place, and there in connection with wars with the people of the Book:

> "Fight those who do not believe in Allah... out of those who have been given the Book, until they pay the *jizyah* in acknowledgement of superiority and they are in a state of subjection." — 9:29

The Holy Prophet made treaties subject to the condition of payment of *jizyah* with certain Magian, Christian and Jewish tribes. But in all these cases, the *jizyah* was a tribute paid by the state and not a poll-tax. Bukhari opens his book of *jizyah* with a chapter headed as follows: "*Jizyah* and concluding of peace with *ahl al-ḥarb* (those at war with Muslims)".[20] Continuing, he is more explicit, remarking under the same heading:

> "And what is related in the matter of taking *jizyah* from the Jews and the Christians and the Magians and the non-Arabs ('*Ajam*)."

The rule of the *jizyah* was thus applicable to all enemy people, and the Prophet's own action shows that treaties subject to the payment of *jizyah* were concluded, not only with the Jews and the Christians but also with Magians. It would be seen from this that the words "those who have been given the Book" used in 9:29, quoted above, must be taken in the wider sense of followers of any other religion. But *jizyah,* which was originally a tribute paid by a subject state, took the form of a poll-tax later on in the time of Umar; and the word was also applied to the land-tax which was levied on Muslim owners of agricultural land.[21]

Jizyah was not a religious tax

Western writers on Islam have generally assumed that, while the Quran offered only one of the two alternatives, Islam or death, to other non-Muslims, the Jews and the Christians were given a somewhat better position, since they could save their lives by the payment of *jizyah.* This conception *of jizyah,* as a kind of religious tax whose payment entitled certain non-Muslims to security of life under Muslim rule, is as entirely opposed to the fundamental teachings of Islam as the myth that Muslims were required to carry on an aggressive war against all non-Muslims till they accepted Islam. Tributes and taxes were levied before Islam, and are levied to this day, by Muslim as well as non-Muslim states, yet they have nothing to do with the religion of the people affected. The Muslim state was as much in need of finance to maintain itself as any other state on the face of this earth, and it resorted to exactly the same methods as those employed by other states.

All that happened in the time of the Holy Prophet was that certain small non-Muslim states were, when subjugated, given the right to administer their own affairs, but only if they would pay a small sum by way of tribute towards the maintenance of the central government at Madinah. There was no military occupation of their territories, no interference at all with their administration, their laws, their customs and usages, or their religion; and, for the tribute paid, the Muslim state undertook the responsibility of protecting these small states against all enemies.

In the later conquests of Islam, while it became necessary for Muslims to establish their own administration in the conquered territories, there was still as little interference with the usages and religion of the conquered people as was possible, and for enjoying complete protection and the benefits of a settled rule they had to pay a very mild tax, the *jizyah*.

It may, however, be said that the Muslim state made a discrimination between the Muslim and the non-Muslim and that it was this feature of *jizyah* which gave it a religious colouring. A discrimination was indeed made, but it was not in favour of the Muslim but that of the non-Muslim. The Muslim had to do compulsory military service and to fight the battles of the state, not only at home but also in foreign countries, and in addition had to pay a tax heavier than that which the non-Muslim was required to pay, as will be shown presently. The non-Muslim was entirely exempt from military service on account of the *jizyah* he paid. So the Muslim had to pay the *zakāt,* a far heavier tax than *jizyah,* and do military service, while the non-Muslim had only to pay a small tax for the privilege of enjoying all the benefits of a settled rule.

The very name *ahl al-dhimmah* (lit., 'people under protection') given to the non-Muslim subjects of a Muslim state, or to a non-Muslim state under the protection of Muslim rule, shows that the *jizyah* was paid as a compensation for the protection afforded; in other words, it was a contribution of the non-Muslims towards the military organization of the Muslim state. There are cases on record in which the Muslim state returned the *jizyah* when it was unable to afford protection to the people under its care. Thus, when the Muslim forces under Abu Ubaidah were engaged in a struggle with the Roman Empire, they were compelled to beat a retreat at Hims, which they had previously conquered. When the decision was taken to evacuate Hims, Abu Ubaidah sent for the chiefs of the place and returned to them the whole amount which he had realized as *jizyah,* saying that as Muslims could no longer protect them, they were not entitled to the *jizyah.*

Further it appears that exemption from military service was granted only to such non-Muslims as wanted it, for where a non-Muslim people offered to fight the battles of the country, they were exempted from *jizyah.* The Bani Taghlib and the people of Najran, both Christians, did not pay the *jizyah.*[22] Indeed the Bani Taghlib fought alongside the Muslim forces in the battle of Buwaib in 13 A.H. Later on in the year 17 A.H., they wrote to the Caliph Umar offering to pay the *zakāt,* which was a heavier burden, instead of the *jizyah.* Muir writes:

> "The tribe deeming in its pride the payment of 'tribute' an indignity, sent a deputation to the Caliph:— They were willing, they said, to pay the tax, if only it were levied under the same name as that taken from the Muslims. The liberality of Omar allowed the concession; and the Beni Taghlib enjoyed the singular privilege of being assessed as Christians at a 'double *Tithe*,' instead of paying the obnoxious badge of subjugation." [23]

Military service was also accepted in place of *jizyah* from some others in the time of Umar.

The manner in which the *jizyah* was levied also shows that it was a tax for exemption from military service. The following classes were exempt from *jizyah:* all females, males who had not attained majority, old people, people whom disease had crippled, the blind, the poor who could not work for themselves, the slaves, slaves who were working for their freedom, and the monks.[24] And besides this: "In the first century… many persons were entirely exempt from taxation, though we do not know why".[25] These two facts — the exemption of non-Muslims unfit for military service, and of the able-bodied who agreed to military service mentioned earlier — lead to but one conclusion, namely, that the *jizyah* was a tax paid by such <u>Dhimmis</u> (i.e., 'people under protection') as could fight, for exemption from military service.

In spite of exemptions on so vast a scale, the rate of *jizyah* was very low. The Muslim was, apparently, more heavily taxed, for he had to pay at the rate of 2½ per cent of his savings, and, in addition, to perform military service. The *jizyah* was also levied in a very sympathetic spirit, as the following anecdote will show. Caliph Umar once saw a blind non-Muslim begging, and finding on enquiry that he had to pay *jizyah,* he not only exempted him but, in addition, ordered that he be paid a stipend from the state treasury, issuing further orders at the same time that all <u>Dhimmis</u> in similar circumstances should be paid stipends.

Islam, *jizyah* or the sword

It is a myth that Muslims were out to impose their religion at the point of a sword, and that Muslim armies were over-running all lands with the message of Islam, *jizyah* or the sword. If this were true, how was it possible for non-Muslims to fight in their ranks? The fact that there were people who never became Muslims at all, nor ever paid *jizyah,* and yet were living in the midst of Muslims, even fighting their battles, explodes the whole theory of Muslims offering Islam or *jizyah* or the sword.

The truth of the matter is that Muslims, finding the Roman Empire and Persia bent upon the subjugation of Arabia and the extirpation of Islam, refused to accept terms of peace without a safeguard against a repetition of the aggression; and this safeguard was demanded in the form of *jizyah,* or a tribute, which would be an admission of defeat on their part. No war was ever *started* by Muslims by sending this message to a peaceful neighbour; history belies such an assertion. But when a war was undertaken on account of the enemy's aggression, it was only natural that the Muslims did not terminate the war before bringing it to a successful conclusion. They were willing to avoid further bloodshed after inflicting a defeat on the enemy, only if he admitted defeat and agreed to pay a tribute, which was only a token tribute as compared with the crushing war indemnities of the present day. The offer to terminate hostilities on payment of *jizyah* was thus an act of mercy towards a vanquished foe.

The only question that remains is whether Muslim soldiers invited their enemies to accept Islam; and whether it was an offence if they did so? Islam was a missionary religion from its very inception, and every Muslim deemed it his birthright to invite other people to embrace Islam. The envoys of Islam, wherever they went, looked upon it as their first duty to deliver the message of Islam, because they felt that Islam imparted a new life and vigour to humanity, and offered a real solution to the problems of every nation. Islam was offered, no doubt, even to the fighting enemy, but it is a distortion of facts to say that it was offered at the point of the sword, when there is not a single instance on record of Islam being enforced upon a prisoner of war; nor of Muslims sending a message to a peaceful neighbouring state to the effect that it would be invaded if it did not embrace Islam.

All that is recorded is that, in the midst of war and after defeat had been inflicted on the enemy in several battles, when there were negotiations for peace, Muslims in their zeal for the faith related their own experience before the enemy chiefs. They stated how they themselves had been deadly foes to Islam and how, ultimately, they saw the truth and found Islam to be a blessing and a power that had raised the Arab race from the depths of degradation to great moral and spiritual heights, and had welded their warring elements into a solid nation. In such words did the Muslim envoys invite the Persians and the Romans to Islam, not before the declaration of war, but at the time of the negotiations for peace. If the enemy then accepted Islam, there would be no conditions for peace, and the two nations would live as equals and brethren. It was not offering Islam at the point of a sword, but offering it as a harbinger of peace, of equality and of brotherhood.

Directions relating to war

The directions given to his soldiers by the Holy Prophet also show that his wars were not due to any desire to enforce religion. It is reported that, in a certain battle fought by the Holy Prophet, a woman was discovered among the slain. On this, he forbade the killing of women and children in wars.[26] Hadith reports relating to this prohibition are repeated very often in all collections.[27] The fact that there is an express direction against killing some 75% of the population, as women and children must be in every community, shows that the propagation of religion was far from being the object of these wars. In some Hadith reports, in addition to women and children, there was also a prohibition against killing people who were taken along with the army as 'labour units'.[28] There is yet another hadith prohibiting the killing of very old men who are unable to fight.[29] Monks were also not to be molested.[30] It was only in a night attack that the Holy Prophet excused the chance killing of a woman or child saying, "They are among them";[31] what he meant was that it was a thing which could not be avoided, for at night children and women could not be distinguished from the soldiers.

The above examples may be supplemented by some others taken from Syed Ameer Ali's *Spirit of Islam.* The following instructions were given to the troops dispatched against the Byzantines by the Holy Prophet:

> "In avenging the injuries inflicted upon us, molest not the harmless inmates of domestic seclusion; spare the weakness of the female sex; injure not the infant at the breast, or those who are ill in bed. Abstain from demolishing the dwellings of the unresisting inhabitants; destroy not the means of their subsistence, nor their fruit trees; and touch not the palm." (ch. 6, *Mohammed's Clemency,* p. 81)

Prisoners of war

The treatment of prisoners of war, as laid down in the Holy Quran and Hadith, also bears evidence of the fact that the idea of enforcement of Islam by the sword is entirely foreign to the conception of Islamic warfare. If the wars, during the time of the Holy Prophet or the early Caliphate, had been prompted by the desire of propagating Islam by force, this object could easily have been attained by forcing Islam upon prisoners of war who fell into the hands of the Muslims. Yet this the Quran does not allow, expressly laying down that they must be set free:

> "So when you meet in battle those who disbelieve, strike the necks; then when you have overcome them, make them prisoners, and afterwards set them free as a favour or for ransom until the war lays down its burdens." — 47:4

It will be seen from this that the taking of prisoners was allowed only as long as war conditions prevailed; and even when the prisoners are taken they cannot be kept so permanently, but must be set free either as a favour or at the utmost by taking ransom. The Holy Prophet carried this injunction into practice in his lifetime. For instance, in the battle of Hunain, six thousand prisoners of the Hawazin tribe were taken, and they were all set free simply as an act of favour.[32] Seventy prisoners were taken in the battle of Badr, and it was only in this case that ransom was exacted, but the prisoners were granted their freedom while war with the Quraish was yet in progress.[33] The form of ransom adopted in the case of some of these prisoners was that they should be entrusted with some work for the Muslims connected with teaching. When war ceased and peace was established, all war-prisoners would have to be set free, according to the verse quoted above.

Slavery abolished

This verse also abolishes slavery forever. Slavery was generally brought about through raids by stronger tribes upon weaker ones. Islam did not allow raids or the making of prisoners by means of raids. Prisoners could only be taken after a regular battle, and even then could not be retained forever. It was obligatory to set them free, either as a favour or after taking ransom. This state of things could last only as long as war conditions existed. When war was over, no prisoners could be taken.

The treatment accorded to prisoners of war or slaves in Islam is unparalleled. No other nation or society can show a similar treatment even of its own members when they are placed in the relative position of a master and a servant. The slave or the prisoner was, no doubt, required to do a certain amount of work, but the condition, in which it was ordained that he should be kept, freed him of all abject feelings. The golden rule of treating the slave like a brother was laid down by the Prophet in clear words:

> "Ma'rur says: I met Abu Dharr in Rabdha and he wore a dress and his slave wore a similar dress. I questioned him about it. He said: I abused a man [i.e., his slave] and found fault with him on account of his mother [addressing him as son of a black woman]. The Prophet said to me: Abu Dharr! You find fault with him on account of his mother, surely you

are an ignorant man; your slaves are your brethren, Allah has placed them under your hands; so whoever has his brother under his charge, he should give him to eat out of what he himself eats, and give him to wear of what he himself wears, and impose not on them a task which they are not able to do, and if you give them such a task, then help them [in doing it]." [34]

The prisoners were distributed among the various Muslim families because no arrangements for their maintenance by the state existed at the time, but they were treated honourably.

War as a struggle to be carried on honestly

It will be seen from what has been stated above, concerning the injunctions relating to war and peace, that war is recognized by Islam as a struggle between nations — though a terrible struggle — which is sometimes necessitated by the conditions of human life; and when that struggle comes, a nation is bound to acquit itself of its responsibility in the matter in an honourable manner, and fight it to the bitter end whatever it is. Islam does not allow its followers to provoke war, nor does it allow them to be aggressors, but it commands them to put their whole force into the struggle when war is forced on them. If the enemy wants peace after the struggle has begun, Muslims should not refuse, even though there is doubt about the honesty of his purpose. But the struggle, as long as it lasts, must be carried on to the end. In this struggle, honest dealing is enjoined even with the enemy, throughout the Holy Quran:

> "And do not let hatred of a people … incite you to transgress. And help one another in righteousness and piety, and do not help one another in sin and aggression." — 5:2

> "And do not let hatred of a people incite you not to act equitably. Be just, that is nearer to observance of duty." — 5:8

This is in a chapter which was revealed towards the close of the Holy Prophet's life. The directions given by Islam purify war of the elements of barbarity and dishonesty in which warring nations generally indulge. Neither inhuman nor immoral practices are allowed.

A hadith is sometimes cited as allowing deceit in war. It is reported about the Holy Prophet that "he called war a deception".[35]

These words were uttered by the Holy Prophet while he was prophesying that the power of both the Persian and the Byzantine empires shall depart in their wars with the Muslims. Evidently these concluding words, "and he called war a deception", explain how these empires will perish. War is a deception in the sense that sometimes a great power makes war upon a weaker power thinking that it will soon crush it, but such war proves a deception and leads to the destruction of the great aggressive power itself. This was what happened in the case of the wars of Persia and Rome against the Muslims. They both had entered upon an aggressive war against the Arabs, thinking that they would crush the rising power of Arabia in a little time. They were drawn into a war with the Muslims which ultimately crushed their own power.

These words have been explained as follows: "The meaning is that war deceives people; it gives them hopes but does not fulfil them".[36] It is only imperfect knowledge of the Arabic language which has led some people to think that this hadith means that it is lawful to practise deception in war. The Islamic wars were in fact purified of all that is unworthy when Muslims were plainly told that a war fought for any gain (which includes acquisition of wealth or territory) was not in the way of Allah.[37]

Apostasy

There is as great a misconception on the subject of apostasy (*irtidād*), i.e., the act of going back to unbelief from Islam, as on the subject of *jihād*. The general impression among both Muslims and non-Muslims is that Islam punishes the apostate (*murtadd*) with death. If Islam does not allow the taking of the life of a person on the score of religion, and this has already been shown to be the basic principle of Islam, it is immaterial whether unbelief has been adopted after being a Muslim or not, and therefore as far as the sacredness of life is concerned, the unbeliever and the apostate are at par.

Apostasy in the Quran

The Quran is the primary source of Islamic laws and therefore we shall take it first. In the first place, it nowhere speaks of someone who becomes an apostate by implication. Apostasy consists in the expression of unbelief or in the plain denial of Islam, and it is not to be assumed because a person who professes Islam expresses an opinion or does an act which, in the view of a learned man or a legist, is un-Islamic. Abuse of a prophet or disrespect towards the Quran are very often made false excuses for treating a person as an apostate, though he may avow in the strongest terms that he is a believer in the Quran and the Prophet.

Secondly, the general impression that Islam condemns an apostate to death does not find the least support from the Quran. The article on *murtadd* in the *Encyclopaedia of Islam* begins with the following words:

> "In the Quran the apostate is threatened with punishment in the next world only." [38]

There is mention of apostasy in one of the late Makkah revelations:

> "Whoever disbelieves in Allah after his belief — not he who is compelled while his heart is content with faith, but he who opens his heart for disbelief — they incur Allah's displeasure, and for them is a grievous punishment." —16:106

Clearly the apostate is here threatened with punishment in the next life, and there is not the least change in this attitude in later revelations, when Islamic government had been established immediately after the Holy Prophet reached Madinah. In one of the early Madinah revelations, apostasy is spoken of in connection with the war which the unbelievers had waged to make the Muslims apostates by force:

> "And they will not cease fighting you until they turn you back from your religion, if they can. And whoever of you turns back from his religion (*yartadda* from *irtidād*), then he dies while an unbeliever — these it is whose deeds are fruitless in this world and the Hereafter. And they are the companions of the fire: in it they will abide." — 2:217

So if a person becomes apostate, he will be punished — not in this life, but in the Hereafter — on account of the evil deeds to which he has reverted, and his good works, done while he was yet a Muslim, become null because of the evil course of life which he has adopted.

The third chapter, revealed in the year 3 A.H., speaks again and again of people who had resorted to unbelief after becoming Muslims, but always speaks of their punishment in the Hereafter:

> "How shall Allah guide a people who disbelieved after their believing and after they had borne witness that the Messenger was true ... As for these, their reward is that on them is the curse of Allah ... except those who repent after that and amend." — 3:86, 87, 89

> "Those who disbelieve after their believing, then increase in disbelief, their repentance is not accepted." — 3:90

The most convincing argument that death was not the punishment for apostasy is contained in the Jewish plans, conceived while they were living under the Muslim rule in Madinah:

> "And a group of the People of the Book say: Affirm belief in what has been revealed to those who believe, in the first part of the day, and disbelieve [in it] in the latter part of it, perhaps they may turn back." — 3:72

If apostasy had been punishable with death, how could people living under a Muslim government conceive of such a plan to throw discredit on Islam, by accepting it and then deserting it the same day?

The fifth chapter of the Quran was revealed towards the close of the Holy Prophet's life, and even in this chapter no worldly punishment is mentioned for apostates:

> "O you who believe! if anyone of you should turn back from his religion, then Allah will bring a people whom He loves and who love Him..." — 5:54

Therefore, so far as the Quran is concerned, there is not only no mention of a death sentence for apostates but such a sentence is negatived by the verses speaking of apostasy, as well as by that *magna charta* of religious freedom in the Quran: *lā ikrāha fi-l-dīn* (2:256), meaning "There is no compulsion in religion".

Hadith on apostasy

It is on the authority of Hadith that the books of Muslim jurists have based their death-sentence for apostates. The words in certain reports in Hadith have undoubtedly the reflex of a later age, but still a careful study leads to the conclusion that apostasy was not punishable unless combined with other circumstances which called for punishment of offenders. Bukhari is explicit on the point. He has two books dealing with the apostates, one of which is called "the Book of those who fight [against Muslims] from among the unbelievers and the apostates", and the other is called "the Book of calling to repentance of the enemies and the apostates and fighting with them". The heading of the first book clearly shows that only such apostates are dealt with in it as fight against Muslims, and that of the second associates apostates with the enemies of Islam.

That is really the crux of the whole question, and it is due to a misunderstanding on this point that a doctrine was formulated which is quite contrary to the plain teachings of the Quran. At a time when war was in progress between Muslims and unbelievers, it often happened that a person who apostatized went over to the enemy and joined hands with him in fighting against the Muslims. He was treated as an enemy, not because he had changed his religion but because he had changed sides. Even then there were tribes that were not at war with the Muslims and, if an apostate went over to them, he was not touched. Such people are expressly spoken of in the Quran:

> "Except those who join a people between whom and you there is an alliance... So if they withdraw from you and do not fight you and offer you peace, then Allah allows you no way against them." — 4:90

The only case of the punishment of apostates, mentioned in trustworthy Hadith reports, is that of a party of the tribe of Ukul, who accepted Islam and came to Madinah. They found that the climate of the town did not agree with them, and the Holy Prophet sent them to a place outside Madinah where the state milch-camels were kept, so that they might live in the open air and drink of milk. They got well and then killed the keeper of the camels and drove away the animals. This being brought to the knowledge of the Holy Prophet, a party was sent in pursuit of them and they were put to death.[39] The report is clear on the point that they were put to death, not because of their apostasy but because they had committed the crime of murder by killing the keeper of the camels.

Much stress is laid on a hadith which says: "Whoever changes his religion, kill him".[40] But in view of what Bukhari's collection itself has indicated by describing apostates as fighters or by associating their name with the name of the enemies of Islam, it is clear that this refers only to those apostates who join hands with the enemies of

Islam and fight with Muslims. It is only by placing this limitation on the meaning of the hadith that it can be reconciled with other reports or with the principles laid down in the Holy Quran. In fact, its words are so comprehensive that they include every change of faith, from one religion to any other religion whatsoever, even to embrace Islam! So the hadith cannot be accepted without placing a limitation upon its meaning.

An instance of a simple change of religion is also contained in Bukhari:

> "An Arab of the desert came to the Prophet and accepted Islam at his hand. Then fever overtook him while he was still in Madinah. So he came to the Prophet and said, Give back my pledge, and the Prophet refused. Then he came again and said, Give me back my pledge, and the Prophet refused. Then he came again and said, Give me back my pledge, and the Prophet refused. Then he went away." [41]

This hadith shows that the man first accepted Islam, and the next day on getting fever he thought that it was due to his becoming a Muslim, and so he came and threw back the pledge. This was a clear case of apostasy, yet it is nowhere related that anyone killed him. On the other hand, the hadith says that he went away unharmed. Another example of a simple change of religion is that of a Christian who became a Muslim and then apostatized and went over to Christianity, and yet he was not put to death.[42] This was at Madinah when a Muslim state was well-established, and yet the man who apostatized was not even molested, though he spoke of the Holy Prophet in extremely derogatory terms and gave him out to be an imposter.

Apostasy and *fiqh*

Turning to Islamic jurisprudence, or *Fiqh,* we find the jurists first laying down a principle quite opposed to the Holy Quran and Hadith, namely, that the life of a man may be taken on account of apostasy. But this principle is contradicted immediately afterwards when the apostate is called "an unbeliever at war whom the invitation of Islam has already reached". And in the case of the apostate woman, the rule is laid down that she shall not be put to death, because women are unable to fight in war due to "the unfitness of their constitution". It is also stated: "The killing for apostasy is obligatory in order to prevent the mischief of war, and it is not a punishment for the act of unbelief". And again: "For, mere unbelief does not legalize the killing of a man".[43]

It will be seen that, as in the case of war against unbelievers, the legists are labouring under a misconception, and a struggle is clearly seen going on between the principles as established in the Quran and the misconceptions which had somehow or other found their way into the minds of the legists. Thus, even the *Fiqh* recognizes the principle that the life of a person cannot be taken for mere change of religion and that, unless the apostate is in a state of war, he cannot be killed. It is quite a different matter that the legists should have made a mistake in defining a state of war by considering the mere ability of someone to fight as the existence of a war condition. The law of punishment is based not on potentialities but on facts.

Notes to Chapter 15

1. Raghib's *Mufradāt*.

2. Lane's Lexicon.

3. *Editor's Note:* In these words, *jihād* is said to be conducted by unbelievers against Muslims!

4. Bukhari, book 25: 'Pilgrimage', ch. 4, h. 1520.

5. Bukhari, book 96: 'Holding fast to the Quran and Sunnah', ch. 10, ch. heading (above h. 7311).

6. Bukhari, book 56: '*Jihād*', ch. headings of chs. 99, 100, 143, 145, 178, respectively.

7. Abu Dawud, book 15: '*Jihād*', ch. 4, h. 2484.

8. *'Aun al-Ma'būd 'alā Sunani Abī Dāwūd,* a commentary of Abu Dawud; comment on hadith referred to in note 7 above, on the authority of Nawawi.

9. Maulana Muhammad Ali is here referring to his book *The Early Caliphate.*

10. *The Caliphate* by Sir William Muir, chapter xvi, p. 120.

11. *Ibid.,* chapter xxiii, p. 172.

12. Bukhari, book 2: 'Faith', ch. 17, h. 25.

13. Bukhari, book 56: '*Jihād*', ch. 28, h. 2826, h. 2827.

14. Bukhari, book 64: 'Military Expeditions', ch. 12, h. 4019.

15. *Hidāyah,* v. 1, p. 537.

16. *Ibid.,* v. 1, p. 540.

17. *Ibid.,* v. 1, p. 541.

18. Bukhari, book 56: '*Jihād*', ch. heading of ch. 180 (above h. 3058).

19. Lane's Lexicon.

20. Bukhari, book 58: '*Jizyah*', ch. 1, ch. heading.

21. The jurists, however, made a distinction by giving the name *kharāj* to the land-tax.

22. *Encyclopaedia of Islam,* first edition, art. *Djizya,* v. 1, p. 1051, col. 1.

23. *The Caliphate,* chapter xix, p. 142.

24. *Hidāyah,* v. 1, p. 571–572.

25. *Encyclopaedia of Islam,* first edition, art. *Djizya,* v. 1, p. 1052, col. 1.

26. Bukhari, book 56: '*Jihād*', chs. 147–148, h. 3014, h. 3015.

27. Muslim, book 32: '*Jihād* and Expeditions', ch. 8, h. 1744a, 1744b (MDS: h. 4547, h. 4548). Abu Dawud, book 15: '*Jihād*', ch. 121, h. 2668, 2669, 2672 (MDS: ch. 111). Tirmidhi, book 21: 'Military Expeditions', ch. 19, h. 1569 (MDS: book 19). *Musnad* of Ahmad ibn Hanbal, v. 1, p. 256; v. 2, pp. 22, 23; v. 3, p. 488.

28. Abu Dawud, book 15: '*Jihād*', ch. 121, h. 2669 (MDS: ch. 111). *Musnad* of Ahmad ibn Hanbal, v. 3, p. 488; v. 4, p. 178.

29. Mishkat, book 19: '*Ādāb al-safar*', ch. 3, sec. 2, h. 3778 (v. 2, p. 251). In some editions of Mishkat, this book is included as part of the previous book '*Jihād*', and the report is in ch. 5, sec. 2.

30. *Musnad* of Ahmad ibn Hanbal, v. 1, p. 300.

31. Bukhari, book 56: '*Jihād*', ch. 146, h. 3012.

32. Bukhari, book 40: '*Wakālat*', ch. 7, h. 2307–2308.

33. Abu Dawud, book 15: '*Jihād*', ch. 131, h. 2690–2692 (MDS: ch. 121). *Musnad* of Ahmad ibn Hanbal, v. 1, p. 30.

34. Bukhari, book 2: 'Faith', ch. 22, h. 30.

35. Bukhari, book 56: '*Jihād*', ch. 157, h. 3027–3030.

36. *Nihāyah* of Ibn Athīr (dictionary of Hadith).

37. Bukhari, book 56: '*Jihād*', ch. 15, h. 2810.

38. *Encyclopaedia of Islam,* first edition, v. 3, p. 736; second edition, v. 7, p. 635.

39. Bukhari, book 56: '*Jihād*', ch. 152, h. 3018.

40. Bukhari, book 88: 'Apostates and fighting with them', ch. 2, h. 6922.

41. Bukhari, book 93: 'Judgments', ch. 47, h. 7211.

42. Bukhari, book 61: 'Virtues of the Prophet and his Companions', ch. 25, h. 3617.

43. For these references see *Hidāyah,* v. 1, p. 576–577.

16. Marriage

Section 1: *Significance of Marriage*

In the foregoing five chapters we have dealt with laws relating to the self-development of man, or to the welfare and development of the community as a whole. These are generally called the laws governing the relations of man to God — the religious duties of man in a stricter sense. But as already stated in the Introduction to this book, the scope of the religion of Islam is very wide and covers the whole field of the relations of people to one another, as well as that of man to God. The object of the laws relating to this part of human life is to teach the individual his duties and obligations to others, and to show him how to lead a happy life in this world in his relations with others.

In all these matters Islamic law imposes certain restrictions upon the free acts of individuals for the benefit of society as a whole, and therefore ultimately for the benefit of each person. The basic principle in the matter of all restrictive ordinances is that a thing which is not disallowed is deemed to be lawful, as the well-known juridical dictum has it: "Lawfulness is a recognized principle in all things". In other words, everything (in which is included every free act of man) is presumed to be lawful, unless it is definitely prohibited by law. This dictum is in fact based on the plain words of the Holy Quran:

"He it is Who created for you all that is in the earth." — 2 : 29

According to this verse, everything has been created for the benefit of man, which leads to the only possible presumption that everything can be made use of by him, unless a limitation is placed, by law, on that use.

Importance of the marriage institution

The most important of the restrictive regulations of Islam are those relating to marriage, which institution is, in fact, the basic principle of human civilization. The Arabic word for marriage is *nikāḥ* which originally means 'uniting'. Marriage in Islam is a sacred contract which every Muslim must enter into, unless there are special reasons why he should not. Thus in the Holy Quran it is said:

> "And marry those among you who are single [to their spouses],[1] and those who are fit among your male slaves and your female slaves. If they are needy, Allah will make them free from want out of His grace. And Allah is Ample-giving, Knowing. And those who cannot find a match must keep chaste until Allah makes them free from want out of His grace." — 24:32–33

In another verse, marriage relationship is given the same importance as blood-relationship:

> "And He it is Who has created man from water, then He has made for him blood-relationship and marriage-relationship." — 25:54

Hadith also lays stress upon living in a married state. The Holy Prophet is reported to have said to certain people who talked of fasting in the day-time and keeping awake during the night, praying to God and keeping away from marriage:

> "I keep a fast and I break it, and I pray and I sleep, and I am married, so whoever inclines to any other way than my practice, he is not of me." [2]

Another saying of the Holy Prophet laying stress upon marriage is worded thus:

> "O assembly of young people! Whoever of you has the means to support a wife, he should get married, for this is the best means of keeping the looks cast down and guarding chastity; and he who has not the means, let him keep fast, for this will act as castration." [3]

Celibacy was expressly forbidden by the Holy Prophet.[4] According to one hadith, "the man who marries perfects half his religion", and another says: "Matrimonial alliances increase friendship more than anything else".[5]

Marriage as the union of two natures which are one in essence

The Holy Quran repeatedly speaks of the two mates, man and woman, as being created from each other:

> "O people, keep your duty to your Lord, Who created you from a single being (*nafs*)[6] and created its mate of the same [kind] and spread from these two many men and women." — 4:1

> "He it is Who created you from a single being (*nafs*) and of the same did He make his mate that he might find comfort in her." — 7:189

Both these verses are generally understood as referring to the creation of the first man and the first woman, but that they signify the relation of man to woman in general is obvious from other verses:

> "And Allah has made wives for you from among yourselves (*anfusi-kum*),[7] and has given you sons and daughters from your wives". — 16:72

> "And of His signs is this, that He created mates for you from yourselves, that you may find quiet of mind in them, and He put between you love and compassion." — 30:21

Thus marriage is, according to the Quran, the union of two souls which are one in their essence.

Multiplication of the human race through marriage

It will be noted that, in the above verses, the multiplication of the human race is mentioned as one of the objects of marriage. But it may be said that the multiplication of the race can be brought about without marriage, as with the lower animals; that is to say, without uniting one man with one woman for their whole life. This would be only true if man lived upon earth like other animals, if there was nothing to distinguish him from them, if there were no such thing as civilization, no society, no sense of respect for one's own obligations and the rights of others, no sense of property and ownership. The family, which is the real unit of the human race and the first cohesive force which makes civilization possible, owes its existence solely to marriage. If there is no marriage, there can be no family, no ties of kinship, no force uniting the different elements of humanity and consequently, no civilization. It is through the family that humanity is held together and civilization made possible.

Feelings of love and service developed through marriage

The institution of marriage is also responsible to a very great extent for the development of those feelings of love and service which are the pride of humanity today. The mutual love of husband and wife — a love based not on momentary passion but lifelong connection — and the consequent parental love for offspring leads to a very high development of the feeling of love for fellow-beings as such, and thus to the disinterested service of humanity. This love is described as a sign of God in the Quran (see 30:21 quoted above). The natural inclination of the male to the female and of the female to the male finds expansion through marriage and is developed, first, into a love for the children, then a love for one's kith and kin, and ultimately into a disinterested love for the whole of humanity. The home, or the family, is in fact the first training ground of love and service. Here man finds real pleasure in the service of humanity, and the sense of service is thus gradually developed and broadened. It is in fact a training ground for every kind of morality, for it is in the home that a man learns to have a sense of his own obligation and responsibilities, to have a respect for others' rights and, above all, to have a real pleasure in suffering for the sake of others. The Holy Prophet is reported to have said: "The best of you is he who treats his wife best".[8]

Section 2: *Form and Validity of Marriage*

Prohibitions to marry

The Holy Quran forbids certain marriage relations, as listed in 4:23 which begins with the words: "Forbidden to you are your mothers, and your daughters, and your sisters". It will be seen from the complete verse that these prohibitions arise from:

1. Consanguinity, as in the cases of mother, daughter, sister, brother's daughter, sister's daughter, father's sister and mother's sister;
2. Fosterage, such as in the case of foster-mother and foster-sister;

3.   Affinity, such as in the case of wife's mother, wife's daughter and son's wife.

Jurists have enlarged the conception of certain relations in the classes of consanguinity and affinity. For example, in the cases of daughter and wife's daughter, all their female descendants are included; and in the case of mother or wife's mother, all female ascendants are included. Step-mothers are expressly prohibited in the Quran: "And marry not women whom your fathers married" (4:22).

As to what constitutes fosterage (*raḍā ʻah* or giving suck), a child is recognized as a suckling only up to the age of two years, in the Quran,[9] and Hadith lays down that foster-relationship is not established unless the child is suckled when hungry.[10]

Marriage relations between Muslims and non-Muslims

The only other ground on which marriage is prohibited in the Holy Quran is *shirk* or associating gods with God:

> "And do not marry female idolaters (*al-mushrikāt*) until they believe; and certainly a believing maid is better than a female idolater even though she please you. Nor marry [believing women] to idolaters until they believe; and certainly a believing slave is better than an idolater even though he please you." — 2:221

Along with this, it is necessary to read another verse which allows marriage with women who profess one of the revealed religions:

> "This day all good things are made lawful for you. And the food of those who have been given the Book is lawful for you and your food is lawful for them. And so are the chaste from among the believing women and the chaste from among those who have been given the Book before you, when you have given them their dowries, taking them in marriage, not fornicating nor taking them for lovers in secret." — 5:5

Thus it will be seen that while there is a clear prohibition to marry idolaters or idolatresses, there is an express permission to marry women who profess a revealed religion. And, as the Quran states that revelation was granted to all nations of the world,[11] and that it was only the Arab idolaters who had not been warned,[12] the conclusion is evident that it was only with Arab idolaters that marriage relations were prohibited, and that it was lawful for a Muslim to marry a woman belonging to any other nation of the world that follows a revealed religion. Christians, Jews, Parsis, Buddhists and Hindus all fall within this category; and it would be seen that, though the Christian doctrine of calling Jesus Christ a God or son of God is denounced as *shirk,* still the Christians are treated as followers of a revealed religion and matrimonial relations with them are allowed. The case of all those people who have originally been given a revealed religion, though at present they may be guilty of *shirk,* would be treated in like manner.

Islamic jurisprudence (*Fiqh*), however, recognizes only the legality of marriage with women belonging to the Jewish and Christian faiths, and this is due to the narrow conception of the words *Ahl al-Kitāb* ('People of the Book') adopted by the jurists. There is no reason why all others who profess a religion and accept a revealed book should not be treated as such.[13]

It may be noted here that, while there is an express mention of a Muslim man marrying a non-Muslim woman who professes a revealed religion, there is no mention of the legality or illegality of a marriage between a Muslim woman and a non-Muslim man. The mere fact however that the Holy Quran speaks of the one and not of the other is sufficient to show that marriage between a Muslim woman and a non-Muslim man is not allowed.[14]

Form and validity of marriage

The very fact that marriage is looked upon as a contract in Islam, shows that before marriage both parties must satisfy themselves that each will have a desirable partner for life in the other. The Quran lays down expressly:

> "…marry such women as seem good to you (*mā ṭāba la-kum*)…" — 4:3

The Holy Prophet is reported to have given such an injunction:

> "When one of you makes a proposal of marriage to a woman, then if he can, he should look at what attracts him to marry her." [15]

The heading of this chapter is: "A man should look at the woman whom he intends to marry". Bukhari also has a chapter headed: "To look at the woman before marriage".[16] Sahih Muslim has a similar chapter, "Inviting a man who intends to marry a woman to have a look at her face and hands", in which is cited the case of a man who had not seen the woman he was going to marry, and the Holy Prophet told him to "go and look at her".[17] In another hadith also, it is reported that when a man made a proposal of marriage to a woman, the Holy Prophet asked him if he had seen her and on his replying in the negative, he enjoined him to see her, because "it was likely to bring about greater love and concord between them".[18]

Since the contract is effected by the consent of two parties, the man and the woman, and one of them is expressly told to satisfy himself about the other by looking at her, it would seem that the woman has the same right to satisfy herself before giving her assent. The consent of both the man and the woman is an essential of marriage, and the Quran lays down expressly that the two must agree:

> "…do not prevent them from marrying their husbands if they agree among themselves in a lawful manner." — 2:232

Proposal of Marriage

When a man, who wants to marry, has satisfied himself about a woman, he makes a proposal of marriage[19] either to the woman in question or to her parents or guardians. When a man has made a proposal of marriage to a woman, others are forbidden to propose to the same woman, till the first suitor has given up the matter, or has been rejected.[20] A woman may also make a proposal of marriage to a man,[21] or a man may propose the marriage of his daughter or sister to a man;[22] generally, however, it is the man who makes the proposal. When assent has been given to the proposal of marriage, it becomes an engagement, and usually a certain time is allowed to pass before the marriage (*nikāḥ*) is performed. This period allows the parties to study each other further, so that if there be anything undesirable in the union, the engagement may be broken off by either party. It is only after the *nikāḥ* has been performed that the two parties are bound to each other.

Age of marriage

No particular age has been specified for marriage in the Islamic law. But the Holy Quran does speak of an age of marriage which it identifies with the age of majority:

> "And test the orphans until they reach the age of marriage (*nikāḥ*). Then if you find in them maturity of intellect, make over to them their property, and do not consume it extravagantly and hastily against their growing up." — 4:6

Thus it will be seen that the age of marriage and the age of maturity of intellect are identified with full age or the age of majority. And as marriage is a contract the assent to which depends on personal liking, as already shown on the basis of the Holy Quran and Hadith, and since this function cannot be performed by anyone but the party who makes the contract, it is clear that the age of marriage is the age of majority, when a person is capable of exercising his choice in matters of sexual liking or disliking. A man or a woman who has not attained to puberty is unable to exercise his or her choice in sexual matters and unable to decide whether he or she will like or dislike a certain woman or man as wife or husband.

It is true that Jurisprudence (*Fiqh*), following the general law of contracts, recognizes, in the case of a marriage contract, the legality of the consent of a guardian on behalf of his ward, but there is no case on record showing that the marriage of a minor through his or her parent or guardian was allowed by the Holy Prophet after details of the law were revealed to him at Madinah.[23] There is no reliable Hadith report showing that marriages were contracted by minors through their guardians in the time of the Holy Prophet, after the revelation of the fourth chapter which identifies the age of marriage with the age of majority. Nor does the Quran mention minors being married or divorced.

Guardianship in marriage

The essence of marriage being then, according to Islam, the consent of two parties, after they have satisfied themselves about each other, to live together as husband and wife permanently and accepting their respective responsibilities and obligations in the married state, it follows from its very nature that the marriage contract requires the contracting parties to have attained puberty and the age of discretion. In Islamic jurisprudence, as regards those who have attained majority there is no difference of opinion in the case of the man, who can give his consent to marriage without the approval of a guardian, but some difference exists in the case of the woman, whether she can give such consent without the approval of her father or guardian. The Hanafi view of the law of Islam answers this question in the affirmative:

> "The marriage contract of a free woman who has reached the age of majority, and is possessed of understanding, is complete with her own consent, whether she is a virgin or has been married before, though it may not have been confirmed by her guardian." [24]

The Shiah view is exactly the same. However, both Malik and Shafi'i hold that the consent of the guardian is essential. Bukhari inclines to the same view as that of Malik and Shafi'i. Some verses of the Quran are quoted by him but these do not speak of a guardian in express words and the arguments based on these verses are defective and doubtful. The Hadith reports cited by him also do not establish that marriage is invalid without the consent of a guardian.

On the other hand, the Holy Quran, as well as Hadith, recognizes a woman's right to marry the man she pleases. Regarding divorced women, the Quran says plainly:

> "… do not prevent them from marrying their husbands if they agree among themselves in a lawful manner." — 2:232

And of a widow the Quran says:

> "Then if they themselves go away [from the late husband's house], there is no blame on you for what they do of lawful deeds concerning themselves." — 2:240

These two verses clearly recognize the right of the divorced woman or the widow to give herself in marriage, and prohibit the guardian from interference when the woman herself is satisfied. This is quite in accordance with a hadith: "*Al-ayyim* (the widow and the divorced woman) has greater right to dispose of herself in marriage than her guardian".[25] The words of another hadith are: "The guardian has no business in the matter of a divorced woman or a widow (*thayyiba*)".[26]

Does the same rule apply to women not married before? Imam Abu Hanifah answers this question in the affirmative. His principle is that, since a woman who has attained the age of majority can dispose of her property without reference to a guardian, so she is also entitled to dispose of her person. However, she might be bashful and, moreover, she has not the same experience of the world as has a widow or a divorced woman. Therefore it is fitting that her choice of a husband should be subject to the check of a father or other guardian, who would guard her against being misled by unscrupulous people. But as the contract, after all, depends on her consent and not on the consent of her guardian, which in fact is only needed to protect her, her will must ultimately prevail and the opinion of Imam Abu Hanifah is more in accordance with the essentials of marriage as expressed by the Quran. He says:

> "Hers is the right of marrying, and the guardian is only sought lest it [contracting the marriage] should be attributed to want of shame."

> "It is not lawful for the guardian to compel a virgin who has attained majority to marry according to his wishes." [27]

Hadith also supports this view, for the Holy Prophet is reported in Bukhari to have said:

> "The widow and the divorced woman shall not be married until her order is obtained, and the virgin shall not be married until her permission is obtained." [28]

Bukhari's next chapter is headed: "When a man gives his daughter in marriage and she dislikes it, the marriage shall be repudiated", and a hadith is quoted showing that the Holy Prophet repudiated such a marriage.[29]

Marriage in *akfā'*

Akfā' is the plural of *kuf'* which means 'an equal' or 'one alike'. The people of one tribe or one family would be *akfā'* among themselves, and people of one race would be *akfā'* among themselves. There is nothing in the Holy Quran or in the Hadith to show that a marriage relation can only be established among the *akfā'*. It is quite a different thing that, generally, people should seek such relations among the *akfā',* but Islam came to level all distinctions, whether social, tribal or racial, and therefore it does not limit the marriage relationship to *akfā'*. The way is opened for establishing all kinds of relationships between Muslims, to whatever country or community they may belong, by declaring:

> "The believers are brethren..." — 49:10

> "And the believers, men and women, are friends (*auliyā'*) of
> one another." — 9:71

When speaking of contracting marriage relationships, the Quran
speaks only of certain forbidden relations and then adds: "And lawful
for you are all women besides those" (4:24). And again it goes so far
as to allow marital relations with non-Muslim women.[30] The Holy
Prophet recommended the marriage of a lady of the tribe of Quraish
of the noblest family, his aunt's daughter, Zainab, to Zaid ibn Haritha
who was a liberated slave; and Bilal, a freed African slave, was
married to the sister of the famous companion, Abdur Rahman ibn
Auf. There are other examples of the same kind in the early history
of Islam. This cuts at the root of the limitation of marriage to *akfā'*,
yet the jurists have insisted on it.

Essentials in the contract

Marriage is called a covenant (*mīthāq*) in the Holy Quran, a covenant
between the husband and the wife:

> "And how can you take it [i.e., the dowry or nuptial gift]
> when you have been intimate with each other and they [i.e.,
> your wives] have taken from you a strong covenant (*mīthāq-*
> *an ghalīz-an*)?" — 4:21

The marriage contract is entered into by mutual consent expressed by the two parties, the husband and the wife, in the presence
of witnesses, and that is the only essential, but it was the practice of
the Holy Prophet to deliver a sermon before the declaration of marriage was made, to give it the character of a sacred contract. A nuptial
gift (*mahr*) must also be settled on the woman, according to the
Quran, but the marriage is valid even if *mahr* is not mentioned, or
even if the amount of *mahr* is not agreed upon.

The expression of the consent requires no particular form or
particular words; any expression which conveys the intention of the
parties in clear words is sufficient. The words of mutual consent may
be addressed to each other by the two parties, but generally it is the
person who delivers the sermon who puts the proposal before each
party, which then gives consent to the proposal.

Mahr or the nuptial gift

The second most important thing in marriage is *mahr,* the dowry or
nuptial gift. The word generally used for dowry in the Holy Quran is

ajr, meaning 'reward' and 'a gift that is given to the bride'. Another word sometimes used in the Quran to indicate the nuptial gift is *farīdah,* literally 'what has been made obligatory' or 'an appointed portion'. The word *mahr* is used in Hadith to signify dowry, or the nuptial gift.

According to the Quran, the *mahr* is given as a free gift by the husband to the wife at the time of contracting the marriage:

> "And give women their dowries as a free gift." — 4:4

The payment of the *mahr* on the part of the husband is an admission of the independence of the wife, for she becomes the owner of property immediately on her marriage, though before it she may not have owned anything. The settling of a *mahr* is obligatory:

> "And lawful for you [to marry] are all women besides those [prohibited], provided that you seek them with your property, taking them in marriage, not committing fornication. Then as to those whom you profit by [by marrying], give them their dowries as appointed." — 4:24

> "And [lawful for you are] the chaste from among the believing women and the chaste from among those who have been given the Book before you, when you have given them their dowries, taking them in marriage, not fornicating, nor taking them for lovers in secret." — 5:5

It would appear from this that the Quran renders the payment of dowry necessary at the time of marriage. Hadith leads to the same conclusion. The payment of the dowry was necessary even though it might be a very small sum.[31] In exceptional cases, marriage is legal even though the amount of *mahr* has not been specified, but it is obligatory and must be paid afterwards. Thus the Quran says, speaking of divorce:

> "There is no blame on you if you divorce women while you have not touched them, nor appointed for them a portion." — 2:236

This shows that marriage is valid without specifying a *mahr.* Hadith also speaks of the validity of a marriage, even though dowry has not been named.[32] But the dowry must be paid, either at the time of the consummation of the marriage or afterwards, and if unpaid in the husband's lifetime, it is a charge on his property after his death. The plain words of the Quran require its payment at marriage, barring exceptional cases when it may be determined or paid afterwards. Imam Malik follows this rule and renders payment necessary at marriage, while the Hanafi law treats it more or less as a debt.

No limits have been placed on the amount of *mahr*. The words used in the Quran show that any amount of dowry may be given to the wife:

> "… and you have given one of them a heap of gold…" — 4:20

Thus no maximum or minimum amount has been laid down. The lowest amount mentioned in Hadith is a ring of iron,[33] and a man who could not procure even that was told to teach the Quran to his wife.[34] The amount of the dowry may, however, be increased or decreased by the mutual consent of husband and wife, at any time after marriage, and this is plainly laid down in the Quran:

> "Then as to those whom you profit by [by marrying], give them their dowries as appointed. And there is no blame on you about what you mutually agree after what is appointed [of dowry]." — 4:24

Generally, however, *mahr* is treated simply as a check upon the husband's power of divorce, and very high and extravagant sums are sometimes specified as *mahr*. This practice is foreign to the spirit of the institution, as laid down by Islam; for, *mahr* is an amount which should be handed over to the wife at marriage or as early afterwards as possible; and if this rule were kept in view, extravagant *mahr* would disappear of itself. The later jurists divide *mahr* into two equal portions, one of which they call 'prompt' (*mu'ajjal*) and the other 'deferred' (*mu'ajjal*). The payment of the first part must be made immediately on the wife's demand, while the other half becomes due on the death of either party, or on the dissolution of marriage.

Conditions imposed at the time of marriage

It is lawful to impose and accept conditions, which are not illegal, at the time of marriage, and the parties are bound by such conditions. The Holy Prophet is reported to have said:

> "The best entitled to fulfilment of all conditions that you may fulfil are the conditions by which sexual union is legalized." [35]

It is also related that the Holy Prophet spoke of a son-in-law of his, an unbeliever,[36] in high terms, saying:

> "He spoke to me and he spoke the truth, and he made promises with me and he fulfilled those promises." [37]

Illegal conditions are those which are opposed to the law of Islam. If such a condition be imposed, the condition is void while the marriage is valid. Examples of legal conditions are that the wife shall not be compelled to leave her conjugal domicile,[38] that the husband shall not contract a second marriage during the existence of the first, that the husband and the wife or one of them shall live in a specified place, that a certain portion of the dower shall be paid immediately and the remainder on death or divorce, that the husband shall pay the wife a certain amount by way of maintenance, that he shall not prevent her from receiving visits from her relatives, that the wife shall have the right to divorce for a specified reason or for any reasonable cause, and so on.[39]

Publicity of the marriage

When the Holy Quran speaks of marriage, it at the same time excludes clandestine sexual relations: "…taking them in marriage, not fornicating nor taking them for lovers in secret" (4:24, 4:25, 5:5). Thus the one fact distinguishing marriage from fornication and clandestine relations is its publicity. The mutual consent of two parties to live as husband and wife does not constitute a marriage unless that consent is expressed publicly and in the presence of witnesses. An essential feature of the Islamic marriage is therefore the publication of the news by gathering together, preferably in a public place. There are Hadith reports showing that marriage must be made publicly known, even with the beat of drums.[40] With the same object in view, music is allowed at marriage gatherings. On such an occasion, girls sang with the beating of drum in the presence of the Holy Prophet.[41] The following hadith on this subject may be quoted:

> "Aishah had with her a girl from among the Ansar whom she got married. The Messenger of Allah came and said:

'Have you sent the young girl to her husband?' And on receiving a reply in the affirmative, he said: 'Have you sent with her those who would sing?' Aishah said: 'No.' Said the Messenger of Allah: 'The Ansar are a people who love singing, and it would have been better if you had sent with her someone to sing thus and thus'." [42]

The presence of witnesses, when so much stress is laid on proclamation, is a foregone conclusion.

Marriage (*nikāḥ*) sermon

The delivery of a sermon before the announcement of marriage is another factor which helps the publicity of the marriage, and, at the same time, serves the double purpose of giving it a sacred character and making it an occasion for the education of the community. When the friends and relatives of both parties have assembled, a sermon is delivered by someone from among the party, or by the Imam, before announcing the marriage itself.

The sermon, as reported from the Holy Prophet, opens with a statement of praise of Allah, asking for His help and forgiveness, and ending with the bearing of witness to the Unity of God and the prophethood of Muhammad. After this, the Holy Prophet would take as his text the following three verses of the Quran:[43]

> "O you who believe, keep your duty to Allah, as it ought to be kept, and do not die except as Muslims." — 3 : 102

> "O people, keep your duty to your Lord, Who created you from a single being and created its mate of the same [kind], and spread from these two many men and women. And keep your duty to Allah, by Whom you demand one of another [your rights] and to the ties of relationship. Surely Allah is ever a Watcher over you." — 4 : 1

> "O you who believe, keep your duty to Allah and speak straight words. He will put your deeds into a right state for you, and forgive you your sins. And whoever obeys Allah and His Messenger, he indeed achieves a mighty success." — 33 : 70–71.

All three verses remind people of their responsibilities in general, and the middle one lays particular stress on the obligations towards women. The sermon of course must elucidate these verses and explain to the audience the mutual rights and duties of husband and wife. At the conclusion of the sermon is made the announcement that such and such a man and such and such a woman have accepted each other as husband and wife, and the dowry is also announced at the time. The man and the woman are then asked if they accept this new relationship, and on the reply being given in the affirmative the marriage ceremony proper is concluded.

The Holy Quran requires witnesses even for ordinary contracts and business transactions, and marriage is a contract of the highest importance, a contract affecting the lives of two persons to an extent to which no other contract affects them. It further requires witnesses even in the case of the dissolution of marriage by divorce.[44] The Hanafi law rightly lays special stress on this point, so that marriage is not valid if at least two witnesses are not there. To procure the best testimony, and one free from doubt of all kinds, it is quite in accordance with the law of Islam that all marriages should be registered.

Walīmah or marriage feast

After the *nikāḥ* is over, the bride is conducted to the husband's house, and this is followed by the marriage-feast called *walīmah*. This feast is another step in the publicity of the marriage, and hence the Holy Prophet laid stress on it. It is related of one of his Companions that the Prophet, on being told of his marriage, prayed for him and told him to arrange for a feast though there be only one goat to feed the guests.[45] On the occasion of his own marriage with Safiyyah, when returning from Khaibar, he gave a feast in which everyone was required to bring his own food with him.[46] Of course this was on a journey, but at the same time it shows the great importance given to the marriage-feast. He also invited his friends to a *walīmah* feast on the occasion of his marriage with Zainab, which is said to have been the most sumptuous of all his *walīmah* feasts, and yet he slaughtered only one goat.[47] In addition to numerous stray references in his collection, Bukhari has devoted several chapters to *walīmah* in particular, with headings such as "The *walīmah* is necessary" and "The *walīmah* [is necessary] though there be only one goat to feed the guests".[48]

Polygamy

As a rule, Islam recognizes only the union of one man and one woman as a valid form of marriage. Under exceptional circumstances it allows the man more wives than one, but does not allow the woman more husbands than one. Thus while a married woman cannot contract a valid marriage, a married man can do it. There is no difficulty in understanding this differentiation, if the natural duties of man and woman in the preservation and upbringing of the human species are kept in view. Nature has so divided the duties of man and woman, in this respect, that while one man can raise children from more wives than one, one woman can have children only from one husband. Therefore while polygyny may at times be a help in the welfare of society and the preservation of the human race, polyandry has no conceivable use for man.

It must be borne in mind that polygamy is allowed in Islam only as an exception. It is expressly so stated in the Holy Quran:

> "And if you fear that you cannot do justice to orphans, marry such women as seem good to you, two or three or four; but if you fear that you will not do justice [between them], then [marry] only one…" — 4:3

This is the passage in the Quran which allows polygamy, and it will be seen that it does not require polygamy; it only permits it and even that permission is conditional. Polygamy is here allowed only when there are orphans to be dealt with, and it is feared that they will not be dealt with justly. This condition relates more to the welfare of society than to the needs of the individual.

The meaning of this verse is really explained by following verse:

> "And they ask you [O Prophet] a decision about women. Say: Allah makes known to you His decision concerning them; and what is recited to you in the Book is concerning widowed women whom you do not give what is appointed for them, while you are not inclined to marry them, nor to the weak among children, and that you should deal justly with orphans." — 4:127

The reference to "what is recited in the Book" is admittedly to 4:3. And the reference in "whom you do not give what is appointed for them… nor to the weak among children" is to the Arab custom, according to which women and minor children did not get a share of inheritance, the recognized usage being that only he could inherit who could ride on the back of a horse and take the field against the enemy. The position was therefore this, that when a widow was left with orphans to bring up, she and her children would get no share of the inheritance, nor were people inclined to marry widows who had children. In 4:3, the Quran has therefore enjoined that if you cannot be otherwise just to orphans, marry *the mothers of such orphans* so that you may thus be interested in their welfare, and for this purpose you are allowed to contract other marriages.

A consideration of the historical circumstances of the time when this chapter was revealed corroborates this conclusion. It was a time when Muslims were compelled to fight battle after battle to repel an enemy bent upon their extirpation. The breadwinners had all to take the field against the enemy, and many had been lost in the unequal battles that were being fought by the small Muslim band against overwhelming forces. Women had lost their affectionate husbands and young children their loving fathers, and these widows and orphans had to be provided for. If they had been left to the mercy of circumstances, they would have perished, and the community would have been weakened to such an extent that it would have been impossible to maintain the struggle for life. It was under these circumstances that the fourth chapter was revealed, allowing the taking of more wives than one, so that the widows and orphans may find a shelter, but only on condition that the husband is just to all of them.

It might be said that other arrangements could be made for the maintenance of widows and orphans. But a home life could not be given to them in any other manner. Islam bases its civilization on home life; and under exceptional circumstances, where monogamy fails to provide a home for widows and orphans, it allows polygamy to extend to them that advantage. Even if it be half a home that the women and children find in a polygamous family, it is better than no home at all. The moral aspect of the question is not the least important. The war had decimated the male population and the number of women exceeded that of men. This excess, if not provided with a home, would have led to moral depravity. Professions may be opened up for women to enable them to earn bread, and Islam has never closed the door of any profession against women. But the crux of the question is not the provision of bread but the provision of a home life and that question cannot be solved without polygamy.

The question of war is not peculiar to one age or one country. It is a question which affects the whole of humanity for all ages to come. War must always be a source of decrease in the number of males, bringing about a corresponding increase in the number of females and a solution will have to be sought by all well-wishers of humanity for this problem. Polygamy in Islam is, both in theory and in practice, an exception, not a rule, and as an exception it is a remedy for many of the evils of modern civilization.

It may be further stated that the institution of polygamy, which was allowed by Islam only as a remedy, has largely been abused by sensual people, but then there are people in every society who would abuse any institution, however necessary it may be to the right growth of human society. In countries where polygamy is not allowed, the sensuality of man has invented a hundred other ways of giving vent to his carnal passions, and these are a far greater curse to society than the abuse of polygamy. Indeed that abuse can be easily remedied by the state by placing legal limitations upon its practice, while the state is quite helpless against the evils which result from its entire rejection.

Section 3: *Rights and Position of Women*

Equality with men in spiritual and material terms

From a material as well as a spiritual point of view, the Quran recognizes the position of woman to be the same as that of man. Good works bring the same reward, whether to a male or a female:

> "I [Allah] will not let the work of a worker among you to be lost, whether male or female; each of you is as the other." — 3:195

There is a verse which lists ten good qualities as being possessed by men as well as women, and ends with the words:

> "Allah has prepared for them forgiveness and a mighty reward." — 33:35

The Quran teaches that Paradise and its blessings are equally for both men and women:

> "And whoever does good deeds, whether male or female, and is a believer — these will enter the Garden..."
> — 4:124, 40:40

Both shall enjoy the higher life:

> "Whoever does good, whether male or female, and is a believer, We shall certainly make him [or her] live a good life, and We shall certainly give them their reward for the best of what they did." — 16:97

Revelation, which is God's greatest spiritual gift in this life, is granted to men as well as to women:

> "And when the angels said: Mary, surely Allah has chosen you and purified you..." — 3:42

> "And We revealed to Moses' mother, saying: Suckle him; then when you fear for him, cast him into the river and do not fear, nor grieve." — 28:7

From a material point of view, woman is recognized as on a par with man. She can earn money and own property just as man can do and therefore she may, if she feels the need, follow any profession:

> "For men is the benefit of what they earn. And for women is the benefit of what they earn." — 4:32

She has full control over her property and can dispose of it as she likes:

> "But if they [i.e., women] *of themselves be pleased* to give you a portion from it [i.e., from their property], consume it with enjoyment and pleasure." — 4:4

Women can also inherit property as men can:

> "For men is a share of what the parents and the near relatives leave, and for women a share of what the parents and the near relatives leave, whether it is little or much — an appointed share." — 4:7

Women not excluded from any activity in life

Women are not forbidden to take part in any activity when necessary, nor is there any injunction in the Holy Quran or the Hadith shutting them up within the four walls of their houses. A study of Hadith shows that, notwithstanding her rightful position in the home, as the bringer up of children and manager of the household, women took interest in all the national activities of the Muslim community. The care of the children did not prevent her from repairing to the mosque to join the congregational prayers,[49] nor was this care an obstacle in her way to join the soldiers in the field of battle to perform a large number of duties, such as the carrying of provisions, taking care of the sick and the wounded, removing the wounded and the slain from the battlefield,[50] or taking part in actual fighting when necessary.[51] One of the Holy Prophet's wives, Zainab, used to prepare hides and to devote the proceeds of the sale to charitable work. Women also helped their husbands in the labour of the field[52] and served the male guests at a feast.[53] They carried on business,[54] and could sell to and purchase from men, and men could sell to and purchase from them.[55] A woman was appointed by the Caliph Umar as superintendent of the market of Madinah.

Seclusion of women

The Holy Quran speaks of a Muslim society in which men and women had often to meet each other:

> "Say to the believing men that they lower their gaze and restrain their sexual passions. That is purer for them. Surely Allah is Aware of what they do. And say to the believing women that they lower their gaze and restrain their sexual passions and do not display their adornment except what appears of it." — 24:30–31

A later revelation, 33:59, supports the same conclusion.[56] According to Hadith, the Holy Prophet is reported to have said to women:

> "It is permitted to you to go out for your needs." [57]

There is an injunction to the Holy Prophet's wives in a verse of the Quran as follows:

> "And stay in your houses and do not display your beauty like the displaying of the earlier days of ignorance." — 33:33

This does not mean that they were not to go out for their needs. It is evidently an injunction against the parading of finery and display of beauty and thus exciting the uncontrolled passions of youth. It cannot and does not mean, as explained by the Holy Prophet himself, that women are not allowed to go out for their needs. Display of beauty and going out for one's needs are quite different things. There is, therefore, no seclusion in Islam in the sense that women are shut up within their houses, for they are as free to move about for their needs, or transaction of their business, as men. Only their needs outside the home are generally fewer than those of men.

The veil

The next question is whether women are commanded to veil themselves when they have to go out for their needs. These needs may be either religious or secular. Two prominent instances of the former are taking part in public prayers and the performance of pilgrimage. If it had been necessary for women to wear veils, an injunction should have been given to wear them on these two sacred occasions, since these are the occasions on which men's sentiments should be purest, and when, therefore, all those things that excite the passions must be avoided. There is, however, not only no such injunction but it was a recognized practice that women came into the congregation of men in mosques unveiled.[58]

It is even admitted by the jurists that women should not veil themselves at prayers and on pilgrimage. In the conditions of prayer it is laid down that the body of the woman must be covered entirely except her face and her hands.[59] The exception of these two parts, it is added, is due to the fact that they must of necessity be left exposed. As regards pilgrimage, there is an express injunction in Hadith that no woman shall put on a veil during the pilgrimage.[60] It is also a well-established fact that the mosques in the Prophet's time contained no screens to keep the two sexes separate. The only separation between the men and the women was that women stood in separate rows behind the men. Otherwise they were in the same room or in the same yard, and the two sexes had to intermingle. In the pilgrimage there was a much greater intermingling of the sexes, women performing circumambulations of the Ka'bah, running between Safa and Marwah, staying in the plain of Arafat and going from place to place, along with men, and yet they were enjoined not to wear a veil.

If, then, as admitted by all, women did not wear a veil when the two sexes intermingled on religious occasions, it is a foregone conclusion that they could not be required to veil themselves when going out for their secular needs whose very performance would be hampered by the veil. And there is no such command either in the Holy Quran or Hadith. In fact, no such injunction could be given when there existed an injunction that women shall remain unveiled in pilgrimage. This injunction rather shows that the veil was adopted simply as a mark of rank or greatness, and the unveiling was required in order to bring all on a level of equality. However that may be, the order to remain unveiled in the pilgrimage is a clear proof that wearing the veil is not an Islamic injunction or practice.

Moreover, the verses requiring both men and women to keep their looks cast down (24:30–31, quoted above) show clearly that, when the two sexes had to intermingle as a matter of necessity, women were not veiled, for otherwise there would have been no need for the men to keep their looks cast down. And to make the matter clearer still, it is added that women should "not display their adornment, except what appears of it". The part that necessarily appears is the face and the hands, and this is also the view of the vast majority of commentators.[61] There is also a hadith according to which the Holy Prophet is reported to have excepted the face and the hands from the parts which were required to be covered:

> "Asma, daughter of Abu Bakr, came to the Messenger of Allah, and she was wearing very thin clothes [through which the body could be seen]. The Messenger of Allah turned away his face from her and said: O Asma, when the woman attains her majority, it is not proper that any part of her body should be seen except this and this, pointing to his face and his hands." [62]

Decent dress

All that the Holy Quran requires is that women should be decently dressed when they go out and that they should not uncover their bosoms. This is made clear in 24:31:

> "And say to the believing women that they ... do not display their adornment except what appears of it. And they should wear their head-coverings over their bosoms."

The practice in Arabia, in pre-Islamic times, of displaying beauty, included the uncovering of the bosom, and hence the injunction relating to its covering. A difference was thus made between the dress of women within their houses and when they appeared in public; in the former case they were allowed to be more at ease in the matter of their dress, but in public they had to be particular so that their very appearance should be indicative of modesty. On another occasion, Muslim women are required to wear a dress whose very appearance should distinguish them from such women as did not have a good reputation:

> "O Prophet! tell your wives and your daughters and the women of the believers to let down upon them their over-garments. This is more proper, so that they may be known, and not be given trouble." — 33:59

It seems that this injunction was required by the special circumstances which then prevailed at Madinah, where the hypocrites would molest a good Muslim woman who went out to transact some business and then offer the excuse that they thought her to be a woman of ill repute. This is plainly hinted in the verse that follows:

> "If the hypocrites and those in whose hearts is a disease and the agitators in Madinah do not stop, We shall certainly urge you on against them, then they shall not be your neighbours in it but for a little while." — 33:60

The Arabic word for over-garment is *jilbāb* and it means 'a garment with which the woman covers her other garments' or a woman's head-covering, or 'a garment with which she covers her head and bosom'.[63] It may be part of an ordinary dress or it may be a kind of overcoat. Nor is the wearing of it compulsory under all circumstances; it is, rather, a kind of protection when there is fear of trouble, and in the case of older women it is dispensed with altogether as stated elsewhere:

> "And as for women past childbearing who do not hope for marriage, it is no sin for them if they put off their cloaks without displaying their adornment." — 24:60

Intermingling of the two sexes

In the struggle of life the intermingling of the two sexes cannot be avoided, and Islam allows such intermingling even for religious purposes, as in prayers and pilgrimage. On all such occasions, the Holy Quran requires women to appear in their simplest dress, or to wear an over-garment which should cover their ornaments, at the same time requiring both sexes to keep their looks cast down. Unnecessary mingling of the sexes is discouraged. Some hadith prohibit a woman being alone in private with a man who is not her near relative[64] unless a near relative is present;[65] but when other people are also present, or one is exposed to public view, there is no harm in being alone with a woman.[66]

The intermingling of the sexes in social functions generally cannot be traced in the early history of Islam, though there are examples in which a woman entertained the male guests of her husband.[67] In fact, much would depend, in these matters, on the social customs of the people, and no hard and fast rules can be laid down as to the limits to which the intermingling of the sexes may be allowed. The great object before Islam is to raise the moral status of society and to minimize the chances of illicit sexual relations growing up between the sexes, so that the home may be a haven of peace for the husband, the wife and the children.

Section 4: *Rights and Obligations of Husband and Wife*

Woman's position as wife

By entering the married state, a woman does not lose any of the rights which she possesses as an individual member of society. She is still free to carry on any work she likes, to make any contract she desires, and to dispose of her property as she wishes; nor is her individuality merged in that of her husband. But she is at the same time recognized as undertaking new responsibilities of life, which carry with them new rights. The Holy Quran settles the following principle:

> "And women have rights similar to their obligations, in a just manner..." — 2:228

These are the rights and responsibilities of the home. Hadith describes her position in the home as that of a ruler:

> "Everyone of you is a ruler and everyone shall be questioned about his subjects; the *Amīr* (the head of state) is a ruler, and the man is a ruler over the people of his house, and the woman is a ruler over the house of her husband and his children, so everyone of you is a ruler and everyone shall be questioned about his subjects." [68]

Thus so far as the home is concerned, the wife has the position of a ruler in it, the home being her territory. By marriage she is at once raised to a higher dignity, acquiring new rights while incurring new responsibilities. Her rights as regards her husband are also affirmed in Hadith, as the Holy Prophet said to a Companion:

> "Your body has a right over you and your soul has a right over you and your wife has a right over you." [69]

Mutual relation of husband and wife

As already stated, the mutual relation of husband and wife is described in the Holy Quran as one of a single soul in two bodies:

> "And of His signs is this, that He created mates for you from yourselves, that you may find quiet of mind in them, and He put between you love and compassion." — 30:21

> "He it is Who created you from a single soul and of the same did He make his mate that he might find comfort in her." — 7:189

The same idea is elsewhere very beautifully described in different words:

> "They [i.e., your wives] are an apparel for you and you are an apparel for them." — 2:187

The closest union of two souls could not be described more aptly.

Islam is, however, a practical religion and it does not shut its eyes to the hard realities of life. It describes the home as a unit in the greater organization of a nation as a whole, and just as in the vaster national organization there is somebody to exercise the final authority in certain cases, so the smaller organization of the home cannot be maintained without a similar arrangement. Hence the husband is first spoken of as being "a ruler over the people of his house" and the wife is then described as "a ruler over the house of her husband and his children". The home is thus a kingdom in miniature, where authority is exercised by both the husband and the wife. But unless one of them is given a higher authority, there would be chaos in this kingdom. The reason for giving the higher authority to the male parent is thus stated in the Holy Quran:

> "Men are the maintainers of women with what Allah has given some of them above others, and with what they spend out of their wealth." — 4:34

The Arabic word for 'maintainers' is *qawwāmūn,* which carries the significance of maintaining or managing. It means that the husband provides maintenance for the wife, and also that he has final charge of the affairs of the home, thus exercising authority over the wife when there is need for it.

Rights of husband and wife

The family concern must be kept going by husband and wife in mutual co-operation. The husband is mainly required to earn for the maintenance of the family, and the wife is responsible for the management of the household and the bringing up of the children. The rights of each against the other are therefore centred in these two points. The husband is bound to maintain the wife according to his means, as the Holy Quran says:

> "Let him who has abundant means spend out of his abundance, and whoever has his means of subsistence restricted for him, let him spend out of what Allah has given him. Allah does not lay on any soul a burden beyond what He has given it." — 65:7

He must also provide for her a lodging:

> "Lodge them where you live according to your means".
> — 65:6

The wife is bound to keep company with her husband, to preserve the husband's property from loss or waste, and to refrain from doing anything which should disturb the peace of the family. She is required not to admit anyone into the house whom the husband does not like, and not to incur expenditure of which the husband disapproves.[70] She is not bound to render personal service such as the cooking of food, but the respective duties of the husband and wife are such that each must always be ready to help the other. The wife must help the husband even in the field of labour if she can do it, and the husband must help the wife in the household duties. Of the Holy Prophet himself, it is related that he used to help his wives in many small works of the household, such as milking goats, patching clothes, mending shoes, cleansing utensils, and so on.

The Holy Quran lays the greatest possible stress on kindly and good treatment towards the wife. "Keep them in good fellowship" and "treat them kindly" is the repeatedly occurring advice of the Quran.[71] So much so that kindness is recommended even when a man dislikes his wife, for:

> "...it may be that you dislike a thing while Allah has placed abundant good in it." — 4:19

The Holy Prophet laid equally great stress upon good treatment of a wife. He is reported to have said:

> "The most excellent of you is he who is best in his treatment of his wife." [72]

> "Accept my advice in the matter of doing good to women." [73]

In his famous address at the Farewell Pilgrimage, he again laid particular stress on the good treatment of women:

> "Keep your duty to Allah with regard to women, for they are the trust of Allah in your hands. ... You have certain rights over your wives, ... and they have rights over you, that you provide for them with kindness." [74]

Privacy

Islam sets great value on the privacy of home life. In the first place, going into houses without permission is strictly forbidden:

> "O you who believe, do not enter houses other than your own houses, until you have asked permission and greeted their inhabitants." — 24:27

And again:

> "O you who believe, let those whom your right hands possess [i.e., those serving you] and those of you who have not attained to puberty ask permission of you three times: before the morning prayer, and when you put off your clothes for the heat of noon, and after the prayer of night. These are three times of privacy for you." — 24:58

These rules aim at creating a better atmosphere of sexual morality.

Section 5: *Divorce*

Marriage and divorce

Though marriage, according to Islam, is only a civil contract, yet the rights and responsibilities consequent upon it are of such importance to the welfare of humanity that a high degree of sanctity is attached to it. But in spite of the sacredness of the character of the marriage tie, Islam recognizes the necessity, in exceptional circumstances, of keeping the way open for its dissolution.

The necessity of divorce has been recognized by almost all people. According to the Jewish law the right of divorce belongs to the husband who can exercise it at his will. Christian law recognizes the right of divorce only when there is faithlessness on the part of either of the parties, but the divorced parties are precluded from marrying again. According to Hindu law marriage once performed can never be dissolved. Islam effected several reforms in divorce. It restricted the husband's right to divorce while recognizing the wife's right to it.

Divorce is permitted under exceptional circumstances

The Arabic word for divorce is *ṭalāq* which carries the literal significance of freeing or the undoing of a knot. In the terminology of the jurists, the *ṭalāq* is called a *khul'* (meaning literally the putting off or taking off a thing) when it is claimed by the wife. Both from the Holy Quran and the Hadith it appears that, though divorce was permitted, yet the right could be exercised only under exceptional circumstances.

The Holy Prophet is reported to have said:

> "Never did Allah allow anything more hateful to Him than divorce."

> "With Allah the most detestable of all things permitted is divorce."[75]

The Quran also approves of the Holy Prophet insisting that Zaid should not divorce his wife Zainab, despite a dissension between them of a sufficiently long standing. He said to Zaid:

> "Keep your wife to yourself and keep your duty to Allah."
> — 33:37

Refraining from divorce is spoken of here as *taqwā,* keeping your duty to Allah or righteousness. Elsewhere divorce is thus discouraged:

> "If you hate them [i.e., your wives], it may be that you dislike a thing while Allah has placed abundant good in it." — 4:19

Remedies are also suggested to avoid divorce as long as possible:

> "And if you fear a breach between the two [i.e., the husband and the wife], appoint an arbiter from his people and an arbiter from her people. If they both desire agreement, Allah will effect harmony between them." — 4:35

The mentality of the Muslim should be to face the difficulties of married life along with its comforts, and to avoid the disruption of family relations as long as possible, turning to divorce only as a last resort.

Principle of divorce

From what has been said above, it is clear that not only must there be a good cause for divorce, but that all means to effect reconciliation must have been exhausted before resort is had to this extreme measure. The impression that a Muslim husband may put away his wife at his mere caprice, is a grave distortion of the Islamic institution of divorce. But though the Holy Quran refers to several causes when divorce may become necessary, it does not enumerate all of them, nor does it strictly limit them to specified cases. If the Christian nations of the modern West cannot agree as to the proper causes of divorce, how could Islam, a universal religion which was meant for all ages and all countries, for people in all grades of civilization, limit those causes which must vary with changing conditions of humanity and society?

The principle of divorce spoken of in the Quran, and which in fact includes to a greater or lesser extent all causes, is the decision no longer to live together as husband and wife. In the Quran, the disagreement to live anymore as husband and wife is called *shiqāq* (from *shaqq* meaning 'breaking into two'). But not even such a breach entitles either party to a divorce, unless all possibilities of agreement have been exhausted. The principle of divorce is, therefore, described in the Quran in 4:35 as quoted above. This verse gives us not only the principle of divorce, which is a disagreement to live together as husband and wife, but also the process to be adopted when a rupture of marital relations is feared. The two sexes are here placed on a level of perfect equality. A "breach (_shiqāq_) between the two" would imply that either the husband or the wife wants to break off the marriage agreement, and hence either may claim a divorce when the parties can no longer live together in agreement. In the process to be adopted, both husband and wife are to be represented on a status of equality; an arbiter has to be appointed from his people and another from her people. The two are told to try to remove the differences and reconcile the parties to each other. If agreement cannot be brought about, a divorce will follow.

All causes of divorce are subject to the condition that one of the parties cannot live together with the other. For instance, if the husband or the wife is unfit for sexual relations, or the husband is absent for a long time, divorce would be justified, but only if the party entitled to it wants it. If both are willing to live in marital agreement, no power on earth can effect a divorce, but if one party finds that she or he is unable to live in marital agreement with the other, it would be a case of _shiqāq_ or breach of the marriage agreement.

This breach of the marriage agreement may arise from many causes or from the conduct of either party; for instance, if either of them misconducts himself or herself, or either of them is consistently cruel to the other, or, as may sometimes happen, there is incompatibility of temperament to such an extent that they cannot live together in marital agreement. Divorce must then follow. If there is such disagreement that the husband and the wife cannot get on together, it is better for themselves, for their offspring and for society in general that they should be separated rather than that they should be compelled to live together. No home is worth the name in which instead of peace there is wrangling. Marriage is entered into as a permanent and sacred relation based on love between a man and a woman, and divorce is only a remedy when marriage fails to fulfil its object.

Wife's right of divorce

It will have been seen that the Holy Quran places the husband and the wife on a perfect level of equality in the matter of divorce. Hadith makes it clearer still. The Holy Prophet is related to have married a woman called Umaima or Ibnat al-Jaun, and when he initiated intimate relations with her, she said that she sought refuge in God from him, that is to say, wanted a divorce; and he granted her a divorce, and sent her off with some presents.[76] Another case is that of a man whose wife came to the Holy Prophet and said that though she did not find fault in her husband regarding his morals or faith but she could not get on with him or could not bear him. The Holy Prophet said: "Will you return to him his orchard [which he had settled upon her as a dowry]?" On receiving a reply in the affirmative, the Holy Prophet sent for him and ordered him to take back his orchard and divorce his wife.[77] These two examples are sufficient to show that the wife had the right to claim divorce on those very grounds on which the husband could divorce his wife.

The right of the wife to claim a divorce is not only recognized by the Holy Quran and Hadith but also in Islamic Jurisprudence (*Fiqh*). The technical term for the wife's right to divorce by returning her dowry is called *khul'* and it is based on the hadith already quoted, and on the following verse of the Quran:

> "Divorce may be pronounced twice; then keep them in good fellowship or let them go with kindness. And it is not lawful for you to take any part of what you have given them, unless both fear that they cannot keep within the limits of Allah. Then if you fear that they cannot keep within the limits of Allah, there is no blame on them for what she gives up to become free thereby." — 2:229

By keeping "within the limits of Allah" here is clearly meant the fulfilment of the object of marriage or performance of the duties imposed by conjugal relationship. The *mahr* (nuptial gift or dowry) is thus a check on the party who wants the divorce; if the husband wants to divorce the wife, the wife shall have the dowry; if the wife wants the divorce, the husband is entitled to his dowry back. But it is the arbiters spoken of in 4:35, and referred to here in the words "if you [arbiters] fear that they [husband and wife] cannot keep within the limits of Allah", that shall decide whether the husband or the wife is responsible for the breach and which of them is entitled to the dowry.

Husband's right of pronouncement of divorce

Though the Holy Quran speaks of the divorce being pronounced by the husband, yet a limitation is placed upon the exercise of this right.

The following procedure is laid down in clear words:

> "And if you fear a breach between the two [i.e., the husband and the wife], appoint an arbiter from his people and an arbiter from her people. If they both desire agreement, Allah will effect harmony between them." — 4:35

> "And if they separate, Allah will render them both free from want out of His ampleness." — 4:130

It will be seen that in all disputes between the husband and the wife, which it is feared will lead to a breach, two arbiters are to be appointed from the respective people of the two parties. They are required first to try to reconcile the parties to each other, failing which divorce is to be effected. Therefore, though it is the husband who pronounces the divorce, he is as much bound by the decision of the arbiters as is the wife.

This shows that the husband cannot repudiate the marriage at will. The case must first be referred to two arbiters and their decision is binding. The Caliph Ali is reported to have told a husband, who thought he had the sole right to divorce, that he would have to abide by the judgment of the arbiters appointed under this verse.[78] The Holy Prophet is reported to have intervened and disallowed a divorce pronounced by a husband, restoring the marital relations.[79] This shows that the authority constituted by law has the right to interfere in matters of divorce. When Muslims are living under non-Muslim rule, if no judge has been appointed by the authorities, the appointment of the judges shall be in the hands of the Muslim community. If, therefore, a Muslim government or the Muslim community makes any rules laying down the procedure of divorce and placing such limitations upon the husband in matters of divorce as are not inconsistent with the principles laid down by the Quran, it would be quite Islamic.

Divorce during menstruation

In the Holy Quran, the subject of menstruation is dealt with as a preliminary to that of divorce, and sexual intercourse is prohibited when the courses are on, as it is said to be "harmful" (2:222). It is owing to this temporary cessation of sexual relations between the husband and the wife that divorce is prohibited during the period when the menstrual discharge is on. It was brought to the notice of the Holy Prophet that Ibn Umar had divorced his wife while she was menstruating. The divorce was declared to be illegal by the Holy Prophet, and Ibn Umar was asked to take back his wife.[80] Thus divorce is only permitted when the woman is clear from the menstrual discharge, there being a further condition that the husband and the wife should not have copulated during that time. Evidently this is meant as a sort of check upon the freedom of divorce.

The waiting time (*'iddah*)

The final breaking off of marital relations is discouraged in many other ways and every chance is afforded to the parties to maintain the conjugal tie, even after differences have arisen leading to divorce. Every divorce must be followed by a period of waiting called the *'iddah*. It is stated in the Holy Quran:

> "When you divorce women, divorce them for their *'iddah* (prescribed or waiting time)." — 65:1

The waiting time is about three months:

> "Divorced women should keep themselves in waiting for three courses (*qurū'*)." — 2:228

A course or *qar'* (singular of *qurū'*) is normally about four weeks but there are variations in the case of different women.[81] In the case of women who do not menstruate, as well as those whose courses have stopped, the waiting time is three months, and in the case of pregnant women, the waiting period is till delivery.[82] The waiting time, among other purposes, serves the purpose of affording the parties a chance of reconciliation. Though they are divorced, yet they still live in the same house, the husband being plainly told not to expel the wife from the house in which she has been living unless she is guilty of misconduct, and a similar advice is given to the wife not to leave the house.[83] This injunction clearly aims at restoring amicable relations between the parties. If there is any love in the union, its pangs would assert themselves during the time of waiting and bring about a reconciliation.

Divorce is revocable

In fact, reconciliation is recommended in plain words when, speaking of the *'iddah,* the Holy Quran says:

> "And their husbands have a better right to take them back in
> the meanwhile if they wish for reconciliation." — 2: 228

Every divorce is thus an experimental temporary separation during
its initial stages, and by making the parties live together, every chance
is afforded to them to re-establish conjugal relations. Even after the
period of waiting has passed away, the two parties are allowed, even
encouraged, to remarry:

> "And when you divorce women and they end their term of
> waiting, do not prevent them from marrying their husbands
> if they agree among themselves in a lawful manner. With
> this is admonished he among you who believes in Allah and
> the Last Day. This is more virtuous for you and purer. And
> Allah knows while you do not know." — 2:232

Remarriage of the divorced parties is thus encouraged and recommended as being better and purer for the parties. The condition
is also laid down that such a revocable divorce, allowing reunion of
the parties, can be pronounced twice:

> "Divorce may be pronounced twice; then keep them in good
> fellowship or let them go with kindness." — 2:229

Irrevocable divorce

After the first divorce, the parties have the right to reassert their
conjugal relations within the period of waiting, or to remarry after the
waiting period is over. A similar right is given to them after a second
divorce, but not after a third. Before Islam, however, while the wife
had no right of divorce, the husband had an unchecked licence to
divorce the wife and to reassert his conjugal rights during the period
of waiting as many times as he pleased.[84] Thus women were looked
upon as mere chattel which could be discarded and taken at will.
Islam not only gave the wife a right of divorce but also checked the
husband's licence to divorce as often as he liked, by declaring that
revocable divorce could be given only twice. It was thus laid down
that, after the second revocation or remarriage, the parties must make
their choice either to live together as husband and wife, or to separate
forever, never thinking of reunion. Hence if even the second experi-
ment failed and the parties were separated by a divorce for the third
time, this was an irrevocable divorce.

Pronouncement of divorce in three forms

The jurists have recognized divorce in three forms. A man would sometimes pronounce divorce three times on one and the same occasion, and this would be understood as meaning that divorce had been given three times. Or a man would divorce his wife three times in one and the same *'iddah,* or period of waiting, by divorcing her once during each of the three times when she was clear of menstruation. Thirdly, there is what the jurists call "the best method of divorcing", in which divorce is pronounced only once, during a time when there is no menstruation, and this is followed by the period of waiting. This last method is the only method recognized by the Quran, in which it is plainly laid down:

> "When you divorce women, divorce them for their *'iddah* (prescribed or waiting time), and calculate the period; and keep your duty to Allah, your Lord." — 65 : 1

The divorce is thus to be pronounced only once and when it has been pronounced, the waiting period follows, and during this time the parties have a right to revocation of the divorce. All other forms of divorce are against the Holy Quran and the practice of the Holy Prophet. These are, in fact, only subterfuges to make the revocable divorce an irrevocable one. The pronouncing of three divorces without an interval seems to have been a remnant of pre-Islamic days. The Holy Prophet is reported to have shown indignation when it was brought to his notice that a certain person had pronounced three divorces together,[85] and a divorce thus pronounced was annulled by him.[86] The revocable divorce of the Quran cannot be made irrevocable as, by this change, a death-blow is dealt to the beneficial spirit underlying the institution of divorce in Islam. Hence, whether divorce is pronounced once or three times or a hundred times during one waiting period, it is only a single divorce, and it is revocable during that period.

Effect of irrevocable divorce

It is clear from what has been stated that irrevocable divorce is the very rarest of things that can happen among Muslims, and it can only occur if the two un-Quranic forms of divorce, to make revocable divorces irrevocable, are brought in. When a man and a woman have found by two experiments, each after a divorce, that they cannot live together as husband and wife, it is absurd on their part to think of remarriage again with one another. Hence the Holy Quran lays down that they shall not remarry after a third divorce, except in one case:

> "So if he divorces her [for the third time], she shall not be lawful to him afterwards until she marries another husband. If he [the second husband] divorces her, there is no blame on them both if they return to each other [by marriage], if they think that they can keep within the limits of Allah." — 2:230

Thus the one case in which marriage with the first husband is allowed, after being divorced for the third time, is that in which a marriage has been contracted with a second husband and that too has proved a failure. If there be such a rare case, the parties to the marriage have probably learned a lesson, through another marital union, to the effect that they should behave better towards each other. An irrevocable divorce, being in itself a rarity according to the teachings of the Quran, a case, like the one spoken of in the verse quoted above, would be a still greater rarity, but still if such a case should arise, the parties are allowed to remarry even after an irrevocable divorce.

Procedure of divorce

Divorce may be given orally, or in writing, but it must take place in the presence of witnesses:

> "So when they have reached their prescribed time, retain them with kindness or part from them with kindness, and call to witness two just ones from among you, and give upright testimony for Allah." — 65:2

Whatever the actual words used, they must expressly convey the intention that the marriage tie is being dissolved. As to whether a divorce would be effective under certain circumstances, there are differences among the various schools of jurists. Evidently, intention is as necessary a factor in divorce as in getting married. While some recognize that divorce is ineffective if given under compulsion or influence, or in a state of intoxication, or in anger or jest, or by mistake or inadvertence, others hold it to be ineffective in some of these cases and effective in others. However, the Holy Quran declares divorce to be a very serious matter, and lays down special procedure to be gone through before it is resorted to.

Li'ān or cursing

The words *li'ān* and *mulā'ana* signify literally 'mutual cursing'. Technically these two words indicate that particular form of bringing about separation between the husband and the wife in which the husband accuses the wife of adultery but has no evidence to support the accusation, while she denies it. The Holy Quran makes adultery a punishable crime, since this act aims at the destruction of the whole social fabric. At the same time it makes an accusation of adultery an equally serious crime, punishable like adultery if strong evidence of adultery is not forthcoming. This is to stop the tongue of slander, which is generally very busy, and does not spare even the most innocent persons. One man has no concern with another's private affairs, but if a man has strong reasons to believe that his own wife is adulterous, the case is quite different. The *li'ān* is suggested in this case, as the means of bringing about separation between husband and wife, for whether the accusation is right or wrong, it is in the interests of both to get separated. The following verses deal with this subject:

> "And those who accuse their wives and have no witnesses except themselves, let one of them testify four times, bearing Allah to witness, that he speaks the truth, and the fifth time [he shall swear] that the curse of Allah be on him, if he is lying. And it shall avert the punishment from her, if she testify four times, bearing Allah to witness, that he is lying, and the fifth time [she shall swear] that the wrath of Allah be on her, if he speaks the truth." — 24:6–9

After the parties have thus borne witness, they are separated forever. It will be noticed that there is no mutual cursing in this case; only each of the parties, while bearing witness of his or her own truthfulness, calls for the curse or wrath of God on himself or herself if he or she tells a lie.

Charitable views of divorce

Divorce is looked upon as a necessity in marital relations, under the varying human conditions, irrespective of moral turpitude on the part of husband or wife. The Holy Quran takes the most charitable view of the necessity for divorce, and therefore recommends as much kindness towards women in the case of divorce as in that of marriage. Again and again stress is laid on this point:

> "Divorce may be pronounced twice; then keep them in good fellowship or let them go with kindness." — 2:229

> "And when you divorce women and they reach their prescribed time, then retain them with kindness or let them go with kindness." — 2:231

> "So when they have reached their prescribed time, retain them with kindness or part from them with kindness". — 65:2

Thus a woman is to be treated with equal kindness and generosity, whether she is a sharer in a man's weal or woe as wife, or one from whom he has been compelled to part company. Marital differences, like other differences, may be as often honest as not, but the Quran recommends that the most charitable view of them should be taken.

Notes to Chapter 16

1. *Editor's Note:* The word "marry" in this verse is *ankiḥū*, meaning *cause them to become married,* i.e., place single people in a state of matrimony.

2. Bukhari, book 67: 'Marriage', ch. 1, h. 5063.

3. *Ibid.,* ch. 2, h. 5065.

4. *Ibid.,* ch. 8, h. 5073.

5. Mishkat, book 13: 'Marriage', ch. 1, sec. 3, h. 2959 (v. 2, p. 71).

6. *Editor's Note:* In 4:1 and 7:189 quoted here, *nafs* may also be translated as 'soul'.

7. *Editor's Note:* In 16:72 and 30:21 quoted here, the Arabic for "selves" (in the word "yourselves") is *anfus,* plural of *nafs.*

8. Ibn Majah, book 9: 'Marriage', h. 1977, h. 1978 (MDS: ch. 50).

9. The Quran, 2:233.

10. Bukhari, book 67: 'Marriage', ch. 22, h. 5102. In Jurisprudence (*Fiqh*), opinions vary as to the number of times or period of time for which the child must have been suckled to establish foster relationship.

11. The Quran, 35:24.

12. The Quran, 32:3, 36:6.

13. *Editor's Note:* Verse 5:5 speaks of marrying "chaste" believing women and "chaste" women of other revealed religions, and it lays down the same conditions for marrying a woman of another religion as for marrying a Muslim woman. This shows that marriage of a Muslim man with a non-Muslim woman is only allowed if the two of them follow the same code of sexual morality as would apply if both of them were Muslims.

14. *Editor's Note:* (1) If a non-Muslim woman becomes a Muslim while married to a non-Muslim, her existing marriage remains valid in Islam. (2) A Jewish or Christian woman marrying a Muslim man would enter a household where her prophets and scriptures are believed in. On the other hand, a Muslim woman marrying a non-Muslim would be entering a household where the Prophet Muhammad and the Quran are not believed in.

15. Abu Dawud, book 12: 'Marriage', ch. 19, h. 2082 (MDS: ch. 17/18).

16. Bukhari, book 67: 'Marriage', ch. 36, ch. heading.

17. Muslim, book 16: 'Marriage', ch. 12, h. 1424a, (MDS: h. 3485).

18. Mishkat, book 13: 'Marriage', ch. 2, sec. 2, h. 2973 (v. 2, p. 74).

19. The word *khaṭaba,* which means 'he addressed (another)', also signifies 'he made a proposal of marriage'. The infinitive noun *khuṭbah* means 'an address' and *khiṭbah* means 'proposal of marriage'.

20. Bukhari, book 67: 'Marriage', ch. 46, h. 5142, h. 5144.

21. *Ibid.,* ch. 33, h. 5120, 5121.

22. *Ibid.,* ch. 34, ch. heading.

23. The Holy Prophet's own marriage with Aishah is sometimes looked upon as sanctioning the marriage of a minor through his or her guardian. However, in the first place, her *nikāḥ* was tantamount only to an engagement, because the consummation of marriage was postponed for five years, to allow her, no doubt, to attain majority. In the second place, the *nikāḥ* was performed in Makkah long before the details of the Islamic law were revealed to the Holy Prophet. Therefore it can be no argument for the marriage of a minor.

24. Hidayah, v. 1, p. 293.

25. Abu Dawud, book 12: 'Marriage', ch. 26, h. 2098, see also h. 2099 (MDS: ch. 24/25).

26. *Ibid.,* h. 2100; see also h. 2101.

27. Hidayah, v. 1, p. 294.

28. Bukhari, book 67: 'Marriage', ch. 42, h. 5136. See also Bukhari, book 89: 'Coercion', ch. 3, h. 6946.

29. Bukhari, book 67: 'Marriage', ch. 43, ch. Heading, h. 5138.

Editor's Note: This hadith occurs again in book 89: 'Coercion', ch. 3: 'Marriage under coercion is not permitted', h. 6945. The woman whose forced marriage was repudiated by the Holy Prophet was Khansa, daughter of Khidham. The same incident is mentioned in another report which relates that a woman who was afraid that she would be married against her will sought the advice of two elderly men of the *Ansar,* and they told her of the case of the repudiation of Khansa's forced marriage (Bukhari, book 90: 'Stratagems', ch. 11, h. 6969). A report in Ibn Majah is as follows: "A girl came to the Prophet and said: 'My father married me to his brother's son so that he might raise his status thereby.' The Prophet gave her the choice [to leave the marriage]. She said: 'I approve of what my father did, but I wanted women to know that their fathers have no right to do that'." (Ibn Majah, book 9: 'Marriage', h. 1874; see also h. 1875. In h. 1873 here the incident of Khasna, daughter of Khidham, is also reported. The chapter containing these hadith is headed: 'He who marries his daughter while she is unwilling'.)

30. The Quran, 5:5.

31. Bukhari, book 67: 'Marriage', chs. 51–52, h. 5149–5150. Abu Dawud, book 12: 'Marriage', chs. 30–31, h. 2109–2112 (MDS: chs. 28/29, 29/30).

32. Abu Dawud, book 12: 'Marriage', ch. 32, h. 2114–2117 (MDS: ch. 30/31).

33. Bukhari, book 67: 'Marriage', ch. 52, h. 5150.

34. *Ibid.,* ch. 51, h. 5149.

35. *Ibid.,* ch. 53, h. 5151. Abu Dawud, book 12: 'Marriage', ch. 40, h. 2139 (MDS: ch. 38/39).

36. *Editor's Note:* His name was Abu-l-'Āṣ and he was married to the Holy Prophet's daughter Zainab since before the Holy Prophet's mission began. He accepted Islam shortly before the conquest of Makkah.

37. Bukhari, book 67: 'Marriage', ch. 53, ch. heading.

38. *Editor's Note:* This condition means that the husband cannot compel his wife to move to a different land or country after marriage.

39. See *Muhammadan Law* by Syed Ameer Ali, p. 248–249.

40. Tirmidhi, book 11: 'Marriage', ch. 6, h. 1088–1090 (MDS: book 9). Nasa'i, book 26: 'Marriage', ch. 72, h. 3369, h. 3370 (MDS: h. 3371, h. 3372). Ibn Majah, book 9: 'Marriage', h. 1895–1900 (MDS: chs. 20–21).

41. Bukhari, book 67: 'Marriage', ch. 49, h. 5147.

42. Ibn Majah, book 9: 'Marriage', h. 1900 (MDS: ch. 21).

43. Mishkat, book 13: 'Marriage', ch. 4, sec. 2, h. 3014 (v. 2, p. 80–81).

44. The Quran, 65:2.

45. Bukhari, book 67: 'Marriage', ch. 57, h. 5155.

46. Bukhari, book 8: 'Prayer', ch. 12, h. 371.

47. Bukhari, book 67: 'Marriage', ch. 70, h. 5171.

48. *Ibid.,* chs. 68, 69, 71, 72, ch. headings.

49. Bukhari, book 10: 'Call to prayer', ch. 162–166, h. 864–870, h. 872–873, h. 875.

50. Bukhari, book 56: '*Jihād*', chs. 66–68, h. 2881–2883.

51. *Ibid.,* ch. 63, h. 2877; and ch. 65, ch. heading.

52. Bukhari, book 67: 'Marriage', ch. 108, h. 5224.

53. *Ibid.,* ch. 78, h. 5182.

54. Bukhari, book 11: 'Friday Prayer', ch. 40, h. 938.

55. Bukhari, book 34: 'Sales and Trade', ch. 67, h. 2155–2156.

56. This verse is dealt with a little further on under the heading *Decent Dress*.

57. Bukhari, book 4: 'Ablutions', ch. 13, h. 147; book 67: 'Marriage', ch. 116, h. 5237.

58. Ibn Jarir Tabari's Commentary of the Quran, vol. 18, p. 84.

59. Hidayah, v. 1, p. 88, 'Conditions of Prayer'.

60. Bukhari, book 25: 'Pilgrimage', ch. 23, ch. heading.

61. Ibn Jarir Tabari's Commentary of the Quran, vol. 18, p. 84, and *Rūḥ al-Ma'ānī*, Commentary of the Quran, vol. 6, p. 52.

62. Abu Dawud, book 34: 'Clothing', ch. 33, h. 4104.

63. Lane's Lexicon.

64. *Editor's Note:* The term for a 'near relative' of a woman is <u>dh</u>ū maḥram, which means one so closely related that marriage with him is prohibited, such as brother, father or son, and includes also her husband.

65. Bukhari, book 67: 'Marriage', ch. 112, h. 5233.

66. *Ibid.,* ch. 113, ch. heading, and h. 5234.

67. *Ibid.,* ch. 78, h. 5182.

68. *Ibid.,* ch. 91, h. 5200.

69. *Ibid.,* ch. 90, h. 5199.

70. *Ibid.,* ch. 87, h. 5195.

71. The Quran, 2:229, 2:231, 4:19, 65:2, etc.

72. Mishkat, book 13: 'Marriage', ch. 11, sec. 2, h. 3114 and h. 3125 (v. 2, p. 101 and p. 103).

73. Bukhari, book 67: 'Marriage', ch. 81, h. 5185–5186.

74. Muslim, book 15: 'Pilgrimage', ch. 19, h. 1218a (MDS: h. 2950).

75. Abu Dawud, book 13: 'Divorce', ch. 3, h. 2177, h. 2178.

76. Bukhari, book 68: 'Divorce', ch. 3, h. 5254, h. 5255.

77. *Ibid.,* ch. 12, h. 5273-5277.

78. Razi, Fakhr-ud-Din, *Al-Tafsīr al-Kabīr*, vol. 3, p. 320.

79. Bukhari, book 68: 'Divorce', chs. 1, 2, h. 5251, h. 5252.

80. *Ibid.*

81. *Editor's Note:* The word *qar'* means the start of a menstrual cycle. The waiting time after divorce is the passing of three menstrual cycles.

82. The Quran, 65:4.

83. The Quran, 65:1.

84. Razi, Fakhr-ud-Din, *Al-Tafsīr al-Kabīr*, vol. 2, p. 372.

85. Nasa'i, book 27: 'Divorce', ch. 6, h. 3401 (MDS: h. 3430).

86. *Musnad* of Ahmad ibn Hanbal, vol. 1, p. 265.

17. Economics and Finance

Property may be acquired in three ways: by earning, by inheritance, and by gift. Acquisition of property by the individual, whether male or female, is recognized by Islam as one of the basic laws regulating human society:

> "For men is the benefit of what they earn. And for women is the benefit of what they earn." — 4:32

Both sexes have also a right to inheritance of property:

> "For men is a share of what the parents and the near relatives leave, and for women a share of what the parents and the near relatives leave…" — 4:7

No limitation is placed upon the property or wealth which an individual may acquire or give away. The Holy Quran speaks even of heaps of gold being in the possession of a man which he may give away to a woman as her nuptial gift (*mahr*) when he enters into marriage with her.[1] Islam is thus opposed to ideologies which recognize no individual right of property; but it is at the same time socialistic in its tendencies, inasmuch as it tries to bring about a more or less equal distribution of wealth.

Unlawful means of acquiring wealth

All unlawful means of acquiring property are denounced:

> "O you who believe, do not swallow up your property among yourselves by false means except that it be trading by your mutual consent." — 4:29

> "And do not swallow up your property among yourselves by false means, nor seek to gain access thereby to the judges, so that you may swallow up a part of the property of [other] people wrongfully while you know." — 2:188

The latter verse alludes to bribery. Robbery and theft are spoken of elsewhere as punishable crimes.[2] Misappropriation is forbidden:

> "Allah commands you to make over trusts to those worthy of them [i.e., to their owners]." — 4:58

Gambling is prohibited as being a false or dishonest means of acquiring property:

> "They ask you [O Prophet] about intoxicants and games of chance. Say: In both of these is a great sin and some advantage for people, and their sin is greater than their advantage." — 2:219

> "Intoxicants and games of chance … are only an uncleanness, the devil's work; so shun it that you may succeed." — 5:90

Intoxicating liquors and gambling are mentioned together in both places, and one of the reasons for their prohibition is that they are an aid to creating mischief and enmity between members of the same society:

> "The devil desires only to create enmity and hatred among you by means of intoxicants and games of chance…" — 5:91

All kinds of lotteries and card games etc., involving a stake, however small the sum involved, fall within the definition of games of chance, and are therefore prohibited by Islam. They not only promote habits of indolence and are thus a negation of honest labour, but also reduce some members of society to penury while others prosper at their expense. Usury, which is dealt with later on, is also prohibited for the same reason.

The Quran on the exercise of property rights

The Holy Quran gives full rights of disposal of property to its owner, whether male or female, but at the same time it requires the owner to be most careful in spending it. There are many injunctions of a general nature to that effect:

> "And the [righteous] servants of the Beneficent [God] are they who … when they spend, are neither extravagant nor

> miserly, and the just mean is ever between these." — 25: 63,67

> "And do not make your hand to be chained to your neck, nor stretch it forth to its fullest extension, so that [afterwards] you sit down blamed, stripped off." — 17:29

But it does not content itself with these general directions, and gives society or the state a right to interfere when money is being squandered by its owner:

> "And do not make over your property, which Allah has made a means of support for you, to the weak of understanding, and maintain them out of it, and clothe them and give them a good education." — 4:5

Here certain owners of property are mentioned who, on account of deficiency or unsoundness in intellect, are unable to manage their own property. The community or the state is enjoined not to give such people control of their property, which is here described as *your property,* because Allah has made it "a means of support for you"; and the rule is laid down that these owners of property should be maintained out of the profits of the property, the management being clearly in other hands.

Thus wealth, though possessed by individuals, is recognized as a national asset, and a check is placed upon the rights of the individual if money in his possession is being wasted. The Quran requires that persons who, on account of weakness of intellect, mismanage their property and squander their wealth should be deprived of control of their property and maintained out of its profits, the control being handed over to some person who is called a *walī* or guardian in 2:282.

Restrictions on disposal of property

Hadith lays great stress on preventing wealth from being wasted. Bukhari says the following in the heading of one of his chapters:

> "There is no charity unless a man has sufficient to give, and whoever spends in charity and he is himself in want or his family is in want or he has a debt to pay, it is more in the fitness of things that the debt should be paid than that he

should spend in charity or free a slave or make a gift, and such a gift or charity shall be annulled, for he has no right to waste the wealth of the people; and the Prophet, may peace and the blessings of Allah be upon him, has said, 'Whoever takes the wealth of the people that he may waste it, Allah will destroy him, unless he is a man well-known for his patience so that he prefers needs of others over his own, though poverty may afflict him', as Abu Bakr did when he gave all his wealth and likewise the *Anṣār* [helpers at Madinah] gave preference to the needs of the *Muhājirs* [emigrants from Makkah to Madinah] over their own." [3]

Here, the individual property of a man is called the wealth of the people, and a man is prohibited from making even charitable gifts when he does not have sufficient to support those dependent on him. According to a hadith, the Holy Prophet is reported to have said:

"Allah hates three things in you: useless talk, and wasting of wealth, and asking or begging frequently." [4]

This hadith, repeated frequently, forms the basis of restrictions which may rightly be laid on owners of property for their benefit. The State is, therefore, entitled to make laws for the benefit of owners of property, placing restrictions on them as to the disposal of that property.

Guardian of minor

A guardian is also appointed to deal with the property of minors. The Quranic injunction on this point is as follows:

"And test the orphans until they reach the age of marriage. Then if you find in them maturity of intellect, make over to them their property, and do not consume it extravagantly and hastily against their growing up. And whoever is rich, let him abstain, and whoever is poor let him consume reasonably. And when you make over to them their property, call witnesses in their presence. And Allah is enough as a Reckoner." — 4:6

A minor is thus not allowed to manage his own property which must be made over to a guardian. If the guardian is rich, he is required to do the work of guardianship honorarily, and if he is poor, his wages would be a charge on the property. The age of majority, according to

Abu Hanifah, is eighteen years in the case of males and seventeen in the case of females, but according to Shafi'i and Ahmad, it is fifteen in both cases.[5]

Honest dealing in business transactions

Subject to certain restrictions, a property owner, whether a male or a female, has the right to sell or barter it. The Holy Quran lays stress on honest and straight dealing in the very earliest revelation:

> "Woe to the cheaters, who, when they take the measure [of their dues] from people, take it fully, but when they measure out to others or weigh out for them, they give less than is due!" — 83:1–3

> "And give full measure when you measure out, and weigh with a true balance. This is fair and better in the end." — 17:35

> "Give full measure and do not diminish. And weigh with a true balance. And do not wrong people of their dues, nor act corruptly in the earth, making mischief." — 26:181–183

Hadith also lays stress on honest dealing, so much so that if there is any defect in a thing it must be pointed out to the intending buyer.[6] The Holy Prophet himself is reported to have written to Adda ibn Khalid as follows:

> "This is the writing by which Muhammad, the Messenger of Allah, has made a purchase from Adda ibn Khalid, the barter of a Muslim with a Muslim, there is no defect in it nor any deception nor an evil." [7]

He is also reported to have said:

> "If the two parties speak the truth and make it manifest, their transaction shall be blessed, and if they conceal and tell a lie, the blessing of their transaction shall be obliterated." [8]

Honesty and *bona fides* in matters of sale are stressed in a large number of reports in Hadith.

General directions relating to sale transactions

There are many other details that are met with in Hadith. A few of these, of a general nature, are briefly noted here. Men and women are expressly mentioned as selling to and buying from one another, so that there is not the least sex disqualification in this respect.[9] While a transaction is being carried on with someone, another should not intervene, but auction is allowed.[10] The withholding of food-stuffs so that they may become expensive is prohibited,[11] and so is the inflation of prices in general. Imaginary sales, when there are no goods to deliver, are prohibited;[12] nor should one sell what one does not possess.[13] The sale of land is not favoured, and it is recommended that a person should not sell his land or house unless he intends to purchase other land or another house with the money.[14]

Mortgage

Mortgage of property, i.e., giving it as security for debt, is also allowed. The Holy Quran expressly allows the giving or taking of a security, possession of which is taken by the mortgagee (2:283); and though this case is mentioned in connection with a journey, the words have been taken by all commentators as conveying a general permission, and reliable reports in Hadith corroborate this conclusion. It is related that the Holy Prophet himself left his shield as security with a Jew when borrowing some barley from him.[15] When a horse was given as a security, the mortgagee was allowed to use it for riding as a compensation for feeding; similarly a milch-animal's milk was allowed to the mortgagee when he fed the animal.[16] Hence it is evident that when agricultural land or a house is mortgaged with possession, the mortgagee can derive benefit from it when he pays land revenue or house tax, or spends money on the upkeep of the property.

Bequest

Subject to certain limitations, an owner of property is also allowed to bequeath his property by making a will. This is discussed in the next section entitled *Inheritance,* under the heading *Bequest.*

Gift (*hibah*)

An owner of property has also the right to dispose of his property by gift. The giving and accepting of gifts is recommended very strongly, and even the smallest gift is not to be despised.[17] A gift is allowed in favour of a son, but it is recommended that similar gifts should be made in favour of other sons.[18] The husband can make a gift to his wife, and the wife to her husband or to other people.[19] Gifts from, and in favour of, non-Muslims are allowed.[20] A gift may also be compensated.[21] The jurists allow a gift for a consideration, and also a gift made on the condition that the recipient shall give the donor some determinate thing in return for the gift. The gift transaction is complete when the recipient has accepted it and taken possession of the gift. It is not allowed to a person to revoke the gift when it has been accepted by the recipient.[22]

While a will is allowed only to the extent of one-third of the property, no such limitation exists on gifts because in this case the owner divests himself of all rights in the property immediately, while in the case of a will, not the owner but the heirs are deprived.

Trusts *(waqf)*

Subject to certain conditions, an owner of property has a right to dedicate his property to a particular purpose. A trust, like a gift, takes effect immediately, and it differs from both a gift and a will inasmuch as the property which is dedicated remains untouched, not being the property of a particular person, and it is only the income drawn from it that is spent on the particular objects specified in the trust deed. Many cases of creating trusts are reported in Hadith. A man created a trust the income from which was to be spent on his poor relatives, and this was done under the Holy Prophet's direction.[23] From this it is evident that a man can create a trust for the benefit of his own relatives. It is made clear in another hadith that a man's son or his wife falls within the definition of his relatives.[24] The man who creates a trust is allowed to draw benefit from it, for he himself may be its manager as well as anybody else, even though this may not be stated in the trust deed.[25] Another hadith states that Umar created a trust in accordance with the directions of the Holy Prophet in favour of the poor as well as his rich relatives and guests, and there are other instances on record in which a trust was created for the benefit of the poor as well as near relatives.[26] The person who creates the trust may also include himself among its beneficiaries.[27]

Section 2: *Inheritance*

Reform introduced by Islam

The reform introduced by Islam into the rules relating to inheritance is twofold: it makes the female a co-sharer with the male, and divides the property of the deceased person among the heirs on a democratic basis, instead of handing it all over to the eldest son, as is done by the law of primogeniture. The Arabs had a very strong tradition that he alone could inherit who smites with the spear, and therefore they did not give any portion of inheritance to such of the heirs as were not capable of meeting the enemy and fighting in battles.[28] Owing to this tradition, not only were all females — daughters, widows and mothers — excluded, but even male minors had no right to inheritance. A woman, in fact, was looked upon as part of the property of the deceased,[29] and therefore her right to property by inheritance was out of the question. Even in the Jewish law she had no better position: "There could have been no question in those days of a widow inheriting from her husband, since she was regarded as part of the property which went over to the heirs. ... Nor could there have been a question about daughters inheriting from their father, since daughters were given in marriage either by their father, or by their brothers or other relatives after the father's death, thus becoming the property of the family into which they married".[30]

At a time when a defensive war against the whole of Arabia was being carried on by a handful of Muslims, Islam declared the prevailing law of inheritance in Arabia, which gave the whole of the property to those members of the family who bore arms, to be unjust, and it gave a new law which put widows and orphans on a level of equality with those who fought for the defence of the tribe and the country. When the change was first introduced, some of the Companions thought it very hard and complained to the Holy Prophet, saying that they were required to make over half the property to a daughter who did not ride on horseback or fight with the enemy.[31] The general principle of inheritance is first laid down in the Holy Quran in the following words:

> "For men is a share of what the parents and the near relatives leave, and for women a share of what the parents and the near relatives leave, whether it is little or much — an appointed share." — 4:7

Inheritance law as contained in the Quran

The law of inheritance is then stated at length in 4:11–12 and 4:176. It may be noted that, as repeated in 4:11–12, in all cases the payment of bequests and debts takes precedence over the shares of the heirs. The heirs take the remainder, as follows.

In 4:11, children are mentioned first:

> "Allah enjoins you concerning your children: for the male is the equal of the portion of two females; but if there are more than two females, two-thirds of what the deceased leaves is theirs, and if there is one, for her is the half."

In their case, only a broad principle is laid down — the male shall have double the share of the female. Thus, all sons would be equal sharers, and so would all daughters, a son however having double the share of a daughter.

Then is covered the case when daughters are the sole children. If there is only one daughter, she takes half the property; if there are two or more daughters, they take two-thirds of the whole. The residue goes to the nearest male members, according to a hadith.[32] Note that the words in the Quran here literally mean "more than two" but these include two as the other case mentioned is that of only one daughter. Compare 4:176, where two sisters are mentioned but they include more than two.

There is apparently inequality of treatment of the two sexes here. The reason is that man is generally recognized as the bread-winner of the family, and that is the position assigned to him in the Quran. In view of his greater responsibilities, he is entitled to a greater share, and therefore the Quran has assigned to him double the share of the female. Keeping this in view, there is real justice and real equality beneath this apparent inequality.

After children, are mentioned parents and husband or wife:

> "And as for his parents, for each of them is the sixth of what he leaves, if he has a child; but if he has no child and [only] his two parents inherit him, for his mother is the third; but if he has brothers, for his mother is the sixth, after [payment of] a bequest he may have bequeathed or a debt. … And yours is half of what your wives leave if they have no child; but if they have a child, your share is a fourth of what they leave after [payment of] any bequest they may have bequeathed or a debt; and theirs is the fourth of what you leave if you have no child, but if you have a child, their share is the eighth of what you leave after [payment of] a bequest you may have bequeathed or a debt. …" — 4:11–12

If children are the only heirs, the whole property will be divided among them as explained earlier. But if there are parents or husband or wife, then evidently it is the residue which is divided among the sons and daughters, because the shares of the others are fixed: one-sixth in the case of each parent and one-fourth or one-eighth in the case of the husband or wife respectively.

In the case where the deceased leaves no children, the shares of the parents and the husband or wife are stated in the above passage. The shares of brothers and sisters of the deceased in this case are specified further on in 4:12 as follows:

> "…And if a man or a woman, having no children, leaves property to be inherited and he [or she] has a brother or a sister, then for each of them is the sixth; but if they are more than that, they shall be sharers in the third after [payment of] a bequest that may have been bequeathed or a debt not injuring [others]." — 4:12

If the deceased leaves neither children nor parents, then after the fixed share of the husband and wife has been taken out, brothers and sisters inherit the residual as the children would have done, which is what is mentioned in 4:176.

Briefly, the inheritance law as laid down in the Quran is this:

1. After the payment of debts and execution of the will, if any, the shares of the parents and husband or wife shall be first taken out. (The shares depend on whether or not there are children, and for parents also on whether there are siblings if there are no children.)

2. After that the rest of the property shall go to the children, the division among them being as mentioned above.

3. If there are no children and there are brothers and sisters, one-sixth if there is only one brother or sister, and one-third if there are more than one, shall go to them. (As the mother's share is specified if there are no children, the father receives the remainder.)

4. If the deceased leaves neither children nor parents, the whole of the property, after the husband's or the wife's share has been taken out, shall go to brothers and sisters.

5. If there is a single female, daughter or sister, she shall take one-half of the property, a single brother following the same rule, and if there are two or more daughters or sisters they shall take two-thirds, the residue going to the nearest male relative according to Hadith.

6.   If a person entitled to inheritance is dead, any living offspring of that person shall take his place; if the father or the mother is dead, the grandfather or grandmother, if alive, shall take his or her place.

7.   All brothers and sisters, whether uterine or consanguine or full, shall be treated equally; if there are no brothers or sisters, the nearest relatives after them, such as father's brothers or father's sisters, shall take their place.

Bequests

The legality of a bequest is clearly admitted in both the verses dealing with the law of inheritance. The property left is to be divided "after payment of a bequest … or a debt" (4:11 and 4:12). The making of a will (*waṣiyyah*) is specially recommended and the Holy Quran speaks of it as a duty incumbent upon a Muslim when he leaves sufficient property for his heirs:

> "It is prescribed for you, when death approaches one of you, if he leaves behind wealth for parents and near relatives, to make a bequest in a kindly manner;[33] it is incumbent upon the dutiful." — 2:180

And the Holy Prophet is reported to have said:

> "It is not right for a Muslim, who has property to bequeath, that he should pass two nights without having a written will with him." [34]

There is also mention of a bequest in a verse which was decidedly revealed later than 4:11–12:

> "O you who believe, call to witness between you, when death draws near to one of you, at the time of making the will, two just persons from among you…" — 5:106

All these verses afford clear proof that a person can make a will with regard to his property.

There are, however, reliable reports in Hadith which place a certain limitation upon the right to make a bequest and, in fact, if no limitations were placed, the injunctions contained in 4:11–12 would be nullified, for there would be no property to be divided among the legal heirs. Sa'd ibn Abi Waqas, a well-known Companion of the Holy Prophet, reported:

"I fell ill in the year in which Makkah was conquered, being almost on the brink of death when the Prophet paid me a visit. I said to him: O Messenger of Allah! I possess much wealth and my only heir is a single daughter; may I therefore make a will with regard to the whole of my property? The Prophet said: No. I then enquired about two-thirds of it, and he again said: No. I then asked him, if I may give away one-third of my property by will, and he approved of one-third, adding: A bequest of one-third is much, for if you leave your heirs rich, it is better than that you should leave them poor, begging of other people, and whatever you spend to seek the pleasure of Allah you are rewarded for it, even for the morsel of food you put into your wife's mouth." [35]

Such reports make it clear that the will spoken of on various occasions in the Quran is a charitable bequest, and not a will for the heirs, and that this bequest was to be limited to one-third of the property, so that the heirs might not be deprived of their share of inheritance, the well-being of the heirs being as good a consideration with the law-giver as charity.

It may also be added that, according to another Hadith report, a bequest is not allowed in favour of an heir: "There is no bequest for an heir".[36] To this are added in some reports the words: "unless the heirs wish it".[37] Thus while generally a will can be made only for charitable objects, and not for heirs, it is permissible to make a will in favour of heirs, if they wish it; so that if they have no objection, any arrangement may be made for the disposal of the property by will. Hence if the heirs agree, a man may either divide the whole property by will, or he may leave the property undivided, fixing the shares of the heirs in the income.

Husband's bequest for maintenance of widow[38]

In connection with bequests it is stated in the Holy Quran:

"And those of you who die and leave wives behind, should make a bequest in favour of their wives of maintenance for a year without turning them out. Then if they themselves go away, there is no blame on you for what they do of lawful deeds concerning themselves." — 2:240

There is nothing to show that this verse is abrogated by any other verse of the Quran. It simply speaks of a bequest on the part of the husband that the widow should be given an additional benefit, a year's residence and maintenance. The latter portion of the verse plainly says that if the widow of her own accord leaves the house, she is not entitled to any further concession, and there is no blame on the heirs of the deceased husband for what the widow does of lawful deeds, i.e., if she remarries after her waiting period of four months and ten days is over. As regards the share of the wife's inheritance spoken of in 4:12, the fourth or eighth part of the property of the deceased husband is hers in addition to what she obtains under this verse, and 4:12 plainly says that anything which is to be paid under a will shall have precedence of the division of property into shares under that verse.

Section 3: *Debts*

Leniency towards debtors recommended

The writing down of debts is an ordinance of the Holy Quran, given in detail in 2:282. That verse also contains the instruction:

> "…and let him who owes the debt dictate…"

The Quran also teaches that debtors should be dealt with most leniently:

> "And if [the debtor] is in difficulty, let there be postpone-
> ment till [he is in] ease. And that you forgo it as charity is
> better for you, if only you knew." — 2:280

These two regulations, i.e., the writing down of debts according to the dictation of the debtor in the presence of witnesses and lenient dealing with those in straitened circumstances, are the basis of Islamic regulations on debts and are supplemented by a large variety of detailed directions and recommendations contained in Hadith. The concern of the Holy Prophet for debtors is reflected in his sayings on this point, of which only a few are as follows:

> "May Allah have mercy on one who is generous when he
> sells and when he buys and when he demands payment of
> debt." [39]

> "Allah will give shelter to His servant who gives respite to
> one in financial difficulty or remits to a debtor." [40]

> "There is no believer but I am nearest to him in this world and the Hereafter … so any believer who leaves behind him property, his relatives shall inherit whoever they may be, but if he leaves a debt, or a family for whom there is none to care, I am his guardian (*maulā*)." [41]

> "I am nearer to the believers than themselves, so whoever of the believers dies and leaves a debt, its payment is on me, and whoever leaves property, it is for his heirs." [42]

These show that the debts of a debtor who is in financial difficulty and unable to pay must either be remitted or paid by the state.

Insistence laid on payment of debts

While the lender is advised in numerous Hadith reports to be lenient and not to exert undue pressure, and to remit some or even the whole of a debt if the debtor is in financial difficulty, the debtor is also told to repay the debt in a goodly and liberal manner, and the Holy Prophet is reported to have said: "Among the best of you are those who are good in payment of debt".[43]

The rich, especially, are told not to postpone payment of debt and postponement in their case is called injustice.[44] The one who contracts a debt intending not to pay it back is condemned.[45] The report has already been quoted (see p. 368) which shows that the payment of debt has preference over spending in charity. In the case of an inheritance, the heirs do not take their shares until all debts have been paid;[46] and when there is a will, the debts must be paid before its execution.[47]

Warning against indebtedness

Though the necessity of contracting debts at times is recognized, and the Holy Prophet himself is reported to have done so on occasions, yet he, at the same time, gave warnings against being in a state of indebtedness. It is related in a hadith that:

> "…he [the Holy Prophet] used to pray very frequently: O Allah! I seek refuge from faults and debts. A man said to him, O Messenger of Allah, it is very frequently that you pray against being in debt; and he replied: A person, when he is in debt, speaks and tells lies and makes promises and fails to fulfil them." [48]

According to another hadith, the Holy Prophet often prayed:

> "O Allah! I seek Your refuge from anxiety and grief, and from lack of strength and indolence, and from miserliness and cowardice, and from being overcome by debt and the oppression of people." [49]

Usury prohibited

It would be seen from what has been stated above that helping those in distress forms the basic outlook of Islam on human society. The prohibition of usury rests on the same basis. Even the earlier revelation at Makkah denounced usury, yet without prohibiting it:

> "And whatever you lay out at usury, so that it may increase through the property of [other] people, it does not increase with Allah; and whatever you give in charity, desiring Allah's pleasure — these will get manifold." — 30:39

Prohibition came later, and is contained in the following verses which are among the latest revelations:

> "Those who swallow usury (*ribā*) cannot arise except as he arises whom the devil prostrates by his touch. That is because they say: Trading is only like usury. And Allah has allowed trading and forbidden usury. To whomsoever then the exhortation has come from his Lord, and he refrains, he shall have what has already passed. … Allah will blot out usury, and He causes charity to prosper. And Allah does not love any ungrateful sinner." — 2:275–276

> "O you who believe, keep your duty to Allah and relinquish what remains due from usury, if you are believers. But if you do not, then be apprised of war from Allah and His Messenger; and if you repent, then you shall have your capital. Wrong not, and you shall not be wronged." — 2:278–279

To these may be added an earlier revelation:

> "O you who believe, do not devour usury, doubling and redoubling, and keep your duty to Allah, that you may be successful." — 3:130

Reasons for prohibition

The prohibition of usury is clearly associated in these Quranic verses with charity, for inasmuch as charity is the broad basis of human sympathy, usury annihilates all sympathetic affection. The usurer is compared to one whom the devil has prostrated by his touch, so that he is unable to rise. Such is, in fact, the usurer who would not hesitate to reduce the debtor to the last straits if thereby he might add a penny to his millions. He grows in selfishness until he is divested of all sympathetic feelings. Usury, moreover, promotes habits of idleness, since the usurer, instead of doing any hard work or manual labour, becomes like a parasite living on others.

In the great struggle that is going on between capital and labour, Islam sides with labour, and by its prohibition of usury tries to restore the balance between the two, not allowing capital to enthral labour. It is in reference to the honourable place that Islam gives to labour that the Quran says that "Allah has allowed trading and forbidden usury," for while trading requires the use of labour and skill, usury does not. To help the distressed one who is in straits is the object of Islam and to reduce him to further straits is the aim of usury, and hence it is that usury is called "war" with Allah and His Messenger.

Hadith on usury

Hadith is equally emphatic against usury. It condemns not only the usurer but also the one who pays the usury,[50] because he helps the cause of usury; and, according to one hadith, the witnesses and the scribe in a usurious transaction are equally blamable.[51] Certain details are also added, describing the exchange of gold with gold and wheat with wheat, and dates with dates, and barley with barley, as *ribā* (usury), unless it is a hand to hand transaction.[52] Another report makes it more clear. Usama reports that the Holy Prophet said: "There is no *ribā* unless there is postponement in payment".[53] This shows that only those cases were treated as usury in which there was a barter only in name, the transaction being really usurious. Gold was given to a person on condition that he would pay a greater quantity of the same after some time, or likewise with wheat. This is clearly a usurious transaction though it was given the apparent form of a sale.

It may be added that a case in which the debtor, of his own free will, paid to the creditor a certain sum over and above the original debt, was not considered a case of *ribā*.[54] This was a case in which the Holy Prophet himself was the debtor, and when he paid back the debt, he paid something in addition.

Interest

The basis of the prohibition of usury is undoubtedly sympathetic feelings towards those in distress, but the word used is *ribā* (literally, an 'excess' or 'addition') which means 'an addition over and above the principal sum lent';[55] and, therefore, though the word is considered by some modern writers to apply only to usurious transactions, it apparently includes all kinds of interest, whether the rate be high or low, and whether the interest is or is not added to the principal sum, after fixed periods. In fact, it would be difficult to discriminate between interest and usury, and indeed all interest has a tendency to assume, ultimately, the form of usury, and becomes oppressive for the debtor, a fact which is borne out by the history of indebtedness in all countries.

It is sometimes argued that the prohibition of interest would be a serious drawback in the carrying on of trade and business transactions and also in the execution of important national projects. It is true that this prohibition, if taken in a broad sense, does not fit in the frame of the modern world conditions, but the high ideal which Islam places before itself is not unworkable, and the great Muslim nation of early days, spread over vast territories, the vanguard of the great nations of the world in the march of civilization, carried the Quranic injunction regarding *ribā* faithfully into practice. The material Western civilization has, however, given rise to conditions in which usury and interest seem to be unavoidable, and Muslims were told so many centuries before by the Holy Prophet Muhammad:

> "A time will come over people when not a single person will remain who does not swallow down *ribā* and if there is anyone who refrains from it, still its vapour (or dust) will overtake him." [56]

Deposits in banks or Government treasuries

Such is the time in which we are living, and until a new civilization is evolved which is based on morality and the sympathy of man for man, some solution has to be sought for the great economic questions which confront the Muslim nations. In the forefront of all these questions is the modern banking system. Is this system in conformity with the Quranic law which prohibits *ribā?* Usury is undoubtedly universally condemned today, though it is still rampant in some places and has demoralized both the lenders and the borrowers, but the banking system with its legalization of interest is looked upon as a necessary condition of economic life and in the prevailing conditions this seems to be unavoidable. Not only Muslims living under non-Muslim governments cannot avoid it but even Muslim states seem to be driven to the necessity of employing it. Take only the question of trade, which is no longer a national but an international concern, and it will be found that it is entirely dependent on the banking system. Now the banking system, if it had to be evolved anew, could have been based on a co-operative system in which capital and labour should be sharers in profit as well as in loss; but, as it is, the modern banking system favours capitalism and the amassing of wealth instead of its distribution. For whatever its defects, it is there, and the dust of *ribā* overtakes the one who does not swallow it, as the hadith says.

Bank deposits

The question of deposits in banks, on which interest is payable, seems to be more or less like the question of trade, a necessity of modern world conditions, which cannot be avoided. The bank receives the deposits not as a borrower but as a trustee, where money is safe and may be withdrawn in need. But at the same time it does not allow the money to lie idle, and draws some profit from it, the major portion of which again comes in the shape of interest. Out of this profit, the bank pays a certain amount to the depositors, the rate of which depends generally on the economic conditions prevailing in the country concerned, or in the world at large. It does not make over the entire profit either to the shareholders or to the depositors, but carries a certain amount to a reserve fund which it can fall back upon in less profitable years, or in case of loss. So far, therefore, as it is a part of the profits earned by the bank, there is nothing objectionable in it, but that profit itself being largely income from interest, the question of *ribā* comes in indirectly.

To be on the safe side, a Muslim depositor may spend the interest he receives on his deposit for a charitable object. In fact, if the depositor deposits his money with the intent that he would not receive the interest for his personal use, and, on receiving the amount from the bank, he makes it over to some charitable institution, he has relinquished the *ribā*, as commanded by the Quran.

(*Author's Note:* It was the founder of the Ahmadiyya movement, Hazrat Mirza Ghulam Ahmad, who first suggested this course. On account of his great anxiety for the propagation of Islam, he directed that the interest on bank deposits should be spent for the propagation of Islam. He particularly laid stress on the point that insistence on receiving the *ribā* was called a "war with Allah and His Messenger" (2:279), and that therefore the money so received should be spent on the struggle which was being carried on for the defence and propagation of Islam.)

Co-operative banks

The co-operative banks are more in consonance with the spirit of the teachings of Islam, as the idea underlying them is the amelioration of the lot of the poor who are thus saved from the clutches of the usurious money lenders. There is, moreover, this difference between an ordinary bank and a co-operative bank, that the former is generally for the benefit of the rich and the capitalists, and the latter for that of the poor and the manual workers. In the co-operative bank, moreover, the shareholders are also the depositors as well as the borrowers of money, and the interest paid to the bank is, more or less, in the nature of a contribution by which the borrower of money also ultimately benefits by receiving dividends.

Interest on business capital

Interest on the capital with which a business is run differs a little from ordinary debt. It is in fact a case in which capital and labour are sharers. Islam does not prohibit a partnership in which one person supplies the capital and the other labour. But it requires that both capital and labour shall be sharers in profit as well as in loss. The payment of interest at a fixed rate means that capital shall always have a profit, even though the business may be running at a loss. It is true that when the business is profitable, the rate of interest may be much less than the profit earned, but in all such uncertainties the viewpoint of Islam is that neither side should have undue advantage or be made to suffer undue loss. If the business is run at a profit, let capital have its due share of the profit, but if it is being run at a loss, let capital also share in the loss. This method is more advantageous for the general welfare of the community than the method of charging interest on capital, which promotes capitalism and is unjust to labour.

Section 4: *Work and Labour*

Islam places great emphasis on the necessity for hard work and the dignity of labour. The principle was laid down in the earliest revelations in unequivocal terms that no one who does not work shall hope to reap any fruit and that the worker should have his full reward:

"… man can have nothing but what he strives for, and his striving will soon be seen. Then he will be rewarded for it with the fullest reward." — 53:39–41

"So whoever does good deeds and is a believer, there is no rejection of his effort, and We surely write it down for him." — 21:94

Equal stress is laid in the Quran on faith and work, "those who believe and do good" being the ever-recurring description of the faithful.

The Holy Prophet himself was an indefatigable worker. While he passed half the night, and even two-thirds of it, praying to God, he was doing every kind of work in the day time. No work was too low for him. He would milk his own goats, patch his own clothes and mend his own shoes. In person he would dust his home and assist his wife in her household duties. In person he would do shopping, not only for his own household but also for his neighbours and friends. He worked like a labourer in the construction of the mosque. Again, when a ditch was being dug around Madinah to fortify it against a heavy attack, he was seen at work among the rank and file. He never despised any work, however humble, despite the dignity of his position as Prophet, as chief of the army and as ruler.

He thus demonstrated through his personal example that every kind of work dignified man, and that one's calling, whether high or low, did not constitute the criterion of his status. "No one eats better food than that which he eats out of the work of his own hand", he is reported to have said.[57] In his other sayings he has made clear that every work was honourable in comparison with asking for charity. His Companions followed his example and the most honourable of them did not disdain even the work of a porter.

The relations between a worker and his employer were those of two contracting parties on terms of equality. The Holy Prophet laid down a general law relating to contracts: "Muslims shall be bound by the conditions which they make".[58] The master and the servant were considered two contracting parties, and the master was bound as much by the terms of the contract as the servant. This was made clear by the Holy Prophet:

> "Allah says: There are three persons whose adversary in dispute I shall be on the Day of Resurrection — a person who makes a promise in My name and then acts unfaithfully, a person who sells a free person then devours his price, and a person who employs a servant and receives fully the labour due from him, then does not pay his remuneration." [59]

The employees of the State, its collectors and executive officers and judges, were all included in the category of servants. They were entitled to a remuneration but they could not accept any gift from the public. Umar was once appointed a collector by the Holy Prophet, and when offered a remuneration he said that he did not stand in need of it. The Holy Prophet, however, told him to accept it and then give it away in charity if he liked.[60] The principle was thus laid down that every employee, every servant, every labourer was entitled to a remuneration.

Trading was one of the most honourable professions and the Holy Prophet had special words of praise for the truthful and honest merchant.[61] People were taught to be generous in their dealings with one another, in buying and selling and demanding their dues.[62] Honesty was to be the basic principle in all dealings.[63]

The cultivation of land and planting of trees was encouraged.[64] It was also stated by the Holy Prophet that whoever cultivates land which is not the property of anyone has a better title to it.[65] Those who had vast tracts of land, which they could not manage to cultivate for themselves, were advised to allow others to cultivate them free of charge:

> "If one of you gives it [i.e., cultivable land] as a gift to his brother, it is better for him than that he takes it for a fixed payment." [66]

It was allowed that the owner of the land should give it to others to cultivate for a share of the produce or for a fixed sum.[67] The ownership of land by individuals was thus recognized, as also their right to buy or sell it or to have it cultivated for them by others. A warning was at the same time given that a people who give themselves up entirely to agriculture, neglecting other lines of development, could not rise to a position of great glory.[68]

Notes to Chapter 17

1. The Quran, 4:20.

2. The Quran, 5:33, 5:38.

3. Bukhari, book 24: '*Zakāt*', ch. 18, ch. heading.

4. *Ibid.,* ch. 53, h. 1477.

5. Hidayah, v. 2, p. 341 and p. 342.

6. Bukhari, book 34: 'Sales and Trade', ch. 19, h. 2079. *Musnad* of Ahmad ibn Hanbal, v. 3, p. 491.

7. Bukhari, book 34: 'Sales and Trade', ch. 19, ch. heading.

8. *Ibid.,* ch. 19, h. 2079.

9. *Ibid.,* ch. 67, h. 2155, h. 2156, and ch. heading.

10. *Ibid.,* ch. 58–59, h. 2139–2141.

11. Muslim, book 22: '*Musaqah*', ch. 26.

12. Bukhari, book 34: 'Sales and Trade', ch. 61, h. 2143.

13. Bukhari, book 34: 'Sales and Trade', ch. 54, h. 2131–2133. *Musnad* of Ahmad ibn Hanbal, v. 2, pp. 189, 190.

14. *Musnad* of Ahmad ibn Hanbal, v. 1, p. 190; v. 3, p. 467.

15. Bukhari, book 48: 'Mortgage', ch. 1, h. 2508, ch. 2, h. 2509, ch. 5, h. 2513.

16. *Ibid.,* ch. 4, h. 2511, h. 2512.

17. Bukhari, book 51: 'Gifts', ch. 1, h. 2566.

18. *Ibid.,* chs. 12–13, h. 2586–2587.

19. *Ibid.,* chs. 14–15, h. 2588–2593.

20. *Ibid.,* chs. 28–29, h. 2615–2620.

21. *Ibid.,* ch. 11, h. 2585.

22. *Ibid.,* ch. 30, h. 2621–2623.

23. Bukhari, book 55: 'Wills', ch. 10, heading and h. 2752.

24. *Ibid.,* ch. 11, h. 2753.

25. *Ibid.,* ch. 12, ch. heading.

26. *Ibid.,* ch. 29, h. 2773.

27. *Ibid.,* ch. 33, h. 2778.

28. Ibn Jarir Tabari's Commentary of the Quran, v. 4, p. 171.

29. See the Quran, 4:19.

30. *The Jewish Encyclopaedia,* Funk & Wagnells Co., 1904, p. 583.

31. Ibn Jarir Tabari's Commentary of the Quran, v. 4, p. 171.

32. "Give the fixed portions (*farā'iḍ*) to those who are entitled to them, and what remains should go to the nearest male" — Bukhari, book 85: 'Laws of Inheritance', ch. 7, h. 6735.

33. Generally the construction of these words is supposed to be, "if he leaves behind wealth *to make a bequest for parents and near relatives,*" the import of the passage thus being that someone who leaves wealth should bequeath it *to parents and near relatives.* Owing to this interpretation the verse is looked upon as being abrogated by 4:11–12. But as already shown, both these verses expressly speak of the bequest and require the property to be divided only after payment of bequest or debt. The interpretation I have adopted makes it consistent with the other verses of the Quran.

34. Bukhari, book 55: 'Wills', ch. 1, h. 2738.

35. Bukhari, book 85: 'Laws of Inheritance', ch. 6, h. 6733; Muslim, book 25: 'Wills', ch. 1, h. 1628a (MDS: h. 4209); Tirmidhi, book 30: 'Wills', ch. 1, h. 2116 (MDS: book 28). According to another version, Sa'd told the Holy Prophet: "I have bequeathed the whole of my property to be spent in the way of Allah". Being asked what he had left for his children, he said: "They are in sufficiently good circumstances". The Holy Prophet advised him to bequeathe one-tenth of his property, but he insisted on leaving still less for his heirs. So the Holy Prophet finally said: "Make a will of one-third of property and one-third is much". See Mishkat, book 12: 'Trading', ch. 20, sec. 2, h. 2940 (v. 2, p. 68).

36. Abu Dawud, book 18: 'Wills', ch. 6, h. 2870 (MDS: book 17). Tirmidhi, book 30: 'Wills', ch. 5, h. 2120, 2121 (MDS: book 28). Ibn Majah, book 22: 'Wills', h. 2713, 2714 (MDS: ch. 6).

37. Mishkat, book 12: 'Trading', ch. 20, sec. 2, h. 2941 (v. 2, p. 68).

38. *Editor's note:* For completion of the subject of bequests, this has been added from the footnote to 2:240 in Maulana Muhammad Ali's English translation and commentary of the Holy Quran.

39. Bukhari, book 34: 'Sales and Trade', ch. 16, h. 2076.

40. *Musnad* of Ahmad ibn Hanbal, v. 1, p. 73.

41. Bukhari, book 65: 'Commentary on the Quran', h. 4781 (under *Surah* 33, v. 6).

42. Bukhari, book 69: 'Supporting the Family', ch. 15, h. 5371.

43. Bukhari, book 40: '*Wakālat*', chs. 5–6, h. 2305, h. 2306.

44. Bukhari, book 38: 'Transferring Debt', chs. 1–2, h. 2287–2288.

45. *Musnad* of Ahmad ibn Hanbal, v. 2, p. 417.

46. *Ibid.,* v. 4, p. 136.

47. *Ibid.,* v. 1, p. 79.

48. Bukhari, book 43: 'Loans', ch. 10, h. 2397.

49. Bukhari, book 56: '*Jihād*', ch. 74, h. 2893.

50. Bukhari, book 34: 'Sales and Trade', ch. 25, h. 2086.

51. *Ibid.,* ch. 24, ch. heading.

52. *Ibid.,* ch. 54, h. 2134.

53. *Ibid.*, ch. 79, h. 2178–2179.

54. Abu Dawud, book 23: 'Commercial Transactions' *(Buyū'),* ch. 11, h. 3347 (MDS: book 22).

55. *Tāj al-'Arūs* and Lane's Lexicon.

56. Abu Dawud, book 23: 'Commercial Transactions' *(Buyū'),* ch. 3, h. 3331 (MDS: book 22).

57. Bukhari, book 34: 'Sales and Trade', ch. 15, h. 2072.

58. Bukhari, book 37: 'Hiring (or Employment)', ch. 14, ch. heading.

59. Bukhari, book 34: 'Sales and Trade', ch. 106, h. 2227.

60. Bukhari, book 93: 'Judgments', ch. 17, h. 7163.

61. Tirmidhi, book 14: 'Business' *(Buyū'),* ch. 4, h. 1209 (MDS: book 12).

62. Bukhari, book 34: 'Sales and Trade', ch. 16, h. 2076.

63. *Ibid.*, ch. 19, h. 2079.

64. Bukhari, book 41: 'Agriculture', ch. 1, h. 2320.

65. *Ibid.*, ch. 15, h. 2335.

66. Mishkat, book 12: 'Trading', ch. 13, sec. 1, h. 2846 (v. 2, p. 48).

67. Bukhari, book 41: 'Agriculture', ch. 8, h. 2328, ch. 11, h. 2331, and ch. 19, h. 2346–2347.

68. *Ibid.*, ch. 2, h. 2321.

18. Food, drink and cleanliness

Islam promotes cleanliness

In addition to rules and regulations for the perfection of self and for the better relations of man with man, there are certain restrictive regulations of a general nature the object of which is to teach people the ways of clean living. These regulations relate to foods, drinks, dress and a number of other things, and have both a physical and a moral value. It is a recognized fact that the food which a person eats, or even his clothing, affects not only his constitution but also the building up of his character, and hence in a complete code of life it was necessary that people should be taught ways of clean eating, clean drinking, clean dressing, clean appearance and clean habits of all kinds. These regulations are sometimes obligatory but very often of a recommendatory nature.

General rules regarding food

The first general rule regarding foods, and which applies to drink as well, is laid down in the following words in the Holy Quran:

> "O people, eat the lawful and good things from what is in the earth, and do not follow the footsteps of the devil. Surely he is an open enemy to you." — 2:168

The Arabic word for lawful is *ḥalāl,* and that for good things is *ṭayyib.* The first condition therefore is that the food and drink made use of should be lawful. Lawful things are not only those which the law has not declared to be forbidden, but even unforbidden things become unlawful if they are acquired unlawfully, for example, by theft, cheating, bribery, etc. The other condition is that it should be *ṭayyib* or "good". The word *ṭayyib* carries the significance of pleasant, delightful, delicious or sweet, and pure or clean.[1] An impure or unclean thing or a thing which offends good taste should, therefore, not be used as an eatable. The same rule applies to drinks.

By adding the injunction "do not follow the footsteps of the devil", the real object of the prohibition is made clear. The Quran recognizes some sort of relation between the physical and the spiritual conditions of man, and there is not the least doubt that food plays an important part in the formation of character.

Moderation recommended

The above rule, to avoid unlawful and unclean things, is supplemented by two other equally important directions of a general nature. The first is an interdiction against excess:

> "...and eat and drink and do not be extravagant; surely He does not love the extravagant." — 7:31

Immoderation may either be in the taking of diet, when one overloads the stomach with food,[2] or it may be in the taking of particular kinds of food. Any food, however good, is injurious to health if taken in excess. Moderation in eating is a guarantee of health. And just as overfeeding spoils the system, underfeeding undermines health. Hence the direction is given:

> "O you who believe, do not forbid the good things which Allah has made lawful for you, nor exceed the limits." — 5:87

In these words, all self-denying practices, by which a person either deprives himself of the necessary quantity of food, or of certain kinds of food, are denounced. Good things which are helpful in building up the system should not be denied.

Prohibited foods

Four things are expressly prohibited in the Holy Quran:

> "O you who believe, eat of the good things that We have provided you with, and give thanks to Allah if He it is Whom you serve. He has forbidden you only what dies of itself, and blood, and the flesh of swine, and that on which any other name than that of Allah has been invoked. Then whoever is driven by necessity, not desiring, nor exceeding the limit, no sin is upon him. Surely Allah is Forgiving, Merciful." — 2:172–173

The same prohibition had already been revealed in 16:115, while the Holy Prophet was yet at Makkah, in nearly the same words, whereas in 6:145, another Makkah revelation, reasons are added for the prohibition, and 5:3, which is the latest revelation on the point, adds several things by way of explanation.

The prohibited foods thus are:

1.   That which dies of itself. According to 5:3, the following are included:

> "the strangled (animal), and that beaten to death, and that killed by a fall, and that killed by goring with the horn, and what wild beasts have eaten".

The flesh is prohibited, but the skin may be used. The Holy Prophet saw a dead goat of which the skin had not been removed and said that what was unlawful thereof was the flesh, and that there was no harm in profiting by its skin.[3] From this may be concluded that other parts, such as bones, may also be made use of. "That which died of itself and that which was torn by beasts" were forbidden by the law of Moses also.[4]

2.   Blood, explained as "blood poured forth" in 6:145. This was also forbidden by the law of Moses.[5]

3.   Flesh of swine. This was also forbidden by the law of Moses.[6] Jesus Christ, like a true Jew, seems to have held the swine in abhorrence:

> "nor cast your pearls before swine".[7]

He is also reported to have cast out a number of unclean spirits which he then allowed to go into a herd of swine, causing it to perish thereby.[8] This shows that he looked upon the animal as unclean. St. Peter compares sinners who relapse into evil to swine who go again to wallow in the mire after they are washed.[9]

4.   The fourth kind of forbidden food is that over which any other name than that of Allah has been invoked at the time of slaughtering it. In 5:3 "what is sacrificed on stones set up [for idols]" is added, and it evidently comes under this description.

The Quran, in 6:145, speaks of the first three forbidden foods, carrion, blood and pork, as *rijs* or unclean things, while the fourth, the invocation of other than Allah's name at the time of slaughtering an animal, is called *fisq* or a transgression of the Divine commandment. The reason for this distinction is that there is uncleanness in the case of first three, since they have a pernicious effect upon the intellectual, the physical or the moral system; while in the fourth case, the spiritual side is affected, as the invocation of other than Allah's name, or sacrificing for idols, associates one with idolatry. In this case the thing is not unclean in itself, like blood or carrion or pork; it is forbidden because the use of such food associates the eater of it with idolatry.

Slaughtering of an animal

According to the law of Islam, all animals that are allowed as food must be slaughtered in such a manner that blood flows out. Four veins are cut off in slaughtering an animal: the windpipe, the oesophagus and the two external jugular veins.[10] The idea underlying this particular manner of slaughter is causing the blood to flow so that the poisons contained in it should not form part of food. The same appears to be the reason for prohibition of blood as food. Fish or other watergame does not require to be slaughtered, and it is allowed irrespective of who has caught it, Muslim or non-Muslim; so also fish which has been thrown out by the sea or river on dry land or which has been left by the water having receded from it, and which has therefore died before it is caught, provided it is not spoiled.[11]

Invoking the name of God on slaughtered animal

It should be further noted that, when an animal is slaughtered, it is necessary that the name of God should be invoked. The Holy Quran lays down plainly:

> "And do not eat of that on which Allah's name has not been mentioned, and that is surely a transgression." — 6: 121

Hence it is necessary that, at the time of slaughtering an animal, the following words should be pronounced: *Bismillāh, Allāhu Akbar* — "In the name of Allah, Allah is the Greatest of all".[12] This practice is traceable to the Holy Prophet. If the man who slaughters the animal forgets to pronounce these words, the flesh of the animal is allowed,[13] but if he omits the words intentionally, there is a difference of opinion. Imam Shafi'i allows it even in this case against the Hanafi view.[14] In slaughtering an animal, any sharp instrument may be used which causes the blood to flow, and the flesh of an animal which was slaughtered by a maid with a stone was allowed.[15]

Thus it is allowed to Muslims to slaughter animals for food, but the condition is here laid down that Allah's name must be mentioned when the animal is slaughtered. There is no doubt that the taking of a life, even though it be the life of an animal, bespeaks a kind of disregard for life, and it is allowed by God, only because the full physical development of man requires the use of the flesh of animals. Mentioning Allah's name at the time of slaughter is a reminder that this act is made lawful only by Divine permission, for the attainment of a necessary purpose. The order is based on moral grounds, and as a safeguard against the development of habits of disregard for human life itself, which is a sad aspect of the development of the material civilization of our day.[16]

The food of the followers of the Book (*Ahl al-Kitāb*)[17] is express-ly allowed in the Quran:

> "And the food of those who have been given the Book is lawful for you, and your food is lawful for them." — 5:5

A Muslim may therefore invite the followers of the Book to his own table and he may eat at their table. But Hadith makes it further clear that the animal slaughtered by the followers of the Book is allowed in this verse. The condition is added that, if the slaughterer is heard uttering a name other than that of God, the flesh is not to be eaten, but if he is not so heard then it is lawful for Muslims to eat it.[18] As stated elsewhere, the words *Ahl al-Kitāb* are applicable to followers of all revealed religions, including the Magi, the Hindus, etc. A certain food (cheese) prepared by the Magi was allowed by the Holy Prophet, though he was told that in its preparation use had been made of what died of itself; and he only said: "Mention the name of Allah over it".[19]

The heading of one of Bukhari's chapters is "Animals slaugh-tered by desert Arabs" (*dhabīḥat al-A'rāb*), and under this is men-tioned a hadith from Aishah according to which certain people came to the Holy Prophet and enquired of him about meat which was brought to them by other people, about which they did not know whether the name of God had been mentioned over it or not. The Holy Prophet's reply was:

> "Mention the name of Allah over it and eat it." [20]

This gives a wide latitude in doubtful and difficult cases where a Muslim must depend on food provided or prepared by other people.

Humane treatment of animals[21]

The Holy Prophet had a tender heart which overflowed with mercy even for animals. It is related that he passed by a camel that had grown extremely lean, so he gave the instruction:

> "Be careful of your duty to Allah regarding these dumb animals; ride them while they are in a fit condition, and eat them while they are in a fit condition." [22]

The Holy Prophet also said:

> "Whoever tills a field and birds and beasts eat of it, it is a charity." [23]

He spoke of a man who drew water from a well to quench the thirst of a dog as performing a good deed:

> "The Messenger of Allah said: 'While a man was walking he was overcome by thirst, so he went down a well and drank water from it. On coming out of it, he saw a dog panting and eating mud because of excessive thirst. The man said, This [dog] is afflicted by the same which afflicted me. So he [went down the well,] filled his shoe with water, caught hold of it with his teeth and climbed up and watered the dog. Allah thanked him for his deed and forgave him.'
>
> People asked: 'O Messenger of Allah, Is there a reward for us in serving the animals?' He replied: 'In every animal having a liver fresh with life, there is a reward'." [24]

According to Hadith, the Holy Prophet is said to have "forbidden the shooting of arrows at tied or confined animals" and to have cursed those people who did so. He also cursed the one who cuts off the limbs of a living animal.[25]

Game

The Holy Quran expressly allows game:

> "The good things are allowed to you, and what you have taught the beasts and birds of prey, training them to hunt — you teach them of what Allah has taught you; so eat of what they catch for you and mention the name of Allah over it."
> — 5:4

Hadith makes it clear that the name of Allah is to be mentioned when letting off the beast or bird of prey.[26] The animal caught may be eaten even though it is killed by the beast or bird of prey.[27] The killing of game by throwing pebbles and hazel-nuts is, however, forbidden.[28] Killing it by arrow is allowed,[29] since the arrow causes the blood to flow. Game shot with a gun must follow the same rule, but in both cases the *Bismillāh* must be uttered before letting off the arrow or firing the gun, and if the game is killed before it is caught and slaughtered, there is no harm. As regards the game of sea or water, it is all considered as slaughtered.[30]

Prohibitions in Hadith and Jurisprudence

According to Hadith, the Holy Prophet prohibited all beasts of prey with a canine tooth[31] and all birds of prey with a claw.[32] The tame ass is also prohibited,[33] but not the wild ass which is allowed,[34] the mule is prohibited but not the horse.[35] Other things are mentioned as not prohibited by the Holy Prophet but he did not eat them. To the prohibitions mentioned in Hadith, jurisprudence (*Fiqh*) adds several more, for example, foxes, elephants, wasps and all insects.[36]

As shown earlier, among things which are allowed much depends on personal likes and dislikes; a thing which may be good (*tayyib*) as food for one individual or one people may not be so for another. Certain things may be good and even useful as food, but their use might be offensive to others; it was due to this that the Prophet said that whoever ate raw onions and garlic, he should not approach the mosque,[37] because the odour would be offensive to others; but there is no harm in taking them in a cooked form,[38] or in some other form in which it may not give an offensive odour, or on occasions when one is not likely to appear in public.

Good manners in eating

It is recommended that hands should be washed before the taking of food and after finishing it,[39] and that when you begin a meal, you should do so with the pronouncement of *Bismillāh,* and that when you finish it you should give thanks to God or say *al-ḥamdu li-llāh.*[40] It was the Holy Prophet's practice to cleanse the mouth with water after taking food.[41] There is also a direction to eat with the right hand.[42] To blow on food or drink is prohibited.[43] Taking of food when in a reclining posture is not recommended,[44] nor eating and drinking while standing,[45] but Ali reported that he had seen the Holy Prophet drinking water while standing.[46] It is also regarded as good manners in eating that you should take only so much in your plate as not to leave anything on it after eating,[47] and that you should take a morsel from what lies near your hand.[48]

Of the Holy Prophet it is related that he would never find fault with the food which he was offered; if he liked it he would eat of it, and if he disliked it he would leave it.[49] Feeding the hungry when one sits at a meal is also regarded as good manners in eating.[50] Eating and drinking in vessels of silver and gold was prohibited,[51] because it is a luxury enjoyed by the rich at the expense of the poor, and is against the democratic spirit of Islam.

Entertainments

For fostering good relations it is recommended that one should have no hesitation in eating at the house of relatives or friends:

> "There is no blame on the blind man, nor any blame on the lame, nor blame on the sick, nor on yourselves that you eat in your own houses, or your fathers' houses, or your mothers' houses, or your brothers' houses, or your sisters' houses, or your paternal uncles' houses, or your paternal aunts' houses, or your maternal uncles' houses, or your maternal aunts' houses, or houses of which you possess the keys, or your friends' houses. It is no sin in you that you eat together or separately." — 24:61

The Arabs had their scruples in eating with the blind, etc., and in this respect they were like many other nations. This verse first removes any such distinction as to whom one may eat with. Then the reference to near relatives and close friends apparently shows that a certain degree of familiarity with them is recommended so that one may eat at another's house if the time has arrived for a meal, though he may not have been invited beforehand. Lastly, the verse speaks of eating together or separately as one likes. Islam thus allows the individual a great latitude in this respect.

Stress is laid on the acceptance of an invitation to a feast:

> "The Prophet said, When a person is invited and he does not accept [or reply], he disobeys Allah and His Messenger." [52]

Entertainment of guests is also emphasized.[53] It is stated that when the Holy Prophet came to Madinah, he sacrificed a camel or a cow to feast his friends;[54] from this it is concluded that when a person comes home from a journey, he should entertain his friends at meals. Inviting the followers of other religions, and accepting their invitation, is expressly spoken of in the Holy Quran:

> "And the food of those who have been given the Book is lawful for you and your food is lawful for them." — 5:5

Hadith recommends social functions in which people should eat together: "Gather together at your meals and mention Allah's name on it, you will be blessed therein".[55] The levelling influence of Islam asserts itself even in eating, and it is recommended that a servant may be seated at the same table as his master, or at least he should be given a part of the food which the master eats.[56] Islam therefore allows no distinction between superiors and subordinates in sitting at the same table at meals, as in standing in the same row at prayers. In its physical as well as spiritual aspects, it is essentially the religion of equality.

Drinks — intoxicating liquors

The drink prohibited in the Holy Quran is described under the name *khamr*. This word indicates veiling, covering or concealing, and intoxicating drink is called *khamr* because it veils the intellect. This word has a common application to intoxicating expressed juice of anything, or any intoxicating thing that clouds or obscures the intellect: "The general application is the more correct, because *khamr* was forbidden when there was not in Madinah any *khamr* of grapes, the beverage of its inhabitants being prepared only from dates... it is sometimes prepared from grains".[57] The wider sense of *khamr*, as prepared from other things besides grapes, is borne out by the Quran as quoted in the next paragraph. According to Umar, when wine was prohibited, it was made of five things: grapes, dates, wheat, barley and honey.[58] Hence *khamr* is intoxicating liquor prepared from anything.

Intoxicating liquors are first spoken of in deprecatory terms towards the close of the Makkah period:

> "And of the fruits of the palms and the grapes, you obtain from them intoxicants and goodly provision." — 16:67

Intoxicants are here spoken of in contrast to goodly provision. The prohibition against their use, however, belongs to the Madinah period and the earliest revelation on this point is that contained in the first long chapter revealed at Madinah:

> "They ask you [O Prophet] about intoxicants and games of chance. Say: In both of them is a great sin and some advantage for people, and their sin is greater than their advantage." — 2:219

This was the first stage in the prohibition of wine, but it was more of a recommendatory nature as it only says that the disadvantages of the use of intoxicating liquors preponderate over their advantages. The next stage was that in which Muslims were prohibited from coming to mosques while intoxicated:

> "O you who believe, do not go near prayer when you are intoxicated till you know what you say..." — 4:43

Finally, intoxicating liquors were definitely forbidden:

> "O you who believe, intoxicants and games of chance ... are only an uncleanness, the devil's work; so shun it that you may succeed." — 5:90

These three stages of the prohibition of wine are clearly mentioned in a hadith.[59] On the last of these occasions, a proclamation was made by command of the Holy Prophet that wine was prohibited, and people who heard the proclamation emptied their stores of wine immediately, so that wine flowed in the streets of Madinah.[60]

As wine is prohibited on account of its intoxication, it is stated in a hadith that every intoxicant is prohibited.[61] Herbs and drugs taken for intoxication and all other intoxicating things are therefore also forbidden; only a drink that does not intoxicate is allowed. It is further related that a man invited the Holy Prophet to a wedding feast at which his wife, the bride herself, served food, and at this feast a beverage of dried dates, over which only one night had passed, was used and there was no objection,[62] because it had not become intoxicant. Malik ibn Anas was asked about *fuqqā‘,* a beverage made of barley or a kind of beer,[63] and he said: "So long as it does not intoxicate there is no harm".[64] *Nabīdh,* or fresh juice of grapes over which not more than a night or a day had passed, is also allowed. Thus certain people are spoken of as having come to the Holy Prophet and asked him what to do with their grapes, and he told them to dry them and then make use of their juice in the evening if they were wet in the morning, and in the morning if they were wet in the evening.[65] But when a beverage becomes intoxicant, even a small quantity of it, that could not intoxicate, is not allowed:

> "That of which a large quantity intoxicates, even a small quantity of it is prohibited." [66]

The question whether a very small quantity may be given as a medicine is quite different. It is true that there is a hadith according to which a man, Tariq ibn Suwaid, was ordered by the Holy Prophet not to make wine, and when he said that he made it to be used as a medicine, the Holy Prophet replied that it was not a medicine but a disease.[67] But this prohibition was, in all likelihood, directed only against the making of wine; and as Nawawi, the famous commentator of *Muslim,* explains, in a serious case when life was in danger, wine could be used to save life, for even carrion and flesh of swine could be used in such a case.

It may be added here that trading in wine was also prohibited by the Holy Prophet,[68] and indeed it was necessary to prohibit both the preparing of wine and trading in it when the use of it was no longer permitted.

Cleanliness recommended

The Holy Quran lays down a general rule on toilet as follows:

> "Say: Who has forbidden the adornment (*zīnat*) of Allah, which He has brought forth for His servants, and the good provisions?" — 7:32

The word *zīnat,* in this verse, has generally been understood to mean apparel, but it has really a wider significance including both the dress and make-up of a person. *Zīnat* has further been explained as including spiritual adornment, such as knowledge and good beliefs;

bodily adornment, such as strength and tallness of stature; and extrinsic adornment such as wealth and dignity.[69] A good toilette is recommended even when going to a mosque:

> "O children of Adam, Attend to your adornment at every time of prayer…" — 7:31

The Quran lays the greatest stress on cleanliness, and literally gives it a place next to godliness when it says in one of the earliest revelations addressing the Holy Prophet:

> "O you who wrap yourself up! Arise and warn, and your Lord do magnify, and your garments do purify, and uncleanness do shun." — 74:1–5

Great stress is laid on outward as well as on inward purity throughout the Quran.

Clothing

No limitations are placed upon the form or quality of clothing, either in the Holy Quran or Hadith. The Holy Prophet is reported to have said:

> "Eat and drink and wear clothes and be charitable, not being extravagant or self-conceited."

Ibn Abbas said:

> "Eat what you like and wear what you like, so long as you avoid two things: extravagance and vanity." [70]

Thus Islam requires no particular dress. A person may choose what he eats and what he wears. Anything which may serve as a covering for the body is allowed, the only requirement being that the clothes should be clean and good.[71] The parts of the body which it is necessary to cover are, in a man, what is between the navel and the knee, and in a woman, all the person except the face and the hands as far as the wrists.[72] Silk is forbidden to men[73] but women are permitted to wear it,[74] which shows that silk is not discarded for men on account of any impurity attaching to it, but because the wearing of it is not in consonance with the hard life which men have to lead to earn their living, and also because it is a luxury, and the money thus wasted would be better spent on the amelioration of the condition of the poor. In some cases even men were allowed to wear silk. Thus, the wearing of silk was allowed to Abdur Rahman and Zubair (two Companions of the Holy Prophet) on account of itching.[75] Those who wear long garments or trail the train of the garment, in order to be looked at or for vanity, are censured.[76]

Notes to Chapter 18

1. Lane's Lexicon.

2. *Editor's note:* Eating comparatively less has been described by the Holy Prophet as a sign distinguishing a believer from an unbeliever: "A believer eats in one intestine and an unbeliever eats in seven intestines" (Bukhari, book 70: 'Food', ch. 12, h. 5393–5397). In the Holy Prophet's household, there were never three days in succession when they ate to the full on all of them (*ibid.,* ch. 1, h. 5374).

3. Bukhari, book 72: 'Slaughtering and Hunting', ch. 30, h. 5531–5532.

4. Leviticus, 17:15.

5. *Ibid.,* 7:26.

6. *Ibid.,* 11:7.

7. Matthew, 7:6.

8. Matthew, 8:30–32. Mark, 5:11–13.

9. 2 Peter, 2:22.

10. Hidayah, v. 2, p. 421.

11. See Bukhari, book 72: 'Slaughtering and Hunting', ch. 12, heading. Note also that the Quran says: "Lawful to you is the game of the sea and its food" (5:96). According to Hadith reports in this reference, the "food" of the sea, as distinguished from its game, means fish thrown out on dry land or found after the water has receded, provided it is not spoiled.

12. Bukhari, book 72: 'Slaughtering and Hunting', ch. 17, h. 5500; *Musnad* of Ahmad ibn Hanbal, v. 3, pp. 115, 183. Imam Ahmad speaks of both saying *Bismillāh* and *Allāhu Akbar,* while Bukhari speaks only of mentioning the name of Allah, which in fact includes both.

13. Bukhari, book 72: 'Slaughtering and Hunting', ch. 15, ch. heading.

14. Hidayah, v. 2, p. 419.

15. Bukhari, book 72: 'Slaughtering and Hunting', ch. 18, h. 5501–5503.

16. *Editor's Note:* This paragraph has been added from the author's English translation of the Quran with commentary, footnote under 6:118.

17. *Editor's Note:* "Followers of the Book" (*ahl al-kitāb*) refers to followers of earlier religions based on revealed scriptures. It is applied principally to Jews and Christians, but by extension includes followers of other revealed religions as well.

18. Bukhari, book 72: 'Slaughtering and Hunting', ch. 22, ch. heading.

19. *Musnad* of Ahmad ibn Hanbal, v. 1, p. 302.

20. Bukhari, book 72: 'Slaughtering and Hunting', ch. 21, h. 5507.

21. *Editor's Note:* This topic has been added from other English writings of Maulana Muhammad Ali.

22. Abu Dawud, book 15: '*Jihād*', ch. 47, h. 2548 (MDS: ch. 44).

23. *Musnad* of Ahmad ibn Hanbal, v. 4, p. 55.

24. Bukhari, book 42: 'Distribution of Water', ch. 9, h. 2363.

Editor's Note: In the next two Hadith reports, the Holy Prophet relates that he was shown hell in a vision, and he saw in it a woman being punished because she kept a cat locked up till it died of hunger. According to the second of the two reports, it was said to the woman (in the vision): "You neither fed it nor gave it water when you tied it up, nor did you set it free to eat insects from the earth" (h. 2365). Thus, just as there is reward from God for those who are kind to animals, there is punishment from God for torturing and afflicting distress on animals.

25. Bukhari, book 72: 'Slaughtering and Hunting', ch. 25, h. 5513–5516.

26. *Ibid.,* ch. 2, h. 5476.

27. *Ibid.,* ch. 3, h. 5477.

28. *Ibid.,* ch. 5, h. 5479.

29. *Ibid.,* ch. 8, h. 5484.

30. *Ibid.,* ch. 12, h. 5493–5494, and ch. heading.

31. *Ibid.,* ch. 29, h. 5530.

32. Abu Dawud, book 28: 'Food', ch. 33, h. 3802–3806 (MDS: book 26, ch. 32).

33. Bukhari, book 56: '*Jihād*', ch. 130, h. 2991.

34. Bukhari, book 28: 'Penalty of hunting on Pilgrimage', ch. 3, h. 1822.

35. Abu Dawud, book 28: 'Food', ch. 26, h. 3788–3790 (MDS: book 26, ch. 25).

36. Hidayah, v. 2, p. 424.

37. Bukhari, book 10: 'Call to Prayer', ch. 160, h. 853–855.

38. Tirmidhi, book 25: 'Food', ch. 14, h. 1808–1809 (MDS: book 23).

39. Abu Dawud, book 28: 'Food', ch. 12, h. 3761 (MDS: book 26, unnumbered ch. between ch. 11 and ch. 12).

40. Bukhari, book 70: 'Food', ch. 2, h. 5376, and ch. 54, h. 5458–5459.

41. *Ibid.,* ch. 51, h. 5454–5455.

42. *Ibid.,* ch. 2, h. 5376.

43. Bukhari, book 74: 'Drinks', ch. 25, h. 5630. *Musnad* of Ahmad ibn Hanbal, v. 1, p. 309, 357.

44. Bukhari, book 70: 'Food', ch. 13, h. 5398–5399.

45. *Musnad* of Ahmad ibn Hanbal, v. 3, p. 199.

46. Bukhari, book 74: 'Drinks', ch. 16, h. 5615–5616; see also h. 5617.

47. *Musnad* of Ahmad ibn Hanbal, v. 3, p. 177.

48. Bukhari, book 70: 'Food', ch. 3, h. 5377–5378.

49. *Ibid.,* ch. 21, h. 5409.

50. *Ibid.,* ch. 1, h. 5373, ch. 11, h. 5392.

51. *Ibid.,* ch. 29, h. 5426; book 74: 'Drinks', chs. 27–28, h. 5632–5635.

52. Abu Dawud, book 28: 'Food', ch. 1, h. 3742 (MDS: book 26). See also h. 3736–3741.

53. *Ibid.,* ch. 5, h. 3748 (MDS: book 26).

54. *Ibid.,* ch. 4, h. 3747 (MDS: book 26).

55. *Ibid.,* ch. 15, h. 3764 (MDS: book 26, ch. 14).

56. Bukhari, book 70: 'Food', ch. 55, h. 5460.

57. Lane's Lexicon.

58. Bukhari, book 74: 'Drinks', ch. 5, h. 5588–5589.

59. *Musnad* of Ahmad ibn Hanbal, v. 2, p. 351.

60. Bukhari, book 46: 'Oppression', ch. 21, h. 2464; book 74: 'Drinks', ch. 3, h. 5582–5583.

61. Bukhari, book 64: 'Military Expeditions', ch. 60, h. 4343–4344; book 74: 'Drinks', ch. 4, h. 5585–5586.

62. Bukhari, book 74: 'Drinks', ch. 9, h. 5597.

63. Lane's Lexicon.

64. Bukhari, book 74: 'Drinks', ch. 4, ch. heading.

65. Abu Dawud, book 27: 'Drinks', ch. 10, h. 3710–3712 (MDS: book 25).

66. *Ibid.,* ch. 5, h. 3681 (MDS: book 25), see also h. 3687.

67. Muslim, book 36: 'Drinks', ch. 3, h. 1984 (MDS: h. 5141).

68. Bukhari, book 34: 'Sales and Trade', ch. 24, h. 2084.

69. Raghib's *Mufradāt.*

70. Bukhari, book 77: 'Dress', ch. 1, ch. heading.

71. Abu Dawud, book 34: 'Dress', ch. 16, h. 4062–4063 (MDS: book 31, ch. 14).

72. *Tāj al-'Arūs* (Dictionary) under the word *'aura.*

73. Bukhari, book 77: 'Dress', ch. 12, h. 5801; ch. 25, h. 5828–5835; ch. 36, h. 5849.

74. *Ibid.,* ch. 30, h. 5840, h. 5842.

75. *Ibid.,* ch. 29, h. 5839.

76. *Ibid.,* ch. 5, h. 5788, h. 5791.

Editor's Note: In the same book of Bukhari (book 77), in ch. 2, h. 5784, it is reported that when the Holy Prophet said that, on the day of Resurrection, Allah would not care to look upon the man who trails his garment behind him out of conceit, Abu Bakr expressed the anxiety that his garment tended to hang low on one side unless he took special care of it. The Holy Prophet replied: "You are not one of those who do it out of conceit". Therefore it is not the long length of a garment which is condemned but the intention by the wearer to show superior status by means of it. According to the next hadith (h. 5785), on the occasion of a solar eclipse when the Holy Prophet hurried to the mosque for the eclipse prayer, he was trailing his garment because of his hurry.

19. The State and Penal Laws

Section 1: The State

Modern conceptions of the state

All modern conceptions of the state have one thing in common: material benefits have so obsessed the views of the civilized world that God and religion have been relegated to the corner of oblivion and the higher values of life are utterly neglected. Modern states are at one in worshipping the two new gods which Western civilization has created in place of the One God Whom it has dismissed as a thing of the past. The Nation and the State are the new idols before which the civilized man has fallen prostrate. And along with the old god Mammon, a new Trinity has emerged in place of the Trinity of the Church. The gain of economic advantages or the acquisition of wealth being the sole consideration of the civilized man, he is prepared to make any sacrifice that is required of him to gain this end, in the name of the State and for the love of the Nation. Wealth, Nation and State have thus the highest place of honour in the heart of the civilized man and he worships these idols. The desire to bow is there in human nature, and if people will not bow before their Maker, they must bow before things of their own making. Objects unworthy of worship have, however, always led humanity to ruin, and the worship of Mammon and its two associates, the Nation and the State, is even now leading civilization to sure destruction.

Every state must necessarily be invested with power, with which it may stop aggression and protect the weak, dealing out fair justice to all. The advance of science has increased this power a thousand-fold. On the other hand, materialistic outlook on life has made man more unscrupulous in the use of his power against fellow man, and with advancement in the conquest of nature, the conquest of self, which alone serves as a check on the tyranny of man against man, has been retarded and thrown to the background. The result is that the increased powers of the state, which must necessarily be exercised through individuals, are being used more for the enslavement and destruction of man than for his deliverance from tyranny and upholding the cause of truth and justice.

Islamic conception of the state

It is to remedy this evil that Islam requires the vesting of state authority in the hands of men who are God-fearing before all. The state which the Holy Prophet Muhammad founded was invested with physical force, as every state must necessarily be, but it was a unique service which he rendered to humanity that he spiritualized the greatest of all human physical forces. The head of the state in Islam is called both an *Amīr,* meaning 'one who commands', and an *Imām,* meaning 'a person whose example is followed', i.e., a person who stands on a very high moral plane. On his deathbed the Holy Prophet gave an indication as to who should succeed him as the head of the Muslim state by appointing Abu Bakr, admittedly the fittest man, to lead prayers in his absence. For a long time this practice was continued, and the head of the state led the prayers.

Righteousness — fear of God and regard for other people's rights — was as necessary a qualification for the ruler as fitness to rule. Spiritual force alone could enable a man to control the powers which temporal authority gives him and which, in the absence of such force, are often in danger of being abused. The head of the state considered himself responsible to God, in the first place, for the exercise of his temporal authority.

The foundations of the state laid down by the Holy Prophet were thus spiritual. They were at the same time democratic in the truest sense of the word. There exists a misconception in some quarters that the Islamic state was a theocracy. The head of the Muslim state never considered himself a representative of God on earth but as a representative of people who had chosen him to serve them; nonetheless, he certainly considered himself responsible to God for every act that he did in the exercise of his authority. All people, including the ruler, had equal rights and obligations and were subject to the same law. The Holy Prophet himself did not claim any rights beyond those which other Muslims had. In the actual working of the state organization, of which he was the founder and the head, there was nothing to distinguish him from the others. Outsiders came and asked: which of you is Muhammad? He lived in the simplest possible manner, and never claimed any superiority on account of his being a ruler. When his soldiers were digging a ditch for the defence of Madinah, he was there with his pick-axe, and when they were removing heaps of dust and stones, he was one of the labourers who were covered with dust. If ever there was a democracy free from all differences of heredity, rank or privilege, it was the democratic state of which foundations were laid by the Prophet Muhammad.

Perhaps history cannot show a greater conqueror than Umar, the second successor of the Holy Prophet, a conqueror and an administrator at one and the same time. Yet he would not stop even his lowest subjects from rebuking him in public. It is reported that an ordinary citizen once interrupted him repeatedly. "Fear God, O Umar!" said the man; and when others wanted to stop him, Umar himself intervened, saying: "Let him say so; of what use are these people if they do not tell me such things?" This monarch of four kingdoms visited a famine-stricken camp at night incognito, and finding a woman with no food to give to her children, he rushed back to Madinah, a distance of three miles, and took a sack of flour on his back to feed the distressed woman and her children. When a servant offered his services to carry the load, he said: "In this life you might carry my burden, but who will carry my burden on the day of Judgment?" Yet when this great servant of the people was lying on his death-bed and a young man lauded his great services, he said: "Enough, young fellow! It is sufficient if the evil I may have done in the exercise of authority is neutralised by any good that I have done".[1] It is such a mental attitude alone which can make men fit for ruling their fellow beings. But such a mentality is created only by a strong faith in God and a feeling of one's responsibility to God.

It was such a responsible government that Islam created, a government by those who realised that above all other things they were responsible to God for everything they did. The ones to be honoured — and entrusting someone with command was certainly doing him honour — were those who paid the greatest regard to their duties. It was such people that were to be placed in authority over others, as the Holy Quran says:

> "Allah commands you to make over [positions of] trust to those worthy of them." — 4:58

In a state, some people have necessarily to be placed in authority over others, but those placed in authority have been repeatedly warned that they would be answerable to God, first of all, for what they did in the exercise of authority. The warning to the prophet-king David is a warning to every true believer:

> "O David, surely We have made you a ruler in the land; so judge between people justly and do not follow [your low] desire that it should lead you astray from the path of Allah. Those who go astray from the path of Allah, for them is surely a severe punishment because they forgot the day of Reckoning." — 38:26

Everyone who was entrusted with any authority was told that he was a ruler in his own sphere and that he was responsible to God for those placed under his trust:

> "Everyone of you is a ruler and everyone shall be questioned about his subjects. The king is a ruler and he shall be questioned about his subjects, and the man is a ruler over the people of his house and he shall be questioned about those under his care, and the woman is a ruler over the house of her husband and she shall be questioned about those under her care, and the servant is a ruler so far as the property of the master is concerned and he shall be questioned about that which is entrusted to him." [2]

The ruler or head of the state is, thus, along with all those persons who hold any authority over others, placed in the same category as a servant. Just as a servant is entrusted with a certain property for which he is responsible to his master, those entrusted with authority of the state, in whatever position they may be, are entrusted with the care of the people and guarding their rights, and for the proper discharge of their duties they are responsible, in the first place, to the Real Master, Who is God, and then to the people who have entrusted him with this charge. The first necessity of a good state organization is this mentality on the part of each one of its members, and the greatest stress is, therefore, laid on this in the Islamic concept of state.

Principle of counsel

The Holy Quran and Hadith, as quoted above, also show that hereditary kingship is foreign to the concept of the state in Islam. Nor is the

Islamic state an autocracy, as uncontrolled authority is not vested in the head of the state. It has already been stated that the law was one for all, and all were one in the eye of the law including the man entrusted with the highest command, and including the Holy Prophet himself who was as much subject to the law as any of his followers. It is stated in the Quran:

> "And when Our clear messages are recited to them, those who have no hope of meeting with Us say: Bring a Quran other than this or change it. Say: It is not for me to change it of my own accord. I follow only what is revealed to me. Indeed I fear, if I disobey my Lord, the punishment of a terrible day." — 10:15

Speaking of the most prominent qualities of Muslims, the Quran mentions an equally prominent quality: "And whose affairs are [decided] by counsel among themselves" (42:38). The chapter in which this verse occurs is entitled *Shūrā* or *Counsel* on account of the great democratic principle of counsel laid down here as the basis of the future state of Islam. This is one of the early revelations, when the Holy Prophet was still leading the life of a helpless and persecuted reformer, and shows how the two ideas of democratizing and spiritualizing the state were blended:

> "And those who respond to their Lord and keep up prayer, and whose affairs are [decided] by counsel among themselves and who spend out of what We have given them." — 42:38

The verse gives prominence to the great acts which are needed to spiritualize man, answering the call of God, praying to God and devoting oneself to the service of humanity, while laying down the principle for conducting the affairs of state. In this verse, Muslims are enjoined as usual to observe prayer and to spend out of what God has given them. Yet between these two injunctions, which always go together in the Quran and which are the basis of a true Islamic life, is placed a third: *And their affairs are decided by counsel among themselves.* This injunction at such an early period is clearly meant to prepare Muslims for transacting the momentous affairs of state and all matters connected with national weal or woe. In fact, the word *amr,* translated here as *affairs,* means 'command', and therefore refers to the Islamic state, the affairs of which must be transacted by counsel.

The verses that follow the above verse also show that the Holy Prophet wanted his followers to be trained on spiritual lines while preparing them for conducting the affairs of the state:

> "And those who, when great wrong afflicts them, defend themselves. And the recompense of evil is punishment like it; but whoever forgives and brings about reform, his reward is with Allah. Surely He does not love the wrongdoers. And whoever defends himself after his being oppressed, these it is against whom there is no way of blame. The way of blame is only against those who oppress people and revolt in the earth unjustly. For such there is a painful punishment. And whoever is patient and forgives — that surely is an affair of great resolution." — 42:39–42

These excellent rules for the defence of the Muslim community, which was being oppressed and persecuted at that time, and for the forgiveness of the enemy that was bent upon its extirpation, clearly show that the basis was herein being laid of the Muslim State, because forgiveness could only be exercised towards a vanquished enemy. It was in their sufferings that Muslims were being told to exercise forgiveness when their turn should come to take revenge upon a fallen enemy. The passion for revenge was thus being obliterated from their hearts from the very beginning and the physical force of the state was spiritualized by making it subject to moral considerations.

Position of the rulers

The Islamic State is a democracy in the truest sense of the word. The Quran tells Muslims:

> "Allah commands you to make over [positions of] trust to those worthy of them, and that when you judge between people, you judge with justice." — 4:58

The section of chapter 4 in which this verse appears deals with granting of kingdom to Muslims, who are here required to entrust the *affairs of state* to people who are worthy of this responsibility. The words that follow ("and that when you judge between people, you judge with justice") corroborate this significance of the word *amānāt* or "positions of trust". The whole verse states the reciprocal duties of the governed and the governors. The Holy Prophet himself has explained the word *amānat* (singular of *amānāt*) as meaning government or affairs of state. He said:

> "When the *amānat* is wasted, wait for the doom. It was said: How will the *amānat* be wasted, O Messenger of Allah? He said: When government (*amr*) is entrusted to those unworthy of it, then wait for the doom".[3]

The first successor to Holy Prophet was Abu Bakr, who was elected the head of the state by the agreement of all parties, and so were the three successors that followed him. When the news of the Holy Prophet's death spread, Muslims gathered together and freely discussed the question as to who should succeed him as the head of the state. The *Anṣār,* the residents of Madinah, were of the opinion that there should be two heads, one from among the Quraish and one from among themselves, but the error of this view was pointed out by Abu Bakr who made it clear in an eloquent speech that the state could have only one head.[4] And so Abu Bakr was elected, being as Umar stated, "the best" of them[5] and "the fittest of the Muslims to control their affairs".[6] Fitness to rule was the only criterion to decide the election, as indeed in the Quranic injunction: "Allah commands you to make over [positions of] trust to those worthy of them" (4:58).

Why the state organization was needed, and what the constitutional position of the head of the state was, was explained by Abu Bakr in his very first address:

> "You have elected me as <u>*Khalīfah,*</u> but I claim no superiority over you. The strongest among you shall be the weakest with me until I get the rights of others from him, and the weakest among you shall be the strongest with me until I get all his rights... Help me if I am in the right, and set me right if I am in the wrong... Obey me as long as I obey Allah and His Messenger; in case I disobey Allah and His Messenger, I have no right to obedience from you."

The head of the state was a servant of the state who was paid a fixed salary for maintenance out of the public treasury, like all other public servants. It was Abu Bakr, the very first successor of the Holy Prophet, who acted on this rule.[7] The head had no special privileges and in his private capacity he could be sued in the court like any other member of the community. The great Umar appeared as a defendant in the court of a judge. Some of the orders given by him to his provincial governors were that they should be accessible at all hours of the day to those who had a complaint to make and that they should not keep a door-keeper who should prohibit people from approaching them. And further that they should accustom themselves to lead hard lives. The head of state carried on the administration with the help of ministers, all important state affairs being decided by a council.

Those entrusted with the work of government, including the head, were required to work for the good of the people. The Holy Prophet is reported as saying:

> "There is no one whom Allah grants to rule people, then he does not manage their affairs for their good but he will not smell the sweet odour of paradise." [8]

They were required to be gentle to the people, as for example when the Holy Prophet appointed Abu Musa and Mu'adh ibn Jabal to govern over Yaman, he instructed them as follows:

> "Be gentle [to the people] and be not hard, and make them rejoice and do not incite them to aversion." [9]

According to Hadith, they were enjoined to lead simple lives and to be easily accessible to those who needed their services,[10] to be Godfearing,[11] to tax the different classes of people according to their capacity, to provide for those who could not earn and to have as much regard for the rights of non-Muslims as for those of Muslims.[12] The Holy Prophet did not introduce any compulsory taxation to fund the war that he was compelled to fight; people were required only to subscribe voluntarily if they felt the justice of the cause.

The state was not only required to maintain uncared-for families but also to pay the unpaid debts which were contracted for a lawful need. The Holy Prophet said:

> "Whoever leaves property, it is for his heirs; and whoever leaves a burden, it shall be our charge." [13]

"Burden" includes both a family to maintain and debts to be paid.

People's obligations

The people's responsibility to the state is to respect its laws and obey its orders as long as they do not involve disobedience to God and His

Messenger. After stating that "Allah commands you to make over [positions of] trust to those worthy of them", in the verse that follows the Quran says:

> "O you who believe, obey Allah and obey the Messenger and those in authority from among you; then if you quarrel about anything, refer it to Allah and the Messenger, if you believe in Allah and the Last Day. This is best and more suitable to achieve the end." — 4:59

This verse lays down three important rules of guidance in matters relating to the welfare of the Muslim community, especially in those relating to affairs of state. These are obedience to God and His Messenger in the first place; secondly, obedience to those in authority from among the Muslims; and thirdly, referring matters to God and His Messenger in cases of dispute with those in authority. God and His Messenger are thus the final authority. The words "those in authority" have a wide significance, so that in different matters relating to the life of man different persons would be in authority.

The first successor of the Holy Prophet, Abu Bakr, in his first address to those who had sworn allegiance to him, said, as already quoted: "Help me if I am in the right, and set me right if I am in the wrong… Obey me as long as I obey Allah and His Messenger; in case I disobey Allah and His Messenger, I have no right to obedience from you". The law of the Quran was to be held supreme and it was the Holy Prophet who had laid down this rule of the supremacy of the law:

> "To hear and obey the authorities is binding, so long as one is not commanded to disobey God; when one is commanded to disobey God, he should not hear or obey." [14]

The Holy Prophet went so far as to say that a black African could be appointed to rule over the Arabs and that obedience was due to him as to any other head.[15]

Thus while it was considered an act of great merit, "an excellent *jihād*", to speak out the truth in the presence of an unjust ruler,[16] active opposition to constituted authority or rebellion against it was not allowed because the Holy Prophet had laid down the condition to hear and obey "whether we liked or disliked, and whether we were in adversity or ease, even if our rights were not granted", and the authority of the head could only be disputed if he committed "open acts of disbelief in which you have a clear ordinance from Allah".[17]

Law making

The law of the Quran was supreme indeed, but there was no ban to making laws according to the needs of the people so long as they did not go against the spirit of the revealed law. On being appointed governor of Yaman, Mu'adh ibn Jabal was asked by the Holy Prophet as to the rule by which he would abide. "By the Book of Allah," was the reply. "But if you do not find any direction in it," asked the Holy Prophet. "Then by the practice (*Sunnah*) of the Messenger of Allah," was the reply. "But if you do not find any direction in the *Sunnah*," he was again asked. "Then I will exercise my judgment," came the reply. The Holy Prophet raised his hands and said: "Praise be to Allah Who has granted the messenger of His Messenger what pleases the Messenger" (see page 44).

The necessary laws were, however, to be made by consultation in accordance with the general command: "And [Muslims are those] whose affairs are [decided] by counsel among themselves" (42:38). It appears from the Quran that people were gathered together for counsel on many important occasions:

> "Only those are believers who believe in Allah and His Messenger, and when they are with him on an important matter, they do not go away until they have asked permission from him." — 24:62

In reply to Ali who enquired as to how to proceed in cases where there was no definite direction in the Quran, the Holy Prophet is reported to have said: "Gather together the righteous from among my community and decide the matter by their counsel and do not decide it by one man's opinion". He definitely directed his followers to take counsel whenever an important matter was to be decided: "Never do a people take counsel but they are guided to the right course in their affair."

Counsel was freely resorted to by the Holy Prophet himself in all important matters. Madinah was attacked three times by the Quraish of Makkah, and every time the Prophet held a consultation with his followers as to how to meet the enemy. On one of these occasions, that of the battle of Uhud, he acted upon the opinion of the majority and marched out of Madinah to meet the enemy, although his own opinion was that the Muslim army should not leave the town. During the battle, when some people disobeyed his orders and this act of theirs caused heavy loss to the Muslim army, he was still commanded to include them when taking counsel:

> "Pardon them and ask Divine protection for them, and consult them in [important] matters." — 3:159

The command "consult them" also refers to the fact that, apparently, it was the taking of counsel and following the majority opinion that had brought about trouble. Yet at such a critical time the Holy Prophet did not waver for a minute from the course of taking counsel in important matters, and just at this juncture we find Divine revelation confirming the principle of adhering to counsel.

Thus the three principles of democracy, namely, the supremacy of the law, the taking of counsel in making new laws and deciding other important affairs, and the election of the head of the state, were laid down and recognized by the Holy Prophet himself.

It was due to these clear directions to make laws for themselves and to decide other important matters by counsel that the first successors of the Holy Prophet had councils to help them in all such matters. It was also in the early history of Islam that the great Imams, such as Imam Abu Hanifah, freely resorted to analogical reasoning in legislation, and *Ijtihād* was recognized as a source of Islamic law along with the Quran and the *Sunnah*.

Scrupulous justice

Justice was declared to be the corner-stone of the state which the Prophet Muhammad founded. No distinction was to be made between friend and foe, allied nations and enemies, those whom one loved and those whom one hated, in dealing equitably. The Quran says:

> "And do not let [your] hatred of a people — because they hindered you from the Sacred Mosque — incite you to transgress. And help one another in righteousness and piety, and do not help one another in sin and aggression, and keep your duty to Allah." — 5:2

> "O you who believe, be upright for Allah, bearers of witness with justice; and do not let [your] hatred of a people incite

you not to act equitably. Be just; that is nearer to observance of duty." — 5:8

The broad principle was also laid down that dishonesty must be punished, and the balance of justice must be held equal between Muslims and non-Muslims and between friends and foes. The Holy Prophet was told in the Quran:

> "Surely We have revealed the Book to you with truth that you may judge between people by means of what Allah has taught you. And do not be one pleading the cause of the dishonest, and ask the forgiveness of Allah. Surely Allah is ever Forgiving, Merciful. And do not contend on behalf of those who act unfaithfully to their souls. Surely Allah does not love him who is treacherous, sinful." — 4:105–107

Commentators of the Quran agree that the occasion of the revelation of these verses was a dispute between a Muslim and a Jew. The Muslim had stolen something and hid it at the Jew's, afterwards accusing the Jew of the theft. The Muslim was supported by his tribe. The Holy Prophet cleared the Jew of the charge and gave judgment against the Muslim, despite the risk of the loss of that tribe at a time when every Muslim hand was sorely needed.

Observance of agreements

Great stress has been laid in Islam on faithfulness to agreements:

> "O you who believe, fulfil the obligations." — 5:1

Respect for all contracts, agreements, leagues, treaties, etc. is taught here, as these are included in the significance of the word 'uqūd, meaning 'ties', translated here as 'obligations'. Nations are particularly enjoined to fulfil their agreements, because they it is who, intoxicated with power, treat agreements as mere scraps of paper:

> "You make your oaths to be means of deceit between you because [one] nation is more numerous than [another] nation. Allah only tries you by this." — 16:92

True to these teachings, the Holy Prophet and his followers stood firmly by their agreements under the most trying circumstances. An example was at the truce of Hudaibiyah. The agreement had just been signed, when Abu Jandal, a convert to Islam fleeing from Makkah, appeared on the scene. He had been severely persecuted at Makkah and showed the scars of his tortures to the Muslims. Under the conditions of the agreement, Muslims could not give him shelter. The Holy Prophet was moved and tried to secure an exception to the rigorous condition, but the other party did not agree to this, and Abu Jandal had to be sent back to his persecutors to be dealt with as they liked. Another example was when, in the time of Umar, the Muslim general, Abu Ubaidah, was obliged to evacuate the occupied territory of Hims, which the enemy was now going to occupy. Abu Ubaidah ordered that the tax received from the people as a condition for their protection should be paid back to them because Muslims could not give them protection any longer. There is not a single instance on record in which Muslims broke their agreement with any other nation. No example of such scrupulous regard for agreements can be found elsewhere.

One of the qualities of those who would be righteous is stated in the Holy Quran to be that they are "performers of their promise when they make a promise" (2:177). The performance of promise on the part of individuals as well as of nations is one of the first essentials of the welfare of humanity, and hence the stress laid upon it by the Quran. Faithlessness to treaties and pledges on the part of nations has wrought the greatest havoc on humanity. Just as no society can prosper until its individual members are true to their mutual agreements and promises to each other, so humanity at large can never have peace unless the nations are true to their agreements.

Section 2: *Penal Laws*

The penal laws of Islam are called *ḥudūd* (singular: *ḥadd*) in Hadith and books of Jurisprudence. In the parlance of the jurists, the word *ḥudūd* is limited to punishment for crimes mentioned in the Holy Quran or Hadith, while other punishments left to the discretion of the state are spoken of as *ta'zīr*.

It should be pointed out at the very beginning of a discussion on the penal laws of Islam that all violations of Divine limits *in a general sense* are not punishable by the state; punishment is inflicted only in those cases in which there is violation of other people's rights. For instance, neglect of prayer, or omission to keep fasts or perform the pilgrimage is not punishable; but the case of *zakāt* is different. *Zakāt* is a charity as well as a tax, and the Holy Prophet appointed official collectors to collect the *zakāt,* which was received in the state treasury, thus showing that its collection was a duty of the Muslim state. Hence it was that when, after the death of the Holy Prophet, certain Arab tribes refused to pay, Abu Bakr, the first Caliph, sent out troops against them, this step being taken because the withholding of *zakāt* on the part of an entire tribe was tantamount to rebellion.

General law of punishment

The punishable crimes in Islamic law are those which affect society; and those spoken of in the Holy Quran are murder, robbery with violence against persons, theft, adultery or fornication and accusation of adultery. Before discussing in detail the various punishments prescribed in these cases, it may be stated that the Quran lays down a general law for the punishment of offences in the following words:

> "And the recompense of evil (*sayyi'ah*) is punishment (*sayyi'ah*) like it; but whoever forgives and brings about reform, his reward is with Allah." — 42:40

This golden rule is of very wide application, since it applies both to individual wrong done by one person to another and to offences of a less particular nature, offences against society. Similar instructions as to the punishment of offenders are given elsewhere in the Quran:

> "And if you take your turn (*'āqabtum*), then retaliate (*'āqibū*) with the like of what you were afflicted with. But if you show patience, it is certainly best for the patient." — 16:126

> "And whoever retaliates (*'āqaba*) with the like of what he is afflicted with (*'ūqiba*), and he is oppressed, Allah will certainly help him." — 22:60

> "Whoever then acts aggressively (*i'tadā*) against you, inflict injury (*i'tadū*) on him according to the injury he has inflicted on you." — 2:194

While in the verses quoted above, and similar other verses, a golden rule is laid down for the individual wronged, that he should in the first instance forgive the offender provided the latter amends by forgiveness, the basis also is ordained of penal laws in general for the protection of society, and that basis, according to all these verses, is that the punishment of evil should be proportionate thereto. Every civilized code of penal laws is based on that principle, and by enunciating this general rule, ample scope is given to Muslim peoples and states to formulate their own penal laws. It is for this reason that the Quran does not go into many details, and speaks of punishment only in cases of the most glaring offences against person and property. It should be further noted that the Quran generally adopts the same word for punishment as for the crime. Thus in 42:40, both evil and its punishment are called *sayyi'ah* (evil); in 16:126 and 22:60, it is a derivative of *'uqūbah* (punishment); and in 2:194, it is *i'tidā'* (aggression). The adoption of the same word *evil* for the crime and its punishment indicates that punishment itself, though justified by the circumstances, is a necessary evil.

Punishment for murder

Undoubtedly the greatest crime known to society is taking away of the life of another person. It is a crime denounced in the earliest revelations:

> "And do not kill the soul which Allah has forbidden except in the course of justice." — 17:33, 6:151

> "And they who… slay not the soul which Allah has forbidden except in the course of justice… and he who does this shall meet a penalty of sin — the punishment will be doubled to him on the day of Resurrection, and he will abide in it in humiliation." — 25:68–69

The punishment of murder is, however, prescribed in a Madinah revelation:

> "O you who believe, retaliation (*qiṣāṣ*) is prescribed for you in the matter of the slain: the free for the free, and the slave for the slave, and the female for the female. But if remission is made to one by his [aggrieved] brother, prosecution [for blood-money] should be according to usage, and payment to him in a good manner. This is an alleviation from your Lord and a mercy. Whoever exceeds the limit after this, will have a painful punishment. And there is life for you in retaliation, you people of understanding, that you may guard yourselves." — 2:178–179

The word *qiṣāṣ,* rendered as retaliation, means retaliation by slaying for slaying, wounding for wounding and mutilating for mutilating.[18] The law of retaliation among the Israelites extended to all these cases, but the Quran has expressly limited it to cases of murder. It speaks of retaliation in wounds as being an ordinance of the law of Moses (5:45), but it is nowhere prescribed as a law for Muslims, who are required to observe retaliation only in the case of the slain. In some Hadith reports it is no doubt mentioned that the Holy Prophet ordered retaliation in some cases of wounds, but this was in all likelihood due to the fact that he followed the earlier law until he received an express commandment to the contrary.

The command to observe the law of retaliation in murder cases is followed by the words "the free for the free, and the slave for the slave, and the female for the female". These were meant to abolish an old Arab custom, for the Arabs before Islam used to insist, when the person killed was of noble descent, upon the execution of others besides the murderer. So it was made clear that whoever the murderer might be, a free man or a slave or a woman, it was the murderer who was to be slain.

An alleviation is, however, allowed in case the person who suffers from the death of the murdered person makes a remission and is satisfied with *diyah* or blood-money. Another case mentioned in the Quran (4:92) in which blood-money takes the place of a death sentence is that of unintentional killing.

Murder of a non-Muslim

The murder of a non-Muslim living under a Muslim state is punishable in exactly the same way as the murder of a Muslim. The Holy Prophet is reported to have said:

> "Whoever kills a *mu'āhad* (a non-Muslim living under the protection of a Muslim state), he shall not perceive the odour of Paradise, and its odour is perceivable from a distance of forty years' journey." [19]

Thus, even from a purely religious point of view, not the least distinction is made between the murderer of a Muslim and a non-Muslim, and therefore any distinction in their temporal punishments is out of the question. And where the Holy Quran speaks of a murderer, it always speaks of the murderer of a *nafs* (person) and not of a Muslim:

> "Whoever kills *a person* unless it is for manslaughter or for mischief in the land, it is as though he had killed all mankind." — 5:32

Ali is stated to have with him a written paper, according to which a Muslim was not to be killed for an unbeliever,[20] but evidently this related to a state of war and not a state of peace; the latter is expressly spoken of in the hadith already quoted. In fact, the rights of non-Muslims in a Muslim state are in all respects at par with those of Muslims, so much so that Muslims are required even to fight in their defence,[21] and the Holy Prophet is reported to have said that their property was like that of the Muslims and their blood was like that of the Muslims.

Alleviation of punishment in murder cases

Hadith speaks of cases of murder in which the murderer's intention is doubtful and, in these cases too, blood-money is to be paid.[22] And where the murderer could not be discovered, blood-money was paid from the state treasury.[23] There does not appear to be any reported case in which the murderer may have been imprisoned in case of unintentional murder, but the *alleviation* of punishment in such cases is clearly provided for in the Quran. The form of alleviation spoken of in the Holy Book is the payment of blood-money but the right of the state to give that alleviation any other form is not negatived.

Punishment for armed robbery

Another crime for which capital punishment may be awarded is robbery by an armed gang, or banditry. In the Holy Quran, this is spoken of as waging war against God and His Messenger:

> "The only punishment of those who wage war against Allah and His Messenger and strive to make mischief in the land is that they should be murdered, or crucified, or their hands and their feet should be cut off on opposite sides, or they should be imprisoned. This shall be a disgrace for them in this world, and in the Hereafter they shall have a grievous punishment, except those who repent before you overpower them; so know that Allah is Forgiving, Merciful." — 5:33–34

It has been accepted by the commentators, by a consensus of opinion, that gangs of robbers, bandits and murderers who create disorder in a settled state of society are referred to in this verse. The punishment prescribed is of four kinds, which shows that the punishment to be inflicted in any particular case would depend upon the circumstances of the case. If murder has been committed in the course of robbery, the punishment would be the execution of the culprit. Where the robbers have committed excesses, one of their hands and feet may be cut off. In less serious cases, the punishment may be only imprisonment. The Arabic words translated as "they should be imprisoned" mean, literally, "they should be banished from the earth", which both Imam Abu Hanifah and Ahmad Ibn Hanbal take as meaning imprisonment. Deportation is included if we take "earth" as meaning a particular country.

Punishment for theft

Theft is the next punishable crime spoken of in the Holy Quran:

> "And as for the man and the woman addicted to theft, cut off their hands as a penalty for what they have earned — an exemplary punishment from Allah. And Allah is Mighty, Wise. But whoever repents after his wrongdoing and reforms, Allah will turn to him mercifully. Surely Allah is Forgiving, Merciful." — 5:38–39

The cutting off of hands may be taken metaphorically, as in the expression *qaṭaʻa lisāna-hū,* literally meaning 'he cut off his tongue', but which means 'he silenced him',[24] and it would simply mean *restraining* the thief by imprisonment or otherwise.

Even if taken literally, it is not necessary to cut off the hands for every type of theft, and this is a fact which all jurists have recognized. Evidently what is meant is that whereas the maximum punishment for armed gang robbery or banditry is death (5:33) if murder has also been committed, the maximum punishment for theft (5:38) is the cutting off of the hand. Therefore it is for the judge to decide which punishment will suit a particular case.

There are several circumstances which go to show that the maximum punishment of the cutting off of hands may ordinarily be reserved for habitual thieves. Firstly, the minimum punishment for banditry, i.e., imprisonment, having already been mentioned in 5:33, may also be taken as the minimum punishment for the much less serious offence of theft, and this would meet the ends of justice. Secondly, the cutting off of hands, being a punishment for the more serious offences falling under armed gang robbery, should also be reserved for the more serious offences falling under theft, and the offence of theft generally becomes more serious when it becomes habitual. Thirdly, the punishment of cutting off of hands, in cases of theft, is called an exemplary punishment and such punishment could only be given in very serious cases, or when the offender is addicted thereto and the milder punishment of imprisonment has no deterrent effect upon him. Lastly, 5 : 39 shows that the object of the punishment is *reform,* and an occasion to reform can only be given if the punishment for a first or second offence is less severe.

It is true that the cutting off of the hand, for even a first crime, is reported in Hadith but this may be due to the particular circumstances of society at the time, and it is for the judge to decide which punishment will suit the circumstances. For instance, according to some reports in Hadith, the hand was cut off when the amount stolen was one-quarter of a dinar or more; according to others when it was one dinar or more.[25] According to another report the hand of the thief was not to be cut off at all when a theft was committed in the course of a journey or on an expedition.[26] Probably some other punishment was given in such cases. There are also reports showing that the hand was not to be cut off for stealing fruit on a tree and the cutting off of the hand is also prohibited in the case of criminal misappropriation.[27] In another hadith it is stated that when a certain person stole another's mantle valued at thirty dirhams from underneath his head, the owner of the mantle offered that he would sell the same to the person who had stolen it, without demanding immediate payment, and the Holy Prophet approved of this arrangement.[28] These examples show that great latitude was allowed to the judge in the choice of punishment.

Punishment for adultery

Adultery, and false accusation of adultery, are both punishable according to the Holy Quran:

> "The adulteress and the adulterer, flog each of them with a hundred strokes, and do not let pity for them detain you from obedience to Allah, if you believe in Allah and the Last Day, and let a group of believers witness their punishment." — 24 : 2

It is generally thought that while the Quran prescribes flogging as a punishment for fornication, i.e., when the guilty person is not married, stoning to death is the punishment for adultery, and that this is based on the Holy Prophet's practice. But the Quran plainly speaks of the punishment for adultery in the case of *married slave-girls* as being half the punishment of adultery in the case of *free married women:*

> "So marry them with the permission of their masters, and give them their dowries justly, they being chaste, not fornicating, nor taking lovers in secret; then if they are guilty of adultery when they are taken in marriage, they shall suffer half the punishment for free married women." — 4:25

Therefore death, or stoning to death, cannot be conceived of as possible punishment in case of adultery as it cannot be halved, while imprisonment or flogging may be. Thus the Quran not only speaks of flogging, and not death, as punishment for adultery, but it positively excludes death or stoning to death.

Flogging

A few words may be added as to the method of flogging. The Arabic word for flogging is *jald* which means *skin,* and the act of flogging signifies hitting or hurting the skin.[29] Flogging was therefore a punishment which should be felt by the skin, and it aimed more at disgracing the culprit than torturing him. In the time of the Holy Prophet, and even for some time after him, there was no whip, and flogging was carried out by beating with a stick or with the hand or with shoes.[30] It is further stated by the same authority that the culprit was not stripped naked for the infliction of the punishment of flogging; he was only required to take off thick clothes such as would ward off the stroke altogether. Baring the back for flogging is forbidden among Muslims, and a shirt or two must be left over the body. It is further related that it is preferable to give the strokes on different parts of the body so that no harm should result to any one part, but the face and the private parts must be avoided.

Stoning to death in Jewish law

As already shown, stoning to death as a punishment for adultery is nowhere spoken of in the Holy Quran nor was it contemplated as the punishment of adultery in this scripture. In Hadith, however, cases are met with in which adultery was punished with stoning to death. One of these cases is expressly mentioned as that involving Jews:

> "Jews came to the Prophet with a man and a woman from among them who had committed adultery; and by his order they were stoned to death near the place where funeral services were held." [31]

Further explanation of this incident is given in another hadith where it is stated that when the Jews referred the case to him, he enquired of them what punishment the Torah prescribed in case of adultery. The Jews tried at first to conceal the fact that it was stoning to death, but on Abdullah ibn Salam giving the reference, they admitted it, and the guilty persons were dealt with as prescribed in the Torah.[32] The Gospels show that such was the punishment up to the time of Jesus.[33] According to a third version of this hadith, which is the most detailed, the Jews who desired to avoid the severer punishment of stoning for adultery said to one another: "Let us go to this Prophet, for he has been raised with milder teachings; so if he gives his decision for a milder punishment than stoning, we will accept it." It is then related that the Holy Prophet went with them to their *midrās* (the house in which the Torah was read), and asked them what punishment was prescribed in their sacred book. They tried to conceal it at first but the truth had to be admitted at last, and the Holy Prophet gave his decision saying: "I give my judgment according to what is in the Torah".[34]

Jewish practice followed by the Prophet at first

These reports leave not the shadow of a doubt that stoning was the punishment of adultery in the Jewish law, and that it was in the case of Jewish offenders that this punishment was first resorted to by the Holy Prophet when he came to Madinah. There are other Hadith reports which show that the same punishment was given in certain cases when the offenders were Muslims, but apparently this was before the revelation of the verse (24:2) which speaks of flogging as the punishment for both the adulterer and the adulteress, it being the practice of the Holy Prophet to follow the earlier revealed law until he received a definite revelation on a point.

A suggestion to that effect is contained in a hadith:

> "Shaibani says, I asked Abdullah ibn Abi Aufa: Did the Holy Prophet stone to death? He said: Yes. I said: Was it before the chapter entitled *The Light* [the 24th chapter] was revealed or after it? He replied: I do not know." [35]

The question shows clearly that the practice of stoning for adultery was recognized as being against the plain injunction contained in 24:2. It is likely that some misunderstanding arose from the incidents which happened before the Quranic revelation on the point, and that that practice was taken as the *Sunnah* of the Holy Prophet. The Khawarij, the earliest Muslim sect, entirely rejected stoning to death (*rajm*) as a punishment in Islam.[36]

There is evidence in Hadith itself that Umar himself, at least in one reported case, and it is a reliable report, punished adultery with flogging as laid down in the Quran in 24:2, and not with stoning to death. According to Bukhari, one of Umar's collectors, Hamzah by name, found that a married man who had committed adultery with his wife's slave-girl had been punished by Umar with a hundred stripes, and he referred the case back to Umar, and Umar upheld his first decision.[37]

Accusation of adultery

A false accusation of adultery is punished almost as severely as adultery itself:

> "And those who accuse free women and do not bring four witnesses, flog them with eighty strokes and never accept their evidence, and these are the transgressors — except those who afterwards repent and act aright; surely Allah is Forgiving, Merciful." — 24:4–5

It may be added here that while in ordinary matters two witnesses are required, in the case of an accusation of adultery four witnesses must be produced.[38] Thus a case of adultery can be established only on the strongest possible evidence. That circumstantial evidence is accepted is shown by the Quran itself in Joseph's case who, when accused of an assault on the chief's wife, was declared free of the charge on circumstantial evidence.[39] There are also a number of Hadith reports showing that circumstantial evidence was accepted when it led to the establishment of a certain fact.

General directions for execution of punishment

Punishment must be inflicted without respect of persons, nor should mediation be accepted in such cases. When, in the case of a certain woman who was guilty of theft, some people sought to intercede on her behalf through Usamah, since she came of a good family, the Holy Prophet was enraged and said, "Do you intercede in the matter of a punishment (*hadd*)?", and then addressed the people in general, saying:

> "Those before you went astray, for, when one of them committed a crime and he was a great man, they would not punish him, and when he was a poor man they would execute the punishment." [40]

Leniency was shown in the execution of punishment when the guilty person showed signs of repentance. A Companion relates:

> "While I was with the Prophet a man came and said: 'O Messenger of Allah, I have committed a sin subject to legal punishment *(hadd),* so inflict it on me.' The Prophet did not ask him what he had done. Then the time for the prayer came and the man offered prayer along with the Prophet, and when the Prophet had finished his prayer, the man again got up and said, 'O Messenger of Allah, I have committed a sin subject to legal punishment *(hadd),* so inflict on me what is in the Book of Allah.' The Prophet said: 'Have you not prayed with us?' He said: 'Yes.' The Prophet said: 'Allah has forgiven your sin', or he said: 'your punishment'." [41]

It is strictly forbidden that a person should be punished for the crime of another.[42] Nor is any punishment to be inflicted on a mad man or a minor.[43] The punishment of the pregnant woman is to be deferred until she has delivered her child.[44]

Supplement by the Editor

In recent years certain misconceptions have spread regarding legal punishments prescribed by Islam due to the misapplication of Islamic law in some Muslim countries as well as misunderstandings by Muslim individuals and communities. These misconceptions are clarified from the Holy Quran and Hadith in the supplement below, compiled by the Editor of this handbook.

1. No punishment for 'blasphemy' or insulting the Prophet

Muslims have the duty to refute, by means of word and speech, any allegations against Islam and the Holy Prophet Muhammad. Apart from fulfilling this duty, they are taught in the Holy Quran and by the Holy Prophet to respond to abuse and mockery *by the following means only:* showing patience, ignoring the abuse, leaving the company of the abusers, and exercising forgiveness. Islam neither requires nor allows Muslims to respond to abuse with fury and rage, call for physical retribution, use violence, or kill the abusers. This is clear from the following verses of the Holy Quran:

1. "And you will certainly hear from those who have been given the Book before you and from the idolaters much abuse. And if you are patient and keep your duty, surely this is an affair of great resolution." — 3 : 186

In a Hadith report, commenting on this verse and on 2 : 109 (this latter verse is quoted further below), it is stated:

> "The Prophet and his Companions used to forgive the idolaters and the followers of previous books, as Allah had commanded them, and they used to show patience on hearing hurtful words." [45]

2. "So bear patiently what they say…" — 20 : 130, 50 : 39

3. "And do not obey the disbelievers and the hypocrites, and disregard their annoying talk, and rely on Allah." — 33 : 48

4. "And bear patiently what they say and turn away from them with a dignified withdrawal." — 73 : 10

5. "And indeed He has revealed to you in the Book that when you hear Allah's messages disbelieved in and mocked at, do not sit with them until they enter into some other discourse…" — 4 : 140; see also 6 : 68.

6. "Many of the people of the Book wish that they could turn you back into disbelievers after you have believed, out of envy from themselves, after truth has become clear to them. But pardon and forgive, till Allah bring about His command." — 2 : 109

7. "Take to forgiveness and enjoin good and turn away from the ignorant." — 7 : 199

8. Once there were four men who spread an accusation of immoral conduct against the Holy Prophet's wife Aishah. Their allegation was ultimately proved to be false. One of them, called Mistah, who was poor, used to receive financial

assistance from Aishah's father, Abu Bakr. After this incident, Abu Bakr swore never again to help Mistah. The following verse was revealed to the Holy Prophet on this occasion:

> "And the possessors of grace and abundance among you should not swear against giving to the near of kin and the poor and those who have fled in Allah's way; and pardon and overlook. Do you not love that Allah should forgive you? And Allah is Forgiving, Merciful." — 24:22

Hearing this, Abu Bakr exclaimed: "Indeed, I certainly love that Allah should forgive me." He then resumed providing assistance to Mistah, as before.[46]

These teachings are borne out by the sayings and actions of the Holy Prophet Muhammad reported in the most authentic of Hadith reports:

1. "No one and no thing has greater patience than Allah upon hearing hurtful words. People call for a son for Him, and [yet] He grants them safety and sustenance." [47] (Note: Christians are meant here.)

2. "Once the Messenger of Allah distributed some battle gains among people. A man of the Ansar said: 'By Allah! Muhammad, by this division, did not intend to please Allah'. So I [the narrator of this report] came to the Messenger of Allah and informed him about it, whereupon his face changed colour with anger and he said: May Allah bestow His mercy on Moses, for he was hurt with more than this, yet he remained patient." [48]

3. "Aishah [wife of the Prophet] said: A group of Jews came to see the Messenger of Allah and they said: *as-sāmu 'alaikum* ['Death be to you' instead of *as-salāmu 'alaikum,* 'Peace be to you']. I understood it and said: 'And upon you be death and curse'. Then the Messenger of Allah said: 'Be calm, Aishah. Allah loves that one should be kind and lenient in all matters'." [49]

4. Suhayl ibn Amr was a prominent opponent of the Holy Prophet Muhammad at Makkah, and a skilled orator of the Quraish tribe, who used to employ his oratory in making speeches defaming the Holy Prophet. He was captured by the Muslims at the battle of Badr and brought before the Holy Prophet. A Companion suggested to the Holy Prophet that Suhayl's front teeth should be pulled out "so that he would never be able to exercise his oratory against you". The Holy Prophet replied without hesitation:

> "Certainly not. I will not mutilate anyone, for God would mutilate me even though I am His Prophet." [50]

There is thus *no legal penalty* in Islam for blasphemy. However, laws may be made to prevent the spread of hate *against any religion,* as the Quran teaches: "abuse not those [gods] whom they call upon besides Allah…" (6:108).

2. No punishment for apostasy

Maulana Muhammad Ali has fully discussed in the chapter on *Jihād* in this book that there is no legal punishment of any kind in Islam for an apostate, i.e., a Muslim who leaves the religion of Islam. See pages 317–322.

3. Rape

Cases reported from certain Muslim countries show that, under Islamic law as administered there, a woman who reports that she has been raped must produce four, male eye-witnesses (as required for an accusation of adultery) to support her claim; if she fails to produce such witnesses then her report of rape is treated as a confession of adultery on her part, for which she is then convicted and awarded the legal punishment. However, the following hadith shows that this is not at all correct:

> "In the time of the Prophet a woman went out for prayer. On the way, a man met her, and he caught her and raped her [lit., 'fulfilled his need from her']. She shouted and he went off. A man passed by her and she said: That man did such-and-such to me. Then a group of *muhājirīn* [Companions of the Holy Prophet who had migrated from Makkah to Madinah] passed by. She said: That man did such-and-such to me. They went and caught the man about whom she thought that he had raped her, and brought him to her. She said: Yes, he is the one. So they took him before the Prophet. When he was about to pass sentence, the man who had [actually] raped her stood up and said: O Messenger of Allah, I am the one who did it. He [the Prophet] said to her: You can go, Allah has indeed forgiven you. And he said some kind words to the man [who had been wrongly caught]." [51]

Here the Holy Prophet accepted the woman's evidence and the identification by her of the attacker. Even the misidentification by her of the attacker was forgiven as it was a genuine mistake.

4. So-called 'honour killings' are illegal in Islam

Hadith reports in Bukhari and Muslim show that the Holy Prophet Muhammad strictly forbade any husband from inflicting his own punishment on a man if he caught his wife with him in the sexual act, or making allegations of this kind against his wife without bringing any witnesses. He instructed that the due process of law should be invoked to establish guilt and award punishment. He warned those who would take the law into their own hands that they themselves would be punished. From this, it follows more generally that no person is allowed in Islam to kill another by accusing him or her of an illicit sexual act, even if he claims to have seen it taking place.

According to a report in Bukhari, a man accused his wife of having sexual intercourse with another man and brought the case before the Holy Prophet:

> "The Prophet said [to him]: Either you bring forth a proof or you will receive the legal punishment on your back. He said: O Messenger of

> Allah, if anyone of us saw a man with his wife, would he go to seek after witnesses? But the Prophet kept on repeating: Either you bring forth proof or you will receive the legal punishment on your back." [52]

By "proof" the Holy Prophet meant four witnesses in accordance with 24 : 4 of the Quran, the legal punishment for accusation without witnesses also being prescribed in that verse. The report says that it was on that occasion that the passage 24 : 6–9 of the Quran was revealed. The swearing of oaths as stipulated in those verses has been dealt with in this book in the chapter on *Marriage* on page 361 under the heading *Li'ān* or cursing. According to the report, both the husband and the wife then took oaths as required in this passage, though the wife hesitated to swear the fifth time. Later, when she gave birth to a child, it resembled the alleged adulterer. The Holy Prophet, learning of this, said: "If it were not for the command which came in the Book of Allah, I would have dealt with her in a different way [i.e., by punishment]".

The very next report in Bukhari is as follows:

> "In the lifetime of the Messenger of Allah, a man accused his wife of illegal sexual intercourse and denied that he was the father of her child. The Messenger of Allah ordered them both [to do the cursing as prescribed in 24 : 6–9], so they did the cursing as commanded by Allah. Then he gave his decision about the child that it would be for the mother, and he separated the cursing couple [by divorce]." [53]

Similarly, according to a report in Sahih Muslim a man put the following predicament to the Holy Prophet:

> "If a man were to find a man with his wife and if he were to talk about it, you would lash him; and if he killed [the man], you would kill him, and if he were to keep quiet he would be consumed by anger." [54]

This question shows that the Holy Prophet would have punished the husband for making a false allegation against his wife if he could not provide proof, and punished him for murder if he killed the other man. The report continues that the Holy Prophet prayed to Allah for an answer, and Allah revealed to him the passage 24 : 6–9 quoted above. Then both the man and his wife came to the Holy Prophet and swore in the manner prescribed. The woman was then free to go, even though the report casts doubt on her truthfulness.

As to sense of "honour", it was reported to the Holy Prophet that a man, Sa'd ibn 'Ubada, a chief of the *Anṣār,* said: "If I found a man with my wife, I would kill him by the sword and not ignore it". The Holy Prophet said:

> "Do you wonder at the sense of honour of Sa'd? I have a greater sense of honour than him and Allah has a greater sense of honour than I have." [55]

By this, the Holy Prophet meant that a person cannot be more moral and more concerned about honour than the Messenger of Allah and Allah Himself.

When Allah and His Messenger, who are the greatest guardians of honour, decency and morality, do not teach the action the man wants to take, how can it be moral for him to do so?

In one version of the same incident in Sahih Muslim, Sa'd ibn 'Ubada himself asked the Holy Prophet: "If a man finds his wife with another man, should he kill him?", and the Prophet replied: "No." In another version, he asked: "If I were to find my wife with a man, should I wait until I bring four witnesses?", and the Prophet replied: "Yes." [56]

Notes to Chapter 19

1. Bukhari, book 62: 'Virtues of the Companions', ch. 8, h. 3700.

2. Bukhari, book 11: 'Friday Prayer', ch. 11, h. 893.

3. Bukhari, book 81: '*Ar-Riqāq* (What makes the heart tender)', ch. 35, h. 6496.

4. Bukhari, book 62: 'Virtues of the Companions', ch. 5, h. 3667–3668.

5. *Ibid.*

6. Bukhari, book 93: 'Judgments', ch. 51, h. 7219.

7. Bukhari, book 34: 'Sales and Trade', ch. 15, h. 2070.

8. Bukhari, book 93: 'Judgments', ch. 8, h. 7150.

9. Bukhari, book 64: 'Military Expeditions', ch. 60, h. 4341–4342.

10. Mishkat, book 17: 'Governing and Judgment', ch. 2, sec. 2, h. 3556.

11. Bukhari, book 93: 'Judgments', ch. 16, ch. heading.

    Editor's Note: Umar ibn Abdul Aziz is also quoted here as saying that a ruler must be intelligent, gentle, of pure character, just, knowledgeable and a seeker of knowledge.

12. Bukhari, book 62: 'Virtues of the Companions', ch. 8, h. 3700. See also note 21 below which refers to h. 3052 of Bukhari.

13. Bukhari, book 43: 'Loans (etc.)', ch. 11, h. 2398.

14. Bukhari, book 56: '*Jihād*', ch. 108, h. 2955.

15. Bukhari, book 10: 'Call to Prayer', ch. 54, h. 693.

16. Mishkat, book 17: 'Governing and Judgment', ch. 1, sec. 2, h. 3534 (v. 2, p. 198).

17. Bukhari, book 92: '*Al-Fitan* (Afflictions, Tribulations)', ch. 2, h. 7055–7056.

18. Lane's Lexicon.

19. Bukhari, book 87: 'Blood-wit (*Al-Diyāt*)', ch. 30, h. 6914. Tirmidhi, book 16: 'Blood-wit', ch. 11, h. 1403 (MDS: book 14). *Musnad* of Ahmad ibn Hanbal, v. 2, p. 186.

20. Bukhari, book 87: 'Blood-wit', ch. 31, h. 6915.

21. Bukhari, book 56: '*Jihād*', ch. 174, h. 3052. This report says that Umar, after he was stabbed, left the instruction for his successor "to fulfil the agreement made with those non-Muslims who are under the protection of Allah and His Messenger, to fight for their security, and not to burden them [with taxes or other obligations] beyond their ability".

22. Abu Dawud, book 41: 'Blood-wit (*Al-Diyāt*)', ch. 3, h. 4501; ch. 19, h. 4547–4555; ch. 26, h 4588 (MDS: book 38, chs. 3, 17 and ch. 24). *Musnad* of Ahmad ibn Hanbal, v. 2, p. 36.

23. Bukhari, book 87: 'Blood-wit', ch. 22, h. 6898. See also book 58: '*Jizyah*', ch. 12, h. 3173.

    Editor's Note: In this case the murderer of a Muslim was suspected to be one of the Jews of Khaibar, but as there was no evidence of the identity of the murderer, the Holy Prophet himself paid the blood-money to the heirs of the victim.

24. *Lisān al-'Arab.*

25. Abu Dawud, book 40: 'Punishments *(Hudūd)*', ch. 11, h. 4383–4387 (MDS: book 37, ch. 12). Nasa'i, book 46: 'Cutting off hand of Thief', chs. 8–10, h. 4906–4956 (MDS: h. 4910–4959).

26. Abu Dawud, book 40: 'Punishments', ch. 18, h. 4408 (MDS: book 37, ch. 19). Nasa'i, book 46: 'Cutting off hand of Thief', ch. 16, h. 4979 (MDS: h. 4982). Tirmidhi, book 17: 'Punishments *(Hudūd)*', ch. 20, h. 1450 (MDS: book 15).

27. Abu Dawud, book 40: 'Punishments', chs. 12–13, h. 4388–4393 (MDS: book 37, chs. 13–14).

28. *Ibid.,* ch. 14, h. 4394 (MDS: ch. 15).

29. Lane's Lexicon.

30. For all references in this paragraph, see *Rūh al-Ma'ānī,* vol. 6, p. 4 and 5.

31. Bukhari, book 23: 'Funerals', ch. 60, h. 1329.

32. Bukhari, book 61: 'Virtues of the Prophet and his Companions', ch. 26, h. 3635.

33. "Then the scribes and Pharisees brought to him a woman caught in adultery. … they said to him, Teacher, this woman was caught in adultery, in the very act. Now Moses, in the law, commanded us that such should be stoned. But what do you say?" (John, 8:3–5)

34. Abu Dawud, book 40: 'Punishments', ch. 26, h. 4450 (MDS: book 37, ch. 25).

35. Bukhari, book 86: 'Punishments *(Hudūd)*', ch. 21, h. 6813.

36. *Rūh al-Ma'ānī,* vol. 6, p. 6.

37. Bukhari, book 39: 'Sureties (*Kafālah*)', ch. 1, h. 2290.

38. For accusation of adultery by a husband against his wife when there are no witnesses, see page 361 under the heading *Li'ān,* and page 432 under *Honour killings.*

39. The Quran, 12:26–28.

40. Bukhari, book 86: 'Punishments', ch. 12, h. 6788.

41. Bukhari, book 86: 'Punishments', ch. 27, h. 6823. See also briefer version in Abu Dawud, book 40: 'Punishments', ch. 9, h. 4381 (MDS: book 37, ch. 10).

42. Abu Dawud, book 41: 'Blood-wit', ch. 2, h. 4495 (MDS: book 38).

43. Abu Dawud, book 40: 'Punishments', ch. 16, h. 4398–4403 (MDS: book 37, ch. 17). Bukhari, book 86: 'Punishments', ch. 22, ch. heading.

44. Ibn Majah, book 21: 'Blood-wit (*Al-Diyāt*)', hadith 2694 (MDS: ch. 36).

45. Bukhari, book 65: 'Commentary on Quran', h. 4566 (on *Surah* 3, v. 186).

46. Bukhari, book 52: 'Witnesses', ch. 15, h. 2261.

47. Bukhari, book 78: 'Good Manners' (*Adab*), ch. 71, h. 6099.

48. *Ibid.,* ch. 53, h. 6059.

49. *Ibid.,* ch. 35, h. 6024. See also ch. 38, h. 6030.

50. *Sīrat Rasūl Allāh* of Ibn Isḥāq; see its English translation, *The Life of Muhammad* by Alfred Guillaume, Oxford University Press, 1955, p. 312.

51. Abu Dawud, book 40: 'Punishments', ch. 7, h. 4379 (MDS: book 37, ch. 8). See also Tirmidhi, book 17: 'Punishments', ch. 22, h. 1453–1454 (MDS: book 15).

52. Bukhari, book 65: 'Commentary on the Quran', h. 4747 (on *Surah* 24, v. 6-9).

53. *Ibid.,* h. 4748; see also h. 4746.

54. Muslim, book 19: 'Invoking Curses', ch. 1, h. 1495a, (MDS: h. 3755).

55. Bukhari, book 86: 'Those who wage war from among disbelievers and apostates', ch. 40, h. 6846. See also Muslim, book 19: 'Invoking curse', ch. 1, h. 1498c, 1499a (MDS: h. 3763–h. 3764).

56. Muslim, book 19: 'Invoking curse', ch. 1, h. 1498a, b, c (MDS: h. 3761–3763).

20. Morals and Ethics

Character-building

One of the earliest works to which the Prophet Muhammad applied himself was the building up of character. His heart ailed for the physical ills of humanity. The slave, the widow, the orphan, the needy, the one in distress, the oppressed and the wronged, had a very high place in his heart, and he would do what he could to help them and to make others feel for them as he himself felt. But moral considerations had a still higher place in his programme of reformation, and long before he introduced any reforms in regard to social relations, sex problems and state organization, he was engaged in the moral uplift of man. All wrongs had to be redressed, later on, by means of laws and regulations, but he was aware that even good laws could benefit humanity only when they were worked out by persons standing on a high moral plane.

It was, therefore, at Makkah and in very early days that, while introducing the high ideals of One God and One Humanity and applying himself to lead people to prayer and charity, the Holy Prophet was equally devoted to raising them to a very high moral level. Good morals and good manners are, according to the Holy Quran and Hadith, the real test of a person's excellence, as shown by the verse of the Quran and the hadith quoted below:

> "Surely the noblest of you with Allah is the most dutiful of you [or best of you in conduct]." — 49:13

> "The best of you are those who have the most excellent morals." [1]

Truthfulness

The Holy Prophet was recognized by friends and foes as the most truthful of people. On repeated occasions, his bitterest enemies had to acknowledge his eminent truthfulness, on account of which he was called *al-Amīn,* 'the Faithful one'. Himself so eminently truthful, he laid stress on truth as the basis of a high character:

> "Surely truth leads to virtue, and virtue leads to paradise, and a man continues to speak the truth until he becomes thoroughly truthful; and surely falsehood leads to vice and vice leads to the fire, and a man continues to tell lies until he is written down a great liar with Allah." [2]

The Holy Quran mentions truthfulness as one of the most prominent qualities that Muslims should possess:

> "…and the truthful men and the truthful women … Allah has prepared for them forgiveness and a mighty reward." — 33:35

Speaking of the great transformation which the Holy Prophet had brought about, the Quran bears testimony to the truthfulness of the Muslims by stating that they "witness no falsehood" (25:72), i.e., do not bear witness to what is false. The Quran also lays down the basis of a society in which people are required to "exhort one another to truth" (103:3), and states repeatedly that it is with truth that falsehood can be challenged and vanquished:

> "Indeed, We hurl the Truth against falsehood, so it knocks out its brains, and lo! it vanishes." — 21:18

> "And say: The Truth has come and falsehood vanished. Surely falsehood is ever bound to vanish." — 17:81

It exhorts again and again that truth is to be adhered to at all costs, even if it goes against one's own interest or interest of one's friends and relatives:

> "O you who believe, be maintainers of justice, bearers of witness for Allah, even if it is against your own selves or your parents or near relatives… So do not follow your low desires, that you deviate. And if you distort [the truth] or turn away [from it], surely Allah is ever Aware of what you do." — 4:135

The principle of truth is not to be deviated from even if it goes in favour of the enemy:

> "O you who believe, be upright for Allah, bearers of witness with justice; and do not let [your] hatred of a people incite you not to act equitably. Be just; that is nearer to observance of duty." — 5:8

And even if one is called upon to speak the truth in the face of a tyrant, it must be done:

> "The most excellent *jihād* is the uttering of truth in the presence of an unjust ruler." [3]

Only truth shall benefit in the final judgment, as it shall take place on "a day when their truth will profit the truthful ones" (5:119). The Holy Prophet enjoys the distinction that he made people walk in the ways which he pointed out. The quality of truth was so ingrained in the heart of his followers that they not only loved it but underwent severest hardship for the sake of truth. When about two centuries later, the critics laid down certain canons to judge the truthfulness of the transmitters of Hadith, they all agreed on one point, that no Companion of the Holy Prophet had ever uttered a deliberate falsehood.

Muslims are also enjoined to be true to their promises. "Those who are faithful to their trusts and their covenants" is a twice occurring description of the true believers (23:8, 70:32), and the righteous are described as "performers of their promise when they make a promise" (2:177). Elsewhere too, it is enjoined:

> "Fulfil the promise; surely the promise will be enquired into [i.e., by Allah as to its fulfilment]." — 17:34

Perseverance and patience

Perseverance is another characteristic on which great emphasis is laid in the Holy Quran and which shone prominently in the life of the Holy Prophet and those inspired by him. Persecuted on all sides, suffering the severest hardships, with no apparent prospects of success, the Prophet stood adamant when threatened with death. He was equally firm when offered worldly temptations. During the flight to Madinah, hidden in a cave with a search party at its mouth, he consoled his single companion, Abu Bakr, with these words:

> "Grieve not, surely Allah is with us." — 9:40

The Quran states clearly that perseverance in the cause of truth brings down angels from heaven to console a person:

> "Those who say, Our Lord is Allah, then continue in the right way, the angels descend upon them saying: Do not fear, nor grieve, and receive good news of the Garden which you were promised. We are your friends in this world's life and in the Hereafter." — 41:30–31

Patience and perseverance are inculcated again and again in the early revelations as well as in the later ones:

> "And we would certainly bear with patience your persecution of us. And on Allah should the reliants rely."— 14:12

> "O you who believe, be steadfast and try to excel in steadfastness…" — 3:200

> "So be patient. Surely the good end is for the dutiful." — 11:49. [4]

Patience and prayers are said to be the two doors through which Divine help is received:

> "O you who believe, seek assistance through patience and prayer; surely Allah is with the patient." — 2:153

Courage

Courage is another great quality on which stress is laid. The heart in which there is fear of God cannot entertain fear of others than God, and this makes a Muslim fearless in the face of severest opposition:

> "Those to whom people said: Surely men have gathered against you, so fear them; but this increased their faith, and they said: Allah is sufficient for us and He is an excellent Guardian. … It is the devil who only frightens his friends, but do not fear them, and fear Me, if you are believers." — 3:173, 175

> "So do not fear the people and fear Me…" — 5:44

> "Do you fear them [i.e., your enemies]? But Allah has more right that you should fear Him, if you are believers." — 9:13

> "Do not fear, surely I am with you — I do hear and see." — 20:46

> "Those who deliver the messages of Allah and fear Him, and fear none but Allah." — 33:39

It was on account of their fearlessness and great moral courage that the Muslims, in the Holy Prophet's time, defended themselves in battles against three to ten times their numbers and won on all occasions. Later, in the battles they had to fight against Persia and the Roman Byzantine Empire, their numbers bore no comparison with the enemy forces, and they were almost always victorious. The courage which they showed on the battle-fields was in fact due to their firm faith.

Humility and selflessness

However, while facing so boldly all opposition to the cause of truth, Muslims were required to develop the quality of humility:

> "And do not go about in the land exultingly." — 17:37

> "And do not turn your face away from people in contempt, nor go about in the land exultingly. Surely Allah does not love any self-conceited boaster." — 31:18

> "Surely He does not love the proud." — 16:23

Humility, in fact, should be deeply rooted in a Muslim's heart because of the five daily prayers when all standing on terms of perfect equality bow down and prostrate themselves before their Lord as one body. The Holy Prophet's own example is a beacon-light in this respect. In his dealings with others he was humble and never placed himself on a higher pedestal. He was their spiritual guide and their ruler, but he was just one of them, being true to his picture as portrayed in the Holy Quran: "I am only a mortal like you" (18:110, 41:6).

Along with humility, selflessness is another great quality with which Islam arms every Muslim to fight the battle of life. There are repeated injunctions in the Quran that God's pleasure is to be the only motive for one's actions, not personal gain or loss:

> "And away from it [i.e., the fire of hell] shall be kept the most faithful to duty, who gives his wealth, purifying himself.

And none has with him any favour for a reward, except the seeking of the pleasure of his Lord, the Most High. And he will soon be well-pleased." — 92:17–21

"And they [i.e., the servants of Allah] give food, out of love for Him, to the poor and the orphan and the captive. [They say:] We feed you, for Allah's pleasure only — we desire from you neither reward nor thanks." — 76:8–9

"And among people is he who sells himself to seek the pleasure of Allah." — 2:207

Other qualities

The quality of **sincerity** should be developed by being first sincere in obedience to God:

"Serve Allah, being sincere to Him in obedience." —39:2 (see also 7:29, 40:14, etc.)

"And they are enjoined nothing but to serve Allah, being sincere to Him in obedience, upright..." — 98:5

Hypocrisy is condemned in the severest terms in the Holy Quran:

"They were on that day much nearer to unbelief than to belief; they say with their mouths what is not in their hearts." — 3:167

"O you who believe, why do you say things which you do not do? It is most hateful in the sight of Allah that you say things which you do not do." — 61:2–3

"So woe to the praying ones, who are unmindful of their prayer, who do good to be seen, and refrain from acts of kindness!" — 107:5–7

All qualities which make man stand on a high moral plane are inculcated one after another. **Thankfulness** is one of them:

"O you who believe, eat of the good things that We have provided you with, and give thanks to Allah if He it is Whom you serve." — 2:172

"If you are ungrateful, then surely Allah is above need of you. And He does not like ungratefulness in His servants. And if you are grateful, He likes it for you." — 39:7

A Muslim is required to be grateful to people as well. The Holy Prophet said: "Whoever is not thankful to people is not thankful to Allah".[5] Thankfulness to people means repaying their kindness, as the Quran says:

> "Is the reward of goodness anything but goodness?" — 55:60

The high morals depicted in the Quran were the morals of the Holy Prophet, and it was in this shape that he wanted to mould the character of his followers. Even a cursory glance at the lives of his Companions and his first four successors, who were the rulers of a vast empire, would show that the Holy Prophet achieved a mighty success in this respect. One of the many descriptions of the high moral plane on which his Companions stood occurs in the Quran as follows:

> "And the servants of the Beneficent are they who walk on the earth in humility, and when the ignorant address them, they say, Peace! And they who pass the night prostrating themselves before their Lord and standing. ... And they who, when they spend, are neither extravagant nor miserly, and the just mean is ever between these. And they who do not call upon another god with Allah, nor slay the soul which Allah has forbidden, except in the course of justice, nor commit fornication. ... And they who witness no falsehood, and when they pass by what is vain, they pass by nobly. And they who, when reminded of the messages of their Lord, do not fall down at them deaf and blind. And they who say: Our Lord, grant us in our wives and our offspring the joy of our eyes, and make us leaders for those who guard against evil." — 25:63–64, 67–68, 72–74

Social conduct

In the moral code of Islam, respect of, and kindness to, parents occupies a very high place. The Quran says:

> "…and do good to your parents. If either or both of them reach old age with you, say no word to them showing annoyance, nor rebuke them, and speak to them a generous word. And make yourself gentle to them with humility out of mercy,

and say: My Lord, have mercy on them, as they brought me up when I was little." — 17:23–24

"And We have enjoined on man concerning his parents … saying: Give thanks to Me and to your parents. To Me is the Eventual coming. And if they strive with you to make you set up partners with Me, of which you have no knowledge, do not obey them, and keep kindly company with them in this world." — 31:14–15

Here disobedience to parents is permitted if there is a clash of duty to one's Maker. Even then, kind behaviour towards them is enjoined. It is reported:

"A man came to the Prophet and asked his permission for *jihād*. He asked: Are your parents alive? The man said, Yes. He said: Then do *jihād* in their way [i.e., stay with them and be of service to them]." [6]

Special emphasis was placed by the Holy Prophet on showing consideration to one's mother, so much so that paradise was described by him to be beneath her two feet.[7] A man once asked the Holy Prophet: "Who has the greatest right that I should keep company with him with goodness?" The Prophet said: "Your mother". The man asked: "Who then?" The Prophet said: Your mother". The man asked a third time: "Who then?" The Prophet said: Your mother".The man asked: "Who then?" The Prophet said: "Then your father".[8]

The Quran, too, specially points out the right of the mother in the verse:

"And We have enjoined on man the doing of good to his parents. His mother bears him with trouble and she gives birth to him in pain. And the bearing of him and the weaning of him is thirty months." — 46:15

Parents were required to be kind and gentle towards their children. The sufferings of parents in providing for and protecting their children was described by the Holy Prophet as "a screen from the fire" for the parents.[9] In one hadith he is reported to have said:

"He is not one of us who does not show mercy to our little ones and respect to our great ones." [10]

The words of this hadith are general and apply not only to those younger or older in age but also to degrees of position and authority.

To do good to one's near of kin is mentioned among the fundamental teachings of the Holy Quran:

> "… but righteous is the one who believes in Allah, and the Last Day, and the angels and the Book and the prophets, and *gives away wealth out of love for Him to the near of kin* and the orphans and the needy and the traveller and to those who ask and to set slaves free and keeps up prayer and gives the due charity." — 2:177

> "And serve Allah, and do not set up any partner with Him, and be good to the parents *and to the near of kin* and the orphans and the needy and the neighbour of your kin and the alien neighbour [i.e., of a different community or religion], and the companion in a journey and the traveller and those whom your right hands possess [i.e., those who are under your charge]." — 4:36

The Holy Prophet is reported as saying:

> "*Rahim*[11] is an offshoot of *Rahmān;* so Allah said [to it]: Whoever makes his ties close with you [i.e., with the *rahim* or womb, meaning relatives] I will make My ties close with him, and whoever severs his ties with you I will sever My ties with him." [12]

The word *rahim* means 'womb' and signifies relationships, and *Rahmān* is an attribute of Allah meaning 'the God of mercy' or the 'Beneficent God'. The hadith signifies that relationship is deeply connected with mercy in its very nature. So whoever makes ties of relationship close by kindness to relatives, God is kind to him, and whoever severs the ties of relationship by ill-treatment towards relatives, God is displeased with him. The plural of *rahim,* which is *arhām,* occurs in the following verse:

> "O people, keep your duty to your Lord, Who created you from a single being and created its mate of the same [kind], and spread from these two many men and women. And keep your duty to Allah, by Whom you demand one of another your rights and to the ties of relationship (*arhām*)." — 4:1

Attention is drawn here to our duties towards other people by enjoining the keeping of duty to the "ties of relationship". Duties towards others are included in ties of relationship because, by declaring the whole of mankind to be descendants of the same mother and father, they are all declared to be, as it were, members of the same family. Therefore, the teaching of Islam to do good to relatives includes the whole of humanity.[13]

Kindness and good relations with one's neighbours are strongly emphasized. In 4:36 quoted above, Muslims are thus enjoined: "be good to… the neighbour of your kin and the alien neighbour". The neighbour of kin means a relative or a Muslim neighbour. The "alien neighbour" means an unrelated neighbour or a neighbour of another religion. The Holy Prophet said:

> "Whoever believes in Allah and the Last Day should not harm his neighbour." [14]

> "Whoever believes in Allah and the Last Day should honour his neighbour." [15]

> "[The angel] Gabriel continued to enjoin me with good treatment towards the neighbour until I thought he would make him heir of the property [of the deceased neighbour]." [16]

> "None of you has faith until he loves for his brother or for his neighbour what he loves for himself." [17]

Kindness and generosity towards one's servants and employees is mentioned in a number of Hadith reports, with the injunction to treat them on a basis of equality, as for example:

> "Whoever has his brother under his charge, he should give him to eat out of what he himself eats, and give him to wear of what he himself wears, and impose not on them a task which they are not able to do, and if you give them such a task, then help them [in doing it]." [18]

The care of the orphan was one of the earliest injunctions that Islam gave, and the Holy Prophet had always shown a deep anxiety for the welfare of the poor and the orphans. The care of the orphan and the poor is described as an uphill task, but one which must be accomplished:

> "But he [i.e., man] does not attempt the uphill road. And what will make you comprehend what the uphill road is? It is to free a slave, or to feed in a day of hunger an orphan near of kin, or the poor man lying in the dust. Then he is of those who believe and exhort one another to patience, and exhort one another to mercy." — 90:11–17

Anyone who pays no attention to this is belying religion:

> "Have you seen him who denies religion? That is the one who is rough to the orphan, and does not urge the feeding of the needy." — 107:1–3

Orphans should not be treated as living on the charity of others but must be treated as brethren: "they are your brethren" (2:220), and strict injunctions are given regarding safeguarding their property:

> "And give to orphans their property, and do not substitute worthless things for their good ones, nor devour their property, adding to your own property. This is surely a great sin." — 4:2

Looking after widows and the poor is an act of the highest merit, akin to *jihād* and worship of Allah. The Holy Prophet said:

> "One who manages the affairs of the widow and the poor person is like the one who exerts himself hard [*mujāhid,* i.e., who undertakes *jihād*] in the way of Allah, or the one who stands up for prayer in the night and fasts in the day." [19] *

Behaviour towards other Muslims

The unity and brotherhood of all mankind is a fundamental conception of Islam. Muslims were, however, particularly exhorted to be kind to one another and to help one another. Believers are frequently described in the Quran as brethren, for example:

> "The believers are brethren so make peace between your brethren…" — 49:10 (see also 3:103, 9:11, 59:10, etc.)

---

* *Editor's Note:* Some aspects of ethics have also been covered earlier in this book. See the chapter *Charity* under 'Conception of charity in Islam' and 'Voluntary charity' (p. 238–241), and the chapter *Marriage* under 'Mutual relation of husband and wife' (p. 349).

The quality of being "merciful among themselves" (48:29) is expressly mentioned. Muslims have been specifically prohibited from deriding others or looking down upon other Muslims with contempt, seeking faults in and being unduly suspicious of one another:

> "O you who believe, do not let a people laugh at another people, perhaps they may be better than they; nor let women laugh at women, perhaps they may be better than they. Neither find fault with one another, nor call one another by [offensive] nick-names. Evil is a bad name after faith; and whoever does not repent, these it is that are the wrongdoers. O you who believe, avoid most of suspicion, for surely suspicion in some cases is sin; and do not spy nor let some of you backbite others. Does one of you like to eat the flesh of his dead brother? You abhor it! And keep your duty to Allah, surely Allah returns to mercy again and again, is Merciful."
> — 49:11–12

Hadith describes Muslims as parts of one structure and compares them to a human body; when one member of it ails, the entire body ails. The Holy Prophet said:

> "You will recognize the believers in their having mercy for one another and in their love for one another and in their kindness towards one another like the body; when one member of it ails, the entire body ails, one part calling out the other with sleeplessness and fever." [20]

Books of Hadith are full of reports of a similar nature, some of which are given below:

> "A Muslim is the brother of a Muslim; he does him no injustice, nor does he leave him alone [to be the victim of another's injustice]; and whoever fulfils the need of his brother, Allah fulfils his need; and whoever removes the distress of a Muslim, Allah removes from him a distress out of the distresses of the Day of Resurrection; and whoever covers the fault of a Muslim, Allah will cover his sins on the Day of Resurrection." [21]

> "Help your brother whether he does wrong or wrong is done to him. The Companions said: O Messenger of Allah! We can help one to whom wrong is done, but how can we help

one when he himself does wrong? He said: Take hold of his hand from doing wrong." [22]

"The Prophet said: 'Believers are in relation to one another as [parts of] a structure, one part of which strengthens another,' and he inserted the fingers of one hand amid those of the other." [23]

"Do not hate one another and do not be jealous of one another and do not boycott one another, and be servants of Allah as brethren; and it is not lawful for a Muslim that he should sever his relations with his brother for more than three days." [24]

In his last pilgrimage sermon at Mina, the Holy Prophet said:

"Surely Allah has made sacred to you your blood and your property and your honour as this day of yours is sacred in this month of yours in this city of yours." [25]

Transformation wrought by the Holy Prophet Muhammad

The most outstanding characteristic of the life of the Holy Prophet is the amazing success which he achieved within the short space of less than a quarter of a century. No reformer brought about such an entire change in the lives of a whole nation inhabiting such a vast country. None, in fact, found his people at such a depth of degradation as the Prophet found the Arabs, and no one raised them materially, morally and spiritually to the height to which he raised them. Twenty-three years' work of the Prophet quite metamorphosed them. Superstition gave place to a rational religion. They were cleansed of deep-rooted vice and bare-faced immorality; and further, they were inspired with a burning desire for the best and noblest deeds in the service of, not a country or nation, but, what is far higher than that, humanity. Old customs which involved injustice to the weak were all swept away, and just and reasonable laws took their place. Those who prided themselves on ignorance became lovers of knowledge, drinking deep at every fountain of learning to which they could get access.

No faith ever imparted such a new life to its followers on such a wide scale — a life affecting all branches of human activity, a transformation of the individual, of the family, of the society, of the nation, of the country, an awakening material as well as moral, intellectual as well as spiritual — as did the religion of Islam.

Notes to Chapter 20

1. Bukhari, book 61: 'Virtues of the Prophet and his Companions', ch. 23, h. 3559.

2. Bukhari, book 78: 'Good Morals (*Adab*)', ch. 69, h. 6094.

3. Mishkat, book 17: 'Governing and Judgment', ch. 1, sec. 2, h. 3534 (v. 2, p. 198).

4. See also in the Quran 11:112 and 42:15 for perseverance in the right path.

5. Abu Dawud, book 43: 'Good Morals (*Adab*)', ch. 12, h. 4811 (MDS: book 40, ch. 11).

6. Bukhari, book 56: '*Jihād*', ch. 138, h. 3004.

7. Nasa'i, book 25: '*Jihād*', ch. 6, h. 3104 (MDS: h. 3106).

8. Bukhari, book 78: 'Good Morals (*Adab*)', ch. 2, h. 5971.

9. Bukhari, book 24: '*Zakāt*', ch. 10, h. 1418.

10. Mishkat, book 24: 'Good Morals', ch. 15, sec. 2, h. 4751 (v. 2, p. 454).

11. *Editor's Note:* This word *raḥim* should not be confused with the name of God *Raḥīm* which means Merciful and occurs in *Bismillāh* after *Raḥmān* or Beneficent.

12. Bukhari, book 78: 'Good Morals (*Adab*)', ch. 13, h. 5988.

    Editor's Note: The words "with *you*" in this hadith address, as it were, the *raḥim* or womb, and mean "with *the ties of relationship*". The next hadith, h. 5989, is similar except that it uses the words "with it" instead of "with you".

13. *Editor's Note:* The explanation of 4:1 given here is taken from Maulana Muhammad Ali's Urdu commentary of the Quran, *Bayān al-Qur'ān*.

14. Bukhari, book 78: 'Good Morals (*Adab*)', ch. 31, h. 6018.

15. *Ibid.,* ch. 31, h. 6019.

16. *Ibid.,* ch. 28, h. 6014 and h. 6015.

17. Muslim, book 1: 'Faith', ch. 17, h. 45a (MDS: h. 170); see also h. 45b (MDS: h. 171).

18. Bukhari, book 2: 'Faith', ch. 22, h. 30.

19. Bukhari, book 69: 'Supporting the Family', ch. 1, h. 5353.

20. Bukhari, book 78: 'Good Morals (*Adab*)', ch. 27, h. 6011.

21. Bukhari, book 46: 'Oppression', ch. 3, h. 2442.

22. *Ibid.,* ch. 4, h. 2444.

23. Bukhari, book 8: 'Prayer', ch. 88, h. 481.

24. Bukhari, book 78: 'Good Morals (*Adab*)', ch. 57, h. 6065.

25. *Ibid.,* ch. 43, h. 6043.

Sources and References

In this edition common words are not transliterated, such as Islam, Quran, Allah, Muhammad, Hadith (in these examples the transliteration would be: *Islām, Qur'ān, Allāh, Muḥammad,* and *Ḥadīth*). Some names may be transliterated only to the extent of placing the 'bar' over the letters *a, i,* or *u,* to indicate that the vowel is long, as a guide to pronunciation. Full transliteration marks are used when the exact form of a word, name or phrase in Arabic needs to be represented, and in all such cases that text is printed in italics.

All references given in this book without an indication of the source are to the Holy Quran, by chapter and verse numbers. In the alphabetical list below, short names of sources, as used when referring to them in this book (e.g., Abu Dawud, Bukhari), are printed in bold.

- **Abu Dawud:** *Sunan* of *Abū Dāwūd* (Hadith collection).
- Ameer Ali, Syed, *The Personal Law of the Mahommedans,* London, 1880.
- Ameer Ali, Syed, *The Spirit of Islam,* Calcutta, 1902.
- **Ash'ari:** *Maqālāt al-Islāmiyyīn wa Ikhtilāfāt al-Muṣallīn* by Abu-l-Hasan Ali ibn Ismail al-Ash'ari.
- **Bukhari:** *Al-Ṣaḥīḥ al-Bukhārī* (Hadith collection).
- *Encyclopaedia of Islam,* first edition, E.T. Brill, Leyden.
- *Fatḥ al-Bayān fī maqāṣid al-Qur'ān* by Siddiq ibn Hasan ibn Ali al-Bukhari, al-Miriya Press, Cairo, 1301 A.H.
- *Al-Hidāyah* by Abu-l-Hasan Ali ibn Abi Bakr al-Marghinani, edition printed in Delhi, 1914.
- Hughes, T.P., *A Dictionary of Islam,* London, 1885.
- **Ibn Jarir:** Ibn Jarīr Ṭabarī, *Jāmi' al-Bayān fī Tafsīr al-Qur'ān,* al-Maimana Press, Cairo.
- **Ibn Majah:** *Sunan* of Ibn Mājah Qazwīnī (Hadith collection).

- **Lane:** *Arabic-English Lexicon* by E.W. Lane.
- *Lisān al-ʿArab* (Dictionary).
- *Al-Mawāqif* by al-Qadi Abdur-Rahman ibn Ahmad, al-Saʿada Press, Cairo, 8 vols.
- *Miftāḥ al-Saʿādah* by Ahmad ibn Mustafa, Hyderabad Deccan.
- **Mishkat:** *Al-Mishkāt al-Maṣābīḥ,* by Shaikh Wali-ud-Din Muhammad ibn Abdullah (Hadith collection). References are to the Arabic-Urdu edition, translated by Maulana Abdul Hakim Khan Akhtar Shahjahanpuri (Lahore, 1985).
- Muir, Sir William, *The Caliphate, Its Rise, Decline and Fall,* Edinburgh: John Grant, Revised Edition, 1924.
- **Muslim:** *Al-Ṣaḥīḥ al-Muslim* (Hadith collection).
- *Musnad* of Imam Ahmad ibn Hanbal, al-Maimana Press, Cairo, 1306 A.H.
- **Nasa'i:** *Sunan* of *Nasāʾī* (Hadith collection).
- *Al-Nihāyah fī Gharībi-l-Ḥadīth wa-l-Āthār* (Dictionary of Hadith) by Ibn Athīr.
- *Qāmūs* (Dictionary) by Shaikh Nasr al-Huraini, Cairo.
- **Raghib:** Al-Rāghib al-Iṣfahānī, *Al-Mufradāt fī Gharīb al-Qurʾān* (Dictionary of the Quran).
- **Razi:** Imām Fakhar-ud-Dīn Rāzī, *Al-Tafsīr al-Kabīr,* al-ʿAmira Press, 1307 A.H., 8 volumes.
- *Rūḥ al-Maʿānī,* Commentary of the Quran by Mahmud al-Alusi.
- **Suyuti:** Jalāl-ud-Dīn Suyūṭī, *Itqān fī ʿUlūm al-Qurʾān,* Cairo, 1318 A.H.
- Suyūṭī, Jalāl-ud-Dīn, *Jāmiʿ al-Ṣaghīr.*
- Suyūṭī, Jalāl-ud-Dīn, *Tārīkh al-Khulafāʾ.*
- *Tāj al-ʿArūs* (Dictionary) by Sayyid Muhammad Murtada al-Husaini.
- **Tirmidhi:** *Al-Jāmiʿ al-Tirmidhī* (Hadith collection).
- *Zād al-Maʿād* by Allama Shams-ud-Din Abu Abdul Malik, known as Ibn Qayyim, Maimaniyyah Press, Cairo, 1300 A.H.

References to the 'six reliable' collections of Hadith

1. In giving references to the 'six reliable' collections of Hadith, namely, Bukhari, Muslim, Tirmidhi, Abu Dawud, Ibn Majah and Nasa'i, we have used the numbering of books, chapters and hadith reports as used in the online resource www.sunnah.com. We have also indicated their numbering in the printed editions published by Maktaba Dar-us-Salam, of Riyadh, Saudi Arabia, in cases where the numbering in these editions is different from that of www.sunnah.com.

2. The above-mentioned sources provide the Arabic text and English translation. The translations quoted in this book are by Maulana Muhammad Ali as in his book *The Religion of Islam*, although in some cases we have amended them a little.

3. Here is a typical example of one of our references:

    Bukhari, book 10: 'Call to Prayer', ch. 54, h. 693.

    This refers to book 10 of Bukhari. The name of the book is 'Call to Prayer', which is a further help in identifying the book and in locating the hadith in other editions of the same collection. Here the chapter number within the book is 54, and the hadith number, which runs sequentially through Bukhari, is 693.

4. Below is an example in which a reference to the edition published by Maktaba Dar-us-Salam (MDS) is added because it is different in some respect:

    Abu Dawud, book 26: 'Knowledge', ch. 3, h. 3646 (MDS: book 24).

    In parentheses, after MDS we indicate *in which respect the reference is different* from the www.sunnah.com reference. In this case in the Maktaba Dar-us-Salam edition, the book number is 24 instead of 26, while the chapter and hadith numbers are the same.

5. *Hadith numbers:* In the resource www.sunnah.com, we find that most often there are three hadith numbers appended to each hadith for different purposes. The first of these is marked as 'Reference' (in bold) and we refer to that whenever it is present. There are other instances where are two hadith numbers, one marked as 'English reference' and the other as 'Arabic reference', and in these cases we use the 'English reference' number. Note that in the MDS edition of *Sahih Muslim* each hadith is prefixed with more than one number (for certain reasons), and in those cases we refer to the first number.

Index

A number by itself indicates a page number, while *n* followed by two numbers indicates a note at the end of a chapter; thus *n* 2:11 refers to chapter 2, note 11. A repeated page number, such as "7, 7", indicates references to two separate places on the same page. In listing frequently-cited sources in this Index, such as Bukhari, index entries include only those places where their names occur in the main text and exclude occurrences which are in the end-notes of the chapters.

www.ingramcontent.com/pod-product-compliance
Lightning Source LLC
Chambersburg PA
CBHW051537030726
47592CB00001B/24